THE
LETTERS AND
PAPERS OF

CHAIM
WEIZMANN

YAD CHAIM WEIZMANN

This publication programme was initiated by Meyer W. Weisgal (1894–1977), Chancellor of the Weizmann Institute of Science and Chairman of the Weizmann National Memorial (Yad Chaim Weizmann). He was General Editor of the Weizmann Letters and Papers 1968–77.

ISRAEL UNIVERSITIES PRESS

Executive Editor: GEOFFREY WIGODER
Administrative Manager: MEIRA BENOUDIZ

Staff Editor and Indexer: BRIAN STREETT; *Biographical Research:* YEHUDA BLUMENFELD

This volume marks the conclusion of the unique series of letters tracing, from his earliest years, the role in Jewish life of the man who led the Zionist Organization throughout the world and became the first President of the State of Israel. The series chronicles the ever-widening significance of the Jewish national movement from its modest beginnings at the turn of the century through successive world crises, the destruction of European Jewry and the birth of a nation. The historical method employed by the international group of scholars engaged on the project has produced a fresh evaluation of the circumstances which have decided questions of peace and war in one of the most sensitive regions of the globe. The companion Series B, comprising two volumes of the Papers of Chaim Weizmann, will follow.

At inauguration of Weizmann Institute of Science, November, 1949. Weizmann, the President of Israel, being escorted by Prime Minister David Ben-Gurion and Harry Levine, a Governor of the Institute. *Behind,* Selig Brodetsky, President of the Hebrew University.

The Letters and
Papers of

Chaim Weizmann

GENERAL EDITOR
BARNET LITVINOFF

VOLUME XXIII · SERIES A
August 1947–June 1952

Editor: AARON KLIEMAN

in collaboration with

NEHAMA A. CHALOM

TRANSACTION BOOKS · RUTGERS UNIVERSITY
ISRAEL UNIVERSITIES PRESS · JERUSALEM
1980

Transaction Books, Rutgers University, New Brunswick, N.J.
ISBN   0   87855   263   4

Israel Universities Press, P.O. Box 7145, Jerusalem
ISBN   0   7065   1319   3

Library of Congress Catalog No. 74-35 4485

CONTENTS

ACKNOWLEDGEMENTS

The cooperation of the following individuals and institutions is gratefully acknowledged:

Dr. Abraham Alsberg, Jerusalem
David Carrington, London
Central Zionist Archives, Jerusalem
Eliahu Elath, Jerusalem
Walter Eytan, Jerusalem
Dr. Michael Heymann, Jerusalem
Israel State Archives, Jerusalem
Thelma Jaffe, Rehovot
Benzion Keren, Jerusalem
Sylvia Litvinoff, London
Doris Moushine, Rehovot
National and University Library, Jerusalem
Israel Philipp, Jerusalem
Public Record Office, London
Truman Library, Independence, Mo.
Benjamin Welles, Washington
Dr. Gedalia Yogev, Jerusalem
Moshe Yuval, Israel Foreign Ministry, Jerusalem

ILLUSTRATIONS

This, the final volume of the Letters of Chaim Weizmann, is dedicated to the memory of Dewey D. Stone, who was cherished by the first President of Israel as one of his greatest friends. It was to a great measure due to the devotion of Dewey Stone that the scientific and spiritual legacy of Dr. Weizmann received its present-day form in the establishment of the Weizmann Institute of Science. Dewey and his life-companion Anne were alike guided by the inspiration they received from the Jewish leader to work for the renaissance of their people in its ancestral homeland.

INTRODUCTION

Chaim Weizmann died at his home in Rehovot on 9 November, 1952, shortly before his 78th birthday. The restless hand which had penned so many thousands of letters, to fill these 23 volumes and encompass an epoch, at last was stilled. Between his earliest surviving letter as a ten-year-old schoolboy in Tsarist Russia and his final one as President of the State of Israel, are recorded not merely the drama and pathos, the achievements and disappointments, of one man's journey through a remarkable life, but the modern history of a people as it struggled for its identity. Others have left correspondence spanning the same period and dealing with the same concerns. They were Jewish voices; but Weizmann alone was *the* Jewish voice.

This volume opens in the summer of 1947, when the fate of Zionism still hung in the balance: the scales of power politics are not necessarily the scales of justice. Weizmann had been replaced by more militant Zionist leaders, and they repudiated his policy based upon restraint and cooperation with Great Britain. The Jews, having suffered the loss of a third of their people in a holocaust, were changed; so was the world as a whole, by the Second World War.

Ten years earlier, the possible partition of Palestine into Arab and Jewish states had been under active discussion, but the scheme was thwarted by an absence of enthusiasm, or direct opposition, from the parties concerned, including Britain. Now it was being debated again, in an atmosphere of Britain's continued obstruction, fierce Arab resistance, a new activism on the part of Palestine Jewry (the *Yishuv*), and the emergence of the Jews of America as a strong Zionist force. With the decline of British strength and the rise of America as the dominant power in the world, the Soviet Union assumed a role at the centre of the international stage as never before. In 1937 Weizmann had been the undisputed spokesman of Jewry. Now he was virtually an outsider, having been deprived in 1946 by the Twenty-Second Zionist Congress at Basle of his position as President of the Jewish Agency and World Zionist Organization.

He regarded his displacement as a betrayal, and his resentment found expression in forthright condemnation of his successors, David Ben-Gurion, the *Yishuv* leader, and Rabbi Abba Hillel Silver of America. The years immediately preceding had been marked for Weizmann by personal tragedy, and chronic ill-health. His grievously defective eye-sight threatened blindness. The septuagenarian might have logically and justifiably sought welcome respite in retirement, perhaps to live out his twilight years in the shelter of the Institute of Science he was building at Rehovot. Instead, he threw himself anew into the political struggle. He did not exclude the possibility of returning to a position of authority.

The United Nations Special Committee on Palestine (UNSCOP) produced, at the end of August 1947, the recommendation that Britain withdraw from Palestine and that the country be granted independence at the earliest practicable date. A majority of the committee further recommended its division into Jewish and Arab states, with Jerusalem and its immediate surroundings as a *corpus separatum* under international trusteeship. This verdict was acceptable in principle though not in detail by the Jewish Agency. Weizmann had consistently advocated a solution through partition since its proposal by the Peel Commission in 1937. And his position within both the Jewish and the non-Jewish world was such that the Agency could not now ignore the strength of his advocacy. He was therefore invited to New York both to present the Zionist case before the Ad Hoc Committee of the United Nations and to play a supportive role in promoting the cause unofficially. Weizmann was regarded as a true statesman rather than a politician, not least by President Truman.[1]

Addressing the Ad Hoc Committee on 18 October, he reviewed the circumstances leading to the conferment of the Mandate upon Britain—a power which would be remembered with appreciation for its great services when the 'sordid consequences of the White Paper pass into forgotten history'. Weizmann contended that statehood was the inevitable and foreseen consummation of the Mandate. If not given independence the Jews would be subjected to the will of the Arab majority, and Jews already had experience of minority status in Arab countries. Yet he retained his belief in the prospect of Arab-Jewish co-operation once a solution based on finality and equality had received the sanction of international consent. Weizmann went on to describe the 'acute phase' of the Jewish problem as mainly concerning the fate of some one and a half million people in Europe and the Orient.

His suite at the Plaza Hotel became the headquarters for this informal diplomacy, a style in which Weizmann excelled. He took the view, and this enabled him to play a key role in Israel's actual establishment, that the ebb of Britain's international authority included also the fading of her imperial impulse. Britain had already departed from India, and this robbed her of any justification for her continued presence in Palestine, which had become a burden

[1] Harry S. Truman Memoirs, Vol. II, *Years of Trial and Hope*, New York 1956, pp. 188–89.

to the British taxpayer and an offence to world opinion. True, he felt that 'if not for the British Government, we would be nowhere', but he saw that the Zionists could not anticipate the support of Britain as the General Assembly's debate on the UNSCOP plan approached. The United States, however, had the requisite strength, resources and prestige both to apply leverage against British opposition and to bring about realisation of the Zionist idea. Weizmann still hoped for a revival of the former Anglo-Zionist relationship, but for the present he concentrated on gaining Truman as an ally. He was to do this directly, through a personal meeting, while the American Zionist leaders largely placed their weight behind great demonstrations to enlist public support, and a sustained campaign in the lobbies of both Houses of Congress. But it was the President alone who could override the pro-Arab arguments of the oil and banking concerns, or of the Pentagon and the State Department. No. 26 (28 Oct. 1947)

Harassment from various Zionist groups, in which the threat of disaffection by a traditional Democratic bloc in the forthcoming Presidential Election was strongly intimated, had alienated Truman. Nevertheless he received Weizmann on 19 November, 1947, thanks to the intercession of the President's old friend and erstwhile business partner, Eddie Jacobson. Thus began a unique relationship between the Democratic President of the United States and the Jewish nationalist, involving four meetings and wide-ranging correspondence during the ensuing years.

Truman himself emphasised their shared interests and experiences. Writing after his surprise election victory of 1948 to acknowledge Weizmann's letter of congratulation, he said: 'We had both been abandoned by the so-called realistic experts to our supposedly forlorn lost causes. Yet we both kept pressing for what we were sure was right—and we were both proven to be right. My feeling of elation on the morning of November 3rd must have approximated your own feelings one year ago today, and on May 14th, and on several occasions since then.'[2]

The General Assembly decision of 29 November, 1947 naturally had this effect upon Weizmann, but he was not oblivious to the trials ahead. Securing the requisite two-thirds majority (the U.N. had voted 33 to 13 for partition) had involved the Zionists in heavy persuasion among several wavering delegations. Nevertheless, as he wrote in a tone bordering on the messianic to William Rappard, an old friend from League of Nations days: 'This thing which is now coming to pass after nearly two thousand years of hope and prayer is not likely to be destroyed through the malevolence of a few people.' No. 103 (27 Dec. 1947)

---

[2] Truman to Weizmann, 29 Nov. 1948 (W.A.).

It had been touch and go, for the coalition of forces ranged against the demand for Jewish statehood included not only Britain and the nations she could influence, but also the anti-Zionists in the highest echelons of the American Government. Neither America nor Britain wished to incur the enmity of the Arab States, which were threatening the use of military force to nullify any move that would render the Arabs of Palestine less than paramount in the whole of the country. How ironic that Weizmann, a private individual and British subject, required a letter of introduction from his country's Ambassador in Washington before meeting Truman in his endeavour to range America against Britain!

Much could intervene between a U.N. resolution and the actual acquisition of sovereignty. Did the British really intend to relinquish control over Palestine? Would the Arabs really go to war to prevent partition? Would the Jews be able to resist effectively? And could the U.S. be relied upon to help carry out the verdict of the world organization? Aware of the dangers, Weizmann urged the *Yishuv* leaders not to hesitate, but to demonstrate before the world their resolve and preparedness to take the ultimate risk of life itself for independence.

He returned to England a very sick man immediately following the U.N. vote, but again consented to sail for America in January 1948, in response to urgent pleas from friends who had become alarmed at American equivocation. Some wished him also to lend his name and presence to such activities as fund-raising. He complained that too many were using him 'as a sort of Wailing Wall'.

No. 117
(19 Jan.
1948)

He was thus on the spot in March, to learn of American readiness to support a trusteeship solution in Palestine in place of partition. This was indicative of differences between Truman's own circle and those, particularly in the State Department, who feared the consequences of an announcement of Jewish independence. Evidently the President was either unable or unwilling to resist. At their second meeting of 18 March, the President reassured Weizmann. But the next day U.S. officials indeed proposed trusteeship. The worried Zionist leader wrote to Justice Felix Frankfurter: 'Every day some new hope is being dangled before our eyes, and when the sun sets, it is nothing but a mirage.' With barely a month left before the Mandate was due to expire, he had the feeling that this second visit to America had been a 'heartbreaking and futile waste of time'. Then, on 14 May, came Truman's announcement of *de facto* recognition of the Provisional Government of Israel, and Weizmann's strategy of personal concentration upon the President was triumphantly vindicated. A message from Tel Aviv quickly followed. It said that Chaim Weizmann had been chosen 'Head of the State'.

No. 129
(31 Mar.
1948)

No. 148
(20 Apr.
1948)

This crowning moment of his long career did not bring Weizmann contentment. The infant state was fighting for its life against invasion from Egypt, Iraq, Jordan, Lebanon and Syria. Britain's hostility had not lessened, and about this he wrote: 'I *cannot* believe it, but alas, I must.' He had a feeling of homelessness—his stay in America had no further point, yet he was unable to travel home to Rehovot and was reluctant to go to London. His wife Vera spoke wearily of their having slept in 19 different places since leaving Palestine in July 1947. They longed finally to rest among their own. They travelled to Europe, where Weizmann had to submit to yet another operation on his eyes. He spent some time in France and Switzerland contacting European statesmen in an effort to gain diplomatic recognition for Israel. But it seemed to him that his fellow-Jews were often their own worst enemies, complicating the task of presenting Israel in a good light. On the assassination by Jewish extremists of Count Folke Bernadotte, the U.N. Mediator in the Arab-Israel conflict who seemed to be exceeding his functions by submitting his own territorial recommendations, Weizmann responded with anger: 'We seem to be doing our best in critical moments to make our task impossible.'

No. 186 (14 June 1948)

No. 257 (21 Sept. 1948)

Ultimately, he and his wife arrived to take up residence in Rehovot late in September and Weizmann's thoughts in this final phase of his life, as reflected in his remaining correspondence, were preoccupied with the powers of his office and the nature of Israeli society, in addition to the country's international standing. He had entertained serious reservations about accepting the Presidency, for he was uncertain as to the intentions of David Ben-Gurion, the Prime Minister, and the other leaders of the state. Was it to be a position of true authority, or merely symbolic? He had no desire to be just a figure-head, but his constant enquiries of the Foreign Minister, Moshe Shertok, on this score elicited little satisfaction—indeed, some of his letters remained unanswered. He wrote sharply, in his own style of English: 'I am not offended, but greatly irritated, because this treatment meted out to me only indicates the lack of respect to your own institutions; and that is a Balkan trait, of which I did not think you would all acquire it so quickly.'

No. 241 (2 Aug. 1948)

In this mood of exasperation, Weizmann confided to Meyer Weisgal and Aubrey Eban, two advisers particularly close to him, of his desire to resign. They counselled patience, and no letter of resignation was despatched. But the plan was never entirely abandoned, for he drafted another letter of resignation to Ben-Gurion, unsent, in January 1951 (No. 343). Second thoughts again prevailed, this time because of his concern lest his resignation adversely affect Israel's image abroad. He remained President until his death.

'A constitution is like a straitjacket,' he had commented. And the

No. 231 (25 July 1948)

Fundamental Laws endowed the President of Israel with only limited authority. While never reconciled to this, Weizmann did make the most of the prestige and moral authority of the office. As though invigorated by the very soil and atmosphere of Israel, a different man began to emerge from his letters. Gone were the depression and the fears for Israel's prospects of survival, to be replaced by a rejuvenating enthusiasm. He became filled with the excitement and the sense of history being made, and more tolerant of those conducting the affairs of government. In contrast to his earlier sensitivity No. 235 to foreign opinion, he expressed the belief to Eban that 'we attach (29 July too much value to finding ourselves in the good company of other 1948) nations . . . losing too much energy on externals'. They would do better to make the state strong, intellectually powerful, 'a model of social and political organization'.

Amidst the casualties and damage inflicted in the War of Independence, he adopted a tone of confidence and pride bordering on chauvinism. He sought help in Switzerland to acquire anti-aircraft No. 262 guns, of which Israel at the time had only 15: 'If we would have the (10 Oct. necessary equipment,' he pleaded, 'we could finish the job in about 1948) a month.' To Leopold Amery, former Colonial Secretary and a con- No. 263 stant friend of Zionism, he was led to conclude: 'I do not think that (24 Oct. an inch of territory will be yielded by the Armies of Israel to anybody.' 1948) Soon he was to see Ben-Gurion in another light, resulting in an evaluation of the Prime Minister far different from his earlier assess- No. 264 ment: 'He reminds me somewhat of Winston [Churchill], who is good (24 Oct. in war and less so in peace,' having thus far shown himself to be 1948) 'thoughtful, calm, resolute and a man of enormous courage'. As to the government as a whole: 'Although many things seem somewhat amateurish and hesitant, they have done extremely well on the whole under very difficult circumstances.'

Weizmann lamented the transformation in Israeli society caused by the influx of European and Oriental immigrants. He described this as arising from 'the moral state of the newcomers who are not imbued with the *chalutz* [pioneering] spirit, like the previous generation'.[3] Despite such concerns his letters continued to reflect the optimism of Israel as the second year of independence ap- No. 305 proached: 'One feels for once that the Almighty is on the side of the (3 Mar. Jews, and one realises how good a partner he can be if he chooses to.' 1949) In the sphere of foreign relations Weizmann was still able to exert considerable influence. Israel's precarious position, even after its admission to the U.N. in May 1949, demanded a continued struggle for legitimacy, security and international recognition. Such problems

[3] Draft letter to James de Rothschild, 19 Nov. 1948, W.A.

as a possible change in the status Israel had given to Jerusalem, the whittling down of territory under Israel's control, economic difficulties, the state's relations with Diaspora Jewry, were never far away. New world leaders had emerged who were unacquainted with the Balfour Declaration and the ensuing 30 difficult years. Weizmann had had understanding and encouragement from, among many others, Lloyd George, Jan Smuts, Thomas Masaryk, Léon Blum, Iraq's King Feisal I, but those were men of a previous era. He could still turn to Winston Churchill, however, even before the latter's return as British Prime Minister in October 1951.

Weizmann felt that by ending Britain's estrangement, the pressure against Israel could be alleviated from the Arab states, which continued to receive military and diplomatic support from a Britain still clinging to a position in the Middle East. Britain's commitment to the Arabs, combined perhaps with resentment at the success of the Zionist experiment, produced new tensions in January 1949, when London threatened military intervention. The crisis passed, with Britain modifying her position and extending recognition to Israel shortly afterwards. Weizmann offers posterity this capsule critique of the British in the Middle East: 'They over-estimated the strength of the Arabs and under-estimated the strength of the Jews. These are two serious mistakes which a Great Power in possession of all the facts should not have made.' No. 263 (24 Oct. 1948)

His last phase, clouded by the virtually complete loss of his sight, and the death of such old comrades as Baffy Dugdale, Stephen Wise and Judah Magnes, all of whom figured so prominently in the Weizmann story, was also marred by developments within the Weizmann Institute of Science. This establishment, so dear to him, was to be his personal legacy to Israel. But he was full of anxiety over its future, for as part of the *Yishuv*'s total defence effort, the Rehovot scientists had switched to war work. This was not in keeping with his vision of the Institute, and there ensued a clash between Weizmann and his longtime scientific collaborator, disciple and friend, Ernst David Bergmann, resulting in termination of Bergmann's position as the Institute's director.

However, the appearance in 1949 of his memoirs, *Trial and Error*, had proved a significant publishing event. The book was immediately recognised as a classic of its kind: an intensely human story and perhaps the most important statement of the Jewish struggle to have come from one man's experience—this despite the many complaints from old Zionists wounded by their omission from the account, and the charges of inaccuracy levelled against it. Furthermore, the first *Knesset* convened that year and formally elected Weizmann as President of the State. Soon afterwards the old leader and his life-partner Vera, to whom he owed so much, left on an official visit to Washington and Paris, with a stop-over at the University of Fribourg, where Weizmann received an honorary doctorate from his *Alma Mater*. Late in 1949, in celebration of his 75th birthday, the greatly expanded scientific complex of the Weizmann Institute was inaugurated. Misgivings were temporarily put aside in a triumph the President was happy to share with his devoted collaborator Weisgal, who had shouldered the immense burden of bringing the project to fruition.

By 1950, his health worsening and his activities reduced almost to the ceremonial, Weizmann's increasingly infrequent letters contain only two enduring themes: inspiration and nostalgia. Like Moses of old, the political leader changes to teacher and guide. His thoughts return with a 'somewhat melancholy pleasure' to early battles in company with Israel Sieff and Simon Marks, who, like No. 335 Harry Sacher, recall for him 'the early days of Manchester and Lon-(23 May don—the years of uphill struggle and spade work'. Yet when re-1950) quired, he could still show that old pride, that old readiness for polemic, which permeate the entire range of this correspondence. Again and again, he availed himself of his special *rapport* with Truman to put Israel's case to her most influential friend when it seemed world opinion was running against the young state.

Chaim Weizmann took his second oath of office from his bed at Weizmann House in Rehovot on 25 November, 1951. The letter which terminates these 23 volumes was written in June, 1952. It took the form of a message to the Anglo-Israel Association in London welcoming the foundation of the organization. How appropriate that the last published statement of this man should record the reconciliation of the two nations that had so long shared his loyalties!

He died on Sunday, 9 November, 1952, and in the Cabinet of Israel specially convened in Jerusalem the Prime Minister, David Ben-Gurion, paid this tribute: 'Chaim Weizmann will take his place in the eternal history of the Jewish people alongside the great figures of its past—the Patriarchs and Kings, Judges, Prophets and spiritual leaders who have woven the fabric of our national life for four thousand years. The entire Jewish people will join in our deep mourning of the passing of the last President of the Zionist Organization and the First President of the State of Israel.'

AARON KLIEMAN

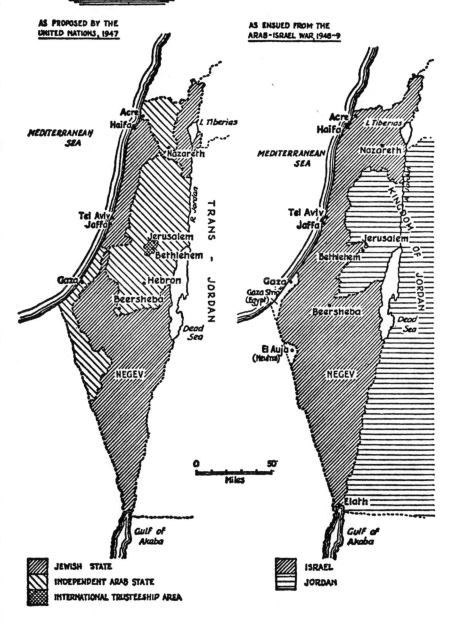

PALESTINE'S FRONTIERS

AS PROPOSED BY THE
UNITED NATIONS, 1947

MEDITERRANEAN
SEA

Acre
Haifa

L. Tiberias

Nazareth

R. Jordan

T R A N S

—

J O R D A N

Tel Aviv
Jaffa

Jerusalem
Bethlehem

Gaza

Hebron

Beersheba

Dead
Sea

NEGEV

Gulf of
Akaba

AS ENSUED FROM THE
ARAB-ISRAEL WAR, 1948-9

Acre
Haifa

L. Tiberias

MEDITERRANEAN
SEA

Nazareth

K I N G D O M

O F

J O R D A N

Tel Aviv
Jaffa

Jerusalem

Bethlehem

Gaza

Gaza Strip
(Egypt)

Beersheba

Dead
Sea

El Auja
(Neutral)

NEGEV

Elath

Gulf of
Akaba

0   50
|_____|
Miles

JEWISH STATE
INDEPENDENT ARAB STATE
INTERNATIONAL TRUSTEESHIP AREA

ISRAEL
JORDAN

LIST OF LETTERS

Reference should be made to the General Introduction to the Series, published in Volume I, for explanations on the structure of the Zionist Organization and associated institutions. A concise Weizmann Chronology will be found on pp. xxxvi–xxxvii of Volume I.

[1] Dates in square brackets are conjectural.

LIST OF LETTERS

ABBREVIATIONS

A.C.	Actions Committee (Zionist General Council)
Cab.	Cabinet Papers
C.O.	Colonial Office
C.Z.A.	Central Zionist Archives
E.Z.F.	English Zionist Federation
F.O.	Foreign Office
H.U.	Hebrew University of Jerusalem
H.W.	Handwritten
I.F.M.	Israel Foreign Ministry
I.S.A.	Israel State Archives
J.A.	Jewish Agency
J.C.	*Jewish Chronicle*
J.D.C.	American Jewish Joint Distribution Committee
J.N.F.	Jewish National Fund
K.H.	*Keren Hayesod* (Palestine Foundation Fund)
Or. Copy	Original Copy
P.R.O.	Public Record Office, London
T.	Telegram
T. and E.	*Trial and Error* (W.'s autobiography; London 1949 edition)
T.W.	Typewritten
U.J.A.	United Jewish Appeal
V.W.	Vera Weizmann
W.	Chaim Weizmann
W.A.	Weizmann Archives, Rehovot
W.W.	World War
(W.)Z.O.	(World) Zionist Organization
Z.G.C.	Zionist General Council—see A.C.
Z.O.A.	Zionist Organization of America

[Chaim Weizmann held no official position in the Zionist movement as this volume opens. At the Twenty-Second Zionist Congress (the first since the war) held in Basle in December 1946, differences between the activist and moderate factions came to a head, with the former prevailing. Consequently, Weizmann was not re-elected President of the W.Z.O. or of the Jewish Agency. Returning to private life, he and his wife Vera spent most of their time at their home at Rehovot in Palestine. In the summer of 1947 they went on vacation to Switzerland. See Introduction.]

1. To Earl Mountbatten,[1] New Delhi. *Flims, 3 August 1947*
English: Or. Copy. T.W.: W.A.

Dear Lord Mountbatten,

I must be forgiven for the delay in answering your kind letter of July 10th[2]; it had to be forwarded to me, as I had left Palestine for a short holiday in the mountains.

I can quite understand that the fact of your becoming Governor-General of the Dominion of India and Chairman of the Joint Defence Council of the two Dominions will make it impossible for you to lend our cause a helping hand. If I had known that at the time I was writing to you, I might not have ventured that suggestion—but then, it drives one almost to despair to realize how few are to-day the men of vision and human understanding and one is tempted to turn to these few, even if one knows the weight of the burden they have to carry already.

The interest you have found in my modest efforts during the War is very flattering for me, and I will be only too glad if Wing Commander Campbell-Johnson[3] will be able to utilize some of the material contained in the attached memorandum[4] in any manner he thinks fit. I venture to think that the idea of developing colonial agriculture as a source of raw materials for the British chemical industry has not lost its appeal even in the post-war period; as a

1. [1] Admiral of Fleet Lord Louis Mountbatten, 1900–79. Member of British royal family; Chief of Combined Operations 1942–43; Supreme Allied Commander, South-East Asia 1943–46. Viceroy of India, March–Aug. 1947; Governor-General of India following partition and independence, Aug. 1947–June 1948. For his war-time association with W. in scientific research, see Vol. XX.
   [2] Mountbatten had replied to a letter of congratulation from W. (Vol. XXII, No. 341) on bringing the problem of India to a successful conclusion. W. suggested that Mountbatten return home via Palestine, and appraise a situation not dissimilar from India's communal clash, 'so that perhaps in future you might take a hand in helping both the Government and the peoples in this country to find a solution'. Mountbatten declined, as he would need to remain in India for some time (W.A.).
   [3] Alan Campbell-Johnson (b. 1913), Mountbatten's Press Attaché formerly on his staff in Combined Operations. He intended writing its war history, and Mountbatten requested W. to describe for him W.'s scheme for the production of synthetic rubber within the British Commonwealth, what might have been achieved, and what caused the project's breakdown.
   [4] Untraced.

1

matter of fact, I believe, it has become even more attractive as such a scheme may make the Empire less dependent on foreign riches.
I remain with my best wishes and regards,

Yours very sincerely,

Ch. Weizmann

2. To Joseph I. Linton,[1] London.   *Flims, 9 August 1947*

English: H.W.: W.A.

August 9th, 1947.

Dear Ivor,

I do hope you'll keep to your plan and come here on August 15th and perhaps you would be able—even if the A.C. is sitting[2]—to see us back to Dover.[3]

I simply dread the going back, and we have made a capital mistake that we undertook to travel from Palestine alone. This made everything extremely difficult apart from the heat. Owing to my bad sight I am not only powerless to help Mrs. Weizmann[4] but am really a drag on her.[5]

Much love,

Yours,

Ch. Weizmann

Dear Ivor,

This letter is not from me—I am the new secretary.
With love,

Maidie[6]

3. To Louis F. Fieser,[1] Cambridge.   *Flims, 22 August 1947*

English: Or. Copy. T.W.: W.A.

My dear Professor Fieser,

Your letter of July 21st[2] has been forwarded to me here, where Mrs. Weizmann and I are taking a few weeks' rest, so far as that is

---

2. [1] Biog. Index, Vol. XIX. Political Secretary of J.A. London Office 1940–48; later Ambassador of Israel to various countries.

[2] The A.C. was due to meet 25 Aug. in Zurich. W. did not plan to attend.

[3] The Weizmanns were due back in London that month.

[4] Vera W., formerly Khatzman (Biog. Index, Vol. I).

[5] Linton replied 14 Aug. (W.A.) that he was arranging for Doris May, W.'s secretary, to accompany them.

[6] W.'s daughter-in-law, wife of Benjamin W.

3. [1] B. 1899. U.S. chemist; professor at Harvard University from 1937.

[2] Untraced.

possible these days. It always makes me very happy to hear from you, and I am deeply thankful and relieved to see that the tragic events of the last few weeks have not daunted your spirits.[3] I hope and pray that by the time we are ready for the dedication ceremonies next spring,[4] all these horrors may be no more than the memory of an evil dream.

We should be most happy and honoured if Professor Kharash[5] would attend the opening. (I believe the Hebrew University is interested in him, too, as a possible candidate for the Chair of Organic Chemistry.) And it would also be a great honour and pleasure to have Dr. Van Niel[6] with us if he felt able to come. I wonder if you could sound him out about it? We should be so grateful if you could.

As regards the two Arab chemists,[7] we shall be delighted to invite them—you know how near to my own heart is the idea of forging links with the neighbouring countries through science, and how anxious I am to do everything possible in this direction. (Naturally, I do not know, and no one can foresee, what effects the general political situation may by then have had on the response to any such move on our part. We must go on hoping!)

With kindest regards to Mrs. Fieser and to you, in which Mrs. Weizmann joins me, I remain,

Very sincerely yours,

Ch. W.

4. To Julian Salomon,[1] Johannesburg.   *London, 5 September 1947*
English: T.W.: W.A.

Dear Mr. Salomon,

Your letter of the 8th August has just reached me here.[2] I am now a private individual, and can speak only for myself, but I hasten to assure you that my view remains, as always, that acts of

---

[3] Apparently a reference to the *Exodus* affair—see No. 5, n. 1.

[4] Of the new Weizmann Institute of Science in Rehovot. The Department of Physics and Physical Chemistry was due to be inaugurated spring 1948.

[5] Morris Selig Kharasch (1895–1957). U.S. chemist; professor at University of Chicago from 1939.

[6] Cornelius Bernardus van Niel, b. 1897. Dutch microbiologist; professor at Stanford, California, 1935–63.

[7] Not identified.

4. [1] Of Witwatersrand University. Not further identified.

[2] (W.A.). Salomon requested W.'s opinion 'as to whether the present acts of violence by the *Irgun* and the Stern group are aiding or detracting from our case at present before U.N.O.'

violence in Palestine[3] or anywhere else, and by whomsoever committed, can advance no cause but the cause of Evil. And whoever,
by aid, comfort or concealment, supports and encourages such acts,
himself becomes an accessory to them.

Yours sincerely,
Ch. Weizmann

5. To the Jewish Agency Executive, London.

London, 6 September 1947

English: Or. Copy. T.W.: W.A.

Gentlemen,

On arrival here on Wednesday evening, I heard that various
Jewish organizations were taking steps to endeavour to modify the
Government decision with regard to the sending of the *Exodus* ship
to Hamburg[1]—but without success. Friends of mine urged me
strongly to make a last minute attempt to see Mr. Bevin[2] personally, and though I was convinced that Mr. Bevin would not see
me, I nevertheless applied for an interview. In view of the probability
of a refusal, I thought it wise to have a preliminary talk with Mr.
Nye Bevan,[3] who promised to see the Foreign Secretary on Friday
morning, and try to impress upon him the desirability of having a
talk with me. Yesterday morning I received a message from Mr.
Bevin's Private Secretary saying that the Minister was sorry but he
could not see his way to arrange an interview for the present. Almost
simultaneously, came a message from Mr. Ivor Thomas,[4] the Under-
Secretary of State at the Colonial Office, who is acting for the

---

[3] Tension in Palestine was at a postwar peak. Late July three members of *Irgun* were
executed by the British; in retaliation two British sergeants were hanged by Jewish extremists.

5. [1] The ship *Exodus 1947*, bearing some 4,550 Jewish refugees, was escorted into Haifa
harbour by the British Navy 18 July. Instead of following their previous policy of interning
the would-be immigrants in Cyprus, the British chose to make an example of this ship in their
efforts to curtail illegal Jewish immigration by returning the refugees to their port of origin in
southern France. The French agreed to accept only those D.P.s who would disembark voluntarily, but after three weeks only some 130 had gone ashore. The British Cabinet, subjected to
adverse international opinion, then brought *Exodus* to Hamburg, where the remainder
were forcibly removed to D.P. camps in the British zone of occupied Germany.

[2] Ernest Bevin (Biog. Index, Vol. XX). Secretary of State for Foreign Affairs in Labour
Government 1945–51.

[3] Aneurin Bevan (1897–1960). Labour M.P.; Minister of Health 1945–51.

[4] Ivor Bulmer-Thomas, b. 1905. On editorial staff of *The Times* 1930–37; Parliamentary
Under-Secretary of State for Colonies 1946–47.

Colonial Secretary[5] in the latter's absence, asking me to come and see him the same afternoon.

Very soon after this, I heard from Mr. Bevan that the Foreign Secretary's refusal to see me was due to the following considerations:

1) He was anxious to avoid any risk of discussing the UNSCOP decision[6] with me, because that might constitute "intervention" in the matter on his part, and this he wished to avoid.

2) So far as the ships were concerned, he thought it would be best for me to discuss the matter first with Mr. Thomas, who would report to him. Later, after hearing Mr. Thomas' report, Mr. Bevin might see me.

The disturbing factor in this communication is the Foreign Secretary's suggestion that he did not wish to see me because I might discuss the U.N. decision (which in fact I did not wish to do, being for the moment concerned only with the boats). But from this remark, and from others, I conclude that the tactics of the Foreign Office will be to refrain from any kind of intervention with the U.N. in this matter, and I feel they may try to induce the Americans to adopt the same attitude. This, of course, would create a very dangerous vacuum, and might render the implementation of the report quite impossible. I should not be surprised if this were, in fact, the design, in which case insistence in the matter of the ships can only exacerbate relations, and give the Foreign Office an opportunity of saying that they are throwing in their hand, and will have nothing further to do with the whole business.

This is why I was anxious—if at all possible—to do something to avoid any open scandal at Hamburg, even at the risk of having the ships turned back to France. That would anyhow be better than starting an international row in Germany.

As I have no standing in any of these matters, I tried my best to get into touch with the Executive in Zurich and London, but could only succeed—and that after much effort—in getting a message to

---

[5] Arthur Creech Jones (Biog. Index, Vol. XXII). Secretary of State for Colonies 1946–50.

[6] The report and proposals of U.N. Special Committee on Palestine were completed 31 Aug. 1947. Its members unanimously endorsed 11 guiding principles, including: that the British Mandate should be terminated and independence granted at the earliest practicable date; that the political structure of the future state or states should be democratic and conform to the principles of U.N.; that Palestine's economic unity should be maintained; and that the sacred character of the Holy Places should be preserved and access to them assured. A majority also recommended partition of Palestine into an Arab state and a Jewish state, with the Jerusalem area as a *corpus separatum,* while a minority filed a separate proposal recommending federalism as the best framework for a unitary, independent Palestine state.

Mr. Kaplan.[7] He did not know where the other members of the Executive were, and was not prepared to take action by himself.

I tried myself, therefore, to get into touch with Mr. Léon Blum,[8] though owing to a PTT strike[9] in France yesterday, it was only this morning that the call came through. I asked him (a) to try and use his influence, as an old colleague, with Mr. Bevin, and (b) if he felt able to do so, to advise the *Exodus* immigrants to agree to land peaceably in France. I naturally made it clear to him that I was speaking as a private individual only.

I am very conscious that all of this may well be too late, as the boats reach Hamburg to-night.

It is most unfortunate that, at a time like the present, with serious trouble obviously brewing, there is not a single responsible person in London on behalf of the Executive. Brodetsky[10] looked in yesterday morning, but has since disappeared, though I am still trying to reach him. Goldmann,[11] who said he would be here to try and see Mr. Bevin again, has so far shown no sign of life. Linton is also not available. It was well known that the ships would be reaching Hamburg over the week-end, and the Executive should have arranged for someone responsible to be in London in case some action might become necessary here. I think the failure to do this is a very serious omission. (Of course, I realise that some of them may have gone to Hamburg—but it is not in Hamburg that any effective action can be taken. It is here.)

I should like to emphasise once more that what worries me most is the indifferent-seeming tactics of the Foreign Office. I may know a little more of what lies behind it all in the course of the coming week, when I shall be seeing the High Commissioner,[12] Colonel Stanley,[13] and Mr. Amery.[14]

It is, of course, no longer any business of mine, but I do feel strongly that we must not let things go by default—and that is just

---

[7] Eliezer Kaplan (Biog. Index, Vol. XVI). Treasurer of J.A. and member of its Executive 1933–48; Israel Minister of Finance from 1948. The Executive met in Zurich late Aug.

[8] Biog. Index, Vol. XI. Served briefly as French Premier 1946–47; then retired from public life except for a short period as Vice-Premier 1948. See No. 7.

[9] I.e., of postal, telephone and telegraph services.

[10] Selig Brodetsky (Biog. Index, Vol. VI). On W.Z.O. Executive 1928–51; President Board of Deputies of British Jews 1939–49; President H.U. 1949–51.

[11] Nahum Goldmann (Biog. Index, Vol. XII). On W.Z.O. Executive from 1935, President 1956–68. Acting President World Jewish Congress from 1949, President from 1953.

[12] Lieut.-Gen. Sir Alan Cunningham (Biog. Index, Vol. XXII). Seventh and last High Commissioner for Palestine, 1945–48.

[13] Oliver Stanley (Biog. Index, Vol. XXII). Secretary of State for Colonies 1942–45.

[14] Leopold S. Amery (Biog. Index, Vol. VIII). Secretary of State for Colonies 1924–29; for India and Burma 1940–45. Zionist sympathiser and friend of W.

what the present attitude of the Executive seems to amount to. It is a most unequal contest that the Executive has been waging with England; for the sake of getting a firm and satisfactory basis for the execution of the UNSCOP report, it is very necessary that we should find some way back to approximately normal relations with Britain. It is already late; I pray that it may not be too late.

This letter is merely to place on record my personal activities in the last two days, and the circumstances in which I felt obliged to act as I did.

I am, Gentlemen,
Yours faithfully,
Ch. Weizmann

6. To Meyer W. Weisgal,[1] aboard Queen Mary.

London, 6 September 1947

English: T.: W.A.

Urge you reply soonest Watt's letter 26/8[2] accepting Macmillan's offer.[3] Delay means missing spring season. Really no point working through Harpers here as Macmillan's better imprint and greater resources. Affectionately,

Chaim Weizmann

7. To Léon Blum, Paris.

London, 8 September 1947

French: Or. Copy. T.W.: W.A.

Mr. President, my dear Friend,

I am writing to you in order to introduce one of my best friends in London, Mr. Sigmund Gestetner,[1] who is coming to Paris with the hope of seeing you and to give you a personal invitation to participate at a Dinner which will be held here in November to initiate collections for a new farm-school for *chalutzim*[2] in Eng-

6. [1] Died 1977; Biog. Index, Vol. X. Executive Vice-Chairman, American Committee for Weizmann Institute of Science in New York 1947; subsequently President of Institute, then Chancellor.
[2] A. P. Watt was W.'s literary agent in Britain and was negotiating publishing rights to his memoirs. Watt's letter, apparently to Weisgal, is untraced.
[3] Negotiations had been taking place for some time with several publishers. In the event, W.'s autobiography, *Trial and Error,* was published in 1949 by Harper & Brothers in U.S. and Hamish Hamilton in Great Britain.

7. [1] Biog. Index, Vol. XX. Industrialist active in Zionist fund-raising; J.N.F. President in Britain from 1950; Treasurer of Weizmann Institute Foundation.
[2] Hebr.: 'agricultural pioneers.'

land. At present we have a very great need for additional facilities to prepare young people for agricultural life in Palestine. It is a project in which Mr. Gestetner has always been very interested; he has devoted much of his time and money to this end, and this is the second or third establishment of its kind which we have as a result of his initiative. It would be a very great pleasure for him, as it would be for us all, if you could accept his invitation and come to England for a few days in November in order to be present at the ceremony.

Naturally, my wife and I would be extremely pleased to see you; I would very much like to discuss the new situation with you, that created by the United Nations Special Committee's latest decision concerning us. There is still, needless to say, much for us to do; and we will have to take precautions against sabotage—from Jewish sources as well as from others. Perhaps, if you can come to London, we shall be able to see Mr. Churchill[3] and rally his powerful support.

I hope very much that you will be able to give us an entire day at least, and that you will let me know as soon as you can fix a date.[4]

With warmest wishes from Mrs. Weizmann as from myself, I am, dear President and friend,

Yours most cordially,

8. To Eliezer Kaplan, Montreux. *London, 16 September 1947*
English: Copy. T.W.: W.A.

My dear Eliezer,

It was very good of you to send me your charming note and your good wishes,[1] which I warmly reciprocate. You have done well to settle down in Montreux for a little; it must be lovely at this time of year, and I hope you will get a really good rest, and feel the better for it.

There is nothing new to tell you from here, except that there is a great deal of heart-searching about the implementation of the majority report. It seems from the press that Great Britain has no intention of making things any easier, though nothing is disclosed about her future intentions. In my opinion, she cannot stay in Palestine without the majority report; but she does not make it clear that she is prepared to go. What would, of course, suit her best is the Mandate without the Jewish clauses—but that seems morally impossible. So everything is very confused and difficult. I do sincere-

---

[3] Winston Churchill (Biog. Index, Vol. X). The British statesman was then out of office.
[4] Blum did not visit England at this time.

8. [1] Untraced.

ly hope that the New Year[2] may bring us some more settled times; I feel we have had enough of all this.

My love to you and your family, and all good wishes for your good health and for the cause. I am already preparing to leave for the States, which I suppose will happen about October 4th.[3]

As ever yours,
Ch. Weizmann

9. To Meyer W. Weisgal, New York.   *London, 17 September 1947*
English: T.: W.A.

For your own information only. Zion. Fed. [of South Africa] just transmitted following message to me from Smuts[1] confidential. "General very anxious you should be at UNO when Palestine Report comes on. This is should your health permit. S[outh] A[frican] delegation will in that case be instructed to keep in close touch with you. It is possible that partition might solve problem, and that chance should not be missed. General sends his warm good wishes to you and Mrs. Weizmann." Affectionately,[2]

Chaim

10. To Akiva Goldstein,[1] London.   *London, 19 September 1947*
English: Or. Copy. T.W.: W.A.

My dear Akiva,

Please convey to all my friends of the *Histadruth*[2] my heart-felt greetings and good wishes for the New Year. May it bring us a stage nearer to the fulfilment of all our hopes.

[2] The Jewish New Year fell 15–16 Sept. 1947.

[3] At J.A.'s invitation, W. was to appear before the U.N. Ad Hoc Committee on Palestine at Lake Success. The Weizmanns left England on 4 Oct. aboard the *Queen Mary*, remaining in U.S. until 17 Dec.

9. [1] Field-Marshal Jan Christiaan Smuts (Biog. Index, Vol. IX). Friend of W. and sympathetic to Zionist cause in discussions leading to Balfour Declaration; South African Prime Minister and Minister of External Affairs 1939–48.

[2] W. cabled Smuts that day (W.A.) that he was about to leave for U.S. and would contact South African delegation as suggested.

10. [1] B. 1903, Russia. Immigrating to Palestine 1921, he was among founders of Kibbutz Ramat David. Then on a *Histadrut* mission in England.

[2] The General Federation of Jewish Labour in Palestine.

You meet[3] at a time of crisis and uncertainty, when the future of Palestine and our National Home is unclear—discernible only to the eye of faith. In such circumstances, you will not expect me to say very much. But there is one thing that can be said, whatever may be the outcome of the great Assembly of the Nations now in session at Lake Success: In the long run, the future of Palestine depends upon us, and not upon anyone else. Our Home will be what we make it. And though our task may be made easier or more difficult by help or hindrance from outside, it remains *our* task, and our first pre-occupation must be its effective execution—with our own hands, and such tools of peace as are available to us. Almighty God is not alone in preferring to help those who help themselves.

I send you all my best wishes for the success of your deliberations, and remain

Very sincerely yours,

11. To Meyer W. Weisgal, New York.   *London, 22 September 1947*
English: T.: W.A.

Am greatly embarrassed by Henry's[1] wire,[2] which places heavy burden on me. Please advise what to do.[3] Affectionately,

Chaim Weizmann

12. To Eliezer Kaplan, Montreux.   *London, 26 September 1947*
English: Or. Copy. T.W.: W.A.

My dear Eliezer,

It was very kind of you to write to me, and I was delighted to have your letter.[1]

We shall be leaving for the States on the *Queen Mary* on October 4th, and intend to stay there till the first week in December. Then

---

[3] Goldstein had requested (11 Sept., W.A.) a message to the founding conference of supporters of *Histadrut* in England.

11. [1] Henry Morgenthau, Jr. (Biog. Index, Vol. XX). Former U.S. Secretary of Treasury. General chairman 1947–50, hon. chairman 1950–53, of U.J.A.

[2] This, 19 Sept. (W.A.), requested W. to visit Pittsburgh, Chicago and Detroit under U.J.A. auspices.

[3] W. wired Morgenthau 29 Sept. (W.A.) indicating his reluctance to take on further engagements, due to the poor state of his health. Should this improve, they could discuss the proposal. See also Weisgal telegram to W., 25 Sept. (W.A.).

12. [1] Untraced.

we may come back here for a few weeks before returning to Palestine. This will be fixed in the course of the next month.

I believe Creech Jones is making a speech to-day, but somehow I don't expect much good to come out of it.[2] The one redeeming feature of the present situation is that peace prevails in Palestine, and I hope it is not going to be disturbed by speeches or any other activities.

I am glad you are making a prolonged stay in Montreux, and hope it will fully restore your health. As for me, I long to get back to Rehovot, where there will be a great deal to be done on the equipment and installation of the new Institute. From all accounts the work is going on well. We have decided, however, instead of building a "settlement" for the scientists (which would cost a lot of money these days) to put up, for the time being, three apartment houses, with flats varying in size from one to four rooms. These would accommodate most of the newcomers, and would carry us over till times are a little easier.

I saw the High Commissioner before he left, and he seemed very pleased that he *is* going back:[3] there had obviously been some struggle about it. He told me very little about higher politics—but I do not think there have been many developments these last days, beyond an unconfirmed rumour that the U.S.A. would be prepared to allow its citizens to join a volunteer army for Palestine. Naturally, the members of such a force would be chiefly Jews. If this were true, it would be the best way out of the difficulty, but so far it is merely a rumour.

We shall be leaving, as I said, on October 4th, and hope to stay about two months, during which there will be a great deal to do. Morgenthau is trying to rope me in for a great many engagements, but much as I would like to help him, I feel I could not face it, or stand the strain.

Write and tell me how you are getting on.

With all good wishes for the coming year, and kindest regards to you and the family from us both, I am

Yours ever,

---

[2] The Colonial Secretary addressed the U.N. Ad Hoc Committee on Palestine (see Bridgenote preceding No. 44) 26 Sept. He stated that his Government endorsed without reservation UNSCOP's view that the Mandate should now be terminated. Britain was prepared to help in effecting any plan on which agreement existed between the Arabs and the Jews. But should the General Assembly recommend a policy not agreeable to both sides, Britain would not feel able to implement it, as she was not prepared to undertake the task of imposing a policy in Palestine by force of arms—text in *Zionist Review*, 30 Oct. 1947.

[3] Cunningham was in England for consultations and vacation.

13. To Sir Wyndham Deedes,[1] London.   *London, 2 October 1947*
English: Or. Copy. T.W.: W.A.

My dear Wyndham,

I can't leave without sending you a word to thank you and Miss MacKinnon[2] for yesterday afternoon, though I doubt if I can make you understand quite what it meant for me. For I had almost come to believe that I had no "goyish"[3] friends—except yourselves. This small and intimate gathering of people whose friendship has stood the test of time and (often) of long separation, has renewed my faith and courage, and I don't know how to thank you enough for that, as well as for the beautiful thing[4] you gave me. I shall leave for the States with a much lighter heart than I had expected, and that is due largely to you, and I don't know how to thank you for it.

We sail on Saturday, and hope to be back early in December; I look forward to seeing you again as soon as possible after our return. Meanwhile, my love and again my heart-felt thanks to you all.

Affectionately, as ever,

Yours,

14. To Felix Frankfurter,[1] Washington.   *New York, 14 October 1947*
English: Or. Copy. T.W.: W.A.

My dear Felix,

Your letter[2] came while I was away in Boston where I delivered a speech, and this explains the delay.

I was delighted to have a line from you and to read your wise words. I have consented to speak at the Forum,[3] although as you may understand, it is out of my purview, but I will try my best.

We had an interesting time in Boston—a great rally of 16,000 people—and I understand that 25,000 had been turned away.[4] Yester-

---

13. [1] Biog. Index, Vol. VIII. Chief Secretary to Palestine Administration 1920–23.

[2] Nancy MacKinnon assisted Deedes in directing activities of the British Association for the Jewish National Home ('Palestine House') aimed at fostering sympathy for the Zionist cause.

[3] Yidd.: non-Jewish.

[4] Allusion unknown.

14. [1] Biog. Index, Vol. VII. Associate Justice U.S. Supreme Court from 1938.

[2] 10 Oct. (W.A.). An affectionate letter of welcome.

[3] *New York Herald Tribune* forum: 'Modern Man, Slave or Sovereign?' W. spoke at the session on 'Spiritual Contributions to the Strength of Man', 21 Oct. Text in W.A.

[4] This took place 11 Oct. at the Boston Garden, sponsored by the Greater Boston Combined Jewish Appeal.

day we had a delightful evening with Harvard professors who turned out in great strength.[5] It was a very informal meeting, but was most interesting and instructive.

Well, I shall be looking forward to seeing you soon. Only now I can begin to make plans, and as soon as they are matured, I shall let you know.

Meanwhile, please accept the fondest love of Vera and myself, also to Marion.[6]

As ever yours,

15. To William Phillips,[1] **North Beverley.** *New York, 16 October 1947*
English: Or. Copy. T.W.: W.A.

Dear Mr. Phillips,

I am most grateful to you for your kind note.[2] I was equally disappointed not having seen you. Possibly there is a chance of your coming to New York in the next two months. In that case, I would ask you to let me know in time so that we might meet.

My speaking engagements are not numerous, happily. Still it is somewhat tiring, but I hope to get through it without mishap.

Things do look a little brighter, although we are not out of the wood yet.[3] The whole problem of implementation and of the interim period loom very largely on our road to the goal as formidable obstacles, particularly as the attitude of Great Britain is neither clear nor, I am afraid, helpful at present. But it may change in the course of this meeting.

You no doubt remember my attitude from the very beginning. I don't believe that any other solution except partition is easy or better. Of course, it all depends on the good will on both sides. Once there is a definite settlement, I am hopeful that both sides may try to "bury the hatchet." It may take time, but it is a possibility.

I hope that your cold has cleared up and you are well again. The

[5] A dinner in W.'s honour at the Harvard Club attended by James B. Conant, President of the University.
[6] Mrs. Frankfurter (d. 1975).

15. [1] 1878–1968. Career diplomat and former U.S. ambassador in Rome; an American member of Anglo-American Committee of Inquiry into the problems of European Jewry and Palestine, formed 1945 (see Vol. XXII).
[2] 14 Oct. (W.A.), regretting inability to attend a luncheon with W. through indisposition.
[3] Noting that Soviet spokesmen had expressed initial approval for partition, Phillips felt that a solution may have been found at last, though he was dubious that this would bring peace unless Jews and Arabs agreed to cooperate.

weather is so lovely and warm that it should help you to get quite well soon, which I sincerely wish.

With best regards from Mrs. Weizmann and myself,

Yours,

16. To Léon Blum, Mansart, France. *New York, 19 October 1947*
French: T.: W.A.

Your friends' attitude very uncertain.[1] Am in contact with André[2] and René[3] but want to talk to you by telephone to explain urgent importance your intervention. Would be grateful if you could cable me[4] Plaza Hotel, New York, when and where I can telephone you without disturbing you. Please give particular attention Jarblum's communication.[5] Sincerely

Weizmann

17. To Gita Dounie,[1] Haifa. *New York, 19 October 1947*
English: T.: W.A.

Distressed to hear Fruma's death.[2] Sending you all our deepest sympathy. Write us Plaza Hotel. Love,

Anka,[3] Vera, Chaim

16. [1] I.e., the French attitude to partition as expressed by their U.N. delegation.

[2] André Meyer (Biog. Index, Vol. XXII). French-born head of New York firm of Lazard Frères. He had fled in 1940 to U.S.

[3] René Mayer (1895–1972). French Minister of Finance 1947–48; Minister of Justice in successive Governments; Prime Minister 1953. W.'s list of engagements (W.A.) indicates that he met both André Meyer and René Mayer 20 Oct., and was due to dine with Alexandre Parodi, leader of French delegation, 22 Oct.

[4] W. telephoned by arrangement 24 Oct., and expressed concern that France might abstain on the U.N. resolution. W. pressed the French not to do this, 'so contrary to all the historical traditions of their country'—note in W.A.

[5] Marc Jarblum (Biog. Index, Vol. XIV). French Zionist leader and socialist influential in winning Blum to Zionist cause; played a significant role in securing France's vote in Nov. 1947. His communication untraced.

17. [1] Sister of W. (d. 1975; Biog. Index, Vol. I). Music teacher.

[2] Fruma Weicman (Biog. Index, Vol. III). Sister of W.

[3] Anna Weizmann (Biog. Index, Vol. I). Sister of W.; on scientific staff of Daniel Sieff Research Institute, and later Weizmann Institute. She was temporarily working in U.S.

18. To Jacob Landau,[1] New York.   *New York, 19 October 1947*
English: Or. Copy. T.W.: W.A.

Dear Mr. Landau,

I am most grateful to you for your letter and for the information contained therein.[2] I have never doubted that you would do all you could to help in this critical time, and I am happy that you did influence Baruch[3] and Swope.[4] From what I understand from George Backer[5] and others, they are extremely helpful and useful, and I am sure that it is largely due to your influence. I hope that you will continue your good efforts, particularly now.

With regard to Mr. Churchill, I would like to say that just at this moment he has more or less withdrawn from Zionist work because he is disgusted by the terrorists and terrorism,[6] and it is not easy to get him back into a proper frame of mind. I have it on best and most reliable authority,[7] and I have never attempted to see him in the last few months. There may possibly be a change now, in view of the new turn of events. I have on purpose included his name amongst the founders of the National Home together with Balfour[8] and Lloyd George,[9] although his role was comparatively small. It would be useful if you would give it prominence in your bulletin and send it on to him. He is rather sensitive.

There is one more matter which seems to be worrisome at present, and that is the attitude of the French. They are feeble and undecided and would probably abstain if you can't convince them to be a little

---

18. [1] 1892–1952. Journalist, founding-director Jewish Telegraphic Agency.

[2] This, 16 Oct. (W.A.), stated that, following W.'s suggestion made some years earlier, a meeting had been arranged between Abba Hillel Silver, the American Zionist leader, and Churchill, during the latter's U.S. visit in 1946. This was achieved through the intercession of Bernard Baruch, via Herbert B. Swope.

[3] Bernard Baruch (1870–1965). U.S. financier, confidant of American presidents; was opposed to Jewish nationalism, but helped the Zionists during the struggle for partition in U.N.

[4] Herbert Bayard Swope (1882–1958). Journalist and policy consultant; associate member and assistant to Baruch on U.S. War Industries Board during W.W.I; director, National Conference of Christians and Jews.

[5] 1902–74. U.S. publisher and prominent New York Democrat; publisher of *New York Post* 1939–42; a Governor of Weizmann Institute of Science.

[6] For Churchill's alienation from the Zionist cause, particularly following the assassination by extremists of Lord Moyne, British Minister Resident in Middle East, on 6 Nov. 1944, see Vol. XXI.

[7] W. was in touch with two men close to Churchill: Sir John Miller Martin, his private secretary, and Leopold Amery. W. and Martin had dined together 15 Oct. (W.'s engagement list, W.A.).

[8] Arthur James Balfour (Biog. Index, Vol. IV). Statesman and philosopher.

[9] David Lloyd George (Biog. Index, Vol. IX). British Prime Minister at time of Balfour Declaration, 1917.

more active. I am seeing them in the course of this week, but I wonder whether you have any more intimate contacts.

I remain with kind regards and hoping to see you during the course of my stay here,

Yours very sincerely,

19. To Samuel Zemurray,[1] New York.   *New York, 20 October 1947*
English: T.: W.A.

Private and Personal

I arrived here a few days ago in connection with the meeting of the United Nations. The situation is such that your help is very much required at this critical stage.[2] Have tried to get in touch with you but so far have failed. Kindly let me know when we can meet. Believe me it is urgent.[3] With affectionate regards, your old friend

Chaim Weizmann

20. To Sir Wyndham Deedes, London.   *New York, 22 October 1947*
English: Or. Copy. T.W./H.W.: W.A.

My dear Wyndham,

I was very glad to read your letter, which I take as an indication that your health so far is stable. I hope it will continue to be so. You have had your share. Many thanks for your letter and invitation, which, of course, I accept gratefully.[1]

It is difficult to prognosticate how things will go. So far it wasn't bad, but to collect a two-third majority is not an easy task, particularly in an organization where the vote of Nicaragua weighs as much as that of the United States. I suppose that is the price one pays for democracy.

We are, of course, having trouble with those countries who have a great Moslem population—France and Holland.[2] They are still

---

19. [1] 1877–1961. Of New Orleans, head of United Fruit Corporation. He and W. had been friends since the 1920s.
[2] Zemurray's influence was strong in the smaller republics of Central America, whose votes would be important in the General Assembly deliberations on Palestine.
[3] They met the following day.

20. [1] Deedes reported (16 Oct., W.A.) on a successful meeting at Palestine House with Richard Crossman M.P. as speaker. He wished W. to address a future gathering there.
[2] In 1947 Holland still possessed Indonesia.

working on the old lines of appeasement, but taking it all in all there is a good chance for the majority report to go through. So far the atmosphere is not unfriendly. The exceptions are, curiously enough, China and India and some of the South American Republics like Argentine. I now hear that France is wobbling, but we might bolster them up in the course of the next few days. It is all rather nerve-wracking, but this seems to be the rule of the road at present.

Nancy [MacKinnon] is right that my stay in London will not be very prolonged. We leave here on Dec. 11, arriving in London about the 16th. We shall certainly stay about three weeks, so that this gives you the possibility of arranging the meeting, although Christmas season may not be the best time to get the people you wish. I think I would prefer no reporters.

Well, my best love to you and all good wishes for your health. Please give my affectionate regards to Nancy.[3]

Yours,

21. To Felix Frankfurter, Washington.   *New York, 22 October 1947*
English: Or. Copy. T.W.: W.A.

My dear Felix,

You overwhelm me with your great kindness, and I feel deeply indebted to you for your expression of opinion about the speech; and I am happy it pleases you, which means a great deal to me.[1]

I am still not in a position to judge how things are going. It is a very ponderous and cumbersome machine, but the attitude of the Americans and the Russians has been excellent so far. The French are difficult just at present. They seem to contemplate abstention and that would in a sense influence Belgium, Holland and possibly Luxemburg. It is lamentable to think that the French who were the vanguard of progress should buckle under Arab threats. Abdul Kerim,[2] like the Mufti,[3] is implacable. They could just as well try and appease a crocodile, and it is extraordinary that they haven't

---

[3] Final sentence handwritten.

21. [1] In an undated note (W.A.), Frankfurter urged a special reprinting of W.'s statement before the Ad Hoc Committee on Palestine (delivered on 18 Oct.—see Introduction). An edition of 1,000 copies was issued by the Overbrook Press of Stamford, Connecticut, in Nov. 1947—the first of many.

[2] Abd el-Krim (1882–1963). Rif tribal leader who had rebelled against the Spanish and the French in Morocco in 1920s, and was given sanctuary by King Farouk of Egypt.

[3] Hajj Muhammad Amin al-Husseini (Biog. Index, Vol. XIV). Former Mufti of Jerusalem, who continued to direct Palestinian Arab resistance to both Zionism and the British Mandate in 1947–48 from Egypt.

learned their lesson yet. If you happen to see Bonnet[4] it might be a good thing to tell him that, in a polite form.

I am not sure when I shall be in Washington but I am certain to go there shortly. I am really looking forward to seeing you and Marion and to hear from you how you are. Meanwhile, please accept our affectionate regards.

Yours ever,

22. To Ludwig Lewisohn,[1] **New York.**   *New York, 22 October 1947*
English: Or. Copy. T.W.: W.A.

My dear Mr. Lewisohn,

It was very good of you to write me, and I appreciate very much your expression of opinion concerning my speech.[2] Coming from you it acquires a particular significance for me.

With regard to your first request, nothing will give me greater pleasure than to fulfil it immediately. I haven't seen you for a very long time, and we might usefully exchange notes. But I am at present under very heavy pressure indeed, which I hope will be reduced very soon. I will then come back to your kind invitation.

With regard to your second suggestion, I am very happy to hear that you will conduct a *Zionist Review*; and it will no doubt be worthy of its editor and of the cause, but under the present circumstances it seems very difficult for me to participate, in any shape or form, in any enterprise of the American Zionist Organization. I have not been in touch with these people either here or anywhere else and have kept myself aloof.[3] You will therefore understand if I do not accede to your request. When we meet I might supplement this letter with some more information.

With kind regards,

Yours very sincerely,

---

[4] Henri Bonnet (b. 1888). French scholar and diplomat; commissioner and Minister for Information, Provisional Government 1943–44; Ambassador to U.S. 1944–45; Vice-President Franco-American Committee.

22. [1] 1882–1955. U.S. novelist and essayist; editor of *The New Palestine* 1943–48.

[2] Lewisohn wrote (20 Oct., W.A.) praising W.'s address before the U.N. Ad Hoc Committee on 18 Oct. He included an invitation to dine, or proposed visiting the Weizmanns. Further, he enquired whether W.'s memoirs were sufficiently advanced for extracts to be published in *The American Zionist Review*, a new periodical to be edited by Lewisohn.

[3] *The American Zionist Review* was to be an organ of Z.O.A., from whose leaders W. was estranged.

23. To Morris D. Waldman,[1] **New York.**   *New York, 23 October 1947*
English: Or. Copy. T.W.: W.A.

My dear Mr. Waldman,

It was very kind of you to write me in such warm terms.[2] Believe me, I appreciate very much a message coming from an old friend with whom we had to work sometimes under very difficult and strenuous conditions.

I know quite well what your work meant—the smoothing over of differences which did exist between us and men like Marshall and Warburg[3]—but I cannot help feeling the difference between the stature of those men and what one sees now. However, that is not only applicable to Jewish life. The level of humanity has been depressed all over the world, and we are no exception. I very often feel that I do not fit any more into this world but that is probably the fate of all elderly people, and one must not let oneself be depressed by these sentiments.

Incidentally, I had the pleasure of meeting Edward Warburg[4] yesterday. He is no doubt one of the young ones, and I was delighted to see his keen interest and his devotion to Jewish work. Of course, he is only one in the family, but one is almost enough nowadays.

I am staying here until the second week in December. I do not know how you are placed, whether you go out much or whether you lead a very quiet life, but I would very much like to see you. Please let me know when and how we can meet. I am going to the Hadassah Convention in Atlantic City tomorrow, and I shall be back on Saturday afternoon.

All the good wishes to which you gave expression are reciprocated from the bottom of my heart.[5]

With very kind regards and best wishes,

Yours,

---

23. [1] 1879–1963. U.S. social worker, active in non-Zionist section of J.A. and Executive Vice-President of American Jewish Committee 1942–45.

[2] Waldman's letter (18 Oct., W.A.), prompted by W.'s address before the U.N. Committee, spoke of W. as 'the outstanding leader of our people'.

[3] Louis Marshall and Felix M. Warburg (both in Biog. Index, Vol. X), were the American Jewish leaders conducting the difficult negotiations leading to the expansion of J.A. in 1929—see Vols. XIII, XIV.

[4] B. 1908. Son of Felix Warburg; chairman of J.D.C. 1941–46; chairman of U.J.A. 1950–55.

[5] Waldman had concluded his letter with a prayer for W.'s health.

24. To Doris May,[1] London.   *New York, 28 October 1947*

English: Or. Copy. T.W.: W.A.

My dear Miss May,

It will be three weeks this coming Thursday since I have arrived in this country, and it seems to me that I have been here an age. The first days were very crowded, and, what with the statement before the UNO and seeing numerous people, it meant a great deal of pressure. It has now subsided a little bit. I have been to Boston and shall still have to visit one or two places. Things are somewhat difficult because of the unusual heat and stuffiness which, for this time of the year, is most abnormal.

You no doubt read in the press and in the various bulletins about the state of affairs in the UNO. It seems to me that on a whole things are not going too badly. The fact that America and Russia have both supported the UNSCOP majority report makes the position much more stable than it would have been otherwise. There are, of course, still a great many hurdles to jump, like the whole problem of implementation. What is going to happen when the British go out, which is the authority which will take over, and the whole financial problem, requires careful thinking. I hear that the people are spending all of their days in endless discussions, and what will follow out of it is difficult to foretell. I see only very few of them and at rare intervals, but I do get an idea of what is going on.

The resolution may come before the Assembly the middle of next month if there is no hitch, and I suppose there will be a great rush for offices; and both Silver[2] and Ben-Gurion[3] are grooming themselves for positions, which is not so bad because they may neutralize each other. News from Palestine about the fights between the *Irgun*[4] and the *Haganah*[5] are rather disturbing, and unless that is quelled at the outset this may have very unpleasant consequences.

I am keeping to my program and am booked to leave on the *Queen Mary* on December 11th. We would arrive in London approximately

---

24. [1] Biog. Index, Vol. XV. W.'s secretary in London 1929–48.

[2] Abba Hillel Silver (Biog. Index, Vol. X). U.S. Reform rabbi, chairman of American section of J.A. He presented the case for an independent Jewish State before U.N., and mobilized American opinion.

[3] David Ben-Gurion (Biog. Index, Vol. IX). Leader of *Yishuv*, chairman of J.A. Executive. Israel's first Prime Minister and Minister of Defence.

[4] *Irgun Zvai Leumi*, Jewish underground armed organization founded 1931, linked with the Revisionist movement in 1937; joined Israel Defence Forces Sept. 1948.

[5] Unofficial military organization of *Yishuv*, founded 1920; on 31 May 1948 became regular army of Israel. It differed from the *Irgun* over both strategy and tactics, though they sometimes cooperated. See Vols. XXI, XXII.

on the 16th and I am anxious to leave for Palestine after about three weeks, so that I would go to Geneva and try to get a plane from there to Palestine. We would also fly to Geneva; so perhaps you and Linton could arrange my trip for an approximate date between the 7th and 10th of January, flying from London to Geneva and from Geneva to Palestine.

Give my best love to Linton and thank him for his letter, and also to yourself. I shall be writing to Linton in a few days.[6]

With affectionate regards,

Yours,

25. To Joseph I. Linton, London. *New York, 28 October 1947*
English: Or. Copy. T.W.: W.A.

Dear Ivor,

Your letter was most welcome[1] as one here hears very little as to what is going on in England. Unfortunately, England's role in Lake Success has been hitherto rather passive. Whether it will remain so, I cannot say. I have seen both Creech Jones and Martin[2] twice and have had some friendly talks, but whether the good will shown by them will not be counteracted from London is difficult to say.

I was glad to hear that the M.P.s are sympathetic to the idea of Great Britain taking part in the implementation. This is always my impression from the conversations with the people here. I was somewhat disappointed that none of our speakers before the UNO have found a few sentences to thank Britain for their services. Whatever may have happened during the regime of the Labor Party, if not for Great Britain we would be nowhere, and many of our people who, at present, lead a good life in Palestine, and are making their contribution to the upbuilding of the country, might have been burned in Auschwitz. It hurts me always to feel that our people are not sufficiently grateful. Gratitude has always been a trait of the Jews, but their manners have deteriorated like everybody else's.

---

[6] See No. 25.

25. [1] 21 Oct. (W.A.). This stated that discussions between Simon Marks, Harry Sacher, Deedes and Linton himself with various M.P.s and Government officials gave him the impression that individual politicians were not opposed to Britain's help in putting the Majority Report into effect, but this did not mean the Cabinet could be persuaded.

[2] Sir John M. Martin (Biog. Index, Vol. XVIII). Under-Secretary of State, C.O. 1945–56. Two meetings only are recorded in W.'s engagement list (W.A.): with Martin 15 Oct., with Creech Jones 23 Oct.

As you may have seen from Miss May's letter, I do not see very much of our people. Eliahu[3] and Aubrey[4] come from time to time to report on what is going on, but the others are always immersed in endless discussions, and I am not aware of the results of these meetings. I hear, however, from Agronsky[5] who has been here for a short time that Silver considers himself the author of the blueprint of the Jewish State, Neumann[6] is the co-author; and when they crack the whip everybody answers "Amen." I never thought that our people can be so supine, but that is the situation, and it argues poorly for the Jewish State.

The fight between the *Haganah* and the *Irgun* is also something which may develop into a great tragedy.[7] It is all too late and it comes at the most inopportune moment. However, I am glad it isn't my responsibility, at present, at any rate.

Write to me, from time to time, and let me know how things are. Incidentally, I have heard that Jowitt, who was here recently, has been carrying on a most violent anti-Semitic propaganda.[8] I may find out more details later on.

I am very amused about Shragai[9] seeing the Archbishop. I suppose he will talk Yiddish to him, because that is the only language he knows well; but I doubt whether the Archbishop could reciprocate.

My best love to you. If you see the children[10] give them my love.

As ever,

Yours,

---

[3] Eliahu Epstein (later, Elath; Biog. Index, Vol. XVIII). Head of J.A. office in Washington 1945–48; subsequently Israel's Ambassador in Washington and London.

[4] Aubrey (Abba) Eban (Biog. Index, Vol. XIX). J.A. Liaison officer with UNSCOP 1947, and on its delegation to U.N. General Assembly. Subsequently Israel's permanent representative at U.N. and Ambassador in Washington.

[5] Gershon Agronsky (later, Agron; Biog. Index, Vol. XVI). Editor *Palestine* (later, *Jerusalem*) *Post*. Subsequently Mayor of Jerusalem.

[6] Emanuel Neumann (Biog. Index, Vol. X). On J.A. Executive; President of Z.O.A. 1947–49, 1956–58.

[7] See No. 24, n. 5.

[8] Sir William (later, Earl) Jowitt (1885–1957). Lord Chancellor 1945–51; member World Committee Chaim Weizmann Memorial 1953–57. Linton had mentioned Marks' meeting with Jowitt and Bevan. Nothing is known of W.'s allegation.

[9] Shlomo Zalman Shragai. B. 1899, Poland. Religious Zionist leader on J.A. Executive 1946–50; Mayor of Jerusalem 1950–52; head of J.A. Immigration Department 1954–68. Linton had written that Shragai was due to discuss Britain's anti-Zionist policy with Archbishop of Canterbury (Geoffrey Fisher).

[10] W.'s son Benjamin (Biog. Index, Vol. V) and his wife, Maidie.

26. To Jan Christiaan Smuts, Pretoria.   *New York, 28 October 1947*
English: Or. Copy. T.W.: W.A.

My dear General,

This is just a note to let you know how grateful I feel that you have put me in touch with your delegation here, whom I have seen twice and with whom we have discussed all the various details. Mr. Lawrence[1] and his colleagues are thoughtful and sympathetic men, and they listened very attentively to what I had to say.

The situation here looks fairly satisfactory, although there are still a good many difficulties to overcome. The main point is the positive attitude both of America and of Russia, and it is almost tantamount to a miracle that these two countries should have agreed on our problem.[2]

It looks as if the UNSCOP majority report is meeting with a great deal of favor. There may be some slight modification here and there, but on a whole it seems to be an excellent basis for discussion. The attitude of the British is more or less neutral, and I for one regret that they have placed themselves into a position whereby their role at present, at any rate, is insignificant. Whatever one may say in criticism of their attitude in the last year or two, or of the work of the British administration in the course of the last twenty-five years,[3] they have carried the burden; and if not for the British Government, we would be nowhere. That is likely to be overlooked at the present time, although I am trying to remind them, but apparently such is the rule of the road.

If I may say so, I miss you here very much. That is no reflection on your delegation, but I am thinking of the old days of 1917–18 and 19;[4] and I thought it would be a historic gesture if you were present at the consummation of what you had begun about twenty-five years ago.

I hope that you all keep well and that you may still consider it possible to come to Palestine this next Spring. It would be grand to have you there and I do hope you will permit yourself the week or ten days necessary for such a trip. I am staying here until December 11th and then returning for a short time to England and from there to Palestine, where we intend to stay about six to seven months.

26. [1] Harry Gordon Lawrence, South African lawyer and politician, whom W. met 11, 27 Oct. See No. 9.

   [2] The Soviet representative, Semyon K. Tsarapkin, joined with U.S. in endorsing partition when he addressed the U.N. Ad Hoc Committee 13 Oct. On 21 Oct. this committee assigned the detailed planning of a partition scheme to a sub-committee of nine supporters of the proposal, including U.S. and Soviet Union.

   [3] W. had contended over the years that an unsympathetic local Palestine Administration was frustrating British policy as laid down in Balfour Declaration.

   [4] Smuts' pro-Zionist influence had been strong at that time.

I would like to take this occasion of expressing to you once again my heartfelt thanks for all you have done and are doing for us.

With my profound respect and sincere wishes, I remain,

Your old friend,

27. To Lord Inverchapel,[1] Washington.   *New York, 30 October 1947*
English: Or. Copy. T.W.: W.A.

Dear Lord Inverchapel,

I am very grateful to you for your kind letter[2] and I would have liked to be able to say when I am coming out to Washington but for the time being it is not yet very definite.

I am most anxious to see you and we have a great deal to say to each other. I have been keeping, somewhat, in touch with Mr. Creech Jones and Mr. Martin.

I would like to see the President.[3] I believe it is rather important and I cannot see him without your introduction, being a British subject. Do you think you can do that for me? I hate to give you more trouble but it seems to be necessary at this juncture.[4]

Thanking you in advance, I remain with all good wishes and kind regards,

Yours very sincerely,

28. To Albert K. Epstein,[1] Chicago.   *New York, 31 October 1947*
English: Or. Copy. T.W.: W.A.

My dear A.K.,

As always, I am happy to receive your letter.[2] I understand very well your good intentions and how you suffer from the state of

---

27. [1] Archibald Clark-Kerr (Biog. Index, Vol. IX). British Ambassador to U.S. 1946–48.

[2] 25 Oct. (W.A.). Indicating that he had just returned from the Middle East, Inverchapel hoped for an early meeting with W. This took place in New York 13 Nov.

[3] Harry S. Truman (Biog. Index, Vol. XXII). The decisive vote in the General Assembly was approaching, and W. was anxious to present the Zionist case to the President.

[4] Simultaneously, W. wrote to David Niles in Washington: 'Supposing the Ambassador refuses to do what I ask, is there another way of seeing the President?' (W.A.).

28. [1] Biog. Index, Vol. XVII. Industrial chemist, and long-time supporter of Daniel Sieff and Weizmann Institutes.

[2] 28 Oct. (W.A.) congratulating W. on his statement to U.N. Epstein saw the UNSCOP recommendation of partition as 'gratifying vindication' of W. against those who had opposed him at the 1946 Basle Congress. He felt that 'we must especially do something to unite the entire Zionist movement, and we must have your counsel and leadership', and wished to discuss practical ideas for making peace in the movement when W. visited Chicago.

affairs which prevails here. But to be quite frank with you, I see no prospect of any peace. With whom do you want me to make peace? The present so-called leaders of the Zionist movement here are not men of peace. They are dictators who may try and force their views, by any means, on the Zionist movement here. They have now made the partition their own program and if you listen to them, they are the sole authors of this idea.

I don't know what practical problems you have in mind. I dread to be dragged in again into the turmoil of debate, controversy and argument at this moment. Should the Jewish State really emerge as a reality out of this meeting, we shall be facing a very dangerous and very responsible period. There will be a rush for offices and in my opinion success depends upon getting new blood into the movement, people of experience in world affairs. We shall be scrutinized and watched zealously, and the position of the Jews, not only inside Palestine but outside, will largely be affected by what we do or fail to do in the Jewish State.

I view the approaching period with great trepidation, still it is both a challenge and a privilege that this task has fallen on the shoulders of the present generation which, unfortunately, has been orphaned by the loss of six million of the best.

I am not yet sure when I shall be in Chicago but shall let you know in good time. Should your way bring you to New York, you know I am always happy to see you and have a talk with you.

Give my best love to your family and to Mr. Harris.[3]

With best regards and affection,

Yours ever,

29. To Aryeh Leon Gellman,[1] New York. *New York, 31 October 1947*
English: Or. Copy. T.W.: W.A.

Dear Mr. Gellman,

Forgive me for answering your kind letter[2] in English, as I have no Hebrew stenographer.

---

[3] Benjamin Harris (b. 1896). Chemical engineer, supporter of Weizmann Institute. Epstein's brother-in-law.

29. [1] 1887–1973. President of *Mizrachi* Organization of America 1935–39 and editor of *Mizrachi* publications 1935–49; settled in Israel 1949; chairman of World *Mizrachi*.

[2] 10 Cheshvan 5708 (24 Oct. 1947, W.A.). This praised W.'s 'new role of prophet to the non-Jews in articulating the abiding ethical values of Judaism'. Gellman pointed out W.'s misreading of a Talmudic reference to the sage, Hillel, in his address to the *New York Herald Tribune* forum (see No. 14, n. 3), and emphasised his admiration for W. despite their differences over the partition formula for Palestine, which Gellman opposed.

It was good of you to write to me and also draw my attention to some misquotation. I must say that the reading of the paper on the Jewish faith and what it does to humanity before the Forum of the *Herald Tribune* was an extremely difficult task for me, because it is a subject about which I have been thinking all my life, but it is not as familiar to me as Zionism or chemistry; and speaking before a non-Jewish audience, chiefly, I had to be extremely careful, and it had taken me a good long time to prepare it.

I would like to add that you are one of the few members of *Mizrachi* who in the course of all these [. . . . .]³ has to say something to me which is different from the usual verbiage, and that is why I appreciate it so much.

With best regards, I am

Yours very sincerely,

30. To Doris May, London.　　　　*New York, 3 November 1947*
English: T.W.: W.A.

My dear Miss May,

I have just heard from Nancy MacKinnon that I am to speak in Palestine House on January 7th.¹ The date is all right as far as I am concerned, except that it brings it very near to my departure for Palestine.

As you know, it is my intention to leave here on December 11th, arriving in London about the 16th and staying there about three weeks to a month. Will you be good enough to secure a plane reservation for both of us and Bergmann,² practically any date after the 7th, the sooner the better, via Swiss Air Geneva. Please let me know, by telegram, how things are going.

I suppose you are watching the press and know what is going on in the UNO. If we are not careful we might get a Jewish State quite soon, with Silver as president and Ben-Gurion as Prime Minister— God help us!

I am sending you my very best love and also to Linton. I am not writing separately because there is very little I have to say at present.

Ever yours,

Ch. Weizmann

---

³ A line missing in extant copy.

30. ¹ See No. 20 and n. 1 there.
² Ernst David Bergmann (Biog. Index, Vol. XVI). Scientific director of Sieff Institute and later of Weizmann Institute; Professor of Organic Chemistry at H.U. from 1952.

31. To Emanuel Neumann, New York.   *New York, 3 November 1947*
English: T.: W.A.

Just received your telegram.[1] Thanks invitation. It is obviously too late for me to attend your dinner.[2]

Chaim Weizmann

32. To Albert K. Epstein, Chicago.   *New York, 10 November 1947*
English: Or. Copy. T.W.: W.A.

My dear A.K.,

As always, I was delighted to receive your very interesting letter,[1] and I fully share your views about the duties and responsibilities which will face us if and when the Jewish State comes about. I equally believe that our forces are much too small for the problems ahead. Whether everybody in Palestine is thinking in these terms, I cannot say. I dare say some are, but they must be isolated groups of people.

I haven't the faintest idea what the leaders of the American Zionists think of it. I don't read their official paper because reading is very difficult for me and I haven't seen any of them all this time. I have seen no signs on their part wishing to heal the rift which they have produced. They seem to be satisfied with the position they have created for themselves and from what I hear their official newspapers give full expression to their self-satisfaction. It is they who have brought about the political advancement which we are witnessing at present, and real Zionist history began after the last Basle Congress. That is typical of all dictators. The real era of Italian history began with the march on Rome,[2] and the years were counted from that date.

31. [1] This (W.A.) read: 'Regret exceedingly extending invitation at late hour. Just brought my attention [that] our dinner chairman, whose responsibility it was [to] extend invitation, took upon himself to assume your presence [at the Jewish] Agency Balfour Day Reception [in] Washington precluded your acceptance. Would be very happy to have you honor us by your presence tonight.'

[2] For W.'s more candid reaction, see following letter.

32. [1] 6 Nov. (W.A.). Replying to No. 28, Epstein proposed: inviting all leaders alienated at the Basle Congress, including W., back into the movement; new orientation within America whereby the movement cease its political activities and concentrate upon practical economic problems involved in building the Jewish State for the anticipated million Jews who would enter Palestine within the next decade; investment by American Jews in Palestinian enterprises through an international loan; furnishing of technical skills by Americans as a stop-gap measure; increasing the number of Jews at institutions of higher learning in Palestine so as to produce specialist personnel.

[2] I.e., the assumption of dictatorial powers by Mussolini, following the march of 28 Oct. 1922.

It is also typical that to the dinner which was given for the 30th anniversary of the Balfour Declaration I was not invited. Only on the eve of the dinner, when the matter became an open scandal and the members of the Executive here had telegraphed their refusal to attend, about 7 o'clock of the same evening, I received a telegram from Mr. Neumann inviting me to the dinner and giving some lame explanation for the omission.[3] I therefore can't see what I can do or anybody else can do to bring about a change in this attitude.

I believe, however, that if we get a Jewish State the whole position of the Zionist organizations in the *Galuth*[4] will change, and it will then be time to reform the position, or if, God forbid, nothing happens, there will be such disappointment followed by chaos in Palestine that I wouldn't like to contemplate it. It is, therefore, advisable for the present to await the developments of the next few weeks.

I shall be glad to talk to you when you are here next Saturday, and I shall hold myself free for the afternoon or the evening as the case may be.

What you write about higher and specialized education in Palestine, as compared with that in this country, is striking and most instructive and constitutes a very powerful reply to those critics who objected to the building of the Weizmann Scientific Center.[5] I think we cannot do enough in the realm of higher learning if we want to get somewhere.

I am making my reply short as I am looking forward to our conversation.[6]

With affectionate regards to you, your family and Harris and his family, I am

                         Yours ever,

33. To Felix Frankfurter, Washington.   *New York, 12 November 1947*
English: Or. Copy. T.W.: W.A.

My dear Felix,

I am delighted at the prospect of seeing you soon, and, believe me, I am looking forward to it very much. As you kindly suggested, I shall see you at 4:30 p.m. on November 17th and then again for dinner on November 18th.

---

[3] See No. 31, n. 1.

[4] Hebr.: Diaspora.

[5] Epstein calculated that two per cent of the American population attended college or university, compared with less than 0.4 per cent in Palestine—1,800 students enrolled in H.U. and the Technion.

[6] They met briefly in New York 16 Nov., as W. was departing for Washington.

I am anxious to see one or two people in Washington, particularly Mr. Lovett[1] of the State Department and Mr. David Lilienthal.[2] The latter is perhaps not within your circle.

Yesterday I spent some time in Princeton seeing Professor Einstein[3] and Professor Oppenheimer,[4] and the projected meeting with Lilienthal is a sequel to my interview with Professor Oppenheimer.

We shall have a great deal to tell each other and meanwhile I am sending you and Marion my best love.

As ever,

Yours,

34. To George S. Franklin, Jr.,[1] New York.

New York, 13 November 1947

English: Or. Copy. T.W.: W.A.

Dear Mr. Franklin,

I would like to thank you for your note of November 11th[2] and to say that I am looking forward to meeting you and your colleagues on the 21st of November and shall be there promptly at 7 o'clock.

I have no special wishes at all but I understand that Jamal Husseini[3] had been speaking before your Council, and I would be most grateful if I could get a stenogram of what he said. Judging from his speech before the UNO, to which I had listened very carefully, his factual data are not all they should be. It is, therefore, important that I know what he said, so that I may correct some of the statements he made.

I don't intend to enter into polemics with him but only limit myself to uncontestable facts, as, for instance, during his speech at Lake Success he made a statement that the Jews have never drained a

33. [1] Robert A. Lovett, b. 1895. Under-Secretary of State in Truman Administration 1947–49; Secretary of Defense 1951–53; special adviser to President Kennedy 1961–63.

[2] B. 1899. Director Tennessee Valley Authority 1933–41; chairman 1941–46; chairman of Atomic Energy Commission 1946–50.

[3] Albert Einstein (Biog. Index, Vol. X).

[4] J. Robert Oppenheimer (1904–1967). Physicist in charge of construction of first atomic bomb as director of laboratories at Los Alamos, New Mexico. Directed Princeton's Institute for Advanced Studies 1947, and chaired General Advisory Committee of Atomic Energy Commission.

34. [1] B. 1913. Authority on international affairs; associated with Council on Foreign Relations from 1945.

[2] W.A. Relates to W.'s leading a discussion of a Near and Middle East group which was considering the problem of Palestine. See also Franklin to W., 5 Nov. (W.A.).

[3] Jamal al-Husseini, b. 1892. The Mufti's cousin and intimate aide; acting chairman of Arab Higher Committee, most powerful political group of Palestine Arab community. Head of delegation presenting Arab case before U.N. in 1947.

single marsh in Palestine. As you may perhaps know, I have been connected with the development both agriculturally and otherwise in Palestine since the earliest days of the Mandate, and I could demonstrate on the map, beyond a shadow of a doubt, the thousands of acres which we have drained and have converted from malaria swamps into excellent land. And this brings me to another small request—whether it wouldn't be possible to have a map of Palestine in the room during the sitting.

Thanking you in anticipation, I am

Yours very sincerely,

35. To Mordecai M. Kaplan,[1] New York.

New York, 14 November 1947

English: Or. Copy. T.W.: W.A.

Dear Dr. Kaplan,

I am very grateful to you for your kind and flattering remarks on my speeches.[2] Coming, as it does, from yourself, it acquires a special significance. You know the high value in which I hold your opinions and the deep respect for your personality which has animated all the time since I had the privilege of knowing you.

I have been extremely busy here this time and I find that it is unwise to try to come to America for a very short time as I did on this visit. But I must get back to London in December as I intend to be home in Palestine by the beginning of January.

Things here have been going well so far but the British declaration of yesterday[3] is rather disturbing. It is a bitter thought that the nation which has helped us to initiate the whole project and has done so much about its practical realization should, at the last moment, bar the way towards the consummation of the great hope, as they seem to be attempting to do now. This declaration, if not modified, will cause us some pain, but things have gone far and I don't think the U.N. will be deterred by this peevish and vindictive statement of the British. It may cause us some trouble in Palestine, but these are all pains of birth.

Please accept once more my deeply felt thanks and with affectionate regards to you and your wife, I am

Yours very sincerely,

35. [1] B. 1881. Rabbi and philosopher; founder Reconstructionist movement and of Society for Advancement of Judaism in New York.

[2] Kaplan to W., 12 Nov. (W.A.), referring specifically to W.'s speech at U.N. and at *New York Herald Tribune* forum.

[3] Sir Alexander Cadogan, British U.N. representative, had announced that the British evacuation of Palestine would be completed by 1 Aug. 1948, and that no British troops would be available for enforcing any settlement against the wishes of either Arabs or Jews.

36. To Jawaharlal Nehru,[1] New Delhi. *New York, 15 November 1947*
English: Or. Copy. T.W.: W.A.

Dear Mr. Prime Minister,

I don't know whether you still remember our conversation in London some years ago on problems of Palestine,[2] and I am happy to say that your great country and our small country have made considerable progress since that time.

Permit me to express my sincerest wishes for the happiness of independent India under your guidance, and which should, I hope, lead to the stability of this important part of Asia.

I am writing at the suggestion of Mr. Pannikar[3] and Mr. Shuva Rao,[4] with whom I have had talks here on the subject of scientific and technical cooperation between Palestine and India. I always cherished the thought that these two countries have a great deal in common and could be of mutual assistance if a veritable cooperation is established, and the best field in which this could be initiated is science.

We have a number of distinguished scientists in Palestine, and I know that some of the Jewish scientists in India who have come over since the early thirties have done fairly well there. The first steps, I think, which could be made in that direction, if you agree in principle, are as follows:

We would send a small group of scientists to India to get in touch with your people, and they could study the questions on the spot and elaborate a practical program.

The other proposal would be that you should send some of your students to do advanced research in physics and chemistry either at the University or at the Research Institutes in Rehovot, and I would be extremely happy to receive them and give them every facility.

Mr. Pannikar, with whom I have discussed these questions, will no doubt speak to you personally on this matter but I was anxious to lay it in writing before you so as to obtain your opinion on this whole subject.

I am staying in this country until December 11th and after that I am leaving for London, The Dorchester Hotel, where I will be spending only about three weeks to a month. From the middle of January until the beginning of July, my address is Rehovot, Palestine.

---

36. [1] 1889–1964. Nationalist leader, disciple of Gandhi. He became Prime Minister when India secured independence, 15 Aug. 1947.

[2] They had met at least once, 20 July 1938, in London. See Vol. XVIII, No. 353.

[3] Kavalam Madhava Pannikar (1895–1963). On Indian delegation to U.N. 1947; Ambassador to China 1948–52, to Egypt 1952–53. W. and Pannikar met 23 Oct., 13 Nov.

[4] I.e., Shiva Rau, journalist. On Indian delegation to U.N. 1947.

Awaiting the favor of your reply,[5] I am, dear Prime Minister, with great respect,

Very sincerely yours,

37. To Eleanor Roosevelt,[1] New York.   *New York, 15 November 1947*
English: Or. Copy. T.W.: W.A.

My dear Mrs. Roosevelt,

I can scarcely tell you how delighted I was for the opportunity to have had a conversation with you[2] and I am most grateful to you for listening so attentively to what I had to say.

I have asked my friends to send you a booklet which represents a collection of documents referring to the Balfour Declaration and cognate subjects. You will find there my treaty with King Feisal,[3] King Feisal's letter to Justice Felix Frankfurter and the statement of the Syrian delegation before the Paris Conference.[4] The reading of these documents should dispel the impression which is so assiduously circulated by the Arabs that it was all done without the consent of the Arabs at that time.

I should like to add, and this is, I am afraid, not in the documents as yet, that the gentleman who was more responsible than anyone else for the issuance of the Balfour Declaration was the late Sir Mark Sykes, who was the Chief Secretary of the War Cabinet,[5] acting under direct orders of the late Mr. Lloyd George and Lord Balfour. He was sent out several times to the East to contact King Hussein, the father of King Feisal and King Abdullah,[6] and who liberated Arabia from the Turks. King Hussein was fully aware of our aims and aspirations which we [?he] approved, and his sons have acted in conformity with his wishes.

---

[5] Replying 2 Dec. (W.A.) without referring to U.N. General Assembly decision in favour of partition three days earlier, and which India had opposed, Nehru expressed gratitude for W.'s wishes on the occasion of India's independence and welcomed the suggestion for co-operation in scientific and cultural activities. He proposed that some of W.'s scientists come to the Indian Science Congress in Jan. 1948 at Patna, Bihar, to consider plans and programmes.

37. [1] 1887–1962. Widow of President Franklin D. Roosevelt; member of U.S. delegation to U.N.

[2] They had met 14 Nov. in U.N. Delegates' lounge.

[3] Feisal I, King of Iraq (Biog. Index, Vol. VIII).

[4] In Jan. 1919, W. and Prince Feisal, as he then was, signed an agreement predicated upon a spirit of mutual respect and assistance between Arabs and Jews in Palestine and the Middle East (see *T. and E.*, pp. 290–95, 306–09; Vols. VIII, IX).

[5] Biog. Index, Vol. VII. Politician and diplomat, expert in Middle East affairs. He was an Asst. Secretary of the Cabinet.

[6] Abdullah Ibn Hussein, King of Transjordan (Biog. Index, Vol. X).

I had seen King Feisal several times, both in London and in the desert. I have met his brother Abdullah in Trans-Jordan and in London. Several of my conversations were carried out in the presence of the late T. E. Lawrence,[7] who had always acted as an interpreter, and there was no shadow of a doubt as to their affirmative attitude towards the whole policy of the National Home and the Mandate. There was also no doubt that at that time they were the authorized representatives of the Arab people; and were King Hussein, King Feisal and Mr. Lawrence alive today, they would be even now. It was always a matter of deep regret to me that King Feisal died so early in life. Things would have gone quite differently between the Arabs and us if he were alive.

Please forgive the length of this letter but I am anxious to leave no doubt in your mind as to our endeavors to have good relations with the Arabs from the very first moment the National Home policy was adumbrated until this very moment.

I remain, with many thanks and best regards,

Yours very sincerely,

38. To Jan Christiaan Smuts, London.   *New York, 15 November 1947*
English: Or. Copy. T.W.: W.A.

My dear General,

I hope you have arrived safely in London[1] and you will get some sort of relaxation from your arduous labors in the last few months. I have been here for something like six weeks and intend to return to London on December 11th.

Our affairs in U.N. have been going quite well. We have met with considerable sympathy and support on the part of your delegation, with whom I have spoken twice, also from America and Russia and many of the other countries. But the statement made by the British yesterday concerning their attitude towards the implementation of partition has created some confusion and disappointment, and is likely to have unhappy repercussions in Palestine.

The British had an opportunity to finish the Palestine story in honor and dignity and go out of the country next summer with the goodwill and appreciation of the civilized world, and I am quite certain that the Jews would have forgotten the troublesome period

---

[7] Thomas Edward Lawrence (Biog. Index, Vol. IX). 'Lawrence of Arabia.' Soldier, archaeologist, Orientalist and author.

38. [1] Smuts was in London for the marriage of Princess (later, Queen) Elizabeth and Philip Mountbatten, Duke of Edinburgh.

and would have only remembered the great contribution which Great Britain has made towards the upbuilding of Palestine.

The declaration made by the British Government last night[2] is likely to affect the good relations of Great Britain with America and other countries and likely to provoke severe criticism, if not condemnation, on the part of many friends of England. In reading the statement, I cannot but feel that it tends to be peevish and vindictive and not at all in conformity with the character of the British as we knew it.

I am deeply pained and grieved. I do not fear that it will jeopardize the whole project, because I believe everybody is determined to go forward without British assistance, if necessary, if they cannot be induced to modify their attitude. I know the Foreign Office is very obstinate and probably aggrieved at the way things have gone. When Mr. Bevin had decided to hand over the whole matter to the UNO he did not foresee, I am sure, that we would meet with such a volume of sympathy and good will.

I am writing to ask you, most respectfully, whether you could, with your great influence, at the last moment, try and bring about a change in the attitude of the Foreign Office.

We may have to face a little more trouble, but on the other hand, the Jews will feel that they are armed with the full moral support of the civilized world, as against the opposite camp which are the Arab States and Great Britain. It is a bitter irony of fate that the very country which has been responsible for the initiation of the project should refuse to cooperate with the United Nations in its consummation, and so indirectly be of assistance to the bitterest enemies of the National Home.

All the delegations with whom I am in contact attach the greatest weight to Palestine as a test case for the United Nations, and the one major issue on which the Great Powers have been able to work together. It is all the more sad to everybody that Britain should refuse to play any positive part and so abdicate from her position of moral leadership.

The whole affair is causing further serious damage to British prestige, instead of redeeming it from past criticism of her handling of Palestine. You can readily understand how painful this is to someone like myself, who has always attached the utmost value to Britain's role in world affairs—especially at a time like this, when the Russians and the Americans should be brought together because of Britain's influence, and not in spite of it.

The press today brings a long statement describing the way in

---

[2] In fact, 13 Nov.—see No. 35, n. 3.

which Britain alleges to dispose of the liquid assets in Palestine. I am enclosing herewith a copy of it together with an article on the same subject.[3] I cannot believe my eyes. It is a high-handed procedure which will be resisted by everybody. Of course, it is only a newspaper story, but it is too circumstantial to be dismissed lightly.

With my profoundest respect and sincere wishes, I am[4]

Sincerely yours,

39. To Alfonso Lopez,[1] New York.   *Washington, 18 November 1947*
English: Draft. T.W.: I.S.A. 105/1/4.

Dear Ambassador Lopez,

I have been obliged to spend the past few days in Washington and have in consequence not been able to communicate with you earlier as I had intended. I have it very much on my mind that as a result of unfortunate misunderstandings arrangements for us to meet had not materialized.[2]

I am most anxious to meet and have a talk with you, and I very deeply regret that owing to circumstances for which neither you nor I were responsible confusion has arisen in connection with the planned appointments.

I expect to be in Washington until Thursday and I trust that you will permit me to get into touch with you again on my return to New York and that on that occasion we may have better fortune in arranging a meeting.[3]

Yours sincerely,
Chaim Weizmann

40. To Henry Morgenthau, Jr., New York.
New York, 20 November 1947
English: Or. Copy. T.W.: W.A.

Dear Mr. Morgenthau,

On arriving from Washington last night,[1] I read your kind letter

[3] A report had appeared that the British were planning to appropriate £12,500,000 from the Palestine Treasury at the termination of the Mandate. The F.O. denied this emphatically. See *New York Times,* 16 Nov. 1947.

[4] See Smuts to Linton (28 Nov., W.A.) for action taken.

39. [1] Member of Colombian delegation to U.N.

[2] They did not meet, as W. left for Washington at short notice for an interview with Truman.

[3] See W. to Lopez, 25 Nov. (W.A.). It is not known whether this took place.

40. [1] W. was in Washington 17–19 Nov. He was received at the White House 19 Nov. by Truman, having held consultations with, *inter alia,* Frankfurter, Eliahu Epstein and Sumner Welles.

of November 14th.[2] Your appeal to me is irresistible, and I have therefore decided to postpone my return for a week so that I can come to Atlantic City on December 13th and, naturally, do my best to assist in the work as much as I can in this short time.

You may be interested to know that I have seen the President and have had a very satisfactory discussion with him concerning the Negev and Aqaba.[3] The effects of this conversation have been very rapid as on my return here I found that instructions have been given to General Hilldring[4] in conformity with my request to the President.

I hope to be able to tell you the details when I see you next. Meanwhile, I beg to remain with very kind regards and many thanks for your invitation,

Yours very sincerely,

41. To Felix Frankfurter, Washington.   *New York, 24 November 1947*
English: Or. Copy. T.W.: W.A.

Dear Felix,

Ever so many thanks for your note.[1] It is always a pleasure to receive a line from you.

I have seen Dr. Rau.[2] He is exactly what you described him to be, and we have made good friends with him and his brother. But curiously enough, the Indian delegation is going to vote against us. I had a long talk with Mrs. Pandit[3] today who is heartbroken about it, and she explains this anomaly by the fact that Nehru's cabinet

[2] (W.A.). Morgenthau urged W. to remain in U.S. to address U.J.A. National Conference in Atlantic City, 12–15 Dec.

[3] The American U.N. delegation intended to propose exclusion of the southern Negev from the Jewish State, and in discussion W. therefore expounded upon the importance of this region for the future growth and economic development of the state, mentioning prospects for overcoming the water shortage either through desalination or via a water carrier from the north. He also described for Truman how Akaba port was imperative for future trade and commerce (*T. and E.*, pp. 560–63; *Israel and Elath*, from the Lucien Wolf Memorial Lecture by Eliahu Elath, publ. London 1966).

[4] John Henry Hilldring, b. 1895. U.S. Asst. Secretary for Occupied Areas following W.W.II. Alternate delegate to U.N. 1947, with specific task of presenting the U.S. view on Palestine problem. Strong supporter of Zionism.

41. [1] Frankfurter stated (22 Nov., W.A.) that he had given Sir B. R. Rau a note of introduction to W. on 17 Nov. He regarded Rau as a wise statesman. It would be profitable for W. to talk with him about future relations between the Jewish State and India.

[2] Sir Benegal Rama Rau (1889–1969). Indian statesman; helped to draft India's Constitution; Ambassador to Japan 1947–48, to U.S. 1948–49. He and W. met 22 Nov. 1947.

[3] Vijaya Lakshmi Pandit, b. 1900. Sister of Nehru; leader of Indian delegation to U.N. 1946–51, 1963; Ambassador to U.S.S.R., and U.S.; President U.N. General Assembly 1953–54; High Commissioner in London 1954–61.

consists, in the majority, of reactionaries, so that the delegation here is helpless. I wonder whether you can talk to these two brothers. They might still do something at the last moment.

The memory of the evening[4] will remain with us for a long time. It went in a flash and I am only sorry that it can't be repeated—but perhaps such things should not be repeated. It would be somewhat like a second *Seder* night.[5]

Our love to you and Marion, and I hope to speak to you after the vote has been cast.

As ever,

42. To Walter Nash,[1] Wellington, New Zealand.

New York, 24 November 1947

English: T.: W.A.

I very deeply appreciate your cable setting out the position of the New Zealand Government regarding the Palestine issue.[2] I assume that by now you will be aware of the further statement last Saturday night by Mr. Herschel Johnson[3] on behalf of the United States, which would appear to go a considerable way towards meeting the point of view indicated in your message, in which you stated that if members of the Security Council and particularly the United States would be prepared to make straightout statements that they would undertake their proportionate share of the task of enforcement New Zealand would feel able to modify its attitude towards the plan. Mr. Johnson stated that the Security Council would be "responsible certainly for the security elements involved in this implementation program" and emphasized that if a situation arose under chapters six or seven of the Charter[4] the United States Government "will perform

---

[4] The Weizmanns dined with the Frankfurters 18 Nov.

[5] The Passover Eve home ritual which, outside Israel, is repeated on the second night of Passover.

42. [1] 1882–1968. New Zealand Minister of Finance 1935–49; Deputy Prime Minister 1940–49; Prime Minister 1957–60.

[2] Nash's cable untraced, but one received 24 Nov. from the New Zealand Prime Minister, Philip Fraser, spoke of the gravity and urgency of the issue. Fraser stated that although favouring partition himself, he feared that an Assembly resolution unaccompanied by Great Power pledges to enforce it would only lead to bloodshed and chaos.

[3] 1894–1966. Deputy Chief, U.S. Mission to U.N. 1947–48; Ambassador to Brazil 1948–53. He charged that the British attitude had set the U.N. an almost impossible task.

[4] Chapter VI of the U.N. Charter deals with 'Pacific Settlement of Disputes' and provides that the Security Council may investigate any dispute and recommend appropriate procedures or methods of adjustment with a view towards its peaceful settlement. Chapter VII pertains to 'Action with Respect to Threats to the Peace, Breaches of the Peace, and Acts of Aggression'.

its duty under the Charter along with other members of the U.N. in carrying out the decision of the Security Council in such a case." In the course of a private conversation today with Mr. Johnson I took the opportunity to refer to your telegram. Mr. Johnson expressed the hope that his statement reported above might meet your reservations. Permit me again to thank you for your generous response to my cable.[5]

Chaim Weizmann

43. To Jan Christiaan Smuts, London.   *New York, 24 November 1947*
English: T.: I.S.A. 105/1/4.

Attitude British delegation here disturbing[1] and may endanger success of all our efforts, which otherwise reasonably certain. Could you use your great influence to induce a more friendly relationship at last crucial hour? Many thanks. Kind regards.

Chaim Weizmann

[The U.N. General Assembly, considering the action to be taken on UNSCOP's Report, decided on 23 Sept. to create an Ad Hoc Committee on the Palestine Question composed of one representative from each U.N. member state, so as to debate the matter further. This committee, on 25 Nov., endorsed the majority proposal in favour of partition by a 25–13 vote. As the General Assembly could not enforce the recommendation, the committee also requested the Security Council to take 'the necessary measures' to implement the scheme. But first the General Assembly was required to vote on the partition scheme, and to carry it a two-thirds majority would be necessary.]

44. To E. Antony Sassen,[1] New York.   *New York, 25 November 1947*
English: Or. Copy. T.W.: W.A.

Dear Dr. Sassen,

    I recall with pleasure our conversation earlier in the Assembly's proceeding.[2] Holland has contributed much to the development

---

The Security Council in such instances may decide what measures should be taken to maintain or restore international peace and security, may call upon the parties concerned to comply with its provisional measures and may also ask members to apply sanctions as well as the use of military force for the sake of peace and global security.

  [5] Untraced; New Zealand voted for partition.

43. [1] In anticipation of the scheduled vote by the General Assembly.

44. [1] B. 1911. Jurist. Netherlands politician and international administrator.
  [2] In continuance of his efforts to persuade undecided delegations, W. had met Sassen 20 Nov.

of the present proposed solution through her signature of the UNSCOP Report and the constructive influence of your delegation on the proceedings of the Ad Hoc Committee.

I most earnestly call your attention again to the grave issues which affect our people at this critical hour. Surely it would be an unforgettable historic tragedy if the solution now so near, on which the reputation and prospects of the United Nations depend, were to be frustrated through the abstention of any responsible delegation. The imperfections and risks of this plan are as nothing compared with the grave consequences to the United Nations and to Palestine if the recommendation fails to secure the necessary majority.

It is a deep sense of historic responsibility which prompts me to address you tonight. I pray God that you will respond in like spirit.[3]

Very sincerely yours,

45. To Harry S. Truman, Washington.   *New York, 25 November 1947*
English: T.: W.A.

Dear Mr. President, at this crucial hour, when difficult Palestine problem is on the verge of a solution which would owe so much to your personal initiative, I address myself to you again. I am aware of how much abstaining delegations would be swayed by your counsel and the influence of your Government. I refer to China, Honduras, Colombia, Mexico, Liberia, Ethiopia, Greece. I beg and pray for your intervention[1] at this decisive hour to bring about a settlement which will go down in history. Please forgive my troubling you again.

Chaim Weizmann

46. To Max Brailowsky,[1] La Chaux-de-Fonds, Switzerland.
New York, 26 November 1947
English: Or. Copy. T.W.: W.A.

My dear Mr. Brailowsky,

Since I wrote you from London[2] about the formation of a Swiss group sponsoring a Technical Physics unit in Rehovot, I have had

---

[3] The Netherlands voted for partition.

45. [1] At the General Assembly four days later, China, Colombia, Ethiopia, Honduras and Mexico abstained. Liberia voted for, and Greece against, partition.

46. [1] Of Beleco Watch Company.
[2] On 27 Sept. (W.A.).

several opportunities of discussing and reviewing the project here in the States. There are undoubtedly a great many important and promising problems which such a group could study; the new Institute in Rehovot, which I expect to be ready in Spring 1948, will give such a group many ideas. I had, e.g. an interesting conversation with Dr. Pekeris,[3] the Director of our future Department of Applied Mathematics, who outlined his program in the field of geophysics and electronics and stressed the point that one should try to manufacture the geophysical instruments—perhaps even in improved design—and some electronic devices. Dr. Pekeris is confident that one could eventually build an electronic computer in Rehovot.

One project which is of immediate interest and which, I believe, I have already briefly discussed with you is the establishment of an optical workshop as the starting point of optical precision manufacturing. One of our future co-workers, who has been with Messrs. Adam Hilger Ltd. in London and has a long experience in this field, has worked out a program for such a workshop and has sent us the enclosed list of the equipment required.[4] Do you think your group could undertake to provide us with that equipment?[5] The space requirements would not be very great; two rooms would have to be added to our present workshop building.

I have also met here again Mr. Bulova[6] who is anxious, as you know, to establish in Palestine a tool and die manufacturing unit in which also young mechanics could be trained, and who is willing to do that in Rehovot. Mr. Bulova will be in Palestine in February or March to see the country and make his final decisions. I feel sure that it will be possible to integrate his plans in our Technical Physics project.

I need perhaps not add that this project has been made even more important and more urgent by the recent political developments, and I would be very grateful to hear from you how far your efforts to create your group in Switzerland have progressed.

I expect to be in Geneva on my return journey to Palestine, and hope to have then an opportunity of seeing you.

Yours very sincerely,

Chaim Weizmann

[3] Chaim L. Pekeris, b. 1908 Lithuania. Head, Mathematical Physics Group, Columbia University 1942–46; at Institute for Advanced Study, Princeton 1946–48; established and headed Department of Applied Mathematics at Weizmann Institute 1948. He and W. met 10 Nov.

[4] Untraced.

[5] Brailowsky and the Swiss Committee of Friends of the Weizmann Institute agreed in Jan. 1948 to supply the equipment.

[6] Arde (André) Bulova (d. 1958). Chairman of Bulova Watch Company and principal trustee of Bulova Foundation.

47. To Ruth Ludwin,[1] Chicago.   *New York, 26 November 1947*
English: T.: W.A.

I take great pleasure in wishing your Convention greatest possible success. During my last [visit] to Meier Shfeyah[2] I was able to appreciate the work of Junior Hadassah,[3] which through hard work has led to the development of a very beautiful place for children in the hills round Zichron. Unfortunately I couldn't see your other establishment nearby, but I might see it on my next visit. I hope your work will receive new impetus from the events through which we are living now. The work of the youth in this country is of particular importance now, as we shall need young men and women to further the building of the State, and particularly people who are nurtured in Western methods and standards. All my good wishes are with you.

Chaim Weizmann

48. To Henry Morgenthau, Jr., New York.
New York, 26 November 1947

English: Or. Copy. T.W.: W.A.

My dear Mr. Morgenthau,

I am writing to tell you how grateful I am to you for your presence last night and for the wonderful address.[1] It lent distinction to the whole assembly, and I know everybody appreciated it.

It was a great privilege to be able to spend part of the evening, at any rate, with you. I knew that you had to go away soon and I understood the reason for it.

Please convey my heartfelt thanks to Mrs. Morgenthau and your family, and in the hope of seeing you soon, I remain with most cordial regards,

Yours very sincerely,

P.S. Our fate is still hanging in the balance and I am afraid there is not going to be a vote until Friday. It is just as well because there are still one or two things which we might do in the interval. I don't

---

47. [1] Vice-President of Junior Hadassah Organization, and co-chairman of its convention in Chicago.

    [2] Children's village in Samaria near Zikhron Yaakov.

    [3] Younger section of Hadassah Women's Zionist Organization. Established 1920 with programme of Jewish education, leadership training and special projects in Palestine.

48. [1] At Dinner sponsored by the U.S. Committee for Weizmann Institute, Waldorf-Astoria Hotel, on occasion of W.'s 73rd birthday; Morgenthau had introduced W.

know whether you could help us with Greece or with the Philippines or with Haiti. Mr. Sumner Welles[2] has promised to do something with Greece. I hope he will succeed.

49. To Stephen S. Wise,[1] New York.   *New York, 26 November 1947*
English: Or. Copy. T.W.: W.A.

My dear Stephen,

You have made me very happy with your beautiful note.[2] I looked around and inquired several times for you and was told that you were there, but I could not discover you. Your note explains the thing and I am deeply sorry for the cause of [your] having to leave so quickly.

I reciprocate all your wishes, and perhaps when the decision comes tonight or tomorrow we might meet and silently offer a prayer to God that we have been privileged both to work for so many years and live to see the fruit of our labors.

With most affectionate greetings to you and your family,

Your old friend,

50. To Jawaharlal Nehru, New Delhi.   *New York, 27 November 1947*
English: T.: I.S.A. 105/1/4.

I solemnly appeal to you at most critical hour of two thousand years Jewish history. Cannot believe that India wishes participate responsibility for tragic disappointment which our national memory could never forget. Defeat of proposal means invitation to Palestine Arabs led by Mufti attack Palestine Jewry, since it involves abdication of United Nations from control and abandonment Palestine to free conflict. Acceptance of proposed decision involves independence for majority both Arabs and Jews, termination of Mandate and good conditions for immediate Arab-Jewish understanding. Immediately after positive Assembly recommendation, myself and friends would seek contacts Arab leaders, discuss harmonious independent

[2] Biog. Index, Vol. XX. U.S. Under-Secretary of State 1933–43.

49. [1] Biog. Index, Vol. VII. Rabbi, leading U.S. communal and Zionist figure. Organized and headed World Jewish Congress 1936–49.

[2] Wise had written that day (W.A.) that indisposition had allowed him to attend only the latter part of the Dinner (see No. 48, n. 1). He had avoided meeting W., since 'my happiness over your birthday and over the great tribute would have overflowed in tears, and I did not wish even for a moment to mar the occasion'. He hoped the imminent U.N. decision would fulfil all that W. merited.

development Western Asia, but this can only follow international decision for establishment Jewish and Arab States. Solemnly ask you not to dispel such great prospects in anarchy ensuing from United Nations inaction. Call your attention support United States, Soviet Union and all progressive Europe to scheme equal Jewish Arab independence in Palestine. Cannot understand how India can wish obstruct such settlement. May sense of historic responsibility peace of Asia guide your country's action.[1] Sincerely,

Chaim Weizmann

51. To Manuel A. Roxas,[1] Manila.   *New York, 27 November 1947*
English: T.: I.S.A. 105/1/4.

I solemnly appeal to you at most critical hour our two thousand years Jewish history. Cannot believe that Philippine Republic, which understands impulse of people fighting for liberation, can wish to participate in frustration of proposal for establishment Jewish and Arab States in Palestine. Defeat of this proposal involves postponement independence, abandonment Palestine to anarchy, grave blow to efficacy United Nations. Draw attention to vast surge of gratitude United States public opinion if Philippines would intervene save situation from intolerable deadlock. Peace of Western Asia depends equal partnership Jewish and Arab States; cannot be ensured by vain attempt subject Jewish nation to Arab majority. Let not your valiant people incur grave responsibility for frustrating important prospect international conciliation under aegis of Great Powers of all Europe, British Dominions and other nations. May deep sense of historic responsibility guide your country's action.[2] Respectfully,

Chaim Weizmann

50. [1] W.'s appeal failed; India was one of 13 countries voting against partition.

51. [1] 1892–1948. President of Philippines from 1946.
   [2] The Philippines, after considerable hesitation, finally voted in favour of partition.

52. To C. David Ginsburg,[1] London.   *New York, 28 November 1947*
English: T.: W.A.

Request you urgently ask your chief[2] instruct his department that they should help in every way at the eleventh hour. Situation requires this intervention. Love,

Chaim Weizmann

53. To Marc Jarblum, Paris.   *New York, 28 November 1947*
English: T.: W.A.

On proposal of French delegation decision which was to be voted tonight has been postponed for twenty-four hours in order that Jews and Arabs should try and come to an agreement. We consider that a very dangerous step. Agreement with Arabs will be much easier after there is a decision of the UNO and not before. Please see friends and obtain definite directives for your delegation, otherwise whole situation endangered.[1] My best to you and Léon [Blum].

Weizmann

54. To Harry S. Truman, Washington.   *New York, 28 November 1947*
English: Or. Copy. T.W.: W.A.

Dear Mr. President,

The gracious manner in which you received me on Wednesday, November 19th, emboldens me to address you in this critical hour which is one of suspense and anguish for me. I am disturbed to hear from unimpeachable sources[1] that two unwarranted rumours are afloat which do us injustice and possible damage.

It is freely rumoured in Washington that our people have exerted undue and excessive pressure on certain delegations and have thus "overplayed" their hand. I am in a position to assure you, my dear Mr. President, that there is no substance in this charge as far as our representatives are concerned. They have had a very limited number

52. [1] Biog. Index.

[2] Ginsburg was then in London advising George C. Marshall, Secretary of State, and the American delegation at conference of Big Four Foreign Ministers, 25 Nov.–16 Dec., seeking a solution to problem of post-war Germany.

53. [1] W. felt that delaying tactics would subject the partition coalition to further, more intense, British and Arab pressure, to detriment of Zionist cause.

54. [1] Unidentified.

of contacts with all delegations and have endeavoured to lay the situation squarely before them. At no time have they gone beyond the limits of legitimate and moderate persuasion. With some delegations, such as those of Greece and Liberia, we have had no more than one conversation throughout the first assembly.

Fears are also expressed that our project in Palestine may in some way be used as a channel for the infiltration of Communist ideas in the Middle East. Nothing is further from the truth. Our immigrants from Eastern Europe are precisely those who are leaving the Communist scene with which they do not wish to be integrated, otherwise they would not leave at all. Had there been a serious attempt by the Soviets to introduce Communist influences through our immigration they could easily have done so in previous decades. Every election, and all observation in Palestine, testifies to the trivial hold which Communism has achieved in our community. An educated peasantry and a skilled industrial class living on high standards will never accept Communism. The danger lies amongst illiterate and impoverished communities bearing no resemblance to our own.

In conclusion, my dear Mr. President, I should like to convey to you how deeply I hope that success will attend your efforts to carry the partition proposal through to success. I hope that this proposal will secure the support of those countries who rightly look to the United States for guidance and leadership. In that success the world will not fail to see a triumph of American statesmanship under your direction and initiative.

I am, Mr. President,

With deep respect,
Yours,
Chaim Weizmann[2]

55. To Serge Koussevitsky,[1] Boston.　　　*New York, 29 November 1947*
English: Or. Copy. T.W.: W.A.

My dear Dr. Koussevitsky,

I could scarcely express in words my deep and warm feeling of gratitude for the wonderful concert with which you honored us on

---

[2] In his memoirs (Vol. II, *Years of Trial and Hope*, 1956, pp. 185–86), Truman published this letter, though with date given as 27 Nov., the final paragraph omitted, and other discrepancies. His version has 'I cannot speak for unauthorised persons' to precede the words 'but I am in a position . . .' in the second paragraph, which ends with 'the present Assembly' rather than 'the first assembly'.

55. [1] 1874–1951. Musical director and conductor of Boston Symphony Orchestra from 1925.

November 25th.[2] It was a rare and beautiful occasion that it is almost a sacrilege to speak about it.

Whether we did meet in our young days or not is very difficult to say now but it did seem to me as if we knew each other all our lives, and it is one of the rare privileges, at the evening of one's life, to find a friend of your calibre.

Once more, my heartiest thanks to you and to your dear wife and may I express the hope that you will still honor us with a visit in Palestine, and the Jewish State will receive you with open arms.[3]

All my best wishes and all my grateful thanks to you and to your orchestra.

Affectionately yours,

56. To Kurt Weill,[1] New York. *New York, 29 November 1947*
English: Or. Copy. T.W.: W.A.

My dear Mr. Weill,

We have not met since your visit to my house in Palestine, and it was a great pleasure to see you again on the evening of the 25th of November[2] and also to hear your beautiful orchestration of the *Hatikvah*,[3] which I hope will be adopted by the Jewish State to be played on the occasion of the first opening of Parliament.

If I remember rightly, you said something about coming over to Palestine again. Perhaps your visit will coincide with the Passover season which, as you may know, is the most beautiful month in Palestine.

With all my good wishes, I remain

Gratefully yours,

57. To Jan Christiaan Smuts, Rome. *New York, 29 November 1947*
English: T.: W.A.

At this milestone in Jewish history[1] I think with feelings of deepest gratitude of your noble friendship and unwavering support through-

---

[2] At the Weizmann Institute Dinner (see No. 48, n. 1).

[3] Koussevitsky conducted the Israel Philharmonic Orchestra in Israel, 1950.

56. [1] 1900–50. Composer. Settled in U.S. 1935 after leaving Germany.

[2] I.e., at the Weizmann Institute Dinner.

[3] Hebr.: 'The Hope'. The anthem was in fact adopted officially by the State of Israel.

57. [1] On 29 Nov. the General Assembly, meeting in plenary session, took the historic decision to partition Palestine into independent Arab and Jewish States. The voting was: for partition, 33; against partition, 13; abstentions, 10; absent, 1.

out the years from 1917 onward for the cause of my people. May God bless and guard you. Affectionately,

Chaim Weizmann

58. To Harry S. Truman, Washington.   *New York, 30 November 1947*
English: T.: W.A.

After the United Nations have approved of the plan which you and your administration have proposed and carried to ultimate success, I feel it my first duty to convey to you the respectful gratitude of my people for your vision and sympathy and for the admirable effort which the American delegation has made under your guidance. May this bond of gratitude be the first link between your great republic and the Jewish State. I beg to add the expression of my personal gratitude for all your kindness and moral support. With deep respect,

Chaim Weizmann

59. To Oswaldo Aranha,[1] New York.   *New York, 30 November 1947*
English: T.: W.A.

The session of the Assembly could not have ended with this historic decision reestablishing the Jewish people to the Commonwealth of Nations if not for your relentless effort and devotion as Chairman of the Assembly. Your understanding for our plight and for the justice of our cause have earned you the abiding gratitude of the Jewish people. I would like to extend to you my personal gratitude for the continuous encouragement and friendliness which you have shown.

Chaim Weizmann

60. To Léon Blum, Paris.   *New York, 30 November 1947*
French: T.: W.A.

Dear Friend, deeply stirred by historic decision United Nations. Would like to send you grateful regards for all you have done for our cause during these hard days of decision. All good wishes to you and your wife and good health from both of us.

Chaim Weizmann

---

59. [1] Of the Brazilian delegation. Chairman of U.N. General Assembly.

61. To Winston S. Churchill, London.   *New York, 30 November 1947*
English: T.: W.A.

As your old friend and admirer I am sending you at this historic moment, to which you have contributed so much since its early inception, my heartiest good wishes and sincere thanks in which my wife joins. To all your historic merits you may add this achievement and the gratitude of an ancient race. Spoke to Randolph[1] yesterday. Affectionately,[2]

                                                    Chaim Weizmann

62. To Sir Reginald Coupland,[1] Oxford. *New York, 30 November 1947*
English: T.: W.A.

Deeply moved by United Nations vote on partition. My thoughts and those of my people go to you who has conceived the idea of partition[2] as a means to give my people a home and the Middle East peace and prosperity. Your name will live in the annals of Jewish history.

                                                    Chaim Weizmann

63. To Richard Crossman,[1] London.   *New York, 30 November 1947*
English: T.: St. Antony's College, Oxford.

I could not let this happy day pass without telling you what source of strength and comfort you have been to me and all of us through these difficult last months since the Inquiry Commission[2] had made the first step towards the solution of our problem. Your courage and passion has proven that there are still champions of freedom and justice in this world, and your name, like that of Zola, will live in the hearts of the Jewish people.

                                                    Chaim Weizmann

61. [1] Randolph Churchill (1911–68). Journalist and author; son of Winston Churchill.
   [2] Churchill acknowledged the message 9 Dec. (W.A.).

62. [1] Biog. Index, Vol. XVIII. Member of Palestine Royal (Peel) Commission 1936–37; Beit Professor of History of British Empire at Oxford 1920–48.
   [2] For Coupland's contribution, see Vol. XVIII.

63. [1] Biog. Index, Vol. XXII. Politician and journalist; member Anglo-American Committee of Inquiry 1945–46; later in British Cabinet.
   [2] Crossman's identification with Zionism and close friendship with W. dated from his service on the Anglo-American Committee.

64. To Sir Alan Cunningham, Jerusalem.

New York, 30 November 1947

English: T.: W.A.

Your Excellency's attitude in all these difficult years and continuous goodwill and friendship to us emboldens us to send you at this historic moment our heartfelt thanks. Difficulties which arose between us and England will be forgotten, and only England's great contribution to Jewish Palestine will be remembered. We are happy that this moment coincided with your term of office. Looking forward to seeing you end of January in Palestine. Gratefully yours,

Vera, Chaim Weizmann

65. To Herbert V. Evatt,[1] New York.   *New York, 30 November 1947*

English: T.: W.A.

After the conclusion of this historic session of the United Nations I would like to thank you on behalf of my people for the untiring efforts you have devoted to the conduct of the Ad Hoc Committee on Palestine. I hope the new State will prove itself worthy of the decision reached. It will see in the great colonising achievements in your country a shining example for its own work.

Chaim Weizmann

66. To Enrique Rodriguez Fabregat,[1] New York.

New York, 30 November 1947

English: T.: W.A.

On this historic day I want to convey to you once more my deep feeling of gratitude for your courageous stand and your passionate endeavor to give back to my people their own homeland. The success of your mission has restored in our hearts faith in the future. Your personal friendship will always be a source of pride to me. God bless you.

Chaim Weizmann

---

65. [1] 1894–1965. Australian statesman; Attorney General and Minister for External Affairs 1941–49; Chairman of U.N. Ad Hoc Committee appointed by General Assembly Sept. 1947.

66. [1] B. 1898. As permanent representative of Uruguay to U.N., he was chosen to serve on UNSCOP and became convinced of the Zionist case.

67. To Jorge Garcia-Granados,[1] New York.

New York, 30 November 1947

English: T.: W.A.

The Jewish people have stood alone for so long that the friendship and sympathy which you have shown us and the passionate efforts which you have made are doubly appreciated. Since I have had the pleasure of knowing you I was confident that our cause would prevail.

Chaim Weizmann

68. To John Hilldring, New York.   *New York, 30 November 1947*

English: T.: W.A.

I cannot let this great day pass without conveying to you my personal thanks and the deep gratitude of my people for your untiring effort in the creation of the Jewish State. You have been a tower of strength. I hope that the bonds of friendship will last for a long time and that you will visit us in Palestine at your earliest convenience. It is only there that we can really give you the reception you so well deserve. Hoping to see you before I leave, I am affectionately,

Chaim Weizmann

69. To Herschel Johnson, New York.   *New York, 30 November 1947*

English: T.: W.A.

The deep gratitude of the Jewish people goes out to you and your colleagues of the United States delegation for the courage and determination with which you have carried the plan of your Government to final success. In these great days the great American tradition of liberty and justice for all which you have upheld has been a source of comfort to all of us. I am personally indebted to you for your kindness and sympathy.

Chaim Weizmann

67. [1] 1900–61. Guatemala's Ambassador to U.S.; served on UNSCOP. Strongly sympathetic to Zionism, he was in close personal contact with W. Subsequently Guatemala's first Ambassador to Israel.

70. To George C. Marshall,[1] Washington.

New York, 30 November 1947

English: T.: W.A.

After the Assembly of the United Nations has cast its decisive vote I feel it my duty to express to you, Mr. Secretary, the gratitude of the Jewish people for the noble part which you personally and your administration have played in solving the millenial-old problem of our country and our people. It will be our earnest endeavor to be worthy of the honor and the challenge of being a member of the United Nations. I hope that the bonds of friendship will last for a long time and that you will visit us in Palestine at your earliest convenience. It is only there that we can really give you the reception you so well deserve.

Chaim Weizmann

71. To James G. McDonald,[1] New York.

New York, 30 November 1947

English: T.: Herbert Lehman Papers.

Deeply moved by the historic event; I must tell you that your constant sympathy and active support have greatly helped me and my people in traveling the difficult road of these last years. As long as men like you are on our side we know we can overcome all obstacles. You will always be a beloved guest and a respected counsellor of the new Jewish State.

Chaim Weizmann

72. To the U.S.S.R. Delegation at U.N., New York.

New York, 30 November 1947

English: T.: W.A.

To your delegation and your distinguished representatives[1] and to your Government my humble thanks and profound respects. You

70. [1] Biog. Index. Secretary of State 1947–49; Secretary of Defense 1950–51.

71. [1] Biog. Index, Vol. XXII. Member of Anglo-American Committee of Inquiry; special envoy to Provisional Government of Israel 1948 and first U.S. Ambassador 1949.

72. [1] During the months of U.N. debate on Palestine, the Soviet delegation included such figures as Andrei Vishinsky, who was to replace Molotov as Foreign Minister in 1949; Andrei Gromyko, Soviet Deputy Foreign Minister and his country's permanent representative to U.N.; Semyon Tsarapkin, Counsellor of Soviet Embassy in Washington.

have placed our people under an eternal debt of gratitude by your
noble action during these days of stress and strain. Cordially and
respectfully,

Chaim Weizmann

73. To Sumner Welles, Oxon Hill, Maryland.

New York, 30 November 1947

English: T.: W.A.

Deeply moved by your telegram and good wishes.[1] I would like to
thank you for all you have done for my people and for your moral
support which has comforted me in these great days. I hope that the
new Jewish State will be worthy of the challenge and will once more
contribute to progress and peace. You were the first I tried to phone
after I received the news.

Chaim Weizmann

74. To Leopold S. Amery, London.   *New York, 2 December 1947*

English: T.: W.A.

Your consistent sympathy and friendship throughout so many years
was a source of pride and encouragement to me, and at this solemn
moment in our history sending you our heartfelt thanks and best
wishes.

Vera, Chaim

75. To Viscount Cecil of Chelwood,[1] London.

New York, 2 December 1947

English: T.: W.A.

On this great occasion sending you my heartfelt thanks for all you
have done in many years in order bring about consummation of
great ideal. Regards.

Weizmann

---

73. [1] Welles wired his congratulations 29 Nov. (W.A.), expressing hope that the new state
would 'serve the cause of peace and world recovery'.

75. [1] Biog. Index, Vol. VII. As Lord Robert Cecil he was Parliamentary Under-Secretary for
Foreign Affairs during time of Balfour Declaration.

76. To Sir Wyndham Deedes, London.   *New York, 2 December 1947*
English: T.: W.A.

You anticipated my message.[1] My thoughts were always with you in this last stage of struggle. Shall never forget our first meeting in your tent, Allenby's Camp.[2] Your great encouragement, consistent friendship and wise counsel contributed greatly towards this success. Looking forward seeing you. Love,

Vera, Chaim

77. To Blanche Dugdale,[1] London.   *New York, 2 December 1947*
English: T.: W.A.

We send you our love and grateful thanks for all you have done to further the cause so brilliantly initiated by your Uncle. Looking forward to seeing you and to rejoice with you. Fondest love.

Vera, Chaim

78. To Joseph I. Linton, London.   *New York, 2 December 1947*
English: T.: W.A.

Kindly transmit Lord Harlech:[1] "On this great occasion sending you my heartfelt thanks for all you have done in many years in order bring about consummation of great ideal. Regards."

Weizmann

---

76. [1] Deedes cabled 1 Dec. (W.A.): 'Warmest congratulations from one who has witnessed for thirty years your noble struggle'.
   [2] They first met 1918 at Gen. Allenby's H.Q. at Bir Salem (Kibbutz Netzer Sereni). W. later recalled in his autobiography: 'It was always a relief to go into Deedes's tent; with him I could speak freely, dream freely' (*T. and E.*, p. 274).

77. [1] 'Baffy' Dugdale (Biog. Index, Vol. XIII). Niece and biographer of Lord Balfour; friend of the Weizmanns and ardent Zionist.

78. [1] William G. A. Ormsby-Gore (Biog. Index, Vol. VIII). Attached to Zionist Commission in Palestine, 1918. Later, Colonial Secretary.

79. To Richard Meinertzhagen,[1] London.   *New York, 2 December 1947*
English: T.: W.A.

To you, dear friend, we owe so much that I can only express it in simple words: May God bless you.

Weizmann

80. To Eleanor Roosevelt, Geneva.   *New York, 2 December 1947*
English: T.: W.A.

You have placed the Jewish people under a deep debt of gratitude for your courageous support of great ideal throughout difficult days. Personally beg you accept my heartfelt thanks. Respectfully,

Chaim Weizmann

81. To James de Rothschild,[1] London.   *New York, 2 December 1947*
English: T.: W.A.

In these stirring days my thoughts are with you and with the memory of your late lamented father.[2] All which you have created in Palestine in the last sixty years is the rock foundation on which we could build, and with your support and continuous interest in all branches of Palestinian activity we shall be able to face the responsibilities which have increased in proportion to opportunities. May God grant you and your wife[3] health and strength to continue work during period of fulfillment on behalf of our people. Best regards.

Chaim Weizmann

82. To Viscount Samuel,[1] London.   *New York, 2 December 1947*
English: T.: W.A.

On the great occasion of momentous decision by UNO I send you my heartiest congratulations and thanks. Your great services our

---

79. [1] Biog. Index, Vol. IX. British soldier, administrator and ardent Zionist.

81. [1] Biog. Index, Vol. VI. On Zionist Commission, 1918.
    [2] Baron Edmond de Rothschild (Biog. Index, Vol. I).
    [3] Dorothy de Rothschild, formerly Pinto (Biog. Index, Vol. VII).

82. [1] Herbert Samuel (Biog. Index, Vol. VII). First British High Commissioner of Palestine, 1920–25.

cause have certainly contributed to consummation this ideal. Affectionate regards to you and family.

Weizmann

83. To Doris May, London.   *New York, 3 December 1947*
English: T.: W.A.

In these stirring days I am thinking of you and your abiding loyalty and cooperation in all these difficult years. You have made my task ever so much easier, and heartfelt thanks to you. Looking forward to seeing you. Affectionately yours,

Chaim Weizmann

84. To the Sokolow Family,[1] London.   *New York, 3 December 1947*
English: T.: W.A.

I reciprocate heartily your good wishes and, like you, the memory of your dear father, my great colleague, was always in my mind during these stirring days. I have often quoted his sayings and his wise utterances which are still guiding us in our path. All good wishes. Affectionately yours,

Chaim Weizmann

85. To Israel S. Wechsler,[1] New York.   *New York, 4 December 1947*
English: T.W.: W.A.

Dear Dr. Wechsler,

I am grateful for your letter,[2] but I am seriously alarmed at the mention that some directors of the Friends of the University would interpret my absence from your meeting as "an unfriendly act."

It is entirely beyond my comprehension how such an interpretation could be given by anybody who knows that for the last 25 years I have supported the University unstintingly and whole-heartedly,

84. [1] Florian (Biog. Index, Vol. II) and Celina, children of Nahum Sokolow (Biog. Index, Vol. I), had sent congratulations to W., stating that, like their father, he had devoted his entire life to Jewish national revival (2 Dec., W.A.).

85. [1] 1886–1962. Neurologist, lecturer at Columbia University; on H.U. Board of Governors from 1930; President, American Friends of H.U.
[2] 2 Dec. (W.A.). This stated that many Board members were extremely disappointed at W.'s inability, which they interpreted as unwillingness, to attend a Dinner for H.U. on 15 Dec.

and there is no reason on earth why my attitude should change towards it now. It is definitely a piece of malevolence and unwarranted intrigue if people spread rumours of that kind, and I hope that you will answer them as they deserve.

I am simply overburdened with duties and the state of my health can hardly stand the strain of these last few days. This should be enough as an explanation by a man in my position and my age. If anybody chooses to insinuate some ulterior motives, it is certainly not my fault and it would be the duty of my friends to dispel such rumours.

I remain, dear Dr. Wechsler,

Sincerely yours,
Ch. Weizmann

86. To Kibbutz Kiryat Anavim, Palestine. *New York, 5 December 1947*
English: T.: W.A.

To you friends go out my heartiest good wishes. Fully understand and sympathize your position.[1] I know you will bear it with your usual courage. You will still be part of us.

Chaim Weizmann

87. To Ignac Moubarak,[1] Beirut. *New York, 5 December 1947*
English: Or. Copy. T.W.: W.A.

My dear Monseigneur Moubarak,

During Dr. Joseph Attie's[2] visit to me he was kind enough to offer to take a letter to your Eminence.

I take great pleasure in sending you a word of greeting and good will on the occasion of the great events which have taken place recently at the meetings of the United Nations.

I know that Your Eminence will accept my assurances that the future Jewish State will use its best endeavors to live in friendly, neighborly relations with our friends in the Lebanon, of whom you are so distinguished a representative. I think the mutual good relations of the two progressive peoples of the Middle East will benefit

---

86. [1] According to the approved U.N. plan of partition, this agricultural settlement, established 1920, was to be within Jerusalem-Bethlehem zone set aside for internationalisation, and would therefore fall outside the Jewish State.

87. [1] Bishop of Maronite Church in Beirut.
　　[2] Jewish communal leader in Beirut.

both Lebanon and Palestine and strengthen the stability and security of this part of the Eastern Mediterranean.

I hope to be in Palestine about the end of next month. I shall come over to Beyrouth and I hope to have the pleasure of seeing you and Monseigneur Arida[3] again.

Meanwhile, I beg you to accept my high regard and respect, and with heartiest good wishes of the season, I remain

Yours very sincerely,

88. To Va'ad Hapoel, Histadrut,[1] Tel Aviv.

New York, 5 December 1947

English: T.: W.A.

Appreciate deeply your kind message.[2] This success due greatly your self-sacrifice and devoted service. Affectionately,

Chaim Weizmann

89. To Mark Vishniak,[1] New York.

New York, 5 December 1947

English: T.W.: W.A.

Dear Mr. Vishniak,

Thank you for your letter.[2]

I have never said anything derogatory about your book; on the contrary, I consider it an interesting and well written biography. All I did remark at the time was that these books, and there are several of them, are taking away some of the interest from my autobiography. But, of course, that isn't anybody's fault. I cannot prevent any one from writing about me if they wish to do so.

Very sincerely yours,

Ch. Weizmann

---

[3] Antoine Arida, Patriarch of Maronite Church in Lebanon.

88. [1] Executive Committee of Jewish Workers Federation.

[2] Cable 30 Nov. (W.A.). This sent workers' greetings on 'fulfilment of a dream bound eternally to W.'s name and labours'.

89. [1] B. Russia, *ca.* 1885. Writer, in youth a member of Social Revolutionary Party. Author of *Doctor Weizmann* (in Russian), Paris, 1939, a biography.

[2] 4 Nov. (W.A.). This stated that Gershon (Hermann) Swet of Jerusalem had informed Vishniak that W. had praised his book. This was some recompense, and he wished to hear it directly from W., since eight years earlier their mutual acquaintance, I.A. Naiditch, had notified him of W.'s demand that the book, then only in Russian, not be translated into English. See Vol. XVIII, No. 237.

90. To Winston S. Churchill, London. *New York, 8 December 1947*
English: T.: W.A.

On eve of Parliamentary debate on Palestine question[1] I venture to call your attention to following considerations: First, Assembly recommendation undoubtedly reflects moral judgment of world. Next to American-Russian agreement most important initiative came from British Dominions, all whom supported resolution together with France, Scandinavian, West European, South American countries. Some press reports which I have seen suggest Assembly's recommendation artificially produced by various pressures, but such reports far-fetched in view of weight of impartial judicial opinion expressed so many quarters. Second, as foremost architect of United Nations you will certainly prefer implementation of Assembly recommendation to its violation. Assertion of Assembly's authority vital for future prestige and efficacy United Nations. Charter must be upheld against menace and intimidation. Third, as one of originators National Home policy and its defender in darkest days you may be gratified at international endorsement that policy and provision made for its realisation. Fourth, while offering Jews some compensation their terrible sufferings this scheme also offers benefits to Arabs. Another unit of Arab independence in addition to seven existing.[2] On original area Palestine Mandate two Arab states, Transjordan and Arab Palestine, now established; therefore Arabs have not done badly and sense of grievance quite unjustified. Thirty million Arabs independent not entitled begrudge small area of freedom to Jews. Myself and friends will strive for harmonious relations Arab world. As Mandate ends I pray for restoration of noble British-Jewish partnership which you and colleagues built thirty years ago and which remains essential for British interest, stability and prosperity Middle East. Cordial regards,

Chaim Weizmann

---

90. [1] House of Commons, 11–12 Dec. Creech Jones announced that British troops would be withdrawn from Palestine by Aug. 1948, but would be available to keep order until the Mandate was relinquished; and that, subject to negotiation with U.N., the Government intended to terminate the Mandate not later than 15 May 1948. Churchill did not participate.
  [2] I.e., Egypt, Iraq, Lebanon, Saudi Arabia, Syria, Transjordan and Yemen.

91. To David Ben-Gurion, Jerusalem.   *New York, 9 December 1947*
English: T.: W.A.

Thanks cablegram.[1] Reciprocate good wishes. Hope for peaceful settlement.

Weizmann

92. To Lord Inverchapel, Washington.   *New York, 9 December 1947*
English: Or. Copy. T.W.: W.A.

My dear Lord Inverchapel,
I have thought that I might still come to Washington and was looking forward to the pleasure of seeing you, but pressure of work here and extreme fatigue make it impossible for me to venture another journey. I will, therefore, not have the pleasure of saying goodbye to you personally, which I regret very much.
I would have liked to talk to you about certain aspects of the situation and the relations between us and H.M. Government. Now that there is a settlement, I would have liked to try to effect a reconciliation between the Jews in Palestine and elsewhere and the British Government and the British people. The strained relations and bitterness are unnatural and in the end harmful to both sides.
Perhaps you will be in London in the course of the next few weeks? I shall be staying there until about the last week in January.[1]
Please accept my good wishes and kind regards.

Sincerely yours,

93. To Robert A. Lovett, Washington.   *New York, 9 December 1947*
English: Or. Copy. T.W.: W.A.

Dear Mr. Lovett,
I had hoped, before my departure from the United States, to call on you for the purpose of expressing the deep gratitude of our people for your Department's initiative and leadership which led to the Assembly's historic decison on Palestine last month.[1]

91. [1] No telegram from Ben-Gurion personally traced.

92. [1] No reply traced.

93. [1] In Marshall's absence at the height of the U.N. debate, Lovett had been in charge of the Palestine issue and was responsible for giving departmental directives to the U.S. delegation in New York.

Not unexpectedly, the immediate results of this decision have included acts of violence in Palestine and the Middle East, but I remain convinced that the Assembly's decision correctly defines the objective conditions of Arab-Jewish harmony, and my colleagues and I will do all in our power to ensure that all these conditions are speedily fulfilled.

In taking the initiative for the Assembly's recommendation, the United States Government has written a notable chapter in the life of the United Nations, whose prestige and prospects will be greatly enhanced by the resolute maintenance of the policy which was approved. I can testify from my contacts and experiences in recent weeks that throughout the Jewish world there is a profound sense of gratitude to your Department and your delegation at the United Nations for the courageous and statesmanlike attitude which you displayed.

I am very sorry to have been unable to say this to you in person, but my health has suffered through strain and tenseness of recent weeks and my medical advisers positively forbid me to leave New York before my departure for London. I therefore hope that you will accept these few written words of appreciation in the cordial spirit with which they are written.

I am,

Very sincerely yours,

94. To Spyros K. Skouras,[1] New York.   *New York, 9 December 1947*
English: Or. Copy. T.W.: W.A.

My dear Mr. Skouras,

I want to take this opportunity to express to you my sincere personal gratitude for your valiant efforts to secure the cooperation of the Greek delegation at the recent session of the United Nations Assembly. Mr. Lubin[2] has told me of the time and energy that you have devoted to our cause.

We regret that we were not successful in securing the affirmative vote of the Greek delegation. However, we are deeply grateful to you for your efforts and cooperation.

I trust that some day in the near future I shall have an opportunity to meet you in person and express to you my appreciation.[3]

Very cordially,

94. [1] 1893–1971. Greek-American President and Chief Executive 20th Century-Fox Film Corporation 1942–62.

[2] Arthur Lubin, motion picture director.

[3] A letter of appreciation was sent likewise 8 Dec. (W.A.) to Joseph Schenk, also of 20th Century-Fox, for his efforts.

95. To Harry S. Truman, Washington.   *New York, 9 December 1947*
English: Or. Copy. T.W.: W.A.

Dear Mr. President,

Before my departure from the United States I feel moved to address a few words to you on the subject of Palestine and the Jewish people.

In recent weeks I have been in close touch with Jewish opinion both in the United States and throughout the world. I can testify from this contact that the Jewish world is dominated by a profound sense of gratitude to you and your Administration for the initiative and leadership which led to the Assembly's historic decision last week. Desultory criticism from certain unrepresentative circles[1] should not be allowed to create any false impressions on this score. Our people everywhere fully understand where their gratitude lies.

Our concern and attention now shift to Palestine itself, and I have been at pains to establish close contact with events there. Our people are deliberately reacting with the utmost restraint to Arab attacks with the aim of avoiding the spread of localized violence.[2] This restraint means sacrifice to us; but I believe that a prudent and unprovocative attitude will best serve our interests and the cause of ultimate peace. We rely on the United Nations and its leading members to remain resolute in defense of the Charter against any intimidation.

The only matter which causes us anxiety is our people's deficiency in the equipment necessary for their defense. The Arabs obviously suffer no such lack. It is a paradox of history that the Jews, who are the only people in the Near East threatened by aggression, are the only people who have not been able to provide freely for their own defense. In our efforts to correct this dangerous position we shall have cause to rely on the good will of your administration; and it is for this reason that I venture to bring the matter to your attention.

In conclusion, Mr. President, may I say how deeply I valued the privilege of meeting you during these crucial days in our people's history and how keenly I felt your sympathy and generous spirit.

I am, Mr. President,

> With deep respect,
> Sincerely yours,

---

95. [1] On 5 Dec. Marshall announced that with growing violence in Palestine the State Department was imposing an embargo on all shipments of arms to Middle East. Many Jews saw this as a significant retreat from America's support of partition, and Jewish opponents of Zionism, such as American Council for Judaism, were encouraged to speak out more vigorously against American support for Jewish statehood.

[2] Arab indignation at the U.N. decision was strong, producing widespread violence in Palestine, particularly in Jerusalem and the Tel Aviv-Jaffa area.

96. To Alexandre Parodi,[1] Washington. *New York, 11 December 1947*
English: Or. Copy. T.W.: W.A.

My dear Mr. Ambassador,

Now that the decision has fallen and your country has supported it, I am anxious to send you a word of greeting and thanks because I know how much you have contributed towards the attitude of the French Delegation.

I know that it wasn't an easy decision for the French Republic to take—they had to choose between political expediency[2] and a moral dictate. True to its tradition, France chose the second.

I had expected to be in Washington and was looking forward to thank you personally, but owing to the strain of the last few weeks, I must forgo any further journeys, and I must limit myself in sending you my thanks and my best wishes in these few simple lines.

I am, dear Mr. Ambassador, with deep respect and high regard,

Yours very sincerely,

97. To Jawaharlal Nehru, New Delhi. *New York, 16 December 1947*
English: Or. Copy. T.W.: W.A.

Dear Mr. Prime Minister,

Let me thank you most heartily for your kind and interesting letter of December 2nd.[1] It reached me here yesterday.

I am leaving tomorrow on the *Mauretania*. You will, therefore, easily understand and forgive that I have done very little in order to carry into effect your most valuable suggestion. We are reaching London on the 23rd of this month and it will be my first duty, and I assure you a most pleasant one, to organize the group which is to go out from Palestine to visit your country. We shall then have time to make all the detailed arrangements and will inform you accordingly.

I myself hope to be in Palestine at the end of January, and if and when your group comes to Palestine, I hope to be able to receive them personally.

I remain, dear Prime Minister, with high regard and respect,

Yours very sincerely,

---

96. [1] B. 1901. Permanent representative of France to U.N. 1946–49.

[2] Principally, France was concerned at repercussions within her Moslem empire.

97. [1] See No. 36, n. 5.

98. To Billy Rose,[1] **New York.** *New York, 16 December 1947*
English: Or. Copy. T.W.: W.A.

Dear Mr. Rose,
My attention has been called to your open letter to me in "P.M." and other newspapers in the country.[2]

Although this is my last day in the United States (I am leaving tomorrow morning for England and Palestine), and as you can readily imagine, I have innumerable things to clear up, I want to acknowledge, at least in a few words, your very interesting and provocative letter.[3]

I am not, of course, in a position to pass judgment on the financial aspects of your proposal and its various ramifications, affecting particularly the campaign for $250,000,000 just decided in Atlantic City.[4] Yet I feel that your proposal merits the most earnest consideration, and I would, therefore, suggest that, if possible, you meet with Mr. Eliezer Kaplan, Treasurer of the Jewish Agency for Palestine, who is now in this country, or still better, get in touch with Mr. Weisgal, whom I believe you know, and he will arrange for a meeting between you and Mr. Kaplan to discuss this matter fully.

I regret I have not the possibility of meeting you personally. I do hope that we shall meet in Palestine.

Very sincerely yours,
Chaim Weizmann

P.S. Mr. Weisgal can be reached at Rh. 4-4200.

---

98. [1] 1899–1966. U.S. showman and Broadway producer.

[2] I.e., in Rose's regular syndicated column 'Pitching Horseshoes'.

[3] Rose wrote that he was addressing a proposal to W. as he had heard Drew Pearson predict on radio that W. would be the first President of the Jewish Republic. Rose hoped Palestine 'doesn't try to put the bite on Uncle Sam' for all the money it would require. Instead, the Zionist leaders should launch a drive for $500 millions of 3 per cent bonds redeemable in 1968.

[4] At U.J.A. National Conference 12–15 Dec.

99. To Moses Schonfeld,[1] New York.   *New York, 16 December 1947*
English: T.W.: W.A.

Dear Mr. Schonfeld,

I know the late Lord Wedgwood's views about Palestine becoming a dominion,[2] and I fully share them.

Whether the Jews in the partition of Palestine will agree to such an idea, I am not prepared to say. This has to be sounded out, and I will do so when in Palestine. There is also the question whether the British Commonwealth would like to receive the Jewish State in its orbit and whether the Jews of America will agree to help in this endeavor. These are all matters of importance which have to be discussed quietly, and I think open propaganda at this moment would only do harm.

I am afraid my time is much too limited at this moment, as I am going away tomorrow, and I shall have to forgo the pleasure of an interview with you.

I remain, with cordial regards,

Yours very sincerely,

Ch. Weizmann

100. To Meyer W. Weisgal, New York.   *New York, 16 December 1947*
English: T.W.: W.A.

Dear Meyer,

In the event that the formalities attending the creation of The Weizmann Foundation shall not have been completed by the time I leave the United States, I want to take this means of advising you that I have decided to transfer and convey to The Weizmann Foundation the manuscript of my memoirs, which have recently been completed, together with all my right, title and interest therein, and for the publication of the same in whole or in part. I hereby authorize you to make the formal transfer to The Foundation in my name

---

99. [1] B. 1910. Merchant, hon. secretary of Wedgwood Memorial Committee in New York. He had been associated with Josiah Wedgwood (Biog. Index, Vol. XI) in 1937–38 in promoting the entry of Palestine as an independent Dominion within the British Commonwealth.

[2] Schonfeld to W., 15 Dec. (W.A.). This stated that 'the Irish and the Boers fought the British with deeper hatred and bitterness than the Jews, yet they have found membership in the Commonwealth advantageous'. He sought a meeting with W. before conducting a campaign in this regard.

and in my behalf in the event that I shall not have done so myself before my departure.

The Foundation shall have the right to publish said manuscript, in whole or in part, and to sell such publication and to use the net proceeds thereof for the purposes of The Foundation. The Foundation shall also have the right to translate said manuscript and to publish and sell any and all translations thereof and to use the net proceeds of such publication and sale for its purposes.

I do also hereby assign, transfer and convey to The Foundation all copyright, motion picture, radio, television, and any and all other rights in and to said manuscript provided, however, that any use of said manuscript shall not vary in substance from the text thereof.

The foregoing assignment and conveyance, and any assignment, transfer and conveyance which I may hereafter make to The Foundation of any kind and description, is upon the condition that the name of The Foundation shall not be changed from its present name. I should like to be able to indicate from time to time the scientific purposes for the application of the funds to be derived from such property or gifts which I may make to The Foundation. I would suggest that after my death, the directors of the Foundation should consult with the Scientific Director of The Weizmann Institute of Science, Rehovot, Palestine, with respect to the nature of the scientific purposes to which the funds derived from such gifts as I may have made to The Foundation shall be applied.

Sincerely yours,
Chaim Weizmann

101. To Sarah Gertrude Millin,[1] Johannesburg.

London, 24 December 1947

English: Or. Copy. T.W.: W.A.

My dear Sarah,

I am just back from America, and find your most kind letter[2] to greet me—I need not tell you how welcome it is, and how warmly I thank you for it. These are indeed days of mighty events—but they don't bring us to the end of our troubles; only to the beginning of another phase. We are to-day rather like a poor young couple, getting married and setting up house with very little means—but

---

101. [1] 1889–1968. South African writer. She and her husband Philip were close friends of the Weizmanns.

[2] 13 Dec. (W.A.), relating to U.N. decision.

perhaps it is not so bad for us that we have to suffer and take risks at the start. We may be all the stronger for it later on.

I am greatly distressed to hear that you telegraphed to us about Michael, and also for my birthday,[3] and had no reply: you may have thought us very remiss and inconsiderate. My secretary, Miss May, who watches over my correspondence, assures me that she has never seen, and has no record, of any telegram or letter from you on either occasion. If they had reached me, I could not possibly have failed to answer. Only yesterday I sent greetings to you through Sir Simon Marks[4] and his wife, who left for South Africa; they will come and see you and give you all our news.

The kindness you both showed us during our time in South Africa will always live in both our hearts,[5] and we have the warmest recollections of your lovely home. You must give us a chance of seeing you in Rehovot: we shall be here for another month or so, but we are booked on a plane leaving here on January 25th, and expect to be home in Palestine by the end of that month, and to stay the whole summer till October or so—by which time I hope things will have settled down. In fact, I hope they will have settled long before then. Do come and see us; I can assure you of a very hearty welcome.

As I said, we are only just back from the States, and your note was the nicest possible greeting on our arrival; we were both delighted to have news of you, and send you our best love.

Yours,

102. To C. David Ginsburg, Washington.   *London, 27 December 1947*
English: Or. Copy. T.W.: W.A.

My dear Dave,

I can scarcely tell you how sorry I am that we have missed each other again.[1] Fate seems to be against us—and the only remedy for this situation is for you to come to Palestine, and *soon*.

My plans are as follows: We hope to leave here on the 25th January by air for Geneva, and to continue from Geneva, also by air, on the 27th, reaching Rehovot on the 28th. This time we intend to stay in Palestine practically the whole year—until the State is set up and

---

[3] Their son Michael W. had been listed as missing in action Feb. 1942. W.'s 70th birthday, 1944, had received world-wide publicity.

[4] Biog. Index, Vol. VI. Merchant, philanthropist, close friend of W. Later, Lord Marks.

[5] The Weizmanns had toured South Africa 1932 (see Vol. XV).

102. [1] Ginsburg had returned to U.S. on termination in London of the Council of Foreign Ministers, 15 Dec.

Tel Aviv scene on the night of the U.N. vote to establish an independent Jewish State.

Food convoy reaches beleaguered Jerusalem, 1948.

the first elections carried through. It will be an interesting, but very difficult, period, and I have no illusions about the submerged rocks we shall have to circumnavigate if we are not to shatter our little ship in the launching. You can help a great deal in this state of affairs by keeping people round you—notably Marshall—informed; they should not expect us to overcome all our difficulties at once, after the long period of demoralisation introduced by the White Paper. We are trying hard to combat the dissident elements, and illegal immigration as well, but these are factors that have developed slowly during the White Paper period. The White Paper was a lawless document, and—in the words of General Smuts, "lawlessness breeds counter-lawlessness."

I go to Palestine with the intention of staying there the whole of the coming year, and of trying to "set the key." It will not be easy. But the *Yishuv* in Palestine consists on the whole of sensible people, conscious of the grave responsibility resting upon them. Judgment on our efforts must not be passed too easily or too swiftly, or without understanding of the inner causes of the scepticism produced by the earlier regime.

I write all this to you because I have been disturbed by some remarks made by Mr. Marshall, who has no doubt been talking here to Mr. Bevin and his friends. Mr. Bevin is our sworn enemy, and his hostility is increased by a sense of frustration. He has twice tried to break us: first through the Anglo-American Committee, which produced a verdict quite contrary to his expectations, and a second time by handing us over to the U.N., which he hoped might bring about the liquidation of the whole affair. But in fact it has done just the opposite. In particular, the united vote of the four Great Powers[2] must have been a bitter pill for Mr. Bevin.

Some of the papers here, no doubt inspired, write constantly of "Jewish influence" and Jewish "wire-pulling"—an easy anti-Semitic device. In fact, quite the contrary is true. So far as I am concerned, I paid three visits only to Lake Success or Flushing Meadows, but even on those visits I could not help noticing that some of the British delegates were working overtime button-holing people. We had neither the opportunity nor the desire to indulge in much of that. But it is easy for non-Jews to credit us with occult powers. I wish you would try and take a suitable opportunity of explaining all this to Mr. Marshall, to whose attitude we all attach the greatest possible weight. I know we have not got many supporters in the

---

[2] On 13 Apr. U.S., Soviet Union, France and China had led a majority of the General Assembly in speedily acting on the British request for a special session of the Assembly. In the event, China abstained from the decisive partition vote.

State Department, and Mr. Marshall's personal views thus acquire an added importance.

A letter from you would still reach me here up to about the 24th January, and I shall be eagerly awaiting it.

Give my love to Leah, and my very best to yourself, as ever,

Yours,

103. To William Rappard,[1] Geneva.   *London, 27 December 1947*
English: T.W.: W.A.

My dear Professor Rappard,

I returned to London from America only three days ago, and feel impelled to take the first opportunity of trying to share with you our joy at the outcome of the U.N. meeting. Though, as you will easily imagine, that joy is not unmixed with a good deal of anxiety as to the future progress of the Jewish State. The attitude of the British in the last few years has made our position very difficult, and for that matter still does; but after all, this thing which is now coming to pass after nearly two thousand years of hope and prayer is not likely to be destroyed through the malevolence of a few people.

On the whole, the U.N. decision was a great moral success—particularly when one thinks that the four Great Dominions voted together against Britain. And—quite contrary to certain interested rumours—the decision was not due to any Jewish wire-pulling: any such insinuation is as untrue as it is harmful. On my (very rare) visits to Lake Success, I could not but notice at least two of the British representatives who were extremely busy lobbying—button-holing practically every delegate. We, on our part, did very little of that; we answered questions when we were asked, and that was about all. Throughout all the weeks of the U.N. discussions, I myself paid just three visits to Lake Success.

But what I really wanted to tell you was something of the deep gratitude we all feel towards you, who, throughout this difficult twenty years, have consistently and unflinchingly supported our cause. What I value most is that you have never hesitated to criticise what was deserving of criticism. May God bless you for everything.

I expect to be leaving here for Palestine on January 25th, and to

---

103. [1] Biog. Index, Vol. XI. Active during early stages of Palestine problem as Director of Mandates Section of League of Nations, and thereafter as Swiss member of Permanent Mandates Commission.

travel via Geneva, where I hope to be from the evening of the 25th till the morning of the 27th, when I am booked to leave by Swissair for Palestine. I very much hope that we may be able to meet some-time on the 26th[2]—if you and Madame Rappard were free to lunch with us that day at the Beau Rivage, it would give us both the greatest pleasure. Should there be any change in our plans, I will let you know in good time.

Meanwhile, please accept our affectionate regards—also to Madame Rappard—and believe me,

As ever yours,
Ch. Weizmann

104. To Israel M. Sieff,[1] London. *London, 29 December 1947*
English: Or. Copy. T.W.: W.A.

My dear Israel,

Your letter of December 9th[2] reached me just at the moment of my departure from America; for this reason it is only to-day that I can reply to it. I thought it preferable to reply in writing so that you can communicate if necessary my answer to Dr. Chain[3] and Dr. Berenblum.[4]

(1) I do not think that the scientific contacts between the Univer-sity and the Institute could have been closer in the past than they have actually been. We have cooperated with our opposite numbers at the University in all those subjects in which there was a mutual interest.

I am fully aware of Dr. Rittenberg's[5] views on the subject. He happens to lay a considerable stress on teaching, and he believes that the members of our staff should have taken a greater part in teaching activities of the University. As you know, this is a contro-

---

[2] In the event, W. had to return to U.S. and did not visit Geneva.

104. [1] Biog. Index, Vol. VI. Merchant, philanthropist, close friend of W. Later, Lord Sieff.

[2] This (W.A.) discussed charges of lack of cooperation in scientific work between H.U. and Weizmann Institute.

[3] (Sir) Ernst Boris Chain, b. 1906. British biochemist and Nobel laureate for role in dis-covery of penicillin, 1945.

[4] Isaac Berenblum, b. 1903. Pathologist specialising in cancer research; member of School of Pathology at Oxford 1936–48; joined Weizmann Institute 1950.

[5] David Rittenberg (1906–70). U.S. biochemist at Columbia University from 1934; was associated with Atomic Energy Commission; later, Governor of Weizmann Institute of Science.

versy of long standing, whether a research man should teach or not. As, in my opinion, this depends entirely on the personal inclination of the scientist, it must be left to the individual. In our case it has been left to the members of our staff as well as to the University authorities to decide whether anything could be gained by their lecturing at the University. I cannot help adding that it has not always been the policy of the University to encourage such members of our staff who would have been willing to lecture to do so.

(2) I agree that our Institute must be in close contact with those departments and members of the Hebrew University who are engaged in the same type of work, but I do not share the belief that the Institute could only do fruitful work if at the University there are already departments staffed with good research workers working on the same lines. On the contrary, it is my conviction that the establishment of a good institute at Rehovot will have a most beneficiary influence on the development of the University. You must not forget that whilst we are in the fortunate position of breaking new ground, the University has already taken a definite shape, and one cannot make fundamental changes by decree.

(3) The only way to go about, if one wants to make changes, is by influencing *gradually* the authorities of the University in the choice of the men they want to appoint to new Departments or to such Departments as become vacant in the course of time. It was particularly for this reason that I recommended to the Board of Governors that Dr. Bergmann should be made a member of the Executive Committee of the University.[6] He is devoting a good deal of his time to the duties of this position.

Of course, it is a good idea to organise an Advisory Council for any appointments at the Hebrew University; but even this can be done much better by people who are already in the country than by people who, at least geographically, are outsiders. It seems to me that the best both Dr. Chain and Dr. Berenblum can do to help the University (and I have spoken to Dr. Rittenberg in the same sense) is that they come to Palestine and help us to make the Institute in Rehovot an institution of such standing that its spirit will automatically influence the life of the University.

I hope I will still have an opportunity of discussing these important questions both with you and with Dr. Chain and Dr. Berenblum, and remain, in the meantime,

Yours affectionately,
Ch. Weizmann

[6] On 6 Mar. 1947—see Vol. XXII, No. 279.

105. To David Bronstein,[1] Toronto.   *London, 30 December 1947*
English: Or. Copy. T.W.: W.A.

Dear Mr. Bronstein,

Thank you very much for your letter of the 5th December,[2] which has only just reached me here. The matter you raise is one which is exercising the minds of many thoughtful Zionists to-day: what, after the establishment of the Jewish State, is to be the function of Zionists outside Palestine? What will be their relationship to the Jewish State?

It is difficult for me, as a private individual, to give a reply off-hand, especially since the problem will no doubt be raised and discussed by the responsible Zionist organs at the first opportunity. But, if I may use an analogy, I would say that the relationship would be not unlike that of (say) American Irishmen to the Irish Free State. Of course, our Jewish problem is more complex and delicate.

As to function, I feel that the Zionist organization should transform itself into a great colonising group—or rather a group for the colonisation of Palestine. But these are merely offhand answers, given entirely on my own responsibility. The whole problem will have to be thoroughly considered and discussed at the next Zionist Congress, which I understand may be called early in the summer.[3] Till then, I think one should just carry on as best one can, and not make any radical changes till the Movement as a whole has had a chance to take a decision, and until the State is actually established, which will not be for the next few months.

I cannot close this note without saying how much I appreciate all the excellent work you have been doing in Canada; it is of the greatest importance to our future, and my thoughts and best wishes are with you.

I remain, with very best regards and personal greetings,

Yours very sincerely,

---

105. [1] National chairman of societies affiliated with the Zionist Organization of Canada.
[2] This (W.A.) enquired on the nature and functions of the Zionist Organization on advent of the Jewish State.
[3] In fact, it convened Aug. 1951.

106. To H.W. Turner,[1] **London.**　　　　*London, 30 December 1947*
English: Or. Copy. T.W.: W.A.

Dear Mr. Turner,

Before leaving for America about two months ago, I sent to Sir Simon [Marks], at his suggestion, a cheque for £4000 for investment purposes. I have no doubt that this money has been disposed of in some satisfactory way, but I find I have no record of what happened to it. I should be greatly obliged if you could let me know whether and how the money has been invested; also whether it has all been invested, or whether any of it remains available?[2]

With many thanks in advance for your help, and all good wishes for the New Year, I am

Yours sincerely,

107. To Blanche Dugdale, Scotland.　　　*London, 1 January 1948*
English: Or. Copy. T.W.: W.A.

My dear Baffy,

I was very happy to get your note[1] and to hear that you will be back here on the 7th. I look forward very much to seeing you. We can dine together almost any evening—I have very few engagements and go out hardly at all these days. The fact is that I am beginning now to feel the reaction after the stresses and strains of New York, and am trying to take things as quietly as I can. So come when you like—you have only to let us know.

When we meet we can discuss everything. One of my first aims here is to try and get the relations between Jews and British re-established on a more normal footing as soon as possible. I believe that to be essential for both sides; and as I am only here for a month, I haven't much time to do whatever I can do at this end.

Please accept my affectionate good wishes for a very happy New Year for you and yours, in which Vera joins me. And in the hope of seeing you soon, I remain, as ever,

Yours,
Ch. W.

---

106. [1] Of Marks and Spencer, Ltd., concerned with directors' personal financial affairs.
[2] Turner replied 2 Jan. 1948 (W.A.), indicating that Marks had invested the funds in Woolworths, South Africa, in the name of W. and Benjamin W. He enclosed a cheque to cover the unallotted balance.

107. [1] 29 Dec. (W.A.).

108. To Meyer W. Weisgal, New York.   *London, 1 January 1948*
English: T.W.: W.A.

Dear Meyer,

I am somewhat alarmed by a letter from Watt, with some extracts from your letter of December 18th to him, which has just reached me.[1] If the expenses on the book already amount to $15,000 it seems as likely as not that all this labour will only lead to my being out of pocket in the end—a prospect which I don't much relish.

I don't know what you advise, but I would certainly like to see matters amicably settled between you, Watt, and the two publishers as soon as possible. As you know, I am quite ignorant in these matters, and must rely on you to make all the arrangements.

As ever,
Affectionately yours,
Ch. Weizmann

109. To Maung Kyi,[1] Rangoon.   *London, 2 January 1948*
English: Or. Copy. T.W.: W.A.

Sir,

I have the honour to acknowledge receipt of your letter of December 18th, 1947,[2] and to thank you for the invitation which the Burmese Government has so kindly extended to me. I very much appreciate it, and shall do my best to combine a visit to Burma with my projected trip to India. The problems of our two countries are in so many respects parallel that I am hopeful that our experience in Palestine may prove of use in furthering Burma's progress towards greater industrial and economic independence.

So far as I can see, my trip to India will not materialise before the later months of 1948, and I would therefore like, if I may, to make a supplementary suggestion. It would, I believe, be very useful if you, and such other experts and colleagues of yours as the

---

108. [1] Weisgal had informed Watt (copy in W.A.) that date of publication in London of W.'s memoirs depended upon Harper's date of publication in New York, not yet determined. He empowered Watt to conclude an agreement with either Hamish Hamilton or Macmillan. Further, he informed Watt that his commission could be paid only after all existing expenses, '$15,000 or more', were recovered.

109. [1] Deputy Secretary of Burmese National Planning Department.

[2] W.A. Having learned from Sir B. R. Rau of W.'s proposed mission to India, Maung Kyi invited W. and his scientific colleagues to visit Burma to advise on techniques of economic and social development, particularly in the fields of hydro-electricity, oil, coal and other minerals.

Burmese Government may select, could pay a visit to Palestine in the spring of this year. We could then have a preliminary discussion of the subjects in which you are interested, and obtain from you many of the data required for adequate preparation of our visit to Burma. You might also be interested to see for yourselves what has been and is being done in Palestine in the fields of science, agriculture and industry.

I was greatly interested in the brief survey of Burma's rich industrial resources contained in your letter, and the following comments, which occur to me on a first reading, are submitted for your consideration:

(1) You probably know that one of the most important projects which we have on hand in Palestine at the moment is a hydro-electric scheme, combined with a scheme for the extended irrigation of dry areas. A substantial proportion of Palestine's electricity supply is already obtained from a hydro-electric plant, and I believe that our experts in this field might be able to be of service to you.

(2) We are in process of establishing, at the Rehovot Research Centre, a Department concerned with geophysical methods; it will be under the direction of a man who has made some outstanding contributions to the development of modern oil-prospecting.[3] He will, I am sure, be very happy to place his experience at the disposal of your Government, and the combined utilisation of coal and oil may well serve as a basis for an organic-chemical industry.

(3) I believe that some of our experts might also be of use to you in the survey of the mineral resources of Burma. This is one of the most important points of contact between our two countries.

(4) Another major problem with which we both have to deal is the transition from an agricultural to an industrial economy. We are endeavouring to combine these two economic domains organically, by using agricultural products as raw material for our chemical industry, and I think you might be interested to see on the spot what we are doing in this field.

I look forward to hearing from you with regard to the above suggestion, which I trust may commend itself to you,[4] and remain, Sir,

> Your obedient Servant,
> Ch. Weizmann

---

[3] Pekeris (see No. 46, n. 3).

[4] Maung Kyi replied 22 Jan. (W.A.), expressing willingness to send experts to Rehovot. W. acknowledged this letter 12 Feb. (W.A.).

110. To Sir Zafrullah Khan,[1] Lahore.   *London, 4 January 1948*
English: Or. Copy. T.W.: W.A.

My dear Sir Zafrullah,
  It gave me very great pleasure to see the news of your new post a few days ago, and I felt I should like to send you my warm congratulations and very best wishes for a long and successful term of office. It falls to you to direct the external relations of Pakistan in the first, most critical, stages of her existence, and to tread a road along which we, in our small State in Palestine, shall soon have to follow you. Many problems will be common to both of us, and it is my earnest hope that it may be possible for us to deal with them together, and in cooperation, for the good of both our peoples.
  I shall be returning home to Rehovot at the end of this month, and shall be there for the rest of the year. Should your travels bring you in our direction, we should be delighted if you could visit us; it would be a great privilege to show you something of our work, and to discuss our problems with you personally.
  With kind regards and all good wishes for the New Year, I am,[2]
                                              Yours very sincerely,
                                                       Ch. W.

111. To Felix Frankfurter, Washington.   *London, 12 January 1948*
English: Or. Copy. T.W.: W.A.

My dear Felix,
  I wanted to send you, as soon as possible after my return here, a note on the situation as I find it, but it is not too easy to do so, since news coming out of Palestine (from all sources I am afraid) is not very reliable, and can be interpreted only in the light of background knowledge, in which I am naturally not very up-to-date at present. Still, I shall try to put down what can honestly be reported from here, and will supplement it as soon as I can from Rehovot.
  The Palestine Administration and security forces seem to have

110. [1] B. 1893. Jurist, appointed Foreign Minister of Pakistan Dec. 1947. He was Pakistan's delegate to U.N. 1961–64 (President of U.N. Assembly 1962); President, International Court of Justice 1970–73. He had visited Palestine in 1945 (see Vol. XXII, No. 58). W.'s letter was prompted by information received from the Orientalist Uriel Heyd, then working for Zionist intelligence in London. This stated that Khan, in Damascus, had given as his personal opinion that partition was the only solution for Palestine, though he himself had tried to prevent it. Khan now counselled the Arabs to allow the Jews to establish their state, but then to boycott it in order to compel the Zionists to join a larger Arab federation. See Heyd to W., 1 Jan. 1948, W.A.
  [2] No reply traced, but the two met in New York 12 Apr.

abdicated: the proof is what is going on in the Old City, where the Arabs seem to have taken possession and closed the gates, forcing even British soldiers to show papers before entering. The Authorities say that the principle of "neutrality" prevents them from acting otherwise than they do—but they are not conspicuously neutral in their handling of *Haganah,* whose members are either completely ignored, or recognised only to be disarmed. And yet—only yesterday one of the most serious Arab attacks so far (the "invasion" across the Syrian frontier) was successfully dealt with by the military and the *Haganah* working together![1]

As regards the ships, the inside story is that it simply was not possible to keep these ships in harbour any longer: the people were in danger of their lives from the Roumanians, and the ships simply had to run somewhere.[2] The [Zionist] Executive was quite powerless to stop them. In fact they were intercepted and taken to Cyprus, where they now are, and I think we can take it that the attempt will not be repeated. We are doing everything we can—but God knows it is hard and heart-breaking to keep these people waiting for months and years—starving, broken, destitute, and hopeless, except for the hope of Palestine. I do wish we could somehow bring this home to Mr. Marshall.

I am rather worried—as you may imagine—about his attitude, for I think he does not realise the position, and am sure that during his stay here recently[3] he must have heard all the Foreign Office arguments, and accepted them at face value. And in my opinion these arguments are far from being valid, and the facts on which they are based frequently open to question—for, as I explained at the start, news out of Palestine, from whatever source, is not very reliable. The Sunday papers to-day describe the situation there in terms which are obviously distorted—if one knows anything of the realities.

It would be a wonderful thing if the U.N. would decide to send out an International Force, even if only a small one; also if the *Haganah* could be permitted to arm itself properly, instead of being disarmed every time a detachment happens to attract the attention of the police. (This seems to be normal procedure these days.)

---

111. [1] Some 600–800 Arabs crossed the frontier and attacked Kfar Szold in northern Palestine 9 Jan. 1948. They were repulsed 10 Jan. by Jews in action together with a British force.

[2] On 1 Jan. the *Pan-York* and *Pan-Crescent,* carrying over 15,000 'illegal' immigrants, were escorted to Famagusta in Cyprus by a British naval force. That same day the *United Nations* succeeded in running the British blockade and landed 537 immigrants on the coast north of Haifa. The Roumanian Government had refused to give the refugees sanctuary.

[3] For the Council of Foreign Ministers.

The Government professes to be in control of the security situation, and does not allow anyone else to help. But where there is cooperation—e.g. on the northern frontier a day or two ago—it does not look as if the situation is at all unmanageable. Another point of the utmost importance is that the Commission[4] should come out to Palestine as soon as possible; otherwise, there is serious danger of spreading anarchy.

We are both well, and intend leaving for Palestine (by air via Geneva) on the 25th January, and should be back home in Rehovot by the 28th. So if you care to drop me a line, you might address it to Rehovot (no further address needed).

Our fondest love to you and yours, and we hope to have the joy of seeing you in Palestine in the not-too-distant future.

As ever,
Affectionately,

112. To James A. Malcolm,[1] London.   *London, 12 January 1948*
English: Or. Copy. T.W.: W.A.

My dear Malcolm,

Many thanks for your letter of the 4th.[2] I have been thinking it over very carefully, but I am afraid I still do not see what purpose would be served by the action you suggest. If a Jewish State comes into being, then the matter will probably adjust itself. At any rate, I don't feel I can give a definite decision in such a matter till I am actually on the spot in Palestine, and have got my bearings there. For various reasons, as you probably know, I am reluctant to write to Mr. Landman;[3] anyhow, you can probably deal with him better than I can, and there is no real point in my mixing in.

With very kind regards, I am,

As ever yours,

---

[4] In recommending partition in Nov. 1947, U.N. General Assembly decided that a Commission consisting of representatives of Bolivia, Czechoslovakia, Denmark, Panama and the Philippines would proceed to Palestine to take over the country's administration from the British and to transfer power to the Arab and Jewish Provisional Governments.

112. [1] Biog. Index, Vol. VII. Merchant of Armenian origin concerned in negotiations leading to Balfour Declaration. He acted for W. in commercial matters and advised him confidentially on political developments.

[2] W.A. This spoke of the desirability of persuading the British that a settlement in Palestine demanded restoration of W.'s leadership, for both the British and the vast majority of the Jewish people had confidence in him. Means had to be found for effecting this.

[3] Samuel Landman (Biog. Index, Vol. V). In 1920s close to W., but later joined New Zionist Organization (Revisionists); during W.W.II returned to W.Z.O.

113. To Josef Cohn,[1] New York.   *London, 13 January 1948*
English: Or. Copy. T.W.: W.A.

Dear Josef,

Thank you very much for your note of the 10th,[2] from which we are glad to see that another parcel is on the way. We are most grateful.

I am sorry to hear that George and Dorothy[3] are worried about our going out. But it is no good sitting here waiting for some improvement; we have to face it, and try to bring the improvement about for ourselves on the spot. I believe myself, from all I hear, that the danger is not too great, given reasonable precautions and care. The main point is to try and see that the U.N. Commission comes out to Palestine as soon as ever possible; that will, I think, have a stabilising effect. I also believe that the British will become more active in maintaining law and order—in the interests of their own prestige if for nothing else—when the Commission arrives. We have already passed, in Palestine, through many such periods of trial, and have come through thus far; so that I believe that with a certain amount of care we can also face what is coming now. Anyhow, we have to get on with the job. I hope by the time they are thinking of coming out, things will have settled down a little.

With kindest regards and renewed thanks for all your help, I am, as ever,

Yours,

114. To Meyer W. Weisgal, New York.   *London, 13 January 1948*
English: T.W.: W.A.

Dear Meyer,

I was delighted to hear your voice on the telephone yesterday, because I had begun to be worried at your silence! Though, truth to tell, I was even more worried when you gave "an attack of economy" as the reason for it. It sounds so very unlike you.

Thank you again for the two parts of the memoirs, both safely

---

113. [1] Biog. Index, Vol. XIX. Represented Sieff Institute in U.S. from 1938, and later the American Committee for the Weizmann Institute.

[2] W.A., notifying W. that parcels (of pencillin and eggs, then in short supply in England) were despatched.

[3] Cohn had written of friends' concern at the Weizmanns' intention of returning shortly to Palestine, where conditions were worsening daily. He specified George Backer and his divorced wife Dorothy (formerly Schiff, and at that time married to William Paley, head of Columbia Broadcasting System).

to hand, and for your letters of the 5th and 7th January.[1] I am
not too sure, though, that I shall be able to meet your wishes about
posting Vol. I back before I leave London. We are leaving on the
24th, and that does not leave me much time. Moreover, I have not
been too well here—what with the reaction after America, and in-
somnia, and a cold, and perfectly wretched weather which has hardly let me outside the door since my return, I am not in much of a
state to concentrate. I have made a start though, and as soon as I
am back in Rehovot, shall get down to it in earnest. I shall sleep
better there, and have more energy for the job. So far as I have got
now, it seems to me that even Volume I, though in general it reads
very well, still needs quite a few minor corrections and amendments
—not major ones of course. But I shall, as I told you, do my very
utmost to keep to schedule.

I understand from Ruskin,[2] who came in a day or two ago
straight from Palestine, that, owing to the uncertain conditions, our
building operations have been slowed down: communications between Rehovot and Tel-Aviv have been none too good. But now
they have built a new road from Tel-Aviv, passing behind Mikweh,
and avoiding all the Arab villages, which shortens the journey by a
good quarter of an hour, and makes it much safer. So I hope that
they will now be able to make up for lost time.

I don't see why the professors should ask for payment as from
January 1st. They should get paid from the date they begin
work—or rather, from the date when they set out for Palestine.
I had a long talk yesterday with Dr. Chain (penicillin) and Dr.
Berenblum. Both are first-class men, and I was delighted to find
them so keen to get out to Rehovot and start work with us.[3]

Have you any definite plans for yourself? Do let me hear as soon
as you have.

Much love from us both,

Yours ever,
Ch. Weizmann

114. [1] W.A. The first letter suggested improvements to the latter part of W.'s memoirs.
The second letter gave an accounting of Weisgal's earlier projection of $15,000 in pre-publica-
tion expenses: typing the manuscript several times, and $12,000 in payments to Maurice
Samuel, who had been engaged intermittently since 1942 in working on the book.

[2] Lewis Ruskin (b. 1905). Manufacturing chemist, closely associated with activities in
U.S. for foundation of Weizmann Institute.

[3] In the event, Chain did not assume an appointment with the Institute.

115. To Meyer W. Weisgal, New York.   London, 16 January 1948
English: T.: W.A.

Letter enclosing Roberts article just received.[1] In no circumstances must this article be published *Collier's* or elsewhere. In any
case prefer say nothing till actually in *Eretz*[2] and certainly nothing
these lines. Rely on you prevent. Important. Please read article
"Palestine Poker," *New Statesman*, January seventeenth[3] and
circulate friends. Distressed hear Eisenman's[4] illness. Have cabled
him.[5] Please keep me informed. Expect you telephone during week-
end. Affectionately,

                                                         Chaim

116. To Felix Bergmann,[1] New York.   London, 19 January 1948
English: Or. Copy. T.W.: W.A.

My dear Felix,

Thank you for your letter of the 10th January.[2] I must confess
that it came as rather a surprise to me, as I hardly see what advantage you will find in going to work at the University, where the conditions are certainly less good than at Rehovot, and where you will
have to devote much of your time to teaching—and probably also
to rather fruitless discussion with your colleagues. Moreover, with

---

115. [1] 12 Jan. (W.A.). The article, by Allen Roberts for *Collier's* magazine, was based on
an interview with Weisgal and purported to reveal W.'s reactions to the U.N. vote. This had
W. describing the Jews of Palestine as 'fully organized' militarily, having courage, initiative,
and intelligence to ward off 'any malefactors', and in possession of 'a variety of military
equipment'.
    [2] *Eretz Israel* (Hebr.): Land of Israel.
    [3] The article expressed concern lest Britain and U.S. hedge in implementation of partition.
It stated that Bevin had a duty to work for an agreed settlement before 15 May; Britain was
obliged to persuade the Arab League that to avoid Russian intervention the U.N. decision
should be accepted by the Arabs of Palestine; the Jews, who had nothing to gain by submission, would be determined to call the British and American bluff.
    [4] Morris Eisenman (1873–1948). Newspaper distributor, founder of *Jewish Daily Forward*
and a former director of Z.O.A. and K.H. He died later that week.
    [5] W.A.

116. [1] B. 1908. Organic chemist and pharmacologist; brother of Ernst D. Bergmann;
on staff of Sieff Institute from 1934; joined H.U. Medical School as associate professor 1949,
professor 1956.
    [2] Untraced. H.U. had for some time been seeking a Professor of Pharmacology. See letter
from D. Werner Senator, H.U. Administrator, to W., 3 Feb. (W.A.), describing the background to the offer to Bergmann and hoping for W.'s consent to his transfer.

the exception of Farkas,[3] the Chemical School there is, in general, definitely below par.

I am not saying all this to try and persuade you to change your mind. But if you want my approval of the decision, then I'm afraid I cannot honestly give it—in your own interests. Of course, you have my consent: you are entirely free to do whatever you think best. One thing, however, I have to add, and that is that the University would have to refund to the Institute your salary for the last year, and the extra expenses involved in your stay in Brooklyn. It is only proper that this should be done, and I think it should be included among the various conditions which you have stipulated. It is both a moral and a financial obligation.

As to the procedure adopted by Dr. Perlzweig[4] and Dr. Friedenwald,[5] in approaching you without even attempting to inform me, I can only express my deep regret. I am constantly hearing suggestions of the desirability of more intimate cooperation between the University and Rehovot, but this is certainly not the way to achieve it.

We are leaving for Rehovot at the end of this week, and shall be back there by the 28th. I hope you will let me know at your earliest convenience when you expect to take up your new duties.

Yours very sincerely,

117. To Rose Halprin,[1] New York.   *London, 19 January 1948*
English: Or. Copy. T.W.: W.A.

My dear Rose,

I am sending you herewith a copy of a letter I have just written to Dr. Felix Bergmann,[2] who has apparently been induced by John Friedenwald to leave Rehovot and take up a professorship at the University. I confess that I find the procedure adopted by the University's representatives in this matter most objectionable. But

---

[3] Ladislaus W. Farkas (1904–48). Professor of Physical Chemistry at H.U.

[4] William Perlzweig (1891–1952). Professor of Biochemistry and Nutrition at Duke University. He had been in Jerusalem during 1947 to advise on matters concerning the organization of the School of Medicine.

[5] Jonas S. Friedenwald (1897–1955). Director, Wilmer Ophthalmological Institute, Johns Hopkins University.

117. [1] Biog. Index, Vol. XVI. President of Hadassah Women's Zionist Organization 1947–51; member of J.A. Executive from 1946.

[2] See No. 116.

it is done now, and you will see from my letter to Felix Bergmann what my attitude is.

In the circumstances, I shall, I am afraid, be rather impatient with future suggestions for closer cooperation between the University and Rehovot. On the intellectual level we have honestly done our best to maintain such cooperation throughout the whole life of the Institute. Farkas, who is at present Professor of Physical Chemistry at the University, worked for many years at the Institute and received his salary from us, because the University was not inclined to take him on. And he is to-day the outstanding man in the Chemical Department there, which can otherwise boast of no particular distinction. Much the same was the case with Saul Adler,[3] who is always short of money for his research work, and never meets with much sympathy from his friends at the University; I have helped him too, in some measure, and have financed some of his researches. Whenever the scientists of the University find themselves in difficulties (and this is, unfortunately, no very rare occurrence), they come to me, and use me as a sort of Wailing Wall.

So to be treated like this by John Friedenwald and Perlzweig (whom incidentally I do not know) is really very trying indeed.

There is nothing I can do about it now, except to hasten Felix Bergmann's departure from Rehovot, but I was anxious that you should know about it, both as a member of the Executive and a leader of Hadassah.

We are leaving for Palestine in a week's time, and I remain, with affectionate regards,

Yours very sincerely,

118. To E. Alexander-Katz,[1] London.   *London, 23 January 1948*
English: Or. Copy. T.W.: W.A.

Dear Dr. Alexander-Katz,

Since seeing you, I have considered very carefully the question of an approach to Field-Marshal Smuts, and have regretfully

---

[3] Biog. Index, Vol. XVI. Parasitologist. Joined H.U. 1924; professor from 1928.

118. [1] Doctor of Law and lecturer in finance and industrial legislation at Haifa Technical College. He was in London on behalf of the Kisch Memorial Fund to help the College. At a meeting, 14 Jan., W. consented to lend his name to a letter which Alexander-Katz wished to send to various potential contributors. Letters were drafted by Miss May, including one to Smuts, in which W. asked his help in contacting certain members of the South African Jewish community. However, W. decided not to sign them, offering Alexander-Katz this explanation (see draft letters, W.A.).

come to the conclusion that it would be improper on my part to ask him to act as an intermediary between ourselves and some of the Jewish South Africans. I am sorry, but I really do not feel that I could write to him in this sense.

As regards the other names mentioned by you, it seems to me that there is no reason for my intervention: an ordinary letter from you setting out the facts, and the purpose of your visit, would probably elicit the response desired. Frankly, I do not feel that, at this crisis in our affairs, I should be asked to use whatever influence I may possess in matters which are, after all, not of front-rank importance from the political point of view. We cannot afford, at a time like the present, to dissipate any of the small stock of goodwill that we can command.

I need not tell you that I am very sorry not to be more helpful; I can only hope that you will understand my position, and understand that much as I would like to help, I do not feel able to do so at present.

Yours very sincerely,

119. To Winston S. Churchill, [Marrakesh]. *London, [January] 1948*
English: Draft: T.W.: W.A.

Dear Mr. C[hurchill],

I hope that you will forgive me for breaking in upon your richly deserved rest with a request for your serious attention.[1] The matter seems to me so vital and so urgent, and at the same time is one which used to be, and I hope still is, so near your heart, that I did not feel justified in leaving it until your return to England. The matter, as no doubt you will have conjectured, concerns Palestine and the future Jewish State. While, naturally, I warmly welcome, with the rest of my people, the great act of historic justice with which the nations of the world have ratified the claims of the Jewish people to a free national existence, I could not but regret the ambiguous, not to say unfriendly attitude of some of the representatives of H.M.G. to the granting of this charter of Jewish liberty. Neither I nor my people will ever forget the noble part played by Great Britain in general, and by such statesmen as the late Lord Balfour, Mr. Lloyd George, and yourself in particular, in our struggle for

---

119. [1] Churchill was in Morocco on vacation following severe indisposition late 1947. W. was forced to change his plans and return to U.S. at short notice. In the event, a final version of this letter was not despatched.

nationhood, and I have taken care to stress this over and over again in my addresses before various UNO committees and elsewhere, not always (I need hardly add) with the unqualified approval of the extremer elements of my own party. But this is not a matter of my personal private feelings and loyalties. The bonds which unite the Jewry of Palestine and the world to Great Britain—and to the great dominions too, particularly after their unanimous support of our cause at Lake Success—still exist, and will, I firmly believe, survive the rising tide of bitterness which at present seems to blind the vision of some of the best Englishmen and Jews alike. But I did not venture to disturb your peace in order to express such pious hopes, however sincere. It seems to me that the UNO decision has radically transformed the political and economic future of the Middle East; a period of sordid frustration is about to yield to a more heroic, but also more perilous, situation: the fate of the Jews will be at stake, and this will affect intimately the relations of the Great Powers; that despite the blunders and misunderstandings of recent years, the peace and happiness of this part of the world—and therefore of Europe and beyond—directly depends upon the closest association of the new Jewish establishment with Great Britain and the British Commonwealth, and that this is appreciated by some of the most clear-sighted and responsible men in the United States and France no less than in Palestine. It is my view that unless a close association between Britain and Palestine, whatever its political or even constitutional form, is firmly established, the consequences will be disastrous to all men of good will and lovers of freedom. It is my fervent belief—the endeavours of a whole lifetime are surety of its sincerity—that even this hour is not too late for the creation of Anglo-Jewish relations based on deep sentiment and principle, as well as on considerations of mutual advantage, and without sacrificing any vital or legitimate interest of the British Empire in its relations either with the Arab world or with the U.S.A.

I am persuaded that what will occur in Palestine within the next year will, for ill or good, profoundly affect the relations of the Powers, and so the immediate future of Europe, perhaps of the world. Because I see the problem as both urgent and critical, and because I profoundly believe that, despite the voices of those who seek to, or cannot help but, darken counsel, British and Jewish interests coincide in this matter, both in the short and in the long run, and because of my faith in the deep insight, sympathy, and magnificent courage which, if I may say so, you have always displayed in guiding the British people, in this as in so many other matters, I venture to write and say how deeply I would appreciate an opportunity of giving you a more detailed exposition of my proposals in a personal interview. I am proposing to leave for Palestine (by air via Geneva) on January 25th.

I feel sure that more than any other great national leader with whom it has been my good fortune to deal, you will understand the anxiety and twofold devotion, to Palestine and England, which prompt my request.

I hope the sun and air of Marrakesh have proved thoroughly enjoyable and salubrious.

[By Jan. 1948 it had become clear that a major effort was necessary to ensure U.S. support for putting the U.N. decision of 29 Nov. 1947 into effect. In Washington Truman, resentful of their pressures, refused to see the Zionist leaders. Reports circulated of his hesitancy to enforce partition for fear of Russian participation in any projected international force for Palestine. The Secretary of Defense, James Forrestal, and the State Department were said to be behind endeavours to reverse the previous American position in favour of partition. The American section of the J.A. Executive therefore decided, despite some opposition, to invite W. to return immediately to New York and take part in the forthcoming political struggle. A cable from Eban went off accordingly, on 23 Jan., the eve of W.'s projected departure from London to Palestine. He acted on this only after it was reinforced by further cables and telephone calls from the Executive itself. Though both were unwell, the Weizmanns left by ship and arrived in New York in the midst of a blizzard on 4 Feb.—see contribution by Eban in *Chaim Weizmann, a Biography by Several Hands,* ed. M. W. Weisgal and J. Carmichael, New York 1963.]

120. To Sir Alan Cunningham, Jerusalem. *New York, 9 February 1948*
English: Or. Copy. T.W.: W.A.

Dear Sir Alan,

Dr. [E. D.] Bergmann is flying tomorrow to Jerusalem and I am taking the opportunity of writing these few words to you.

Mrs. Weizmann and I were on the eve of our departure to Palestine, indeed, we had already sent our luggage off in advance, when I received an urgent request from New York to come to the United States. It was not easy for us to change our plans but serious decisions were impending in America and we decided to go there for a few weeks.

The journey on the *Queen Mary* was very strenuous and we were two days late in reaching New York. Unfortunately, I caught a chill the day after our arrival, and I still keep to my bed under doctor's orders. I hope, however, to be able to resume activities in the course of a couple of days.

I shall try to make my stay in America as brief as possible, as I am very anxious to go to Palestine. Mrs. Weizmann and I look forward very much to seeing you soon. We can imagine the difficult and trying time through which you are now passing.

With warmest good wishes from Mrs. Weizmann and myself.

Yours very sincerely,

Chaim Weizmann

121. To Harry S. Truman, Washington. *New York, 10 February 1948*
English: Or. Copy. T.W.: W.A.

My dear Mr. President,

I was on the eve of leaving for Palestine last week from London when I received an urgent call to return to the United States in view of the crisis which had developed in the affairs of Palestine. It was not easy to postpone my departure for Palestine because I felt that I should be with my people at this critical time. In deciding, however, to return to the United States, I was largely swayed by the hope that it might be possible for me to have an opportunity of meeting with you once more and of trying to be of some help in these difficult and anxious days.

I have heard today that you will be shortly leaving Washington for a trip to the Caribbean. I well understand how heavily occupied you must be in these circumstances, and I would not venture to intrude on you at this moment were not the situation, in my opinion, so serious. Time is of the essence, and if the present trend of events is not halted the crisis might well end in catastrophe, not only for my people but for Palestine and indeed the United Nations.

Remembering the kindness and understanding which you showed to me on the last occasion when I was in the United States, I am emboldened to ask you respectfully to receive me during the course of the next few days before your departure and to spare me a few minutes of your precious time.[1]

With many thanks and good wishes, I am

Respectfully yours,

Chaim Weizmann[2]

---

121. [1] Matt Connelly, Truman's personal secretary, replied 12 Feb. (W.A.). He was asked to tell W. that to his great regret Truman would be unable to see him before his return to Palestine, due to the conflict in their respective schedules. The President was due to leave Washington on 20 Feb. and 'his calendar between now and then is completely filled'. In his memoirs, Truman recalled having been so disturbed at the pressure being brought to bear that 'I put off' seeing W. (*Years of Trial and Hope,* 1956, p. 188).

[2] According to V.W.'s personal diary (W.A.), W. asked Ginsburg and Frankfurter to draft this letter. Herbert Bayard Swope and George Backer came to W.'s suite 8 Feb. to polish the text and Josef Cohn flew to Washington to deliver it personally to the White House.

122. To Sir Robert Robinson,[1] Oxford.   *New York, 12 February 1948*

English: Or. Copy. T.W.: W.A.

My dear Robinson,

I am writing to tell you that after careful consideration we have reluctantly decided to postpone the solemn opening of the [Weizmann] Institute for a few months until the situation in Palestine, which at present is very unstable, becomes clarified. It is difficult to foretell when this is likely to happen, but we are hopeful that things may settle down by October.

I am deeply sorry that all arrangements have been upset in that way, but this is part of the tribulation through which we are going at present. Will you kindly take note of this, and I hope that no inconvenience has been caused to you and to Gertrude.

I am staying here another few weeks and hope to be passing through England on my way to Palestine sometime in March.

With my very best regards to you and Gertrude, I am

Yours very sincerely,

123. To Felix Frankfurter, Washington.   *New York, 23 February 1948*

English: Or. Copy. T.W.: W.A.

My dear Felix,

Eban has brought me your message to the effect that you would be good enough to arrange for me to see Mr. Marshall. I would, of course, like to have this opportunity of talking to him, although I have come to fear that any attempt on our side to see these men will always be misinterpreted as "pressure". This idea of the Jews exercising undue pressure is preposterous, but still, we are being constantly accused of it, particularly in the articles of Mr. Alsop.[1]

My state of health at present is such that I cannot determine yet when I shall be able to get up and move about without any danger of a relapse. The doctor seems to be optimistic, and I think we shall call in a specialist, and then we might be able to determine a little more exactly. Meanwhile, it is a very great nuisance to be incapacitated and have the trip which has caused me so much trouble and effort

---

122. [1] Biog. Index, Vol. V. Professor of Chemistry at Oxford 1930–55. He and his wife, Gertrude, an organic chemist, had worked with W. in Manchester and were close friends of the Weizmanns.

123. [1] Joseph and Stewart Alsop wrote a syndicated column for *New York Herald Tribune* 1946–58.

almost ruined by this unexpected development. However, I must not complain too much and must bear it with patience.

I send you and Marion my fondest love and remain,

Affectionately yours,

124. To Ernst David Bergmann, Rehovot.   *New York, 9 March 1948*
English: Or. Copy. T.W.: W.A.

My dear David,

I have not been writing much to you for the reason which you know. From the moment you left I came down with a cold, which has affected, to some extent, my heart; and I had to be very careful and practically stay in bed the entire time. I am definitely on the mend now but this was a severe warning. I have, naturally, done very little and could not go to Washington to see those people whom I intended to see. I hope to do so next week, all being well.

I have had a long conversation with Bulova and two conversations with Herscher,[1] who seems to be a very keen and very level-headed fellow, and I asked him to put down in writing his ideas, projects and intentions. To my great satisfaction, I find this morning that he has promptly followed my request, and I enclose herewith a copy of his most interesting letter.[2]

I am sorry that I shall not be in Palestine when they come out, but it will be up to you and to the others to convince him that the place for the workshop is Rehovot, not Tel-Aviv and not in Haifa. If he wants to serve the institutes it certainly cannot be placed anywhere else but Rehovot. I am quite convinced you will all know how to handle him. The workshop as planned in this letter would be a unique thing and a very great contribution to our institutes.

My plans, as you can imagine, are all in the air. But it seems that in a month's time or so we shall be able to move from here, go to London for the shortest possible time and then proceed to Palestine, if you will have us. I am most anxious to go there and if I cannot go to Palestine I shall be, to all intents and purposes, homeless. The idea of staying in the Dorchester again is a nightmare to me and to Mrs. Weizmann. She, of course, as you can imagine, has been very worried; but I am glad to say that during the last two days she has picked up a little.

---

124. [1] Seymour Herscher, Bulova's aide. The two described their plan for establishing a tool and die shop in Palestine during a visit to W. 2 Mar. They wished to contribute to Palestine's industrial development by making precision equipment for local manufacturers serving the workshop of the Institute at Rehovot (see Herscher to W., 8 Mar., W.A.).

[2] W.A.

I send you and Miss Goldschmidt[3] all my fondest love. I am thinking of you all, all the time, and praying ardently for your safety. Give my best regards to Bloch[4] and the other workers. Mrs. Weizmann joins me in all the good wishes.

I remain,

Most affectionately yours,

125. To Doris May, London.　　　　*New York, 10 March 1948*
English: Or. Copy. T.W.: W.A.

My dear Miss May,

I have to thank you for your letters,[1] and I think by now you know the cause of my silence. What with the very bad crossing and a great deal of mental anxiety that brought about a breakdown, I have been kept in bed for slightly over a month. In fact, I have not been able to do anything at all, and so far my trip has been, to all intents and purposes, rather useless, apart from a few desultory conversations with various people, including Mr. Creech Jones, which was not too edifying.[2] I hope to be up in a few days and slowly resume some of my duties, but it will have to be very slowly indeed.

The general news you know. There is nothing very decisive yet, and things move like on a fever chart, up and down, more downs than ups.

Today we are all under the impact of the terrible news about the suicide of Masaryk,[3] and things begin to look terribly like before the last war. I always thought that two wars in one generation ought to suffice, but we may not be spared the third one. God help us all.

Forgive the somewhat sombre tone of this letter but what can one say nowadays.

---

[3] Frieda Goldschmidt (1899–1971). Chemist; with Sieff Institute from 1934.

[4] Benjamin M. Bloch (Biog. Index, Vol. XVII). Physicist, Administrative Director of Sieff Institute from 1936, and later of Weizmann Institute.

125. [1] These, 9, 12 Feb. (W.A.) discussed British Press coverage of Palestine and expressed concern over Baffy Dugdale's health.

[2] Creech Jones and W. met 18 Feb., 4 Mar. At the earlier meeting W. spoke angrily of Bevin's 'apparent Hitler complex'; the British were leaving behind 'organised chaos' in Palestine, and he wanted Creech Jones to know that nothing could compel the settlers to leave their Negev homes. There was only one alternative to a Jewish State—extermination (record of discussion in W.A.).

[3] Jan Masaryk (Biog. Index, Vol. XX). Czech Foreign Minister, and close friend of the Weizmanns. He was killed in a fall from his office window, reported as suicide, after President Benes had been forced to accept a predominantly Communist Government in Czechoslovakia.

I very much hope that you are well and am looking forward to seeing you again in about five or six weeks.

As ever,
Affectionately yours,

126. To Sir Leon Simon,[1] New York. *New York, 15 March 1948*
English: Or. Copy. T.W.: W.A.

My dear Leon,

This is the first day I got out of bed after my somewhat prolonged illness, and your letter[2] as well as the correspondence concerning the Medical School has been read out to me today.

It is, I am afraid, a matter of some considerable complexity, and it is difficult for me, at present, to utter an opinion on it. However, I agree, in principle, [to] the idea that it is much better to begin on a modest scale and let the thing evolve than to wait indefinitely until all the funds for a large scale development are available, which is never the case.

In view of the unfortunate position today in Jerusalem, there is no great urgency to take a decision now, and as I hope to be in Palestine in April, I shall have an opportunity of discussing the situation on the spot.

There is, however, one remark that I would like to make at once. It is essential, I think, to secure one or two first class people for the fundamental subjects of the school. It is time that the University should have some few outstanding personalities to which the world could look as personifying learning at the Hebrew University. This is no reflection on Doljansky[3] or the others. They are, no doubt, very competent people or even more, but I am thinking of men of international reputation, and we must try and secure them. There are some to be found in Europe and in this country.

With best regards,

Yours very sincerely,

[On 2 Feb. the U.N. Palestine Commission, after 26 meetings, issued a report appealing to the Security Council to take speedy action to avert a catastrophe in Palestine on termination of the Mandate and withdrawal of British administrative services. Representatives of the 'Big Four' discussed this during ensuing weeks and

---

126. [1] Biog. Index, Vol. V. Hebraist and retired British civil servant, he was chairman of H.U. Executive Council 1946–49.

[2] 7 Mar. (W.A.), enclosing the proposals for a Medical School—see No. 116, n. 4.

[3] Leonid Doljanski. Head of Department of Experimental Pathology, Cancer Research Laboratories. Killed in Arab attack on convoy to Mount Scopus—see n. 4 to No. 142.

on 19 March recommended to the full Security Council that it take further action 'by all means available to it to bring about an immediate cessation of violence and a restoration of peace and order in Palestine'. But the same day the U.S. delegate caused great surprise by submitting to the Security Council a U.S. Government proposal that the partition plan be suspended and replaced by U.N. trusteeship over Palestine instead.

This reversal of the U.S. position shocked W. particularly, as the day before, 18 March, he had been granted the meeting with President Truman which he had sought for two months and for which he had returned to America. Truman's reluctance had been overcome at the last moment through the personal intercession of his old friend Eddie Jacobson (see *Years of Trial and Hope,* pp. 188–91). At the interview, lasting nearly an hour, W. pressed for the lifting of the U.S. embargo on arms, American support for partition, and the right for Jewish immigrants to enter Palestine during this transitional period and without any external limitations following statehood. W. found the President 'sympathetic personally' and still indicating 'a firm resolve to press forward with partition'—*T. and E.,* p. 577.]

127. To Doris May, London. *New York, 23 March 1948*
English: Or. Copy. T.W.: W.A.

My dear Miss May,

This is to inform you that we are booking passage on the *Queen Mary* leaving here April 7th; so that we may reach Southampton on the 12th. We propose to stay about a week in London and then proceed to Palestine by air. We are trying to book on Swiss Air from here but if we fail, will send you a telegram, and you might book from London. I cannot travel, in my present state, in an ordinary plane. It must be pressurized, and I believe that the Swiss planes going to Palestine are of that nature, and so are the French planes.

I need hardly tell you that the trip here was not very successful. The unexpected and sudden let down by the American Government will, I am afraid, have tragic effects, and the only thing which is left for us to do is to go on with our own work and await better times.

I don't know what Ben-Gurion's proclamations mean[1] but it seems that the British administration in Palestine is deteriorating and that they have abandoned a considerable portion of the Jewish district between Haifa and Tel Aviv and that the Jews have taken over. If

---

127. [1] The U.S. proposal to shelve the partition plan was categorically rejected by J.A. and *Va'ad Leumi* in a joint statement issued 23 March. The statement declared that a Provisional Jewish State would be proclaimed not later than 16 May, upon termination of the Mandate. After expressing 'regret and astonishment' at the change of attitude on the part of the U.S., the statement indicated that the *Yishuv* would oppose any scheme designed to prevent or postpone statehood, would reject trusteeship even for a short period, would cooperate with the U.N. Commission to implement partition, would do its utmost to minimize the chaos produced by England and would persist in the Jewish desire for peace with the Arabs.

this process goes on and it is consolidated, it might lead in a natural way to a Jewish State which, I am sure, will be eventually recognized by the other powers.

I don't think that the trusteeship business will ever work. It is a still-born project produced on the spur of the moment by some fertile brain in the American State Department. It is an insincere attempt to placate some part of Jewish public opinion, but I don't think anybody is being taken in by it.

Will you kindly see Mr. Ronus and secure an apartment for us in the Dorchester. We would rather like to have something different than our old apartment, which has become dreary since our own furniture has been taken out. We want a bedroom, sitting room and dressing room overlooking the park.

With all good wishes and affectionate regards,

Yours very sincerely,

128. To Rose Halprin, New York.   New York, 25 March 1948
English: Or. Copy. T.W.: W.A.

My dear Rose,

It was very good of you to write me your charming note[1] and to send me the Purim gifts. I reciprocate it most heartily, and through you I beg to thank the members of Hadassah for their kind thoughts.

It is never given to us to win things easily and perhaps it is as well that we have to go the hard way. There are still, in my opinion, many difficult days ahead of us, but we shall outlive our enemies and adversaries as we have done in our long past.

This year's Purim is unfortunately without a Mordecai,[2] but the feast of liberation is really Pesach.[3] Let us hope that these four weeks will bring some clarification in the confusion created by the British and American "statesmen".

With all good wishes to you and to the members of Hadassah, in which Mrs. Weizmann joins me, I am

Affectionately yours,

129. To Felix Frankfurter, Washington.   New York, 31 March 1948
English: Or. Copy. T.W.: W.A.

[On 25 March W. issued a statement in condemnation of the positions adopted by both England and, more recently, the U.S. He asserted that to prolong foreign rule

---

128. [1] W.A.   [2] I.e., as in Book of Esther.   [3] Passover.

and delay a final solution based on independence was to increase confusion and bloodshed; to make Arab consent a condition for settlement of the dispute was to rule out all chances of a settlement; to abandon a judgement under pressure of Arab violence was to give an incentive to further violence. The recent U.S. declaration consequently 'is thus built on a triple fallacy and goes against everything that long experience has taught'. W. professed an inability to understand how the British authorities could allow foreign Arab forces to cross freely into Palestine and leisurely prepare for war against the Jews and against a Resolution of the U.N. In 'exposing everything and everybody in the country to destruction by lawless hordes, the Mandatory Government has acted against its own best traditions, and left a tragic legacy to the country's future' (W.A.).]

My dear Felix,

You overwhelm me with your kindness,[1] and I am cherishing your letters, which represent to me perhaps the happiest events during this very difficult stay in this country. I appreciate deeply what you say about Marion and please convey to her the same sentiments I express to you.

In going about in this somewhat shabby world of ours, very often reminiscences of my youth well up in me, and I think of one great figure which always dominated my feelings in my young days, particularly at a time of great stress, like the pogroms at the end of the eighties and the beginning of the nineties.

There was a venerable old rabbi in Berdyezeff near Kiev. It was a city almost exclusively Jewish. The name of the rabbi was Rabbi Levy Yitzchak,[2] a pious, saintly man, and when things went hard with his flock and with the people around him he used to betake himself to the great synagogue at a time when there was nobody there and go up to the Ark, open the doors, pull the curtain and enter into a conversation with the Almighty—something of the following nature: "God of Israel, I have come to ask you to give me an account as to why you persecute your people so much and so often. You have done enough harm. It is about time you should stop and if you won't I will call you to court (*Din Torah*)." I am sure the great rabbi felt considerable relief after having spoken thus, and it is very unfortunate that even this sort of comfort is not given to us, and we have to carry the pain in us until the heart breaks and the moral force begins to ebb.

At a time like this, it is essential that old friends like you and me should keep together, and that is why I feel so deeply about your

---

129. [1] See Frankfurter to W., 26 Mar. (W.A.), commending W.'s statement of the previous day.

[2] Levi Isaac of Berdichev (c. 1740–1810). *Hasidic* rabbi and outstanding personality; founder of *Hasidism* in Central Poland, and also active in Lithuania and the Ukraine.

letters. Every day some new hope is being dangled before our eyes, and when the sun sets, it is nothing but a mirage. How long, oh God, how long?

With love, affection and gratitude to you both, I am

Your old friend,
Chaim Weizmann

130. To Sigmund Gestetner, London.   *New York, 31 March 1948*
English: Or. Copy. T.W.: W.A.

My dear Sigmund,

This is a short note to let you know that we are leaving on the *Queen Mary* on the 7th of April, due to arrive in Southampton on the 12th. I hope it will be possible for you to meet us, which would make us very happy.

As on present advice, we should stay about a week or a little more in London and then leave for Palestine going by air from Paris. But the latter proposition is subject to change in accordance with what the conditions in Palestine will be at the time. So I am not giving out that I am going. On the contrary. We shall discuss and decide everything in London.

There is nothing much new that I can tell you from here. The Americans change their views about Palestine almost every week, and this has thrown the whole affair into great confusion and has caused considerable distress to everybody. One has to wait for the next few meetings of the UNO and possibly for the special meeting which is to be called in about three weeks to a month. Whether anything definite will emerge, I don't know. Meanwhile the 15th of May is approaching very rapidly, and I cannot say that I view this day with an easy heart.

Give my love to Simon [Marks] and Israel [Sieff]. I understand that the former has returned from South Africa. I have had a very nice telegram from Smuts.[1]

With very kind regards and all good wishes from both of us to you, I am

Yours ever,

130. [1] 29 Mar. (W.A.), describing the U.S. trusteeship proposal as an interim measure. Smuts personally saw no alternative to partition, but 'nobody wishes it to be achieved through massacres and international complications, and some interim measures may yet prevent irremediable mischief'. He concluded: 'My deep sympathy and warm good wishes go to you, my old friend, who have laboured so hard for the cause and been wounded in the struggle for it. May your work yet be crowned with success before the end'.

131. To Oscar Wolfsberg,[1] Jerusalem. *New York, 31 March 1948*
English: T.W.: W.A.

My dear friend Wolfsberg,

Your lines always arrive at the right moment[2] and always carry a certain amount of comfort with them.

I can feel with you and with the *Yishuv,* and I am greatly concerned with what you say about the deterioration. I do hope that the morale won't break. If that goes, everything goes. If that remains intact we may suffer but we shall pull through. This is my firm conviction. I wish I were with you now and be able to speak to you the same words personally, but it may not be very long before we meet. I wouldn't like you to spread this information.

By the time you get this note Passover will be on our doorsteps— the Feast of Liberation—when in every Jewish household they will be repeating the text that in every generation there arose enemies who wished to destroy us, but they failed. The present enemies of today, in spite of their number, in spite of their arrogance, in spite of the support which they might get from various quarters, in spite of the fact they find us standing alone and almost friendless, will fail because God will protect his people.

I send you once more my heartfelt thanks, my best wishes and sincere affection.

As ever,
Yours,
Ch. Weizmann

132. To Dewey Stone,[1] Beverly Hills. *New York, 1 April 1948*
English: T.: W.A.

Dear Dewey, had long talk with Freda Kirchwey.[2] Convinced she and her associates through the powerful Liberal instrument at their

131. [1] Later, Yeshayahu Aviad (Biog. Index, Vol. XIV). Religious Zionist leader; Israel envoy in Scandinavia 1948–49.

[2] Letter of 22 Mar. (W.A.), reassuring W. that their cause would triumph if they remained united.

132. [1] 1900–77. Merchant and communal leader; personal friend of W. National chairman of U.J.A. 1955–63; chairman of American Committee and of Board of Governors of Weizmann Institute, of which he was a generous benefactor.

[2] 1893–1976. President of Nation Associates, a liberal organization which published *The Nation.* She and the director, Lillie Shultz, helped to influence American public opinion on behalf of the Zionist cause, particularly through *The Nation,* and advised J.A. representatives and W. in gaining access to U.S. governmental circles (see, e.g., Kirchwey to W., 17 Mar. 1948, W.A.).

command can do magnificent job. Urge you most strongly please speak your California friends, view to securing their aid.[3] I understand initiative actually emanated there. Would not bother you with this if did not think it important. Will speak to you before my departure. Affectionate greetings you, Anne.[4]

Chaim Weizmann

133. To Frieda Goldschmidt, Rehovot.　　*New York, 2 April 1948*
English: Or. Copy. T.W.: W.A.

My dear Miss Goldschmidt,

I should have written to you before, but things were much too confused, and I wasn't able to give any definite information, and even now I am still undecided about my plans.

I am leaving here for London on the 7th, getting there on the 12th, and it is only in London, in the light of events which are going to happen between now and the 20th, that I shall be able to decide whether I am going to Palestine or whether I shall stay in England and Switzerland or wherever the case may be. At present I am more or less in the position of a refugee—I can't stay here, I am not very anxious to stay in London, and I don't know where to go.

Should I not go to Palestine, I will need some of my clothes which I sent on sometime ago in the big bag, namely, some of my good shirts, some of my lighter underwear (the wool and cotton), some of my socks, some of my pajamas; and there must be one or two good suits of clothes which I may be able to wear in London and Switzerland. I must leave it to you as I don't remember what I have there.

Mr. Weisgal will be travelling back from Palestine to London and he could bring the stuff. If it is difficult for him to take it or too expensive, you might send it on by air freight, or there may be other people travelling so that it could be distributed. By the time Mr. Weisgal travels back I shall know for certain what my plans are and telegraph to you.

I am glad this visit here is finished. It was useless and one painful frustration. I wish I would have gone to Palestine direct and not have accepted the invitation to come here, but there is no use crying over spilt milk.

[3] The Nation Associates sought Jewish financial support to continue their public relations campaign. W. also requested assistance from J.A. in Jerusalem (W. to Weisgal, 13 Apr., W.A.).

[4] Dewey Stone's wife.

I hope you are well and not too worried, and please write to me to the Dorchester Hotel.

I send you all my affectionate greetings and remain, as ever

Yours,

134. To Ernst David Bergmann, Rehovot.   *New York, 2 April 1948*
English: Or. Copy. T.W.: W.A.

My dear David,

You will read my letter to Miss Goldschmidt, and I needn't go over the same ground.

The situation here is worsening every day, and the last decision of the UNO to call a special meeting of the Assembly[1] can only mean that they will cancel the decision taken on November 29th, and what they will substitute for it God only knows. It will certainly be nothing good. And so all the worry and all the trouble and all the work has ended in smoke, and that all is the result of American militancy and the quarrel with England which has certainly been influencing America all the time.

I am undecided as to what to do and, as you will read, can only decide around the 20th in London. I have a reservation on a plane leaving Paris the 23rd, which will get me to Palestine in eight hours. I still hope I shall be able to take it.

I shall be very happy to receive a letter from you in London at the Dorchester and to hear how the work is going on in the Institute. That is about the only comforting positive thing left, and please give me all the details.

Yesterday I had a long and interesting talk with Katchalsky,[2] who gave me an account of his work, which seemed to be most interesting and opens up great vistas. I am glad to have met him. He is a very nice fellow.

My love to you, my sister [Anna], Dr. Bloch and my heartiest regards to all the workers.

As ever,

Yours,

---

134. [1] The Security Council passed two resolutions 30 Mar., calling on Arabs and Jews to conclude a truce, and calling for a special session of the General Assembly to reconsider the situation in Palestine.

[2] Ephraim Katchalsky (later Katzir, b. 1916). Biochemist. He was in New York 1947–48 as Research Fellow at Columbia University and Brooklyn Polytechnic Institute. In May 1948 he returned to Rehovot. Professor of Biophysics, Weizmann Institute 1949–73. President of State of Israel 1973–78.

135. To The Weizmann Foundation, New York.

English: Or. Copy. T.W.: W.A.   *New York, 5 April 1948*

Gentlemen,

In connection with the gift of the manuscript of my Memoirs which I have made to the Foundation, pursuant to my letter of December 16th, 1947,[1] addressed to Mr. Meyer W. Weisgal, I wish to advise you that in connection with the work that was done on the preparation of the manuscript during the last few years there has been expended the sum of $13,565.85, principally for editorial work, typing and miscellaneous expenses.

These expenditures are, of course, a first charge upon any income which may be received from the sale of any rights for the publication of the Memoirs, and it is my understanding that in accepting the gift of the manuscript which I have made to the Foundation, and of all of the rights thereto, pursuant to the said letter of December 16th, 1947, the Foundation will assume the repayment of the said sum of $13,565.85 incurred in preparation of the manuscript. Herewith is an itemized list of these expenses.[2] These funds should be paid to Mr. Meyer W. Weisgal, who, at my request, over a period of time, has advanced this money.

The Foundation is likewise requested to assume the agreement which was made on [my] behalf with Mr. Maurice Samuel[3] for fees and royalties in connection with his work on the preparation of the manuscript. The terms of this agreement are contained in a letter from Mr. Maurice Samuel to Mr. Meyer W. Weisgal, dated November 29th, 1947, copy of which is enclosed herewith.[4]

Sincerely yours,
Chaim Weizmann

136. To Sigmund Gestetner, London.   *New York, 7 April 1948*
English: T.: W.A.

View General Assembly[1] compelled postpone departure about fortnight. Love.

Vera, Chaim

135. [1] See No. 100.

[2] The list itemized $5,600 paid to Samuel 1943–45, $7,000 paid him in 1947, plus other expenses (W.A.).

[3] Biog. Index. U.S. author and popular exponent of Zionist ideology, he had assisted in the writing of W.'s memoirs.

[4] (W.A.). Samuel was to receive a 15 per cent royalty on all copies over 20,000 sold in U.S.

136. [1] Responding to a call from the Security Council, the U.N. Secretary-General, Trygve Lie, announced that a special session of the General Assembly would begin 16 Apr. to re-examine the Palestine problem. See No. 134, and n. 1 there.

137. To Harry S. Truman, Washington.   *New York, 9 April 1948*
English: T.W.: Photostat W.A.

Dear Mr. President,

I had intended to take the liberty of addressing you in writing immediately after the interview which you kindly accorded me on March 18th. The events which followed,[1] however, impelled me to wait until I could formulate some clearer impressions on the new situation which has developed. In inviting your consideration of my views at this time, I wish to thank you, Mr. President, for the personal kindness which you have so often shown me, and for the sympathetic interest which you have constantly devoted to the cause of our people in its grave ordeal.

I noted with satisfaction that in your statement of March 25[2] you indicated that the United States had not abandoned Partition as the ultimate political settlement in Palestine. I welcome this assurance because my long experience of this problem has convinced me beyond doubt that no more realistic solution exists. Palestine is inhabited by two peoples. These peoples have separate political aspirations and common economic interests. The settlement by Partition and economic union recognizes this logic. Partition is further reinforced by the support of two distinguished investigating Commissions[3] (in 1937 and 1947), by the binding force of the General Assembly's Resolution and by the fact that a virtual Partition is now crystallising in Palestine. Jews and Arabs are both mature for independence and are already obedient in a large degree to their own institutions, while the central British Administration is in virtual collapse. In large areas Jews and Arabs are virtually in control of their own lives and interests. The clock cannot be put back to the situation which existed before November 29. I would also draw attention to the psychological effects of promising Jewish independence in November and attempting to cancel it in March.

It is the logic of partition and of the present situation in Palestine which compelled me to go on record against the idea of Trusteeship. One fails to see how any of the admitted difficulties of Partition are avoided by Trusteeship. The problem of enforcement becomes even more acute as neither the Arabs nor the Jews of Palestine have ac-

---

137. [1] See Bridgenote preceding No. 127.

[2] On 25 Mar. Truman issued a statement declaring that U.S. had raised the issue of Trusteeship only after every effort had been exhausted to find a way of carrying out partition peacefully. Further, Trusteeship did not prejudice the character of the final settlement, but was meant to fill the vacuum shortly to be created by termination of the Mandate (J. Snetsinger, *Truman, the Jewish Vote and the Creation of Israel,* New York 1974, p. 98).

[3] The Royal (Peel) Commission (see Vol. XVIII) and UNSCOP.

cepted Trusteeship, which appears likely to deprive each of them of Statehood. It is proposed to institute a Trusteeship in a country threatened by foreign Arab aggression, torn by internal warfare, and already moving inexorably towards Partition under a valid international resolution. The proposal is made without any assurance that a trustee is available, that Arabs or Jews will cooperate, that the General Assembly will approve an agreement or that any effective measures can be improvised by May 15th.

The difficult but clear course of implementing Partition is thus replaced by a leap into the unknown, and I am forced to regret, Mr. President, the great increase of trouble, danger and responsibility which must ensue for the United States from the unfortunate reversal on March 19th, with its inauguration of new uncertainty and new political conflict.

If I may venture to leave you, Mr. President, with one or two reflections on the major aspects of the problem, I would sound a note of solemn warning against any prolongation of British rule in Palestine. As you may know, I have cherished the British-Jewish relationship all my life. I have upheld it in difficult times. I have been grievously disappointed by its recent decline. It is because I hope for its renewal that I tremble to think of the wave of violence and repression which would sweep Palestine if the conditions and auspices of the recent unhappy years were to be continued under British, or indeed any foreign, rule. I also know how passionately the British people desire the end of this troubled chapter. Should your administration, despite all this, press for any prolongation of British tenure, it would incur a responsibility for terrible events and, almost certainly, the equal resentment of the British and Jewish peoples.

I recall that it is exactly two years since the Anglo-American Committee so emphatically endorsed your moving plea for the immediate admission of 100,000 Jews from the Displaced Persons Camps to Palestine.[4] They are still in those camps. Reports have reached me of the grave effect produced on their dwindling resources of hope and morale by the United States declaration of March 19th. I cannot for a moment believe, Mr. President, that you would be a party to the further disappointment of pathetic hopes, which you yourself have raised so high. Their hope is solely for personal and national integration in a Jewish State in Palestine.

In conclusion, I am convinced that the present situation in Palestine is making a profound impact on the conscience of the American people. Having recognized the right of our people to independence last November, the great powers now expose them to the risk of

[4] See Vol. XXII.

extermination and do not even grant them the arms to provide for their own defense. Arab aggression is now more confident than ever. Arabs believe that an international decision has been revised in their favour purely because they dared to use force against it. Mr. President, I cannot see how this belief can honestly be refuted. The practical question now is whether your Administration will proceed to leave our people unarmed in the face of an attack which it apparently feels it is unable to stop; and whether it can allow us to come directly or indirectly under Arab domination which is sworn to our destruction.

The choice for our people, Mr. President, is between Statehood and extermination. History and providence have placed this issue in your hands, and I am confident that you will yet decide it in the spirit of the moral law.[5]

Respectfully yours,
Ch. Weizmann

138. To Doris May, London.   *New York, 12 April 1948*
English: T.W.: W.A.

My dear Miss May,

As you know already from my telegram,[1] we shall be leaving here on the 29th of April by the *Queen Elizabeth,* arriving about the 4th of May in London. How long we shall remain in London depends upon the connections with Palestine, where we should like to go if at all possible. But all that depends upon the position there, which, in my opinion, seems to be deteriorating more every day. If we cannot go to Palestine, we shall stay in London for a month or so and then go on to Switzerland.

There is nothing much to report from here. The special meeting of the Assembly begins on Friday. What will be the outcome of it remains on the knees of the gods. There seems to be chiefly confusion about everything. What is meant by the American proposal of Trusteeship nobody knows, including the Americans themselves, and therefore there is a chance for those people who know what they want in these babel of proposals, and the one thing which seems to be successful is a Trusteeship for Jerusalem alone. That would take away a great deal of our trouble and would at least secure the lives and peace of a hundred thousand Jews. The Partition scheme

---

[5] A copy of this letter went to Marshall. No reply was received from Truman.

138. [1] 7 Apr. (W.A.), informing her of his change of plans.

for the rest of Palestine would, I think, fall into line almost automatically, because while the people are talking, Partition is going forward, and the Jewish population of Palestine is creating the necessary organs of a State, since the administration of that country is completely broken down.

This was a very tiresome and difficult stay, which has been complicated by a fairly long illness. I am looking eagerly forward to my returning to England. It seems that I shall be able to stay in London about nine days and go to Palestine after that—if there is still a Palestine to go to. But that we shall be able to decide when we meet.

Will you kindly give my love to the children. They seem to have been under a misapprehension about my arrival. As soon as the postponement of my departure was fixed, I rang up Benjy and told him about leaving on the 29th of April, and I was surprised to hear from Simon Marks this morning that I was expected there today by the *Queen Mary*. There seems to be a lack of coordination.

Well, all the best to you.

Affectionately,
Yours,
Ch. Weizmann

139. To Viscount Samuel, London.   *New York, 12 April 1948*
English: Or. Copy. T.W.: W.A.

Dear Lord Samuel,

Forgive the delay in answering your letter of March 15th,[1] but I have not been well for weeks.

I have read with great care your statement, and I am very grateful to you for sending it to me, but I must say quite frankly that I see no advantage in this project over a clear cut project of Partition. From a purely Arab point of view, I think a Bi-National State represents much more danger than a limited area in the form of a Jewish State. A Bi-National State may, in the eyes of the Arabs, eventually become a domination of the Jews over the whole of Palestine. However, you may have seen my statement, which was published sometime ago in the press here (I understand also in London), and I adhere to the views expressed therein. The Arabs would offer the

139. [1] Samuel sent W. a copy of a memorandum (W.A.) he was about to send to U.N. Secretary-General, in which he called for a bi-national state to be administered upon termination of the British Mandate by U.N. Trusteeship Council. He informed W. that one of his primary motivations was to head off 'open and unrestrained civil war' in Palestine, 'with the sacrifice of thousands of splendid young lives'.

same resistance to a Bi-National State as they do to Partition because nothing will satisfy them except domination over the whole of Palestine as a unified Arab State.

I hope all is well with you. We shall be returning to London at the end of this month, and I remain with best regards,

Yours very sincerely,

Chaim Weizmann

140. To Leonard J. Stein,[1] London. *New York, 12 April 1948*
English: Or. Copy. T.W.: W.A.

My dear Leonard,

I would like to thank you for your very interesting letter of March 30th.[2] I need not emphasize the point which you so rightly make in your letter that a great deal of the trouble through which we are going at present is in some degree a consequence of the [1946] Basle Congress. That the nemesis came so quickly doesn't make things easier, and it is very difficult to say what can be done at present. The relations with the Mandatory Power have deteriorated beyond repair, at any rate, as far as it is visible from here, and there is nobody here who either could or would make an attempt to improve such relations. If anything can be done at all, it must be attempted in London.

I hear that Creech Jones is coming here this week. In spite of everything, I have maintained friendly relations with him, and I shall, of course, see him. But he isn't a strong man. Neither did he behave too tactfully when he had an opportunity to sweeten the situation. However, I am going to see him.[3]

With regard to the position in Palestine, there is a tendency of having a truce, but so far the attempts of the U.N. have not been crowned with success, and the failure is due to the intransigent attitude of the Arabs. The only thing which seems to me to offer some hope is an international trusteeship for Jerusalem, which is feasible and which everybody agrees can be carried through. If that is settled, a very substantial part of the difficulties would be solved, and it is a

---

140. [1] Biog. Index, Vol. VI. Barrister and Zionist historian. President of Anglo-Jewish Association 1939–49.

[2] W.A. This arrived shortly after Samuel's letter (see No. 139), and was strikingly similar in tone. Given the existing hazards, Stein wondered whether there was not something to be said for a 'breathing-space' enabling 'what is essential' to be preserved. These misgivings, he added, were felt all the more keenly because the present Zionist leadership failed to inspire confidence.

[3] They met several times during this period, e.g., 19 Apr. and 5 May.

matter which concerns not only the Jews but everybody. If the Jerusalem problem is out of the way, I think the Partition program for the rest of Palestine might go through without much friction. We might have to make some slight territorial concessions.

I don't know whether you realize in London that the main trouble in Palestine is due to the presence of foreign troops[4] which have invaded the country and came there for the purpose of looting and murdering. The Palestine Arabs, if left to themselves, would not give us much trouble. In fact, they are prepared to enter into a compromise. At least that is the report which one gets from the country. It was a first class disaster that these foreign Arabs have been allowed to enter the country in full daylight over the highroads with their armored cars and ammunition—and in great quantities. That is stretching neutrality a little too far. Still with all that, I agree that one has to try to restore the good relations, if possible, and on my part I am prepared to do what I can when I come home.

Meanwhile, I thank you once more for your letter, and I am looking forward to meeting you as soon as I arrive in London. Miss May will tell you about my movements.

With all good wishes,

Affectionately yours,

141. To Felix Frankfurter, Washington.   *New York, 13 April 1948*
English: Or. Copy. T.W.: W.A.

My dear Felix,

I am sending you a copy of the letter which I have sent to the President yesterday.[1]

As I have already told you, I may be in Washington next week, but that really depends upon Dave Niles,[2] whom I have seen yesterday, and who has promised to arrange an interview with the President. If I am in Washington, I shall be hoping to see you, and we might talk over the whole situation. Meanwhile the Americans are bringing forward various proposals which, in my opinion, are all

---

[4] Arab irregular forces had entered Palestine from neighbouring countries, especially Syria, and were engaged in daily attacks upon a number of Jewish settlements in the north and around Jerusalem.

141. [1] See No. 137.

[2] David K. Niles (1890–1952). Administrative assistant to the President and his adviser on minorities. He maintained close ties with the Jewish leadership.

destined for the wastepaper basket. They don't seem to think these things out and hold themselves open to ruthless criticism on the part of everybody, which is a very great pity.[3]

Affectionately yours,

142. To Ernst David Bergmann, Rehovot. *New York, 14 April 1948*
English: Or. Copy. T.W.: W.A.

My dear David,

I have just sent you a telegram[1] expressing my surprise that I have heard nothing from you all this time. As far as I understand it, the postal communications are still holding good, and I am therefore disturbed that there is no letter either from you or from Meyer [Weisgal], except the cable which I received yesterday.[2] I don't know whether the advice given in this cable has been done with your consent and cooperation or whether it is Meyer's own opinion. I hope that you will send me a clear telegram on receipt of this letter and also follow it up by a letter while air-mail service is still in existence.[3] Otherwise we may be cut off for a long time, which will only increase the distress.

The latest news about the assassination of the doctors surpasses in its cruelty anything which I have read hitherto.[4] On the other hand, I can't help feeling that this is an act of retaliation for the senseless

---

[3] The U.S. representative submitted a number of 'tentative proposals' to the Security Council 5 Apr. concerning administration of the suggested trusteeship. After a second informal meeting 7 Apr., the French delegation issued a formal statement criticizing the American proposal for its failure to provide adequately for implementation and enforcement.

142. [1] 14 Apr., W.A.

[2] This, 13 Apr. (W.A.) stated: 'Rehovot divine. The place [i.e., the Institute] magnificent. The work diligent. The spirit splendid. Wish you were with us, yet the answer [to whether W. ought to come] is no'.

[3] Bergmann wrote both to W. and V.W. 18 Apr. (W.A.). To the former he explained that whereas previously he and Bloch had advised the Weizmanns to proceed to Palestine, they were now less enthusiastic as the Arabs had begun using heavy artillery. This was essentially the reason why Weisgal and most others opposed their coming. To Vera, Bergmann gave as his reasons the likelihood of the Syrians and Egyptians employing bombers in the coming struggle, and the pettiness and inattention which would be shown by the *Yishuv*'s leaders, who were 'small fry, concerned with the job at hand' and 'very jealous of their position'. Nevertheless, he personally felt that 'if our supreme hour has come, you both would feel it very wrong not to be here'.

[4] On 13 Apr. a Jewish convoy in Jerusalem, consisting of medical staff, nurses and members of the H.U. faculty, was attacked and virtually annihilated by Arab bands while on the road to Mount Scopus and the Hadassah Hospital. The bodies of 78 Jews were found on the road.

and cruel murder of 250 Arabs by the *Irgun*.[5] That the activities of the *Irgun* have not been curbed hitherto is a bad testimony to the maturity of the Jewish community in their capacity of running a State. However, I don't know fully the circumstances, and therefore, shall not say any more.

How far has the Institute been completed and has everything which has been bought arrived? Dr. Stern[6] has returned to this country, and I had a letter from him asking me to see him, which I have refused to do on the plea that I don't interfere in the administrative details. I don't know whether any of the younger men have actually gone off, or if they have also shied away.

We are staying here, as you know, until the 29th, and then going on to London, where we shall find ourselves about the 3rd or 4th. Our intention is to fly to Palestine on the 13th from Paris, unless there is an absolute injunction against it on everybody's part. So far, I am inclined to ignore the advice given in Meyer's telegram because I feel I ought to go there, and we have been in greater danger during the blitz in London.

There is very little to report from here. Everything is centered on the news from Palestine.

Mrs. Weizmann joins me in sending you both all the best. With much love to you and Meyer, I remain

As ever,
Yours,

P.S. I suppose your movements are confined to Rehovot and Tel Aviv. Is the road from Rehovot to Tel Aviv safe?

143. To Edward Jacobson,[1] Kansas City.   *New York, 16 April 1948*
English: T.W.: W.A.

My dear Mr. Jacobson,
There is now only a fortnight left before I shall leave this country. It may be that I shall still be in Washington on business, but I would like to take this opportunity of thanking you very cordially for your

---

[5] I.e., in the capture of the Arab village of Deir Yassin near Jerusalem four days earlier by members of *Irgun* and Stern Group operating independently of *Haganah*.

[6] Kurt G. Stern (1904–56). U.S. biochemist. Professor at Brooklyn Polytechnic Institute 1944–56.

143. [1] 'Eddie' Jacobson (Biog. Index). Haberdasher, long-time friend and former business associate of Truman in Kansas City.

great kindness and for the service which you have been so good as to render me during my stay in Washington.[2]

I hope to have an opportunity to do so personally. Meanwhile I send you my best wishes and kind regards and remain,

As ever,

Ch. Weizmann

144. To Meyer W. Weisgal, Tel Aviv.   *New York, 17 April 1948*
English: T.: W.A.

Moshe[1] cannot act without express instructions from Kaplan. Therefore preferable you discuss direct with Kaplan.[2] Wire your plans.[3] Affectionately,

Weizmann

145. To Frank W. Buxton,[1] Brookline, Mass.
New York, 19 April 1948
English: Or. Copy. T.W.: W.A.

Dear Mr. Buxton,

It was very good of you to write to me, and your lines have made me very happy.[2] I remember both with joy and sadness our meetings in Jerusalem and Rehovot, and so much has happened since which has obscured the decisions of your [Anglo-American] Com-

---

[2] See Bridgenote preceding No. 127. A similar letter (W.A.) was sent to Frank Goldman and Maurice Bisgyer, President and Executive Director respectively of *B'nai Brith,* who had intervened with Jacobson and enlisted his help in approaching Truman. For the most detailed and authoritative record of the circumstances, see Frank J. Adler, *Roots in a Moving Stream* (Centennial History of Congregation B'nai Jehuda of Kansas City), publ. by the Congregation 1972.

144. [1] Moshe Shertok (from 1949, Sharett; Biog. Index, Vol. XVI). Then head of J.A. Political Dept., he was representing the Jerusalem section of the Executive in New York.

[2] Relates to Freda Kirchwey's public relations programme against rescission of partition by the special session of U.N. General Assembly, of which she gave W. a copy 7 Apr. (W.A.). The Nation Associates would conduct the programme, involving Press and radio, leading to recognition of an independent Jewish Government. But funds were required, and she informed W. that implementation of the programme depended on Shertok. W. supported her proposal — see No. 132.

[3] See No. 147.

145. [1] 1877–1974. Formerly Editor of *Boston Herald,* and a Pulitzer Prize winner, he had been a member of Anglo-American Committee of Inquiry.

[2] 17 Apr. (W.A.), hoping that reports of W.'s illness were inaccurate; he still supported partition and found America's erratic course distressing.

mittee. Still I believe something will come out of the welter of blood and sorrow through which we are wading today. If you can only get the U.N. to carry into effect the decision about the international status of Jerusalem, that would take a heavy burden off our shoulders and relieve us of a great difficulty. I think the rest of Jewish Palestine could look after itself, the U.N. or no U.N.

I am not so sure that Meltzer[3] is right regarding England's stay in Palestine. The government may want to keep its grip on the country, but they would need to pass new legislation to that effect, and I don't think that the House [of Commons] would take to it very kindly. But one never knows in this cynical age what changes may be taking place.

I thank you for your inquiries about my health. I have not been well for sometime but I feel much better just now. I am leaving for England on the 29th of this month. My intention was to stay a few days in England, then go on to Palestine. But I am advised not to proceed at once but to wait for further developments. I shall, therefore, remain in England longer than I thought, and if I can't go to Palestine I propose to go to Switzerland and stay there until things have settled down and I am allowed to go. I have become something of a refugee. I can't very well stay in England; neither here. And I can't join my people in Palestine. Let's hope it will change.

Do you ever meet your other colleagues of the Commission?[4] I saw something of Jimmy McDonald here, but he has gone to South Africa. I have never met the others. I thought, however, that Phillips has been inclined to take your view. Aydelotte[5] I always considered incorrigible. I think that your point of view will triumph in the end, after a good deal of suffering has been inflicted on all of us.

Are you at all likely to be in New York before the 29th? It would be good to see you. I don't think I will be likely to leave this city.

---

[3] Julian L. Meltzer (1904–77). Journalist, later Executive Vice-Chairman, Yad Chaim Weizmann, Director of Weizmann Archives and Managing Editor, *Weizmann Letters and Papers*. At this time correspondent for *New York Times*. Buxton enclosed Meltzer's despatch (unpublished) describing the Palestine disorders as a ploy used by England to ensure her continued presence there should no international force to institute U.N. trusteeship emerge.

[4] Buxton thought the U.S. members of the committee were now divided, with Bartley Crum, James G. McDonald, Paul Hannah of the Commission's advisory staff, and himself still in favour of partition. Judge Joseph Hutcheson, Frank Aydelotte and William Phillips opposed.

[5] Frank Aydelotte (1880–1956). President, Swarthmore College 1921–40; President, Association of American Rhodes Scholars, 1930–56, and member of other international foundations.

Well, I send you my very heartiest regards and thanks for your friendly letter. All good wishes.

Yours ever,
Chaim Weizmann

146. To Samuel I. Rosenman,[1] New York.   *New York, 19 April 1948*
English: T.W.: W.A.

Dear Judge Rosenman,

I thought it might be useful for you to have the enclosed *aide-memoire*[2] which gives, in a summarized form, the points which we touched upon this afternoon.[3]

You will remember I mentioned that if Jerusalem were to be taken over by the Trusteeship Council and the Jews relieved of the defense of the City and surrounding district, which properly should be the function of the United Nations, then we would be in a better position to look after ourselves in the territory of the Jewish State. I have since spoken to friends who have just come back from Palestine,[4] and they confirm my predictions that the Arab staying power would not last long, but would begin to crumble. There have already been many desertions from the Arab bands, and this process is likely to continue if the Arabs do not receive external aid and encouragement. Indeed, were it not for the tacit support which the Arabs drew from the unwillingness or the inability of the British to

---

146. [1] Biog. Index. Counsel to Presidents Roosevelt and Truman.

[2] A memorandum, 'The Present Position of the Palestine Problem' (W.A.). Written following the Security Council's call for a truce in Palestine on 16 Apr., this contained the following desiderata: An embargo on arms to the Arab countries as well as to the two communities in Palestine; U.S. leadership in internationalising Jerusalem and thus alleviating the plight of its besieged Jewish population; return by U.S. to its earlier policy of supporting establishment of the Jewish State; detailing of steps U.S. should take to facilitate statehood, which 'in any case the Jews of Palestine intend to proclaim' on 15 May. The memorandum called for a warning to the Arab States not to commit aggression, the immediate despatch to Palestine of the U.N. Palestine Commission, recognition of *Haganah* as the militia responsible for maintaining law and order, and the granting of facilities to *Haganah* to acquire adequate arms.

[3] W.'s diary (W.A.) indicates that he and Rosenman met 18 Apr. In the renewed effort at gaining Truman's firm support, Rosenman became the focal figure. A member of the committee on campaign strategy for the Democratic Party in preparation for the forthcoming National Convention and presidential election, he had weekly meetings with Truman. He had approached W., offering his help, but insisted that this be kept secret. Rosenman proceeded to Washington and on 23 Apr. was able to report to W. in confidence that Truman was fully intent upon extending immediate recognition to the Jewish State ('Report on Dr. Weizmann's Visit to U.S.A.', W.A.).

[4] Especially Col. David Marcus.

keep inviolate the frontiers of Palestine, from their failure to preserve law and order because they did not wish to clash with the Arabs, and their unhelpful attitude toward the U.N. Commission, the security situation would not have deteriorated to the extent it did; and many lives, Jewish, Arab and British, could have been saved. The hesitations of the United States and finally the change of policy during the early stages of the Security Council meetings also helped to worsen the situation in the country.

Looking forward very much to hearing from you soon, I remain with best wishes and kindest personal regards,

Yours very sincerely,

Ch. Weizmann

147. To Moshe Shertok, New York.   *New York, 19 April 1948*
English: Or. Copy. T.W.: W.A.

Dear Moshe,

We have received the following cable from Meyer who spoke to Kaplan about Freda Kirchwey's request:[1] "Kaplan beset staggering problems; believes if Moshe desires can do it without reference here."

Kaplan says you can do it. You say Kaplan can do it. This is the usual way of not doing anything. That it is wise to dismiss a request from Freda Kirchwey, who has done so much for us, in this lighthearted manner, I am not prepared to agree. I understand that your Finance Committee consists of Chaim Greenberg,[2] Rose Halprin, Emanuel Neumann and Gottlieb Hammer.[3] You should have no difficulty if you really wish to pass it through this Committee. I wouldn't like to dismiss Miss Kirchwey with some empty promises. If you definitely can't or don't wish to do it, please let me know.

It's really not my business. I am simply doing it because I think Miss Kirchwey's activity is of great value.

With all good wishes,

Yours sincerely,

Chaim Weizmann

---

147. [1] See No. 144, and n. 2 there.

[2] 1889–1953. Socialist-Zionist editor. Director of J.A. Department of Education and Culture in U.S. from 1946.

[3] Gottlieb Hammer, b. 1911. Zionist official. Comptroller American section of J.A. 1944–49.

148. To Ernst David Bergmann, Rehovot.   *New York, 20 April 1948*
English: Or. Copy. T.W.: W.A.

My dear David,

I was very glad to receive your very long letter,[1] which gave me all the detailed information about the research which you carry on, I presume together with your collaborators. My own criticism of it is that it is too many-sided and too much for a limited group of people, and unless you have a very considerable number of collaborators, it doesn't seem wise to attempt so many things at once. However, you know best, although my experience has shown me that you overstrain yourself and overestimate the limit to which you can go. I would, therefore, advise most energetically to curtail some of the work, which does not seem to me to be of equal importance or of equal character, and from so many subjects one could select some which have priority, leaving the others aside for the time being. Anyhow, I am very grateful to you for having given me an insight into what is going on. Needless to say, I wish you every conceivable success.

My stay here is drawing to an end, and I am not sorry that it is so. It was the most heart-breaking and futile waste of time I have ever experienced. I have been brought over here apparently for some purpose which is still not clear to me. I had a beastly crossing, and was ill for weeks after that. I have been once at the U.N. and said my piece,[2] and since that time I had comparatively little to do, except occasionally seeing some people and trying to instil some ideas into their block-heads. Whether this is worth all the effort, I doubt very much. Well, this experience will teach me not to be a fool in the future and not to answer these pressing invitations unless I know beforehand what is to be done. I am definitely under the impression that probably Mr. Silver and Mr. Neumann didn't want me at all to take part in their work, and Moshe and the other friends were too cowardly to assert their point of view. But the only comfort in this situation is that there is nothing lost. Nothing has happened and nothing will happen apparently, and when the show is all over, we shall have spent a great deal of money, wasted a great deal of time, made quite a number of speeches, but the result will be very small.

The news I got from Rehovot through the people who have just

---

148. [1] 19 Apr. (W.A.). This was a progress report on the research activities of each scientist at the Institute.

[2] There is no explicit evidence of W.'s visit to the U.N. during this stay in U.S. Several delegates called upon him in his suite at the Waldorf-Astoria (W.'s diary).

come back, and also Meyer's telegram,[3] seem to indicate the place is very wonderful and is ready to be worked in. But unfortunately you will have only very few workers to populate these large and beautiful laboratories and we have to possess our soul in patience until this storm has blown over. Stern has definitely resigned, and he seems to be followed by a few others. Frankly, I am not sorry. We ought to be able to get better men, and if we look out for them in France or even amidst the German-Jewish scientists, we probably could get them easier and cheaper.

I don't know when you think we shall be able to start work regularly, and I am naturally extremely sorry that I can't come out and see the place for myself. At present I am gradually acquiring the mentality of a refugee. I am anxious to leave here. I have nothing to do in England, and I can't go to Palestine.[4] I am anxiously awaiting news that the situation has changed so that we may come out as soon as possible.

I am afraid that even letters will not be coming and going regularly, and one will have to wait for an occasion to send them. There seems to be some idea that the air-mail post will be working, and so you might write by it.

Will you please give my best regards to my sister and thank her for her note;[5] also to the rest of my family when you see them, and to Miss Goldschmidt, Dr. Bloch and to all the workers at the Institute.

I remain most affectionately,

Yours,
Chaim Weizmann

149. To Meyer W. Weisgal, Tel Aviv.   *New York, 20 April 1948*
English: T.W.: W.A.

My dear Meyer,

I was most grateful to receive your very interesting letter.[1] I have just written a rather longish note to David,[2] which you will no doubt read, and there is very little which I have to add to it except to say

---

[3] See No. 142, n. 2.

[4] Weisgal had cabled 19 Apr. (W.A.): 'Extremely sorry. Fear true nature situation unrealized your end. Believe you should postpone definite decision fortnight, awaiting developments.'

[5] Anna W. to W., 12 Apr. (W.A.).

149. [1] 14 Apr. (W.A.), describing his impressions of Palestine and of the Institute.

[2] See No. 148.

once more that I am most anxious to get away and am counting the days. It was an absolutely futile waste of time here. I have seen some people, but really, it was not worthwhile for the sake of this sort of activity to go through the ordeal of a crossing in mid-winter and being sick, and at the end, to add insult to injury, you are not giving me a visa to come to Palestine, which I think is very wrong of you. I am still hoping to find a telegram when I come to London, which will be about the 4th of next month, that I may come, because the military situation may improve. This would compensate me for all the heart-breaking experience here.

At any rate, I am very happy that you like Rehovot and that you are able to do your work, as I hope you and Shirley[3] enjoy it.

I wish you a very good *Yontif,*[4] and Vera joins me in this wish.

With very much love, I am

Yours ever,

Ch. Weizmann

150. To Alexander Sachs,[1] **New York.**　　　*New York, 21 April 1948*
English: Or. Copy. T.W.: W.A.

My dear Alex,

I am most grateful to you for your letter and for sending me the copies of the Intelligence Report concerning the Middle Eastern countries.[2] If this bloc of countries would not be artificially bolstered up by Anglo-American money, they would present no difficulty or danger to us. It is only the combination of the Anglo-American bourgeoisie and the Egyptian pashas which constitute the chief cause of our trouble. But even that won't hold very long.

As you know, I am staying here only a very few days, and I am leaving on the 29th. I shall be very busy the next three or four days, but I would be grateful still to see you for a moment after that, so as to take leave and thank you for all your kindness to me.

Wishing you an excellent *Pesach,*[3] I remain

Yours,

Ch. Weizmann

---

[3] Weisgal's wife.

[4] Yidd.: 'festival', referring to Passover.

150. [1] Economist (1893–1976) formerly on W.Z.O. staff. At this time employed by Lehman Corporation.

[2] 17 Apr. (W.A.). Sachs enclosed the 8 Apr. issue of the Intelligence Unit of the London *Economist,* entitled 'Middle East Morass'. This spoke of the belt of Arab countries along the under-belly of Russia as open to Communist influence or invasion, due to the pervasive corruption of the local leadership supported by London.　　　[3] Passover.

151. To Jan Christiaan Smuts, Pretoria.   *New York, 21 April 1948*
English: T.: W.A.

We are reaching decisive point in deliberations. Attitude of New Zealand and Australia demanding fidelity to Assembly Resolution and resistance to aggression has raised morale and hopes of all here.[1] Similar attitude by South African delegation in conformity long tradition would be most helpful. Your old friend,

Chaim Weizmann

152. To Albert K. Epstein, Chicago.   *New York, 5 May 1948*
English: Or. Copy. T.W.: W.A.

Dear A.K.,

Please forgive the delay in answering your very interesting letter.[1] I don't know really the cause of this delay except that somehow I wasn't feeling too well and work was going very slowly.

I share your sentiments fully, and as you know, I never attach too much value to external political forms, and I always knew that the deciding factor in shaping such forms will be our performance in Palestine. Of course, one should always bear in mind that there may be such a political regime which would interfere with practical activities. Such was the case these last few years, which were dominated by paper. But there is a hope that we may get a clear run for the next few years, and I hope we shall not miss the opportunity as we did at the early beginning of the Mandatory regime. From 1922 until 1932 we could have done everything if we would have seized the occasion, but we have failed lamentably, and we have paid for it all these years. I hope that this is not going to be repeated.

I have still to thank you and Harris for the kind greeting which you have sent me for *Pesach*. I need hardly tell you that I reciprocate it most cordially.

My stay here is drawing to an end. We shall be going to London on the 22nd[2] for a few weeks and then to Switzerland. There will

---

151. [1] Australia, New Zealand, Soviet Union and Sweden were calling for implementation of the partition plan. Smuts replied 26 Apr. (W.A.) that South Africa would support them, and press for a truce.

152. [1] 22 Apr. (W.A.). This criticized the Zionist leadership for their militancy. According to Epstein, the most important consideration was not a Jewish State but the perpetuation of the Jewish people. He personally was concerned only that immigration be allowed.

    [2] W. had postponed his return to London, previously scheduled for early May, as he had a relapse diagnosed as 'chronic passive pulmonary congestion' (physician's report, W.A.).

probably be something to do in connection with the General Assembly in Paris in September,[3] but after that we intend to go to Palestine.

Are you likely still to be in New York before I go away? Please let me know.

I remain with the very best wishes to both you and Harris and to your families.

Affectionately yours,
Chaim Weizmann

153. To Walter J. Baer,[1] Zurich.   *New York, 7 May 1948*
English: T.W.: Baer Papers, Zurich.

My dear Walter,

This is a note to let you know that we intend to come to Switzerland either the end of June or the first week in July, and we would like to find a suitable, quiet and nice place, but it mustn't be too high because with my present state of health, I can't stand height. I don't know how high Villars is. We would very much like a quiet and good hotel.

The stay here this time was not very happy. I was ill most of the time and couldn't do very much. We shall be going away on the 22nd to London first, so that you can address your reply to the Dorchester Hotel. You could also give me your telephone number in the letter so that I can speak to you when I reach London.

There is nothing new yet in our political struggle. It is going on. The only new feature of the situation is the sudden collapse of the Arab world, and all the threats which were held over our heads for so many years were merely the inventions of our enemies who used it in order to keep Jewish activities down. The Arabs are running away from all the cities of Palestine—Jaffa, Haifa, Jerusalem, Safed. Many of them will, of course, return; but it will be a different state of affairs, when they do come back. I don't think much will come out of the meeting this season. Perhaps in September—and it all depends upon the facts which the Jews are creating on the spot meanwhile.

I hope all is well with you and Ducia[2] and the children; also with Werner and his family.[3] I am looking forward to seeing you and I remain,

Affectionately yours,
Chaim Weizmann

[3] This was its next scheduled session.

153. [1] Biog. Index, Vol. XVI. Swiss banker and friend of W.
[2] Baer's wife.   [3] Baer's youngest brother.

154. To Harry S. Truman, Washington.   *New York, 13 May 1948*
English: T.W.: Photostat W.A.

Dear Mr. President,[1]

The unhappy events of the last few months will not, I hope, obscure the very great contributions that you, Mr. President, have made toward a definitive and just settlement of the long and troublesome Palestine question. The leadership which the American government took under your inspiration made possible the establishment of a Jewish State, which I am convinced will contribute markedly toward a solution of world Jewish problems, and which, I am equally convinced is a necessary preliminary to the development of lasting peace among the peoples of the Near East.

So far as practical conditions in Palestine would permit, the Jewish people there have proceeded along the lines laid down in the United Nations Resolution of November 29, 1947. Tomorrow mid-night, May 15th, the British Mandate will be terminated, and the Provisional Government of the Jewish State, embodying the best endeavors of the Jewish people and arising from the Resolution of the United Nations, will assume full responsibility for preserving law and order within the boundaries of the Jewish State; for defending that area against external aggression; and for discharging the obligations of the Jewish State to the other nations of the world in accordance with international law.

Considering all the difficulties, the chances for an equitable adjustment of Arab and Jewish relationship are not unfavorable. What is required now is an end to the seeking of new solutions which invariably have retarded rather than encouraged a final settlement.

It is for these reasons that I deeply hope that the United States, which under your leadership has done so much to find a just solution, will promptly recognize the Provisional Government of the new Jewish State. The world, I think, would regard it as especially appropriate that the greatest living democracy should be the first to welcome the newest into the family of nations.[2]

Respectfully yours,

Ch. Weizmann

---

154. [1] Cohn again travelled to Washington to deliver this message personally to the White House (see Eban, *op.cit.*). W.'s appeal was reinforced by a formal request for American recognition submitted 14 May by Eliahu Epstein on behalf of the Provisional Government of Israel. Truman's *de facto* recognition was forthcoming at 6 p.m. Washington time 14 May.

[2] Truman sent W. a note 15 May: 'I appreciated very much your letter of May thirteenth and I sincerely hope that the Palestine situation will eventually work out on an equitable and peaceful basis' (W.A.).

155. To David Ben-Gurion, Tel Aviv.   *New York, 14 May 1948*
English: T.: W.A.

My heartiest greetings to you and colleagues in this great hour. May God continue give you strength carry out task which has been laid upon you and to overcome difficulties still ahead. Please accept and transmit following message to *Yishuv* in my name. "On this memorable day when Jewish State arises after two thousand years I send expressions of love and admiration to all sections of *Yishuv* and warmest greetings to its Government now entering on its grave and inspiring responsibility. Am fully convinced that all who have and will become citizens of Jewish State will strive their utmost live up to new opportunity which history has bestowed upon them. It will be our destiny create institutions and values of free community in spirit our great traditions which have contributed so much to thought and spirit mankind. At this moment I think with special gratitude and affection of our fighters and workers who have borne burden building Jewish Palestine and who now sustain brunt and sacrifice of its defense. It's not easy for me think of peaceful farmers Nahalal, Ein Harod, or youth our Jewish cities, in role soldiers active service. In days of Ezra our forefathers built with one hand while defending themselves with other. We called upon today act in this tradition. It is profound desire our people establish relations harmony and mutual respect with their Arab fellow citizens, with neighbouring Arab States and with all other nations in human family. As British Mandate ends we think with gratitude of vision which inspired its inauguration. We also think of those nations, big and small, who under auspices of United Nations contributed their share to international decision which confirmed our right to statehood. My thoughts are with *Yishuv* in this solemn and fateful hour. May God's blessings rest upon you all."

Chaim Weizmann[1]

---

155. [1] On 15 May a cable from Tel Aviv signed by Ben-Gurion, Kaplan, Golda Meyerson (later, Meir), David Remez and Shertok conveyed the following message to W.: 'Greetings to you upon establishment of the Hebrew State. Of all those living, no one contributed as much as you to its creation. Your position and help at this stage in our struggle encouraged all of us. Looking to the day when we shall be privileged to see you at the head of the State—when it enjoys the blessings of peace. May we go from strength to ever greater strength' (W.A.).

156. To Herbert B. Swope, New York.   *New York, 14 May 1948*
English: Or. Copy. T.W.: W.A.

Dear Swope,

I am very much obliged to you for sending me your letter[1] to Bernard Baruch. I think your letter correctly reflects all the available knowledge on Surinam and the possibilities it offers for Jewish settlement.

I remember that this matter has been talked about sometime ago,[2] and everybody whom I have consulted, just for information, assured me that the coast is a white man's grave. As for the settlement in the uplands, which is covered with tropical forests, this may be, from a hygienic point of view, more suitable, but there is no road and no communication, and the tropical forest has got to be cut down before one could think of any settlement. And so the matter is unpractical from every point of view, and I am very glad that you have given your views so clearly to B.B.

You will have, no doubt, heard that the Jews in Palestine have declared the Jewish State today—and so the new chapter in our history has been opened.

Affectionately yours,
Chaim Weizmann

157. To Sol Bloom,[1] Washington.   *New York, 16 May 1948*
English: Or. Copy. T.W.: W.A.

Private and Personal

Dear Congressman Bloom,

Before my departure from this country, I would like to take the opportunity of sending you my heartfelt wishes and thanks for all the valuable assistance which you have rendered to the cause of the Jewish National revival throughout this difficult period.[2] I think

---

156. [1] This, 13 May (W.A.), warned Baruch against a visitor who intended approaching him regarding a plan to promote Jewish settlement in Surinam.

[2] This region was one of many considered in late 1930s as a possible alternative to Palestine for Jewish refugees.

157. [1] 1870–1949. Congressman from New York 1923–49; the ranking Democratic member of the House Foreign Affairs Committee.

[2] Bloom had canvassed representatives of several countries, including the Philippines, Haiti and Liberia, on behalf of partition in Nov. 1947. While conferring with the President 12 May, Bloom suggested that Truman arrange to have the U.S. become the first nation to recognize the Jewish State (see J. Snetsinger, *op. cit.,* pp. 66, 104).

the consummation of our hopes which has now taken place ought to constitute by itself the richest reward, and any words of mine are really superfluous.

I hope you will be given many years to continue your good work and that we shall be able to count upon your help and advice to meet the difficulties which, I fear, we may still have to overcome in the near future.

With warmest regards,

Yours very sincerely,
Chaim Weizmann

158. To Public Rally,[1] New York.   *New York, 16 May 1948*
English: Message: Or. Copy. W.A.

I deeply regret that indisposition makes it impossible for me to join this great gathering tonight in an expression of solemn joy and deep thankfulness for the rise of the Jewish State to new and independent life. Blessed is the generation which has worked for it and has been found worthy to witness it. It is a generation which will be remembered in ages to come with that which left Egypt and stood before Sinai.

The recent confirmation by international judgment of our right to an equal place in the family of nations closes a two thousand year chapter of injustice, homelessness, and frustration in our history. We remember the six million martyrs of the last and bitterest trial of our exile, as we enter the new era in a spirit of rededication to the fundamental truths expounded by our prophets and sages. With God's help we shall continue to build the State of Israel on foundations of justice and equality for all its inhabitants and with good will and brotherhood toward the neighboring Arab States, and indeed to all peoples of the world. If our young men and women are engaged in deathly strife, it is not a quarrel of our seeking. We have always stretched out the hand of friendship to the Arab people, and we shall continue to do so. It is timely to recall the understanding of our cause and of our peaceful purposes which Arab leaders showed after the First World War, and the Treaty, which it was my privilege to sign with Emir, later King, Feisal, who represented the Arab people at the Peace Conference. I am confident that with their sense of reality the Arab States will recognize that the Jewish State is now a permanent part of the world order: and that the obligations which they have undertaken toward the United Nations Organization will

---

158. [1] At Madison Square Garden the same evening.

speedily bring them back to tranquil paths. They will find the Jewish State always ready and eager to enter into neighborly relations and to join with them in a common effort to increase the welfare and prosperity of the Near East.

My thoughts today are with the *Yishuv,* whose pioneers and workers are bearing burdens and heavy sacrifices in defending their Homeland. We honor those who have fallen. They have given their lives that the Jewish people may live. The road of statehood is beset with many difficulties and obstacles, but I am confident that we shall overcome them with tenacity and courage, with faith in the justice of our cause.

This is also a moment of great pride for the Jews of the United States, who have contributed so much to the Jewish national revival in Palestine. I do not doubt that the full measure of their support and encouragement will be forthcoming to sustain the Jewish State in the ordeals which it now confronts. Though there have been some disappointments in recent months, I feel sure that American Jews will never forget the services and assistance which the President, the Government and the people of the United States have rendered in those actions whereby the United Nations last November gave historic recognition to Jewish nationhood. It is particularly gratifying that it was the President of this great democratic country who was first to give recognition and extend a welcome to the State of Israel. It is my cherished hope that the Jewish State will deserve well of the American people and of peace-loving nations throughout the world. I would urge the Jewish people everywhere to gather round the State of Israel in vigilant and wholehearted support.

Finally, I should like to say a few words of deep appreciation for the work carried out in the past few months by Dr. Silver, Mr. Shertok, Dr. Neumann, and their colleagues, who represented the Jewish cause so worthily in the United Nations. The burden on them was grievously heavy but they have discharged their responsibilities and the tasks laid on them in a manner which deserves well of the Jewish people and of Israel.

159. To Jan Christiaan Smuts, Pretoria. *New York, 16 May 1948*
English: T.: W.A.

Now that Balfour Declaration has been consummated by establishment State of Israel I take opportunity of expressing to you as one of architects of Declaration and most constant supporter of Jewish cause my deepest appreciation and gratitude for manifold kindnesses which you have shown to Zionist Movement and to me personally during intervening years. I understand that new State has approached you for recognition, and I venture express hope it will be possible for you to crown your lifelong encouragement of our national aspirations by giving speedy recognition. I am confident that Israel will make every endeavor to live up worthily to precepts of our ancient sages and prophets and fulfill vision which inspired those who initiated the work in 1917. Affectionately and devotedly yours,[1]

Chaim Weizmann

160. To Moshe Shertok, Tel Aviv.   *New York, 16 May 1948*
English: T.: W.A.

Warmest good wishes to you on beginning your important and responsible work as Foreign Secretary of our new State. May God's blessing be upon your activities always and particularly in these critical days. Have cabled Smuts as requested.[1] Affectionately,

Chaim

161. To David Ben-Gurion, Tel Aviv.   *New York, 17 May 1948*
English: T.: W.A.

Many thanks your cable seventeenth May.[1] Am proud of great honor bestowed upon me by provisional Council of Government of State of Israel in electing me as its first President. It is in humble spirit that I accept this election and am deeply grateful to Council for confidence which it has reposed in me. I dedicate myself to service of land and people in whose cause I have been privileged to labor these many years. I send to Provisional Government and people of Israel this expression of my deepest and most heartfelt affection invoking blessing of God upon them. I pray that struggle forced upon us will speedily end and will be succeeded by era of peace and prosperity for people of Israel and those waiting to join us in construction and advancement of new State. I regret that this moment I am not with our people, but my thoughts and prayers are especially

---

159. [1] South Africa recognized Israel shortly afterwards.

160. [1] See No. 159; see also Shertok to W., 16 May, W.A.

161. [1] Ben-Gurion's telegram (W.A.) read: 'Provisional Council of State of Israel at opening of its inaugural meeting elected you as its President. Please accept our heartiest good wishes. We hope to see you soon with us in peaceful and prosperous State of Israel.'

with those who are bearing brunt and sacrifice of Israel's defense. Future of Israel will not be unworthy of those who have fallen, and Zion shall be redeemed in justice.

Chaim Weizmann

162. To Samuel Rosenman, New York. *New York, 17 May 1948*
English: T.W.: W.A.

My dear Judge Rosenman,

This is the first letter which I am writing since the news of last night has reached me.[1] It is only proper that it should be addressed to you who have contributed so much of your effort and wisdom towards bringing about some of the happy results during the past few days.

Even in this moment I feel that I must ask you again to be so good and impress upon the President the necessity of two additional steps: first, the lifting of the embargo on arms in such a way as to permit supplies being sent to those defending the new State; secondly, a warning to the Arab States that they should stop their destructive and murderous attacks and withdraw their irregular troops and regular forces. I fear that the debate in the Security Council which started off so unhappily on Saturday[2] is not likely to have any deterrent effect on the Arabs and may, indeed, encourage them to increase their violence. The only way, it seems to me, is for the President to take personal action in the same way as he did in regard to the recognition of the Jewish State. Otherwise I fear that the trouble may assume very serious proportions.

I am still not out of bed but I hope to be so in a day or two. I shall then try to contact you, and if you are out of town I shall speak to your wife. In the meantime, I should like once more to express to you my sincere gratitude and to send you affectionate greetings, in which Mrs. Weizmann joins me.

Yours ever,
Ch. Weizmann

---

162. [1] See No. 161, n. 1.

[2] The Security Council convened 15 May to consider an Egyptian note saying that Cairo had decided to intervene in Palestine to 'establish respect for the laws of universal morality and the principles recognized by the United Nations'.

163. To the Dugdale Family, London.   *New York, 18 May 1948*
English: T.: W.A.

Deeply distressed hear of Baffy's death.[1] It is an irreparable loss to your family and to us an unforgettable great personal friend and friend of the cause.

Vera, Chaim Weizmann

164. To Countess Lloyd George,[1] Criccieth, Wales.
New York, 19 May 1948
English: T.: W.A.

Deeply moved by your kind cable,[2] which I much appreciate. Name your husband will always have honored place in history of Jewish national revival, which now culminated in establishing of State of Israel. With best wishes and warmest greetings,

Chaim Weizmann

165. To James de Rothschild, London.   *New York, 19 May 1948*
English: T.: W.A.

Deeply touched by your and Dorothy's message of good wishes.[1] It is fitting that at this moment we should recall with gratitude the great initiative taken by your honored father and the worthy manner in which you carried on his important work. Vera joins me in sending you both our warmest and affectionate greetings.

Chaim Weizmann

---

163. [1] She died 15 May, in Scotland.

164. [1] D. 1972. She was Frances, widow of late Prime Minister David Lloyd George.

[2] She had wired 18 May (W.A.): 'My warmest felicitations on your appointment. How glad my husband, your friend, would have been at this fitting ending to plans you both made thirty years ago. Best wishes for your return to health and a speedy solution of Israel's difficulties'.

165. [1] They cabled (17 May, W.A.), offering heartfelt congratulations on the historic role 'you have and we hope will continue to play in destiny of our people'. This was among the flood of congratulatory telegrams and letters received by W.

166. To Albert Einstein, Princeton.   *New York, 20 May 1948*
German: T.W.: W.A.

Dear Professor Einstein,

I find it difficult to express what pleasure your letter gave me.[1] Your words are noble and full of wisdom and, as you know, I attribute great importance to them. It is a great consolation to me to hear from you in these difficult and complicated times. Please accept my heartfelt gratitude.

I shall do my best to do justice to the great task, but the attitude of the British worries me greatly now, and I shall try and talk to the people in London, although Bevin is not an easy person. I intend to leave here next week and hope to be in America again in late autumn, before finally settling down in Palestine.

May I repeat how grateful I am, and wish you the best of health. I look forward to seeing you soon, and remain,

Yours very sincerely,
Ch. Weizmann

167. To Benjamin V. Cohen,[1] Washington.   *New York, 21 May 1948*
English: Or. Copy. T.W.: W.A.

My dear Ben,

Thank you very much for your letter of the 17th.[2] It was kind of you to send congratulations and I much appreciate them.

It certainly is a long and difficult road which we have travelled since we worked together more than a quarter of a century ago in "77."[3] But our dreams have come true, and now we shall have to work harder than ever and lean more heavily on those of our friends who have given constant support through the intervening years.

With affectionate greetings,

Yours sincerely,

---

166. [1] Einstein wrote 19 May (W.A.) of his satisfaction that Palestine Jewry had placed W. at the head of the new State. The Great Powers still wished the Jewish State harm, but despite this he was confident all would be overcome.

167. [1] Biog. Index, Vol. IX. Lawyer and Presidential adviser; helped in drafting U.N. Charter.
[2] W.A.
[3] Cohen served at Z.O. headquarters 1919–21, at 77 Great Russell Street, London, as adviser to the Zionists during period of Paris Peace Conference and San Remo Conference.

168. To Berl Locker,[1] **London.**   *New York, 21 May 1948*
English: Or. Copy. T.W.: W.A.

My dear Berl,

I am sending you just a line, firstly, to thank you for your telegrams and messages and good wishes, which I heartily reciprocate.
We are now entering upon a new period in life and work, and I hope
that you will carry on with the same zeal and devotion as you did
hitherto, to the honor of yourself and your Party[2] and the Movement.

These lines are carried by Goldmann,[3] and I am anxious that you
should arrange the work between yourself and him in a brotherly
manner, as neither he nor you have had any misunderstandings
throughout your long period of cooperation. There is enough to do
for both of you, and the line of demarcation can be easily established.
These arrangements are purely temporary, and after a short while,
everything will have to fall into a permanent, definite pattern. However, I am sure that you will talk it over in a friendly way between
you, and if my support and mediation are required, you know I
shall be more than happy to do what I can.

So far as my own movements are concerned, we shall be leaving
here by next Wednesday, the 29th, going to Paris, for reasons which
Dr. Goldmann will explain to you. I hope I will be able to see you
there. We will stay in Paris a fortnight and then we shall proceed to
Switzerland. I shall advise you of my addresses and movements in
good time.

My affectionate regards to you and Malka,[4] and I remain, as ever,

Your old friend,
Chaim Weizmann

---

168. [1] Biog. Index, Vol. XV. Labour Zionist leader on J.A. Executive engaged in political
work in London, principally with British Labour Party.

[2] The Palestine Labour Party (*Mapai*).

[3] Goldmann's mission was as unofficial representative of the Provisional Government, and
there was as yet no clear division of functions between the new State and W.Z.O., which had
hitherto been Locker's responsibility in London. See No. 181; see also D. Ben-Gurion, *Israel:
A Personal History,* New York 1971, pp. 136–37.

[4] Malka Locker, b. 1887. Yiddish poet and essayist; wife of Berl.

169. To Queen Elisabeth of Belgium,[1] Brussels.
New York, 23 May 1948
English: T.: W.A.

Greatly honored at your Majesty's gracious message,[2] for which we beg to express our heartfelt thanks.

Vera, Chaim Weizmann

170. To Sir Benegal Rama Rau, New Delhi. *New York, 23 May 1948*
English: Or. Copy. T.W.: W.A.

My dear Sir Benegal,

I am writing in connection with the conversation which I had the pleasure to have with you when you were here.[1] You will recall that you have touched upon the question of scientific collaboration between some of your scientific institutions in India and the research institutes in Rehovot, Israel. I gave expression at the time to the thought that we would be most happy if such a collaboration could be established, and I have suggested that some of your young scientists might come to Rehovot sometime in the summer.

As things stand now, I shall not be in Rehovot before the end of September or middle of October, and therefore, I would be very happy if you would let me know when they could best come. I can assure you that we shall be happy to receive them as honored guests and give them all the facilities which they might require for their scientific pursuits.

Conversely, we would then decide when I am to go out to India and to Burma, because I have received a very pressing invitation from the Burmese Government and also a program of the problems which they would like to discuss.[2] Meanwhile, we have one first-class scientist who is both a physicist and a geologist and who would be prepared to go out very soon and make a general survey. He would probably suggest the kind of other scientists who should join him. His name is Professor Chaim L. Pekeris. He is an applied mathematician, dealing with problems of physics and technology, many-sided and very much to be recommended.

---

169. [1] Queen Elisabeth (1876–1965), widow of Albert I, King of the Belgians. Together they had visited Palestine as W.'s guests in 1933.
[2] 22 May (W.A.).

170. [1] See No. 41.
[2] See No. 109 and ns. 1, 3 there.

Perhaps you will be kind enough to let me know what is the most convenient time for this gentleman to come out and to whom he should address himself when he gets out to India. I suppose he would have to go to Delhi.

I shall be grateful for all information which you would be good enough to give, and would you kindly address your reply in care of Mr. Walter Baer, Bergstrasse 54, Zurich, Switzerland, where I intend to be in the next few months. I shall be leaving here next Wednesday, going directly to France and Switzerland where I shall stay until October.[3]

I hope all is well with you, and I remain with kind regards and high respects,

Yours very sincerely,
Chaim Weizmann

171. To James Fergusson,[1] Kilkerran, Scotland.

New York, 24 May 1948

English: Or. Copy. T.W.: W.A.

Dear Mr. Fergusson,

Thank you very much for your letter of the 17th of May.[2] The death of Baffy came as a great shock to Mrs. Weizmann and myself. We still cannot reconcile ourselves to the thought that we shall not see her again. London will not be the same for us without her. It is a comfort, as indeed it must have been to her, that before she passed away she knew that the dream which she had shared with us for so many years had come true.

Miss May has sent us the letter Baffy had written to her on the 13th of May, in which she wrote that she was looking forward to coming to London to meet us all and where she would hear the news of all that was happening in Palestine. The name of Baffy Dugdale will find a sure and honored place in Jewish history. We have had few non-Jewish friends who have served the cause with such constancy and with such great devotion.

---

[3] Rau replied 8 July (W.A.), having first discussed the subject with Nehru. He was due at The Hague mid-Aug., and hoped for a meeting with W. in Switzerland.

171. [1] B. 1904. Succeeded to baronetcy 1951. Writer and Scottish public servant. Son-in-law of Mrs. Dugdale.

[2] (W.A.). He had written how Mrs. Dugdale's final hours, at his home, were made happy on hearing of Israel's creation as culmination of the process begun by her uncle, Lord Balfour, in 1917.

We had hoped to leave for England, but in the present circumstances we thought it best not to do so, and shall spend a little while in France and Switzerland before returning to Israel.

Mrs. Weizmann and I are very grateful to you and Frances[3] for your good wishes. We send you our warmest and most affectionate greetings.

Yours, ever,

172. To Louis Finkelstein,[1] New York.　　　*New York, 24 May 1948*
English: Or. Copy. T.W.: W.A.

Dear Dr. Finkelstein,

Thank you very much for your letter of the 20th of May.[2] I am very grateful for this expression of good wishes on the occasion of my election. Please accept my sincere appreciation and convey it also to the members of the Faculty of the Jewish Theological Seminary of America.

May I take this opportunity of expressing to you my warmest thanks for so readily offering your private *Sefer Torah*[3] as a gift to be presented to President Truman on the occasion of my visit to Washington.[4] I know what it means to part with such a treasured possession. My only excuse for taking advantage of your generosity is that it is the most fitting gift we can at this time present to the President.

With renewed thanks,

Yours sincerely,

173. To Harry S. Truman, Washington.　　　*New York, 26 May 1948*
English: T.W.: Truman Library.

Dear Mr. President,

Before leaving the shores of the United States, I should like to express to you my warmest thanks for the friendly reception which

---

[3] Fergusson's wife, daughter of Mrs. Dugdale.

172. [1] B. 1895. Conservative rabbi, scholar and educator. Professor of Theology at Jewish Theological Seminary 1931, he became President 1940 and was Chancellor 1951–72.

[2] (W.A.). Finkelstein had sent W. congratulations and offered the prayers of his colleagues at the Seminary.

[3] Hebr.: Scroll of the Law.

[4] W. had accepted Truman's invitation for an official visit to the White House and residence at Blair House. Their meeting took place 25 May, W. presenting Truman with the Scroll (see *T. and E.*, pp. 587–88).

you accorded me yesterday and for the kind hospitality given to Mrs. Weizmann and myself and to the members of my party at Blair House.[1] This official visit, coming soon after the recognition given to the new State of Israel, will be a source of satisfaction and encouragement to my people.

I trust that the two questions of military assistance, and of financial help for constructive work and for the absorption of Jewish Displaced Persons, will receive urgent and favorable consideration. I shall not go into the details here as these are contained in the *aide memoire* which I had the opportunity of leaving with you.

There is, however, one matter to which I only made brief reference and which is of some importance to us. We are anxious that the United States recognition of the State of Israel should be put on a regular basis by an exchange of diplomatic representatives. In anticipation of this arrangement, we have designated Mr. Eliahu Epstein, who is now acting as the representative of the Provisional Government of Israel in this country, as the prospective Minister in Washington. Mr. Epstein, a Palestinian with intimate knowledge of the whole Middle East, has spent the last three years in Washington as the representative of the Jewish Agency for Palestine and has done invaluable work in explaining our aims, problems and activities. I am confident that he will be successful in the new task of increasing the ties between Israel and the United States and of deepening the friendly relations between the two peoples. I hope, Mr. President, that it may be possible for the United States to appoint a Minister to Israel at a very early date.[2]

In taking my leave of you, Mr. President, I should like warmly to commend Mr. Epstein in whom I have every confidence.

Yours very sincerely,

Ch. Weizmann

MEMORANDUM TO THE PRESIDENT

FROM: CHAIM WEIZMANN

SUBJECT: ISRAEL'S TWO BASIC PROBLEMS.

1. Israel is now wrestling with two basic problems: first, national survival in the face of Arab aggression supported by the British; second, the resettlement and rehabilitation of the homeless DPs.

2. There is little hope that the Arabs will accept the cease fire order without crippling limitations. The British still feel that they can divide American opinion and render American policy irresolute; the Arabs still rely on guidance and assistance by the British.

173. [1] See No. 172, n. 4.
   [2] See No. 195, n. 1.

Only action can bring peace to the Middle East, and the most effective action with the British and Arabs is a modification of the arms embargo established by the United States.

3. Military aid is thus the first basic problem which confronts the new State. It requires especially anti-tank weapons; anti-aircraft weapons; planes; and heavy artillery. By American standards the needed quantities are extremely limited but in the context of the current activity in Israel they may well be decisive. Above all speed in the provision of such arms is urgently necessary. Would it be possible to make limited quantities of these weapons available from depots or other storeplaces in the Middle East?

4. The second basic problem confronting Israel arises from the desperate situation of the Jewish DPs. Israel plans to empty the camps at the rate of 15,000 persons per month. To transport, equip, house, and rehabilitate these impoverished people requires expenditures which by Israel's standards are enormous, and which must be made at a time when Israel is engaged in a struggle for national survival.

5. Israel is now applying to the Export-Import Bank for a loan. It was thought that funds could be obtained more speedily in this way rather than by requesting at this time a gift or a grant. Israel can and will satisfy the necessary banking requirements. An indication from you, Mr. President, that you are sympathetic to our application would make certain that speedy action, so urgently required, will be forthcoming.

25 May 1948

174. To Leopold S. Amery, London.   *Paris, 6 June 1948*
English: T.W.: W.A.

My Dear Friend,

I must apologize for the delay in answering your most interesting and important letter.[1] The last few days in New York were hectic and we were overwhelmed with correspondence of all sorts and even on board ship there was comparatively little peace.[2]

The events of the last few weeks have proved your prognosis to

174. [1] 19 May. Amery confessed to mixed emotions over the birth of Israel and W.'s appointment. On the one hand, it was a fitting recognition of his life's work. On the other hand, the State was beset with deadly peril from the start, which Amery thought due in the main to the 'reckless irresponsibility' of the present British Government and to 'a general apathy and weariness' of the British public (I.S.A. 93.03. 67/2).

[2] The Weizmanns left the U.S. 27 May aboard *Mauretania*, reaching Paris 2 June.

be more than correct. We are surrounded by deadly peril and our small community in Israel is fighting desperately and bravely against very heavy odds. Five Arab States are flinging their soldiers and their armour into the battle against us, and there seems to be no doubt, from what one reads in the press and hears from Israel, that British neutrality is merely a cover for the moral and military assistance being given to the Arabs, who are out to destroy the young State. I hope that they will fail, but the deterioration of relations between Israel and Great Britain is one of the gravest consequences of this war. Neither side can well afford these resentments. But when I think of the destruction wrought in the ancient city of Jerusalem, where many shrines must have been gravely damaged, when I think of the constant shelling of our University, our Library, our Hospital on Mount Scopus, it all fills me with dismay, anger and shame, that British officers should have helped the Arabs in this vandalism. But I am convinced that we shall survive and that Israel will emerge as a strong, progressive, democratic community, which in the end will contribute to the revival of the Middle East.

We shall be here another two weeks and then proceed to Switzerland where we shall be staying at the Grand Hotel et Righi Vaudois at Glion sur Montreux. I intend to be back in Paris for the General Assembly of the U.N.O. in September. Are you likely to come over to Switzerland this summer? I know that you are not doing any more climbing, but perhaps you would care to visit old haunts. We are likely to spend 5 to 6 weeks, or even more in Switzerland, that is July and the greater part of August. It would be a great joy to see you there.

Once more, many thanks for your letter and with affectionate regards to you and to Mrs. Amery from both of us.

I remain, as ever,

Your devoted friend,
Ch. Weizmann

P.S.—I enclose herewith a telegraphic report of a speech made by Mr. Ben-Gurion a few days ago.[3]

---

[3] Speech to State Council in Tel Aviv, 3 June (copy in W.A.). This surveyed Israel's successful effort after three weeks not only to retain control over the Jewish areas, but also to take the war to the enemy. These successes were despite British support, aid and advice to Israel's enemies.

175. To the Government and People of Israel.   *Paris, 9 June 1948*
English: T.: C.Z.A. 1210, London File.

On *Erev Shavuoth*[1] send Government and people of Israel my heart-felt greetings and affection. Renewed Israeli State is first historic *bikurim*[2] after over eighteen centuries. Hope and pray that Israel may grow in moral, spiritual and physical strength and live in peace and security, yielding ripened fruit worthy of ancient glories of our history. *Shalom uvracha*[3] and *chag sameiach*[4] to Israel. *Lehitraot.*[5]

Chaim Weizmann

176. To Gidon Schocken,[1] Tel Aviv.   *Paris, 11 June 1948*
English: Or. Copy. T.W.: W.A.

My dear Mr. Schocken,

I am more than grateful to you for your kind and thoughtful letter which was re-addressed here from New York.[2]

I was distressed to read about the bombing of the *Ha'Aretz* offices and the loss of lives accompanying it.[3] But it was a comfort to read that the wonderful modern press which I remember having admired so much has not been damaged, and you can continue publication without much interruption. Let us hope that you will soon be able to restore your office to its previous state of efficiency.

Please convey my kindest regards to Gustav,[4] and I hope the whole thing will not cause him too much additional trouble.

There is very little I have to say about myself at present. We have returned from America somewhat tired as usual. The reception here was rather warm, although the question of recognition does not seem to be too near, but I also hope not too far.[5] All the west of Europe is under pressure from Mr. Bevin, who is gradually qual-

---

175. [1] Hebr.: 'Eve of Pentecost' (Feast of First-Fruits).

   [2] Hebr.: 'the first-fruits.'

   [3] Hebr.: 'peace and blessings.'

   [4] Hebr.: 'happy holiday.'

   [5] Hebr.: '*au revoir.*'

176. [1] B. 1919. Son of Salman Schocken (Biog. Index, Vol. XII). Then with family publishing company; served British army 1941–46; Jewish Brigade 1944; in Israel Defence Forces 1949–59; adviser *Bank Leumi Le-Israel* from 1960.

   [2] 25 May (W.A.), extending congratulations to W.

   [3] An Egyptian air-raid on Tel Aviv struck the premises of the daily *Haaretz,* causing four deaths.

   [4] Gershom Gustav Schocken, b. 1912. Brother of Gidon. Editor and publisher of *Haaretz* from 1939.

   [5] See No. 179.

ifying as our greatest enemy. But they will have to recognize the existence of a State, and they may find that it is in their interest to change their tactics, which do not reflect too much credit on British statesmanship. They certainly try to damage us, but in the end it will recoil on them.

I am sick at heart when I think of the destruction on the Mount Scopus, and possibly this Truce[6] may leave it [*sic*] to some permanent peace, which I am sure, we all wish for.

Let me thank you once more for your kind letter and please convey our greetings to Mrs. Schocken and to the rest of your family in Israel.

With ever so many regards,

I am in old friendship,

Yours

177. To Isaiah Berlin,[1] Oxford. *Paris, 12 June 1948*
English: Or. Copy. T.W.: W.A.

My dear Isaiah,

To thank you for your letter[2] would sound banal—now that I have at last succeeded in reading it (with Miss May's help). We have been trying for several days to decipher it, but had only got bits; now I have had it read to me in full—and can find no words. Only to say: God bless you for it.

It is difficult, and not very profitable, to deal with details in a letter, and as I shall probably not be in London for some time, I would like to send you the warmest possible invitation to come and join us here, either next week-end or the following week-end, when we could talk everything over. I think we could give you a pleasant time—and there is one thing in particular that I want very much to discuss with you.

In a letter I can only say that I would like your advice as to whether I should or should not write to Winston [Churchill]. I had a charming letter from Amery, to which I have replied.[3] But I doubt whether Winston wishes to hear from me directly: you know he always says that whenever I see him or write to him it means he has a sleep-

---

[6] The truce in the fighting, called for by the Security Council, came into effect 11 June.

177. [1] Biog. Index, Vol. XX. Political scientist; Fellow of New College, Oxford 1938–50.
[2] 6 June (W.A.). Berlin felt that despite efforts by F.O. to thwart statehood, even this bastion of pro-Arab sentiment believed that Israel had come to stay. He thought Churchill alone could change Britain's attitude, 'and I shall try and do my best to get the facts to him'.
[3] See No. 174 and n. 1 there.

less night! Well, you will know that I don't wish to give him any such thing. I should greatly value your advice.

But above all, come! Please wire me on receipt of this letter.[4]

I have been overwhelmed with letters and telegrams and what-nots, and it is only now that I am beginning to get through the accumulation. I am trying to get through as much as possible while Miss May is here, but seem to be constantly invaded.

Again—please come!

With all my regards and good wishes,

Yours ever,

Ch. Weizmann

178. To Isaac A. Naiditch,[1] New York.   *Paris, 12 June 1948*
English: Or. Copy. T.W.: W.A.

So very many thanks for your dear letter.[2] You must please forgive both the delay in answering it, and the typescript: my eyes still don't let me write by hand, and since arrival here we have been overwhelmed with visitors, telegrams, telephone calls, and all sorts of crises, so that it is only to-day that I am able to get down to replying to the letters I most want to answer.

These are indeed great days—and it is a privilege to live in them. They are anxious ones, too, but I am greatly comforted and encouraged by the consciousness that they are shared, as so much of my life has been shared, with you and the very few old friends whose affection and confidence have defied the years, and will, I know, continue to defy them. The shadows of troubles to come already darken my path, but I have no doubts at all of the ultimate outcome: if we work on, with faith, honesty of purpose, and confidence, we shall win through.

In all friendship and affection, as ever,

Yours,

---

[4] No reply from Berlin traced.

178. [1] Biog. Index, Vol. VI. Philanthropist, formerly European K.H. leader; friend of W. from youth.

[2] 17 May (W.A.).

179. To Moshe Shertok and David Ben-Gurion, Tel Aviv.

Paris, 12 June 1948

English: Or. Copy. T.W.: W.A.

My dear Moshe and my dear Ben-Gurion,

I have been here just over a week, and I meant to write to you before this, but I have been snowed under—letters, telegrams, visitors, requests of all kinds, and it is only now that I am beginning to get straight. Not that the quantities have diminished, but things have become more orderly. I always thought that nothing could be worse than New York, but Paris is almost as bad, and the general amenities of life are slower here than in America.

There is nothing very much to report from here, except perhaps on the problem of recognition. I have tried gently to sound the people here. M. Bidault[1] has been very amiable, but they are obviously hesitant and frightened mostly of their own Arabs in North Africa, but to a lesser degree they find themselves under pressure from England, to which—as they say—they do not attach too much importance. Both M. Léon Blum and M. René Mayer advise me not to press the matter: it will come. I believe they are right. I would like, however, to have your opinion about it, which you might indicate by telegram; if you wish me to do a little more in this direction I shall gladly do so. On France's recognition the whole Western Bloc and Italy really depend. The Italian Ambassador, whom I met yesterday at a dinner party, indicated quite clearly their fear of England. I think we must try to overcome it, but I shall do nothing till I hear from you. As I am staying here until the end of this month, you could still send me a telegram on receipt of this letter.[2]

I was dreadfully sorry to hear of the death of Colonel Marcus.[3] I saw him before he left. I understand that he was a great soldier and a very fine fellow—something like Orde Wingate.[4] It is, I am afraid, a terrible loss.

I wonder whether you are intending to make use, in Washington, of men like David Ginsburg and others in the service of Israel? I have seen a good deal of him, and was greatly impressed by his efficiency,

---

179. [1] Georges Bidault (b. 1899). Intermittently French Foreign Minister 1944–48, 1953. Premier 1946, 1949–50.

[2] Shertok cabled 18 June (W.A.) that he was immersed in routine work in connection with implementation of the truce but would keep W. informed of major developments.

[3] David ('Mickey') Marcus (1902–48). U.S. soldier. Recruited by J.A. in 1947 to advise *Haganah*. At time of death he was commander of Jerusalem front.

[4] Biog. Index, Vol. XVIII. British soldier. He played a leading role against the Arab rebellion 1936–39, establishing close contact with *Haganah* and *Yishuv* leaders.

judgment and devotion. There are a few men like him, and I think it would be extremely valuable to have such an element in the country. It would also help our relations with the U.S.

I do sincerely trust that you will build up the Administration not on party lines, and that you will not use the famous "key,"[5] but select your men and women on merit. Forgive me for offering all this advice, but much will depend on our first steps, and now is the time to correct the mistakes which many years of Zionist routine have introduced into our system. We shall, no doubt, make new mistakes, but we must use the opportunity to get rid of the old ones.

I do not know what you foresee at the end of this truce. It will probably last more than a month. I understand that the Mediator[6] may press for a revision of frontiers, and for our relinquishment of the Southern Negev, including Akaba. I would not agree to this, certainly not so far as Akaba is concerned. It will be a dagger in our backs if it falls into the others' hands. You remember how we fought for it at Lake Success.

Well, I don't wish to bother you with more at present, except to wish you all the luck in the world, health and strength and—above all—peace.

Please acknowledge the receipt of this letter by telegram.

Affectionately yours,

Ch. Weizmann

P.S. I have had here an opportunity of getting to know Dr. Goldberg[7] rather better, and of seeing him at work. As a result, I feel I ought to tell you that I think it essential for him to have the same rank as Fisher.[8] He does not wish to be of superior rank, but he is certainly entitled to equality of status, and I hope that you will agree with me and will be able to arrange this. Please let me know about it.

---

[5] A system for allocating positions and offices on basis of party affiliation rather than merit.

[6] Count Folke Bernadotte (Biog. Index). Appointed U.N. Mediator in Palestine 20 May.

[7] Abraham Goldberg (later Gilboa; b. 1905). Consul of Israel and Immigration Officer, Paris 1948–54.

[8] Maurice Fischer (1903–65), Israel Ambassador to France 1948–53.

180. To Dewey Stone, Boston.   *Paris, 12 June 1948*
English: T.: W.A.

Your telegram received.[1] Shall do all I can but please send me detailed telegraphic instructions what you want me to write to Jacobson.[2] Best love to all.

Chaim Weizmann

181. To Leopold S. Amery, London.   *Paris, 13 June 1948*
English: T.W.: W.A.

My dear Amery,
    I shall be writing to you fully in a day or two.[1] Meanwhile, this is just a note to introduce to you my very good friend and colleague of many years' standing, Dr. Nahum Goldmann. He is coming to London tomorrow, with the mission from the Government of Israel of trying to re-open relations between Israel and Britain. If I may say so, he is the most suitable man in our ranks—both by training and natural inclination—for this rather delicate task.
    On his arrival in London tomorrow he will be most anxious to see you; also Salisbury[2] (whom he already knows), Stanley, and, if possible, Mr. Churchill.
    I should be deeply grateful to you for any help and advice you may be good enough to give Dr. Goldmann in these matters.
    With thanks in anticipation, and best regards as ever from Mrs. Weizmann and myself to you both, I am

Affectionately yours,
Ch. Weizmann

180. [1] 11 June (W.A.). This indicated that the two men had been in telephone contact regarding a new initiative to reach and influence Truman. Stone urged W. to send Jacobson instructions on 'what you would like his friend [Truman] to do now on the overall question'. Stone added: 'Jacobson trying hard to help but needs the stimulation and advice from you. No one else can be effective'.
    [2] W. requested Weisgal to visit Jacobson in Kansas City, and cabled Jacobson accordingly (W. to Jacobson, 14 June, W.A.). Weisgal reported: 'I did go to Kansas City to see your friend the haberdasher, and he, in turn, saw the other haberdasher [Truman] and indicated to him that... the boundaries will stand and that he is fully aware of all the British shenanigans. As he himself put it, "They have pulled the rug from under me before. They will not do it again." This had reference to the State Department, Mr. Loy Henderson, and their allies in Whitehall. Apparently the old boy is determined to make good. His appointment of [James G.] McDonald [as special U.S. representative to Israel] is a good sign' (Weisgal to W., 23 June, W.A.).

181. [1] No such letter traced.
    [2] Robert Gascoyne-Cecil, 5th Marquess of Salisbury (1893–1972). Secretary of State for Dominion Affairs 1940–42, 1943–45; for Colonies 1942; for Commonwealth Relations 1952; Leader of House of Lords 1942–45, 1951–57.

182. To Moshe Shertok, Tel Aviv. *Paris, 13 June 1948*
Code: T.: W.A.

Press here reports two boats left Marseilles with young immigrants and arms.[1] Feel very strongly we bound be most scrupulous and correct in abiding by conditions ceasefire[2] not laying ourselves open any accusations of violating international law and mutually accepted agreements as this would gravely prejudice our general position. Am convinced you feel same way and will take all necessary action to secure correct behaviour our representatives everywhere. Regards.

Chaim Weizmann

183. To Moshe Shertok, Tel Aviv. *Paris, 13 June 1948*
English: Or. Copy. T.W.: W.A.

My dear Moshe,

I am somewhat exercised in mind because I have heard nothing from you for quite a long time. Decisions are pending, and I know very little about them, though you will remember that we agreed that I should so far as possible be kept informed about things. I know you are overwhelmed with work, but I still feel it to be essential that we should keep in touch.

So, for instance, I know nothing about the state in which our draft constitution at present finds itself. I am naturally interested, among other things, in knowing as soon as possible "what the President looks like". There are, as you know, several sorts of President: the American type, the French type, the Swiss, the Czech, and no doubt others. I have no idea what the draft looks like, but I would like to say now that I would certainly not care to be the French brand of President; nor yet the American—which would be unsuitable for a state like ours, and I neither desire nor claim any such position. But you will understand that I do not wish either to be a mere figurehead, and I would like you to take this into serious consideration.

Of course it is all still provisional, but I think it is as well to be clear about it from the start. I would therefore feel greatly obliged

---

182. [1] The *Irgun* forces, independent of *Haganah*, had denounced the truce. On 22 June they sought to unload a ship, the *Altalena*, with 800 immigrants and laden with arms, on the beach north of Tel Aviv. The Government's demand that the ship be placed under its authority was rejected, and Ben-Gurion ordered that force be used to secure the *Altalena's* compliance. In the ensuing action 15 lives were lost and the ship sunk. See Ben-Gurion, *op. cit.*, pp. 165–77.

[2] The cease-fire terms included a provision that war materials were not to be imported into the country or territory of any interested party.

if some information could be vouchsafed to me. (David Ginsburg spoke to me about it in Washington—though I was not clear whether he had any definite ideas on the subject or not.)

You can always address a letter here; if I have already left, it will be forwarded to Switzerland (address: Glion-sur-Montreux, I think Hotel Righi). Anyhow, it is a small place, and letters will no doubt find me.[1]

With all good wishes, I am   Yours ever,

184. To Moshe Shertok, Tel Aviv.   *Paris, 13 June 1948*
English: Or. Copy. T.W.: I.F.M. 2449/150414.

My dear Moshe,

Forgive me for worrying you again over administrative matters— but they are almost inevitable in this present stage of our affairs.

This time it is a question of our friend Linton, who is at your disposal either for the Foreign Office in Israel or for the London Legation. I think myself he might be more useful in London—but that is for him and you to decide together, and is not for me to say. As you know, he has served us loyally for many years, is intelligent, hard-working, and conscientious, and certainly very devoted. He could remain in some way attached to me, and I have offered him this quite frankly and sincerely; but he would prefer a rank which would make him a permanent member of the administration, rather than just a personal post with the President. And I think he is right.

But whether in London or Jerusalem he feels he should have appropriate status, both in view of his long service, and in order to have the necessary scope to do his best work for us. We have not so very many people with his experience and qualifications. A rank such as "Counsellor" in our Foreign Office might meet the case.

I leave it of course entirely to your judgment. He has deserved a post where he can use his abilities to the full, and I hope you may see your way to meet his wishes. Of late he has been working a good deal with me, to my complete satisfaction. I would not like him to suffer because this has kept him away from the London office.[1]

With best regards,
                                                        Yours ever
                                                        Ch. Weizmann

183. [1] Shertok cabled 13 June (W.A.) that the question of a draft constitution was at a 'complete standstill'; no immediate progress was likely.

184. [1] Linton was formally appointed a member of the Foreign Service. As no rank of Counsellor existed, and because the establishment of an Israeli Legation in London seemed unlikely in the early future, given Britain's non-recognition of Israel, Shertok wished Linton to assume the post of Consul-General in London and deputy to Goldmann—see Walter Eytan, Director-General of Israel Foreign Ministry, to Linton, 12 July (copy in W.A.).

185. To Walter Elliot,[1] **London.** *Paris, 14 June 1948*
English: Or. Copy. T.W.: W.A.

My dear Walter,

Forgive me for having been so slow in answering your letter.[2] It gave me great happiness and touched me deeply that you should have felt moved to write to me as you do, and I find it difficult to say what is in my heart without being "un-English." So I will just say "God bless you for it," and hope you will understand all that that means.

Indeed, these are great, if anxious, days. But how right you are to say that, however great events may be, they are not so great as human relationships. I am so very glad to think that Baffy heard the news and rejoiced in it before she died. Thank you for sending me the story of her last day—my grief at her going is assuaged a little by the thought that it was such a happy one, and so typical of all she loved. Perhaps, too, it is well for her that she is spared the anxieties and uncertainties of the last few weeks, and all the miserable tangle of the British attitude towards us, which would assuredly have saddened her as much as it saddens me. For forty years I have lived and thought and felt with the English, and I need not tell you that what is happening now is agony for me—the cutting away of half my life.

Yet, though I do not minimise the difficulties of our infant State—indeed, their shadows already fall heavily across my path, I have no doubts at all of the ultimate outcome. With faith, honesty of purpose, and hard work, we shall win through.

I fear we shall not be in London again for some time. We shall be here for another fortnight, and after that in Switzerland (Glion-sur-Montreux, Grand Hotel et Righi Vaudois). I suppose there is no chance of seeing you? There is so much which is difficult to say in a letter—specially when I cannot write with my own hand. Do let me know.

With kindest personal regards from us both to both of you, I remain as ever,

Affectionately yours,

---

185. [1] Biog. Index, Vol. XIII. British Conservative politician; strong Zionist sympathizer.
[2] 3 June (W.A.). In congratulating W. upon being chosen President, Elliot spoke of the stupendous events being overshadowed for him by the death of his close friend, Baffy Dugdale. He described her last days and how she had yearned to see W.

186. To Richard Meinertzhagen, London.   *Paris, 14 June 1948*
English: Or. Copy. T.W.: W.A.

My dear Friend,

If I have been slow in replying to your dear letter,[1] it is purely for technical reasons—I have been overwhelmed with correspondence and (still worse) with visitors, and am only now able to get down to writing the letters I really want to write. You must please forgive the typescript—my eyes still don't let me write by hand.

I cannot possibly find words to tell you how much your letter has meant to me in consolation and encouragement. These are great, but anxious, days, and the shadows of the dangers which the infant Israel will have to face already darken my path. One of the heaviest of them is the attitude of England—or rather of the British Government. You know that I have lived and felt with the English for forty years. With you I still believe that English interests and Israel's in the Middle East are complementary and inseparable—but it is heart-rending to have to stand by and watch a British Government trying its hardest to destroy both Israel and the only sure bastion of Britain's own safety in the Levant. . . I *cannot* believe it, but alas, I must. I cling to the hope that soon there will surely be a change of heart—and with it a change of policy towards a more natural, more human, line. . .

But all this is not telling you what I set out to try and tell you—I wish so much that I could write with my own hand!—what your letter meant to me. Because, for me, human relationships have always tended to overshadow events—even great events. And perhaps the keenest personal pleasure that the re-birth of Israel has brought me has been your assurance that our long friendship and cooperation in the work still endure, and the confirmation it brings to my conviction that Mr. Bevin is *not* England, to my faith that "the other England" will yet arise.

When it comes to the point, what can I really say, except "God bless and keep you always"? I suppose there is little chance of seeing you here—where we shall be for another ten days or so—but even if not, I want you to know what comfort you have given me, and how deeply grateful I am to you for your friendship and confidence and help through all these years. That is something which can never be taken away from us—as inalienable as the soil of Israel itself—and for it I give humble and grateful thanks to Israel's God and yours.

As ever, yours in deep affection,

Ch. Weizmann

186. [1] 1 June (W.A.) He wrote in moving terms of the events surrounding the birth of Israel.

187. To Moshe Shertok, Tel Aviv.   *Paris, 14 June 1948*
English: T.W.: I.F.M. 2449/150414.

My dear Moshe,

Confirming my letter of yesterday, I would like to let you know that I shall be here till the end of the month, and afterwards at Glion-sur-Montreux (Grand Hotel et Righi Vaudois). If you have my passport ready, please send it there. So far I continue to use my British passport, and naturally shall be glad to have my own as soon as possible.

You might perhaps also advise me whether if I don't come till the end of September the delay is too long? My trouble is that the heat affects my health, so it is difficult to come earlier.

So far I have no idea where the offices of the Israel Government are or will be situated, or where—and when—we shall have to build. I would like to know that I shall have an office somewhere—whether Sarona or Tel Aviv or wherever the seat of the Government may be. I think it can hardly be expected that I shall conduct presidential business from my home in Rehovot—nor yet from the Institute. I would be very grateful for some information about this.[1]

How is the Mediator getting on? Please try to keep me fully informed.[2] Much love.

As ever yours,
Ch. Weizmann

188. To Meyer W. Weisgal, New York.   *Paris, 14 June 1948*
English: T.W.: W.A.

My dear Meyer,

I am most grateful to you for your kind letter of the 8th, with its enclosures.[1] I am dealing with them now.

I agree with your suggestion about the title of the book—except that I thought it was to be *Through Trial and Error*.[2] But I daresay

---

187. [1] Replying 20 June (W.A.), Shertok assured W. that a building suitable for the presidential office would be especially adapted in the Government complex at Sarona in Tel Aviv before W. assumed his duties.

[2] As reflected by his subsequent reports (W.A.), Shertok strove to keep W. fully informed on developments.

188. [1] W.A. This dealt with aspects of W.'s autobiography and enclosed two letters from Gershom Schocken, one giving his opinion of the manuscript, which was to be published in Hebrew in *Haaretz,* the other a letter of congratulations for W. to sign as part of a testimonial honouring *Haaretz* on the 30th anniversary of its foundation.

[2] Weisgal suggested omitting 'Through'.

it makes little difference. I shall see what I can do about the epilogue, and, as I mentioned to you before I left, I am doing a few lines about Léon Blum, which you can fit in somewhere. Miss May (who is here for a very short few days) will post them on to you.

I also agree about the dedication to Mrs. Weizmann. Perhaps we say:

"For My Wife—my comrade and life-companion."

I hear from Rehovot that there has been some slight damage to the workshop. I don't think it amounts to very much—in money, something like £300 worth. Let us hope that with the truce there may eventually come some permanent settlement—though that is perhaps too much to hope for so soon.

I was terribly sorry to hear about Harry's[3] boy. I do hope he may still recover. I have sent them a wire to your address,[4] as we haven't theirs to hand.

With best love from us both to you and Shirley and the children,

As ever yours,

Ch. Weizmann

P.S.   Please give our best love to Reva.[5] Would you ask her if she remembers writing for me to Miss Goldschmidt about sending some summer clothes, etc. to Paris or Switzerland for us? I think I did, but can't be sure.

[In June 1948 Bernadotte submitted a blueprint for a negotiated settlement between Arabs and Jews in which the Negev, part of the proposed Jewish State in the 1947 U.N. partition frontiers, would be transferred to an Arab State in exchange for Israeli acquisition of Western Galilee. As discussions continued into September, the U.N. General Assembly was informed of a decision by the United Kingdom to support the Bernadotte plan in its entirety. Washington, which hitherto had been wavering, aligned itself with London when Marshall urged the General Assembly to accept Bernadotte's conclusions in their entirety as the best possible basis for bringing peace. W. had long been apprised by his correspondents in both capitals of Anglo-American discussions aimed at coordinating policy on this issue. Zionist efforts were therefore directed at preventing such a coalition and focused upon convincing Truman of the necessity of retaining the Negev as part of Israel.]

[3] Harry Levine (1895–1977). Merchant. Z.O.A. treasurer 1945; treasurer, American Committee for Weizmann Institute from 1944; world treasurer from 1950.

[4] He did not recover. W. sent condolences to the family through Weisgal (W.A.).

[5] Reva Ziff (later, Stern). Secretary of Weizmann Institute Committee in New York, and W.'s secretary there 1947–48.

189. To C. David Ginsburg, Washington.   *Paris, 15 June 1948*
English: Or. Copy. T.W.: W.A.

My dear Dave,

It seems a very long time since I have seen you or spoken or written to you. I find myself quite busy in Paris, very much against my expectation. The Jews ooze out of every corner and the infectious American habit of handshaking has crossed the Atlantic.

I hope you and Leah are well.

The object of my writing to you is a certain uneasiness in my mind concerning the frontiers. The British plan seems to be that they would recognise us if we are prepared to give up our claim on the Negeb and possibly on some part of Northern Galilee. We shall not agree to it on any account and I am anxious that this matter should be made perfectly clear in the most authoritative form, both to the President and to Mr. Marshall. If you think that it may be useful for me to write to the President, I shall do so. Felix [Frankfurter] could talk to Mr. Marshall. I am sure that any attempt to deprive us of the Negeb would be resisted violently in Israel and would lead to bloodshed. It has been adjudicated to us by the UNO and we will in time make something of it. In the hands of the Arabs it will remain a forbidding desert. I am sure that you understand the position and I need not labour the point too much.

I am here until the end of the month, leaving on the 29th. My address in Switzerland is provisionally: c/o Walter Baer, Bergstrasse 54, Zurich.

Please keep me informed, and give my kindest regards to David Niles, Bob Nathan[1] and other friends.

I would appreciate a telegram on receipt of this letter.

With much love to you and Leah from both of us,

Yours ever,

190. To Joseph I. Linton, London.   *Paris, 15 June. 1948*
English: Or. Copy. T.W.: W.A.

Dear Ivor,

I have sent you messages through Miss May, but I am most anxious to confirm them in writing.

I am somewhat worried about the negotiations which our friend Goldmann is carrying on in London. It is quite clear that the British

---

189.[1] Robert Nathan, b. 1908. U.S. economist. He had previously been advising J.A. on Palestine's development and was then guiding Israeli representatives in their first official contacts in Washington.

Government would be ready to recognise us if we are prepared to give up the Negeb and perhaps some part of Northern Galilee. The Negeb also means Akaba. I would not agree to it, on no account. We have fought for it at Lake Success, we had the support of the President of the United States of America. You remember, I have travelled to Washington especially to see him about it. And besides, to have the Egyptians close to our Southern borders is something which I cannot stomach. I am also sure that in Israel it will be resisted by force of arms and it will all lead to bloodshed. I think it must be made politely but abundantly clear to the people at the War Office, especially to people like Charteris.[1] If they wish (the British and not the Egyptians), to have a base in the Negeb or an airfield, I would be generous on that point, but I would go no further.

I expect you to be here for the weekend and bring me all the news from London.

With kind regards,

Yours ever,

191. To C. David Ginsburg, Washington.   *Paris, 16 June 1948*
English: Or. Copy. T.W.: W.A.

My dear Dave,

Enclosed you will find the *Daily Telegraph* article to which reference is made in my telegram of to-day.[1]

The disturbing feature of it is the alleged cooperation between England and U.S.A. for the purpose of reducing the Territory of the Jewish State to something insignificant. The British do not seem to cease their intrigues and there is no end to their machinations. It may be that the State Department is working hand in hand with them, but I am sure that the President would not lend himself to it. I think we ought to bring the whole matter before the Judge Rosenman. Give him my kindest regards, and tell him that it is important to counteract all these nefarious attempts.

Possibly our friend Ed. Jacobson from Kansas City, the President's friend and ex-partner, might be useful. Meyer can advise you on this matter. But it is essential to stop the whole thing once and for

190. [1] Sir Martin Charteris, b. 1913. Formerly served in Intelligence in Palestine. Private Secretary to Queen 1952–77. Provost of Eton from 1977.

191. [1] Telegram to Weisgal (W.A.), referring to *Daily Telegraph* of 14 June as giving credence to the proposed plan to detach the Negev.

all. The British are determined to reduce the Jewish State to a coastal strip from Haifa to Tel Aviv and to reward the Arabs by territory which they take away from us.

Please cable to me what you are doing.

Much love to both of you,

Yours ever,

192. To Josef Cohn, New York.   *Paris, 20 June 1948*
English: Or. Copy. T.W.: W.A.

My dear Josef,

Very many thanks for your interesting letter.[1] I shall of course be looking forward to meet with Mr. Sumner Welles[2] when he is out in Switzerland in August. What my address in Switzerland will be at that time I cannot determine now, but it will probably be: Grand Hotel et Righi Vaudois at Glion s/Montreux. I will be able to let you know in good time if there is any changement.

I expect that Adele[3] will turn up some time this week and we shall be very glad to see her.

I have not written anything to the Judge [Rosenman], but it is just as well to keep him posted. We are not out of the woods yet, and the British are making every attempt to do us real harm. They would cut our territory by at least 50% if they succeed, and I am not sure that they are not working hand in hand with some people in the State Department. Neither do I think that Bernadotte is a particular friend of ours. He constantly speaks of effecting a permanent settlement between us and the Arabs, and I am certain that he is thinking of appeasing the Arabs by giving them chunks of our territory, either in the Negeb or in the North, or both. This will be resisted at all costs, and the President, who was so helpful in the matter of the frontiers, ought to be warned and kept fully informed. He has promised to keep an eye on Henderson[4] and I hope he will do it. The intention of the British is to keep the country in a ferment

---

192. [1] This, 16 June (W.A.), informed W. of activities in U.S., especially his own efforts, together with Eban, in keeping Rosenman abreast of developments.

[2] Welles' book *We Need Not Fail* had just been published. It described the need, from an American point of view, for a permanent settlement in Palestine on basis of the 29 Nov. Resolution. See also No. 218.

[3] Adele Levy, sister of Lessing Rosenwald, President, American Council of Judaism. Wife of David M. Levy, psychiatrist.

[4] Loy Henderson, b. 1892. Director of Near Eastern and African Affairs at State Department 1945–48. Regarded by the Zionists as one of their principal opponents in State Department, sharing the views of British F.O. Appointed U.S. Ambassador to India 1948.

and to fish in troubled waters. You will, no doubt, warn our good friends in Washington of this state of affairs. I did write a note to David Ginsburg, but Felix [Frankfurter] and Ben [Cohen] ought to be told about it too. There is real danger ahead.

We are staying on for another 10 days or so and then going on to Switzerland. My address there will be: Grand Hotel et Righi Vaudois, Glion s/Montreux. My intention is to be in Switzerland until the end of August.

I expect to be in Israel in the early days of October. By that time most of the building ought to be ready. The disturbances seem to have slowed down the building program considerably.

We have seen Dorothy Paley here,[5] and we shall see her again at the end of this month.

That is all for the present. Give my best love to Meyer [Weisgal], Aubrey [Eban], and to our friends in Washington.

Yours ever,

193. To Samuel I. Rosenman, New York. *Paris, 22 June 1948*
English: T.W.: W.A.

My dear Judge Rosenman,

I hope that you have returned safely from your trip to the West and that you have joined your family again.

We have had a very good trip back and we have been staying all the time in Paris, seeing quite a number of people, and now we shall be going off to Switzerland in a week's time. Our address there is: Grand Hotel et Righi Vaudois, Glion s/Montreux.

There is nothing particularly new here and there are no sensational developments in London, as far as I understand also in Lake Success. But I have the uncomfortable feeling that an attempt is going to be made to curtail our frontiers. How and when it is going to be done I do not know, but the British seem to think that we have got too much and we ought to give up the Southern part, the so called Negeb, bordering on Egypt. That would mean also the loss of Akaba, which one day may become a very important port on the Red Sea leading to India. This must be prevented at all costs. You will remember that we have got the agreement of the American Delegation to Akaba and the Negeb, owing to the intervention of the President, and I hope that he will not withdraw his support, so that we may continue our work in this district. For your information I would like to say that there is quite a number of settlements established there,

---

[5] On 17 June (W.'s diary).

and a goodish number of *Haganah* troops are stationed in the Negeb. Still the British may use the Egyptians in order to attack us; in fact, some Egyptian troops have penetrated into the Negeb, but so far they are being held.

You have, no doubt, heard or read that the British are causing us a good deal of difficulty, and we are looking forward to the time when their troops will leave the country, and all this sad episode will come to an end. I understand that they have advanced the date of their departure very considerably. By the middle of July there should be no British troops in Palestine.

Meanwhile our own Government has taken over the various services, and, in spite of initial complications, they seem to be working quite well. There is a great enthusiasm and confidence prevailing and every one who comes from Israel seems to be bright and happy in spite of all the difficulties with which the new regime has to battle.

I hope that you will keep an eye on the problem of the frontiers, and perhaps you might be so good as to have a word with Mr. Aubrey Eban, who is fully informed about the situation and would gladly come and talk to you if you ask him. Dr. Joseph Cohn, who lives at the Salisbury Hotel, will easily put you in touch with Eban. Eban is our representative at Lake Success, a gentleman of very high qualifications and integrity.

Please remember me to Mrs. Rosenman and I remain, with all best wishes and my thanks in anticipation,

Yours very sincerely,

Ch. Weizmann

194. To Eliezer Kaplan, Tel Aviv.   *Paris, 23 June 1948*
English: Or. Copy. T.W.: W.A.

My dear Eliezer,

You have, no doubt, received my note concerning the Hebrew University.[1] I hope to have your answer in due course.

This time I would like to address you on a matter which has a somewhat personal character. You no doubt remember my son Benji. He is anxious to be associated with the Citrus Board. I may say confidently that he is a good specialist in the matter of fruit, buying, selling, grading, packing and preserving. He has been working for Marks and Spencer for many years and has established excellent connections, both in Covent Garden, London, as well as in Italy and Spain.

---

194. [1] 14 June (W.A.), concerning allocations for H.U.

Remez,[2] who is here, has advised me to write to you about it. I have already written about it a few days ago to Dr. [E.D.] Bergmann,[3] who knows Benji very well, and whom you could consult. He is naturally prepared to spend a good deal of time in Israel and also abroad.

Anything you will do in this matter to help me will be greatly appreciated.

I remain with all kind regards, as ever,

Yours,

195. To James G. McDonald, New York.　　*Paris, 24 June 1948*
English: T.: Herbert H. Lehman Papers, New York.

Am more than delighted your appointment[1] and am looking forward for fruitful cooperation in Israel for the benefit of all. Affectionately.

Chaim Weizmann

196. To Moshe Shertok, Tel Aviv.　　*Paris, 24 June 1948*
Code: T.: W.A.

Democratic, peace-loving nation which seeks create place for itself in world community and United Nations will allow full expression view dissident elements but cannot and will not permit any action[1] in derogation State policy representing majority will. If you agree you might publish the above statement over my name.[2] Regards.

Chaim Weizmann

[2] Moshe David Remez (Biog. Index, Vol. XVI). Chairman of *Va'ad Leumi* 1944–48; Minister of Transport in Provisional Israel Government.

[3] 20 June, W.A.

195. [1] As special representative of U.S. to Provisional Government of Israel.

196. [1] Relates to *Altalena* action (see No. 182 and n. 1 there). The Provisional Government issued a decree 22 June making civil disobedience an act of treason to the State and ordering the arrest of *Irgun* members and other dissident elements.

[2] Ginsburg provided this text, with the suggestion that such a statement be despatched. He further suggested (with Epstein's agreement) that W. cable Truman expressing satisfaction at McDonald's appointment (Ginsburg telegram, 23 June, W.A.). See No. 198.

197. To David Ben-Gurion and Moshe Shertok, Tel Aviv.

Paris, 24 June 1948

Code: T.: W.A.

Consider action *Mizrachi*[1] members, particularly outside inter-ference of Rabbi Berlin,[2] as undermining State authority. Kindly wire what you propose to do.[3]

Chaim Weizmann

198. To Harry S. Truman, Washington.   *Paris, 24 June 1948*

English: T.: W.A.

Allow me to express to you my heartfelt thanks for the appointment of James McDonald as special representative to Israel. I am certain that this appointment will give deep satisfaction to the community of Israel and to Jewry generally. Respectfully and with all regards.

Weizmann

199. To C. David Ginsburg, Washington.   *Paris, 25 June 1948*

English: Or. Copy. T.W.: W.A.

My dear Dave,

I am most grateful to you for your telegram received yesterday and I have transmitted your suggestion to Shertok.[1] If he agrees, he can publish the statement over my name.

I enclose a copy from a letter which I have written to Shertok.[2]

---

197. [1] Following the *Altalena* affair, the Minister of Religions, Rabbi Judah L. Fishman (Maimon) of the religious party *Mizrachi,* and Moshe Shapiro, of its worker's wing *Hapoel Hamizrachi,* who held the Immigration and Health portfolios, resigned 23 June. They urged that all *Irgun* suspects be released to prevent civil war. *Mizrachi's* elder statesman, Meir Berlin, held Ben-Gurion personally responsible for the crisis by assuming too much authority, and proposed a public inquiry. This was accepted with himself appointed to the inquiry committee. But he declined to serve, due to objections as to its composition. (*Palestine Post,* 24 June 1948).

[2] Meir Berlin (later Bar-Ilan; Biog. Index, Vol. XIV). President, World *Mizrachi.*

[3] This early Cabinet crisis was largely resolved 24 June when the two ministers withdrew their resignations. That day the Government's action against *Irgun* was endorsed by the Council of State in Tel Aviv by 24 votes against 7, with 5 abstentions. Simultaneously, all armed organizations were proscribed, with the exception of *Haganah,* and steps were taken to re-organize the army on a unified basis (*Palestine Post,* 25 June 1948).

199. [1] See No. 196 and n. 2 there.

[2] See No. 201.

I do not know the circumstances, and as you will gather from my letter I am not well informed. I am greatly perturbed by their attitude.

There is nothing much to report from here, except that we are battling with the problem of recognition by the French. I have seen the Authorities, the Prime Minister, the Foreign Secretary and other Ministers.[3] They all solemnly promised to deal with the matter quickly, but I am sceptical.

With all the best wishes, I remain, as ever,

Affectionately yours,

Ch. Weizmann

200. To Meyer W. Weisgal, New York. *Paris, 25 June 1948*
English: T.W.: W.A.

My dear Meyer,

I was delighted to have got you on the phone, because I could not explain your silence. I am glad that you are back in New York, and I am looking forward to your next telephone communication on Monday.

I shall be leaving here on Tuesday, for Switzerland, going to Zurich first, where my address will be: c/o Walter Baer, Bergstrasse 54, just dodging the World Jewish Congress,[1] which will be sitting in Montreux. From July 6th onwards, my address will be: Grand Hotel et Righi Vaudois, Glion s/Montreux.

I am sending you a copy of a letter to Shertok, and that will give you an idea of what I think and what I feel.[2] I cannot say that I am terribly happy about what is going on, and I think that they are trying to bite off more than they can chew. Whether it is possible to put the brake on from here, I do not know.

I am looking forward to your letter which you are sending through Blumenfeld,[3] and meanwhile, I am sending you my best love.

As ever,

Yours,

Ch. Weizmann

---

[3] W.'s diary indicates meetings with Bidault, Foreign Minister, 7 June; Daniel Mayer, Labour Minister, 7, 18 June; Jules Moch, Interior Minister, 22 June; René Mayer, Defence Minister, 11 June; Robert Schuman, Premier, 26 June. He also had at least three meetings with Blum, 5, 7, 19 June.

200. [1] The Second Plenary Session of World Jewish Congress, under leadership of Wise and Goldmann, was due to open 27 June at Montreux.

[2] See No. 201.

[3] Joseph ('Ossinka') Blumenfeld (Biog. Index, Vol. V). Brother-in-law of V.W., he was a chemist acting for W. in development of various processes.

P.S. Please do not forget about the tea, and if you have a good opportunity send a supply of American cigarettes, Philip Morris and partly Pall Mall. But do not send it by post. Also, kindly ask Joseph [Cohn] to get me a few refill cartridges for my pen, which is a Norman ball-pen.

201. To Moshe Shertok, Tel Aviv.   *Paris, 26 June 1948*
English: T.W.: I.F.M. 2449/150414.

My dear Moshe,

I am most grateful to you for your letter.[1]

I had a long talk with Fisher,[2] who gave me an idea of what is going on in the country. Of course, I fully realize how difficult it must be to get things going, with the enemy at the gate and internal frictions. Neither the *Irgun* nor the *Mizrachi* appreciate the great harm which they are doing to the integrity of the State. One can expect little from the *Irgun,* but I thought that the *Mizrachi* might know better. I was particularly disturbed by the outside intervention of Rabbi Berlin, and I am sure that he [*sic*] will not allow the party bosses to run the Government.

With regard to the Presidency, I am in full agreement with you, that the American model would not suit our conditions, but I do not think that the French model is more desirable. I think that the middle course approximates to the Czech model. I am not thinking of it because I may have to serve as President, but more as a general proposition, in the interest of the State. There must be some institution not torn by party strife, and which stands above them.

I am somewhat disturbed about some remarks in your letter to Goldmann, concerning the boundaries and, particularly Jerusalem.[3] If we try to press for revision, we open the door to all sorts of intrigues and we may lose everything. I have recently had word—which is supposed to be a message from the President of the U.S.—that he adheres to the boundaries, as they emerged from the discussions in the U.N.O. It would be a great mistake, for which we might have to pay heavily, if we reopen now the question. I quite agree that the Christian world has not shown much piety with regard to

201. [1] 20 June (W.A.), replying to Nos. 182–84, 187.

[2] On 25 June, upon the latter's return from Israel.

[3] Possibly relates to the State Council's view that Jerusalem was under jurisdiction of the Jewish Government (see Ben-Gurion, *op. cit.,* p. 182). According to the U.N. Partition Resolution it was to be internationalised, but it had been cut off from food and other supplies, bombarded by the Arab Legion, and under siege. The Jews had opened a road to Jerusalem, relieving the New City, in April.

Jerusalem, but if we tamper with the status of Jerusalem, we shall render ourselves guilty in the eyes of the very same Christian world of disobeying the resolutions of the U.N.O., and whatever they might overlook in the case of the Moslems, they will not do in our case. We must press for the internationalisation of the city, and possibly Bernadotte might be helpful. But I am really fearful of opening up new questions, which may come to fall outside the decisions of the U.N.O.

This again applies to the problem of Western Galilee, which is outside the boundaries as adjudicated to us. As much as I would like to see it incorporated in the Jewish State, I think one has to go very slowly. On the other hand, I agree with B.G., that the Negeb and Akaba are all-important. Moreover, this has been assigned to us at Lake Success, and we should therefore keep it. If Western Galilee does not contain any Arabs, it will come into Jewish hands in due course. Of course, one must guard against the danger of having it ceded to the Lebanon. In brief, I am very fearful of revising too much.

I hope you will find the work of Bernadotte satisfactory.[4] I am afraid that Fisher has grave misgivings, but he may be unduly pessimistic. Fisher also mentioned that your department is not sufficiently staffed for the enormous quantity of work which has fallen to it. I wonder whether it is not worth your while trying to obtain some assistance from the U.S. I think if David Ginsburg would be invited to come to Israel, and offered a suitable position, he might be willing to accept, and he would be invaluable. The same might be true about Linton. I do not think he relishes the prospect of staying in London.

I have just seen Mr. Blumel,[5] who has returned from Israel, on a whole very pleased with what he has seen. He expressed very high admiration for B.G. and yourself, also for some of your other colleagues. But the main criticism which he has made was that the regime is still very much influenced by party views. You will remember that I mentioned the same thing in one of my letters to you, warning against the "key" principle.[6] I need not tell you that even the Russian Government has abandoned this system. I hope that this advice will be taken to heart, and I may be forgiven for offering too much criticism. I am not doing so in any carping spirit.

I was also informed that there is a considerable opposition to

---

[4] The U.N. Mediator was about to draw up his proposals for a final settlement of the Palestine question.

[5] André Blumel (Biog. Index, Vol. XXII). Lawyer, close to Blum; President of French Zionist Federation 1955–60.

[6] See No. 179.

the Government, and I believe that the main reason is due to what I have stated above.

My stay here is coming to an end, and I shall be leaving for Switzerland next Tuesday, the 29th. We shall stay at the Grand Hotel et Righi Vaudois, at Glion s/Montreux.

There was only one important problem which I was trying to solve here; namely the recognition of Israel by France. The example of France is very important for the rest of Western Europe and even England. I have seen Prime Minister Schuman, the Foreign Secretary, and other Ministers.[7] They were lavish and generous in their promises and in their expressions of sympathy for Israel. But so far, I have received no definite commitment when the recognition will take place. There are two important reasons responsible for the delay: the attitude of England and the Arabs of North Africa. The best I could do after having spoken to everybody was to hand the matter over to the care of Mr. Samuel Spanien,[8] whose name is, no doubt, familiar to you in connection with the trial of Mr. Blum.[9] He is a highly competent and respected person. He has good contacts with the Government and he is a good Zionist. I did all that on the advice of Mr. Blum and our other friends here.

My letter is getting unduly long, and I better conclude it for today in the hope that I shall have more time in Switzerland and write to you again.

Fisher tells me that you are overworked and I am not surprised, but you must really—in the interest of the State—take a holiday, if it is only a short one. And it must not be a busman's holiday, but a real one. In the end it will economise time and effort, and do not let yourself run down too low. You had a great deal [*sic*] in Lake Success and the present effort comes on top of it.

Much love from both of us to you all.

As ever,
Yours,
Ch. Weizmann

[7] See No. 199, n. 3.

[8] Son of Joseph Spanien, pioneer of French Zionism (Biog. Index, Vol. VI).

[9] After the fall of France in 1940, Blum was indicted by the Vichy Government on charges of war guilt and was brought to trial at Riom. Due to his brilliant defence the trial was suspended, though Blum remained in prison until 1945.

202. To Doris May, London.   *Paris, 27 June 1948*
English: Or. Copy. T.W.: W.A.

My dear Miss May,

Ever so many thanks for your kind letters and the various enclosures.[1] Our stay here is coming to an end. It was a somewhat hectic time and I shall be glad to get to Switzerland. We are leaving on Tuesday morning.

I have had a long letter from Meyer, mostly about the book, and I enclose a copy of a proposal which Meyer is making for an epilogue, to be written by me. It is a terrible nuisance. He wants about 3000 to 5000 words.[2]

Do you think you could enlarge and fill out the framework which he has produced? Do not write a text, I shall have to do it myself, but just expand the facts a little more. I do not remember them all, but I am sure you will. For instance, he speaks about two trips to America, and for the life of me I do not remember the dates. Perhaps you could enlighten me on it.

There is nothing to report from here and I remain,

Affectionately yours,

Ch. Weizmann

203. To Meyer W. Weisgal, New York.   *Paris, 27 June 1948*
English: T.W.: W.A.

My dear Meyer,

You need not apologize for the length of your letter.[1] Your letters are always interesting and full of meat.

I am sorry that I cannot do very much to help you in your troubles, but what would life be for you if there were no troubles; you have to invent them.

I am glad to read that you see some daylight in your attempts to get an agreement between the various prima donnas.[2]

---

202. [1] Her letters 20, 24 June (W.A.), reported incidental news from London and had enclosed Shertok's letter to Goldmann mentioned in No. 201.

[2] See No. 203 and n. 4 there.

203. [1] 23 June (W.A.).

[2] Weisgal spoke of his preoccupations in publication and serialisation of W.'s memoirs, which involved a number of conflicting interests: Harpers, the *New York Herald Tribune*, the Yiddish-language *Jewish Daily Forward, Haaretz,* Hamish Hamilton, Macmillan, and Watt, the literary agent.

Can you tell me whether you have been giving some thought to the formation of the foundation,[3] which would deal with the fees coming in from all this enterprise. I understand that the money would not go to me, but to the foundation. Perhaps in your next letter you might let me know something about it.

What you say about acknowledgments is only too true, and there are three people I would like to mention: yourself, Maurice Samuel and Miss May, and there is also a dedication to Mrs. Weizmann and perhaps to the memory of Michael Weizmann. I do not know whether you can combine these two, but Harper would advise you.

The epilogue business is rather a nuisance,[4] coming as it does now, on top of a heavy period, and I shall have to see what I can do in the holidays. Well, I shall try to deliver something in time to be embodied in the book. Whether it shall be printable I cannot guarantee. I shall send you the material when it is ready. I think I have answered all your questions.

There is nothing much to report from here from the political front. I have been trying hard to see whether the French Government would recognize Israel, but so far nothing much has happened. They all speak very sweetly, but there is no performance. I think they are frightened of England and of the Arabs.

I shall be leaving here on Tuesday the 29th, staying a few days in Zurich, so as to escape the World Jewish Congress, and then going on to Glion over Montreux.

When are you likely to come out to Europe or to Israel? We intend to go there in September. My great trouble is that I do not see any vehicle which could carry me there. There are practically no boats going, and if there is a boat, there is a risk of running into the Egyptian blockade. I can only travel in a pressurized plane. For the present they have stopped circulating between Paris and Israel. I hope they will begin again in September. You might make discrete inquiries whether we could not get a destroyer or a pressurized plane from America.

I think the appointment of McDonald and the whole behaviour of the President are a splendid encouragement. The trouble here is Great Britain, but I believe they cannot persist in their attitude very much longer.

[3] The Weizmann Foundation. See No. 100.

[4] Weisgal had suggested subjects for W. to touch upon in his epilogue, covering the period following the U.N. Resolution of Nov. 1947.

I am afraid my letter is dull, but I do not have very much to say at present, except to send you very much love, also on behalf of Mrs. Weizmann, for you and your family.

As ever,
Yours,
Ch. Weizmann

204. To Josef Cohn, New York.   *Zurich,*[1] *30 June 1948*
English: T.: W.A.

Please inform Weisgal, Eban, Ginsburg, Judge Rosenman am greatly disturbed by rumors about change frontiers under British pressure. We must on no account agree to it. Wire situation[2] Bergstrasse 54. Regards.

Chaim Weizmann

205. To Sir Reginald Coupland, Oxford.   *Zurich, 6 July 1948*
English: Or. Copy. T.W.: W.A.

My dear Professor Coupland,

It was very good of you to send me this note,[1] which I appreciate deeply. You need not have felt any qualms about writing. Neither you nor we are to take the responsibility for Mr. Bevin's deeds. His time will come and it won't be easy for him. I would not like to bear the burden of his conscience. I am not sure yet when I shall come to England. It is not easy for me to do so before the British Government has recognized Israel. I have a feeling, however, that this recognition is not far away. As soon as it takes place I shall come to England—if only for a day or two.

My address here remains until further notice "Hotel Righi

---

204. [1] The Weizmanns left Paris for Switzerland the previous day.

[2] The British were believed to be behind Bernadotte's views as described in Bridgenote preceding No. 189 and No. 215, n. 2. Cohn replied 2 July (W.A.) that in response to W.'s plea Rosenman was to see Truman that day; Eban would be writing a detailed report; Ginsburg was about to fly to Zurich to see W.; and Weisgal would 'spread the word' among U.S. Jewish leaders. Moreover, Bartley Crum had immediately made strong representations through his channels, emphasizing the resentment of the Christian world at suggestions that the special status of Jerusalem be altered.

205. [1] Coupland's note of congratulations, undated and written in pencil, was delivered to W. by Isaiah Berlin (W.A.).

Vaudois, Glion sur Montreux." Are you contemplating coming out here for a short time? I can promise you a very good time indeed. We are both sending you our fondest love and remain,

In old friendship, yours,

Ch. Weizmann

206. To Harry S. Truman, Washington.   *Glion, 7 July 1948*
English: Or. Copy. T.W.: W.A.

My dear Mr. President,

Let me first thank you most heartily for your very kind reference to myself, which I find quoted in your message to the Pittsburgh Zionist Convention.[1] It was very generous of you to say these things and to express your good wishes. I need hardly say that this is reciprocated by a great many Jews throughout the world.

I take the liberty of addressing you most respectfully on a few points which seem to me of importance.

a)   From all the news which has been reaching me in the last few weeks, and it came from authentic sources,[2] it was quite clear that the Foreign Office (and I say advisedly the Foreign Office and not the British Government) has spared no effort to hinder the coming into being of the young Jewish State. I am not sure why this policy has been pursued by the British Foreign Office and what are the reasons at the back of it. But the fact is incontestable.

I now hear that there is some change of heart and that they have reached the conclusion in London that the Jewish State has come to stay and that the Arab attacks have ended in a dismal failure.

b)   Instead of annihilation they are now planning amputation. It is constantly being mooted in the press that the Negeb ought to go to the Egyptians.

We all gratefully remember how much you have contributed towards the incorporation of the Negeb into the Jewish State. I believe that an indication on the part of the American Government to the British Authorities in favour of the Negeb remaining within the Jewish State would go a long way towards stopping the propaganda for the detaching of the Negeb from the State of Israel.

c)   There is one more point to which I am anxious to draw your attention. I would like to enclose a telegram which our foreign min-

---

206. [1] Z.O.A. Annual Convention, 3 July. Truman recalled his recognition of Israel as 'one of the proudest moments of my life' and mentioned the privilege of welcoming its President to the White House (W.A.).

[2] See, e.g., Ginsburg's report to W., 1 July (W.A.).

ister, Mr. Shertok, has addressed to our representative in the United States.[3] It is quite possible that this telegram already came to your notice. It is self-explanatory and there is little doubt about the authenticity of its contents. The last paragraph seems to indicate that even after the truce efforts will be made to renew the troubles in the new State.

If I may venture a suggestion, I believe that an effective way to counteract these machinations would be an instruction to your representatives in the various Arab States that they should make it clear to the Authorities that the United States views with disfavour these hostilities towards Israel.

I am certain that such an instruction, if couched in appropriate terms, would go a long way towards neutralizing the activities of various agents responsible for disturbing the peace.

It is fortunate that Mr. James McDonald is already in Israel or would be there very soon. I am quite sure that he could be very helpful in this respect and know that you will hear from him very soon a full report of the situation.

I apologize for the length of my letter and for worrying you with these troubles, but I am anxious that the young State of Israel should have a fair chance, and I am emboldened to take this step, knowing your intrinsic sympathy and sense of justice.[4]

I beg to remain, my dear Mr. President,

Respectfully yours,
Ch. Weizmann

207. To Aubrey Eban, New York. *Glion, 9 July 1948*
English: Or. Copy. T.W.: W.A.

My dear Aubrey,

I have read your report with great interest.[1] Before it came into my hands, I wrote a letter to the President, of which I enclose a copy.[2] It does not cover all the points which you have raised, but some at any rate, and it might prove helpful.

You will find my address on the head of this letter, and if and when I leave this place, letters will be forwarded. I would be grate-

---

[3] Untraced.

[4] No reply traced.

207. [1] W.A. The report was sent via Goldmann, 22 June, and W.'s copy was delayed. It summarized the position at U.N. and British intentions regarding territorial concessions by Israel.

[2] See No. 206.

ful to receive communication from you directly, however compressed it may be, and not via Goldmann or anybody else. Mr. Goldmann is always travelling and as postman is not too reliable.

I was interested to read your opinion about the Count.[3] I have never seen or heard anything about him except that he was negotiating on friendly terms with our old friend Mr. Himmler,[4] and that was enough to put me against him. I think I am not mistaken if I say that he is just a stooge of the British, and unless one presses him hard, I am afraid harder than Moshe [Shertok] is likely to do, he will do us no good, because unfortunately his opinion may carry some weight with the UNO. Happily, McDonald may act as an antidote. I have heard something about McDonald's desire of coming to see me before he definitely goes out.[5] I do not know his address, neither do I know what his plans are. But it would be most desirable to arrange for such a meeting. Please telegraph to me on receipt of this letter. I hope that you and Mrs. Eban are very well and that you are not overworking in the American heat. Once more I beg of you to keep me posted even if it is only a short bulletin.

All my best wishes to both of you,

Yours ever,

208. To Moshe Shertok, Tel Aviv.   *Glion, 9 July 1948*
English: T.W.: I.F.M. 1854.

My dear Moshe,

I am still awaiting the promised report.[1] I thought that at present, while the truce is on,[2] you may have a little freer time, but that

[3] Eban wrote that the key to the situation lay in the degree of British influence upon Bernadotte, and that his apprehensions regarding the Mediator were shared by U.N. Secretary-General Trygve Lie. The general feeling was that the Mediator was likely to recommend Jewish concessions to the Arabs, unless Israel impressed him with a sense of firmness or America would act as counter-balance to British pressure.

[4] In the final weeks of the war Bernadotte sought to mediate between Germany and the Allies. Himmler met him 24 Apr. 1945 without Hitler's knowledge. The mediation proved abortive, due to Allied insistence upon unconditional surrender, but Bernadotte obtained release of 20,000 Scandinavians (Jews among them) and thousands of Jewish women, from German camps in exchange for German prisoners in Sweden (Bernadotte, *The Curtain Falls*, 1945).

[5] See No. 209, n. 2.

208. [1] See Shertok to W., 20 June (W.A.), undertaking to keep W. fully informed of political developments, especially the negotiations with Bernadotte.

[2] The truce was to terminate 8 July. The Mediator was unable to obtain agreement by both sides to an extension, and fighting broke out again that day. After ten days of renewed hostilities, during which Israel improved her military position, both sides consented to the new truce ordered by the Security Council, effective from 18 July.

does not seem to be the case, and I shall possess my soul in patience a little longer, but not too much longer. You no doubt have a number of good secretaries to whom you could easily dictate a long statement. I only wish to know the facts and can draw my own conclusions.

At present, I have to rely on crumbs of information coming through Goldmann or Aubrey. I consider it not good enough.

There is very little to report from here. I have tried my best in France to get them to recognise our State, but they seem to be reluctant for two reasons: There is always the Arab argument which is valid for French North Africa, but I am certain that the greater hindrance is the relentless British pressure. The British realize that once the French have recognised it would promptly be followed by "Benelux" countries and by Italy, and this would isolate England.

Goldmann is always optimistic when he returns from London, but to be quite frank, I am not prepared to share this optimism. He is in London just now, and I am eager to hear what news he is going to bring. There will be no recognition until the truce is over, and that may last some time.

Meanwhile I am anxious to hear something about the progress of the constitutional project.[3] Will you be good enough to ask Leo[4] to send me a rough draft if he has produced one. I am going into a few weeks' vacation, and it is a wonderful opportunity to study such dull writings as constitutions. My advice would be not to produce a fully fledged constitutional project but have for the time being something very general which would serve as a guide in the first two years, and let experience teach us what is the best form suitable to our conditions. We shall have for the first ten years a very heterogeneous population coming from all corners of the earth, and it will not be easy to assemble them under the cover of one constitution, which shall be drawn up now after such a short time of our existence. It is quite possible that the very same ideas have crossed your mind, and you may take mine for what they may be worth.

We have been discussing here with some Swiss friends[5] the project of a loan, but there are not many details available: how and on what objects the money is to be spent, and it will be essential to give some information to that effect when the larger banking houses in this and other countries are approached.

I think Kaplan ought to prepare a full memorandum indicating in large features how he proposes to spend the money. I am quite

[3] I.e., a draft constitution for the State.
[4] Leo Kohn (Biog. Index, Vol. XI). Political secretary of J.A., Jerusalem 1935–48; political adviser to W. 1948–52.
[5] Walter Baer and his circle of banking associates.

sure that such questions will be asked. I understand that the banks are on a whole sympathetic, and some of the Jewish public here would participate in such a loan generously, which is all to the good. I have not got the faintest idea how much money you wish to borrow and what are the interests which the Government is prepared to pay. But I am sure that Kaplan will have the necessary information at the disposal of his agents here.

In conclusion, I would like to give you a few indications concerning my own movements: I am now going to Glion s/Montreux et Hotel Righi Vaudois. I would like to stay there until the end of August and probably proceed to France in preparation for the Assembly, which is taking place mid-September. I do not know whether it is necessary for me to stay for the Assembly proper. That is probably not the case. I would therefore try and leave for Israel at the end of September, arriving there about the Eve of *Rosch Haschanah*,[6] which, I believe, is October 3rd. Of course there may be changes, depending upon political circumstances, but this is roughly the plan I would like to adhere to. I send you all my best wishes and do please find time to write. Corresponding with you is like bombarding an invisible enemy.

All the best,

Yours ever,
Ch. Weizmann

209. To Meyer W. Weisgal, New York.   *Glion, 9 July 1948*
English: T.W.: W.A.

My dear Meyer,

I was very happy to receive your letter,[1] which as usual is full of news. I read with a certain amount of scepticism your remark about Eban's intention to write a long political report. This has become a stereotyped formula which a) is never carried out and b) I detest.

Usually it ends in a copy of a letter to Mr. Goldmann and I have to pick up the crumbs from his table. This is also true for the gentlemen in Israel and I shall have to change all that. I would be de-

---

[6] The Jewish New Year.

209. [1] This, 1 July (W.A.), dealt primarily with the Weizmann Foundation and the intention for it to receive all proceeds from royalties on W.'s autobiography, perhaps for the creation of a permanent memorial at Rehovot in the name of Michael W.

Emanuel Neumann and Abba Hillel Silver, Jewish Agency leaders, during the U.N.
deliberations on the Palestine problem in New York.

May 13, 1948

The President
The White House
Washington, D. C.

Dear Mr. President:

The unhappy events of the last few months will not, I hope,
obscure the very great contributions that you, Mr. President, have
made toward a definitive and just settlement of the long and troublesome Palestine question. The leadership which the American government
took under your inspiration made possible the establishment of a
Jewish State, which I am convinced will contribute markedly toward a
solution of world Jewish problems, and which, I am equally convinced
is a necessary preliminary to the development of lasting peace among
the peoples of the Near East.

So far as practical conditions in Palestine would permit,
the Jewish people there have proceeded along the lines laid down in
the United Nations Resolution of November 29, 1947. Tomorrow mid-
night, May 15th, the British Mandate will be terminated, and the
Provisional Government of the Jewish State, embodying the best endeavors of the Jewish people and arising from the Resolution of the
United Nations, will assume full responsibility for preserving law
and order within the boundaries of the Jewish State; for defending
that area against external aggression; and for discharging the obligations of the Jewish State to the other nations of the world in
accordance with international law.

Considering all the difficulties, the chances for an
equitable adjustment of Arab and Jewish relationship are not unfavorable. What is required now is an end to the seeking of new
solutions which invariably have retarded rather than encouraged a
final settlement.

It is for these reasons that I deeply hope that the
United States, which under your leadership has done so much to
find a just solution, will promptly recognize the Provisional Government of the new Jewish State. The world, I think, would regard it
as especially appropriate that the greatest living democracy should
be the first to welcome the newest into the family of nations.

Respectfully yours,

Chaim Weizmann

A letter to Truman, No. 154.

lighted to see McDonald[2] and I am not so sure that questions of protocol are involved. However he knows best. Thank you for giving me all the information about the foundation, and I have nothing but to express my satisfaction regarding it.

About the plan of creating a memorial for Michael: I am in full agreement with it in principle, but as you rightly say, the form of it will depend largely upon the amount of money which will be available when the book appears. Incidentally, I would like to ask you whether there is much in the book concerning Mr. Churchill, his relations with us, and particularly with me personally. I am asking this question because Mr. Churchill's book has just appeared,[3] and there is not a single word in it either about Zionism or about Palestine or about his various negotiations with me throughout these years. It is no doubt a studied omission; possibly something may appear in his other volumes, but I doubt it. Should my supposition be true, I think I ought to say something about it in the epilogue. It will no doubt produce an outburst on the part of Winston, but I really do not care. Please advise me on the matter.[4] I have naturally not received Mr. Robinson's[5] formula,[6] and that is gone the way of all promises. Will you please point out to Aubrey with all my respect and affection, that I rather will have no promises at all than broken ones. They are not a stable Government yet. Still they have learnt the art of breaking their word, as if they were very old established Governments. It would be excellent if you could come over for a few days here before definitely going over. You must bear in mind that we shall be moving on to Israel at the end of September.

Regarding the acknowledgments, I think they could best be covered by a few sentences in the preface. When do you want the preface written?

The question of my transport to Palestine is a very serious one. You have read recently that the Egyptians have attacked a boat[7] which was carrying food to Palestine, and nobody seems to protest

[2] Questions of protocol arose regarding McDonald's contemplated visit to W. en route to his assignment as U.S. representative in Israel. W. had yet to be sworn in as President and was still residing abroad.

[3] The first volume of Churchill's study of W.W.II, *The Gathering Storm*. Two later volumes contained favourable references to Zionism.

[4] See Weisgal to W., 13 July (W.A.), advising that he considered reference to Churchill's omission in the epilogue as unnecessary.

[5] Jacob Robinson (1889–1977). Jurist, diplomat, historian; legal adviser to delegation of J.A., and later Israel, to U.N. 1948–57.

[6] On the powers of the President. The formula was to be embodied in Kohn's draft constitution.

[7] On 11 July Cairo announced that a unit of the Egyptian Navy had intercepted a sailing vessel bearing arms and *matériel* en route from Cyprus to Tel Aviv, and brought it to Gaza (*Haaretz*, 12 July 1948).

against this piracy. I would certainly advise our people to raise it with the State Department. Therefore I am somewhat worried about my own transport. Dave Ginsburg, when he was here, told me something about corvettes, which we are supposed to have in the Mediterranean, manned and armed. One could either go by them or they could accompany any ship carrying us. But I have no knowledge of any details, and it may be as well to ascertain them and let me know. There is not too much time to waste.

And will you kindly get in touch with Dave, who will be back in the States by now. Find out the details and whether such a corvette could meet me in Marseilles. Otherwise one would have to make other arrangements. Bear in mind that I cannot fly!

I am troubling you with all these questions, which are really the business either of Aubrey or of Eliahu [Epstein]. But I am sure that they are too highly placed for my liking, and I prefer to deal with a common citizen.

My love to you and Shirley and to the children from both of us,

As ever, yours,

Ch. Weizmann

210. To Joseph I. Linton, London.   *Glion, 11 July 1948*
English: T.W.: W.A.

My dear Ivor,

Many thanks for your letter.[1] Goldmann spoke to me last night, after he had seen the people at the Foreign Office. He reports a change of heart and a desire to be helpful. Why this should suddenly happen, I do not know. But let us hope he is right. He tells me that the British have definitely informed the Arabs that they are not going to support them if the hostilities continue. As the Arabs are very short of ammunition, hostilities would really stop if the British stopped supplies. I hope that they will do it. I never could understand what good it does to anybody to have the Arabs assassinating innocent people in Palestine for no reason at all. However all that is inscrutable. Goldmann tells me he is going to stay a whole week in London, and then go on to Palestine for the meeting of the A.C.[2] Why they should be running about is also incomprehensible to me. It is a godless waste of money, of which we have not too much. Yesterday, I was told by a very reliable man[3] a story of horrid waste.

---

210. [1] 5 July (W.A.), reporting on discussions with F.O. officials.

[2] The A.C., or Z.G.C., was the ruling body of W.Z.O. in intervals between Zionist Congresses.

[3] Unidentified.

If this fellow were not so reliable I would certainly not believe it, because the waste seems to go into thousands of Pounds, and responsible for it are young men, Moshe's bright boys.[4] Whether they are so bright I do not know, but they certainly get through a considerable amount of public money. When I get to Palestine, I will try to know a little more about it and—if possible—stop it.

How are things in London? Is there really any chance of recognition by England, as Goldmann seems to think? I shall be glad to hear a little more precise information. Martin should be able to throw some more light on it. Will you please remember me to him very kindly when you speak to him next.

I remain,
Affectionately yours,
Ch. Weizmann

211. To Doris May, London.   *Glion, 11 July 1948*
English: Or. Copy. T.W.: W.A.

My dear Miss May,

Many thanks for your note.[1] I shall be glad if you could ascertain from Nathan[2] what it is all about.[3] It has probably nothing to do with me, but he wants something, if I know him well. I am glad that there is no news. From various sources I hear that Aubrey Eban is writing me a long report. It must be very long indeed, because so far weeks have passed, and there is no sign of this report.

Since we became a Government, we have learnt the art of procrastination. Let me know what is doing in London. Here the weather seems to have made up its mind to improve somewhat. I hope it will last.

All the best to you,

With kind regards,
Yours,
Ch. Weizmann

---

[4] Nothing known of such allegations of waste, nor which of Shertok's personnel are referred to.

211. [1] Written on 7 July (W.A.).

[2] Lord Nathan (Biog. Index, Vol. XVII). Lawyer and politician; Minister of Civil Aviation 1946–48. Legal adviser to Zionist institutions.

[3] Nathan's contemplated visit to W. (specific purpose not stated) was postponed on being informed that W.'s doctors had forbidden visitors for several weeks (Miss May to Nathan, 7 July, W.A.).

212. To Samuel I. Rosenman, New York.   *Glion, 11 July 1948*
English: T.W.: W.A.

My dear Judge Rosenman,

I should have written to you before really, but there is nothing sensational here. All the news come from your side and it was not much either, since we parted.[1]

I hear from Josef[2] that you consider the situation satisfactory, and that is all to the good. The main object which is in danger are the frontiers. The press in England is constantly harping on the tune that the Negeb has to be given to the Arabs, which really means to the British. And they will no doubt bring forward this plan at the next meeting of the Assembly, and may succeed unless there is American counter-pressure. You know they are relentless and will not sit quiet either until they have achieved their object, or until they are definitely convinced that there is no hope of achieving such object. The latter case may only be if the Americans tell them, quite strongly, that they should leave their hands off this matter.

I have written on the subject to the President quite briefly,[3] and I hope that he will bear it in mind, particularly as he was so helpful in securing for us the proper frontier. Things in Palestine are still in a dangerous state, and unless the Security Council issues a definite warning to the Arab States that sanctions will be taken against them, the trouble will always continue. The worst offender is Egypt, because they are so full of their own troubles (famine, disease, etc.) that they use Palestine as a diversion, and again, the only way of preventing them from continuing is a severe admonition on the part of the Authorities of the UNO.

There is nothing further I have to report from here except perhaps letting you know what my movements are. I shall be staying in Switzerland until [it] is time to go to Israel, which I think is to be at about mid-September. But of course a great deal depends upon political developments which are still hidden in the future.

I hope all is well with you and Mrs. Rosenman, and I presume that you will be taking a holiday somewhere where it is cooler than New York.

I remain, with many kind regards to both of you,

Yours very sincerely,

Ch. Weizmann

---

212. [1] When W. left the U.S. in May.

[2] Cohn cabled 9 July (W.A.) that he and Eban, at a discussion with Rosenman upon the latter's return from his weekly meeting with Truman, had received a most encouraging report.

[3] See No. 206.

213. To Elias Schein,[1] Bucharest. *Glion, 11 July 1948*

French: T.W.: W.A.

Dear Schein,

It is with the greatest of pleasure that I have read your good wishes and I thank you very much.[2] I remember our peregrinations in Rumania,[3] and the fears which tormented us that anti-Semitic students would attack our train.

Despite all that, I have very pleasant memories, above all of our visit to Kishinev.[4]

How is everything with you? Are you able to work and follow your profession? I am in Switzerland for a few weeks, after which I intend returning to Israel. Perhaps we will meet there. I would be very happy if we could.

In the meantime, I send you my very best wishes, and I hope that you will soon be able to be with us.

With all good wishes,

Yours very sincerely,

Ch. Weizmann

214. To Aubrey Eban, New York. *Glion, 12 July 1948*

English: Or. Copy: T.W.: W.A.

Dear Aubrey,

Your letter, which has been announced so often, has not come yet and there is no reason for me to write to you at all after such behaviour except for the urgency of letting you know the contents of Linton's letter,[1] which seems to me very grave. Whether you are able to do anything with it, I do not know. I would have written

---

213. [1] Served as W.'s secretary during his visit to Rumania in 1927.

[2] 27 June (W.A.), congratulating W., and referring to hopes of visiting Israel in the near future; for this 'I beg you to help us.'

[3] In 1927 the antisemitic student leader, Corneliu Codreanu, formed the Archangel Michael League, precursor of the Iron Guard, which instituted attacks upon synagogues.

[4] For W.'s visit to Rumania, and threats from antisemitic students, see Vol. XIII, Nos. 299, 305.

214. [1] See No. 215 and ns. 1, 2 there.

myself to the President but I cannot do it now because I have been telegraphing to him on various matters lately.[2]

With all good wishes,

Yours very sincerely,

215. To Joseph I. Linton, London.   *Glion, 12 July 1948*
English: T.W.: W.A.

My dear Ivor,

I have received your note[1] concerning the Bernadotte scheme,[2] which, of course, is something utterly inacceptable. If it is a result of

---

[2] Eban had transmitted a draft cable to W., via Weisgal, for despatch to Truman 11 July (W.A.). W. apparently sent the cable, although no record of its despatch has been traced. Eban's draft read: 'While I have not been able to consult with the Government of Israel, the urgent crisis of the hour compels me to address this personal appeal to you. By rejecting the extension of the truce and renewing their aggression, the Arab States have issued a challenge both to Israel and to all defenders of the peace. I pray that you may see the urgent necessity of extending full American recognition of Israel, modifying the embargo in favor of Israel's defense, and leading the United Nations towards the discharge of its responsibility for suppressing acts of aggression, thus earning the immortal gratitude of our people and the praise of all peace-loving men.'

215. [1] Linton's two communications of 5, 9 July (W.A.) referred to the Bernadotte proposals. The first spoke of likelihood that the Mediator's plan was the outcome of an Anglo-American agreement, and was possibly intended to safeguard British interests and strategic needs. The second noted that Bernadotte's long-term plans were not considered by at least some in Whitehall to have been either wise or timely.

[2] See Bridgenote preceding No. 189. Bernadotte's suggestions for the solution of the Palestine crisis included: 1) Palestine and Trans-Jordan to form a Union; 2) the boundaries of the Arab and Jewish areas to be determined by negotiation; 3) the Union to promote common economic interests, to operate and maintain common services, including customs and excise, to undertake development projects, and to coordinate foreign policy and measures for common defense; 4) these functions to be exercised through a Central Council; 5) subject to these provisions, each member of the Union to exercise full control over its own affairs; 6) immigration within its own borders to be within competence of each member of the Union for two years, after which immigration would have to be adjusted in terms of the common interests of the Union and, in the event of disagreement, could be determined by the binding decision of the U.N. Economic and Social Council according to the principle of economic absorptive capacity; 7) religious and minority rights to be guaranteed by U.N.; 8) the Holy Places to enjoy similar protection; 9) persons who, because of conditions created by the conflict in Palestine had left their normal places of abode, to have full liberty to return to their homes without restriction and to regain possession of their property.

In an annex Bernadotte proposed specific territorial changes, such as the inclusion of the Negev in Arab territory and Western Galilee in Jewish territory, inclusion of Jerusalem in Arab territory but with municipal autonomy for the Jewish community and special arrangements for the protection of the Holy Places, establishment of a free port at Haifa (including the oil refineries) and at Lydda airport, and consideration to be given to the status of Jaffa as an Arab enclave within the Jewish area.

an Anglo-American agreement, it makes it still worse. I am sending copy of your letter to Meyer [Weisgal], asking him to do all he can to stop these machinations. The only man who can stop it is the President himself.

I would have written to the President at once, but I prefer to wait a few days because I have just telegraphed to him on some other matter,[3] and I do not wish to worry him too much.

They will go on digging at us until there is nothing left of the Jewish State except Tel Aviv, and it seems to me that we are in for a hard struggle.

As ever yours,
Ch. Weizmann

216. To Samuel I. Rosenman, New York. *Glion, 12 July 1948*
English: T.W.: W.A.

My dear Judge Rosenman,

I regret very much the necessity of troubling you again, but the contents of the enclosed letter are self-explanatory.[1]

It is evident that the State Department will spare no trouble in order to destroy every hope of bringing into effect the resolution of 29.11.47, and it is largely depending upon the President to stop all these manoeuvres once and for all.

We really ought to be given a chance to begin our work and not always have to tremble for the existence of our small territory. I do beg of you to see the President and to explain to him how impossible life is made for us by these constant intrigues. It is like children pulling out a young plant in order to look at the roots.

Will you be so kind and let Josef know the result.[2] He would then telegraph to me.

I beg to apologize for the trouble once more, and remain with many thanks and kind regards to both of you,

Yours ever,
Ch. Weizmann

[3] See No. 214, n. 2.

216. [1] Linton to W., 5 July. See No. 215, n. 1.

[2] Rosenman replied 20 July (W.A.) that disturbing international events, marking the entry of the Cold War into a more acute phase over Berlin, made it seem that everyone was living on the edge of a precipice with the choice of war or peace 'perpetually out of our own hands'. As to Israel's security, he assured W. that he was seeing Cohn and Eban frequently, and they kept him apprised of developments.

217. To Meyer W. Weisgal, New York. *Glion, 12 July 1948*
English: T.W.: W.A.

Dear Meyer,

I beg to enclose a letter just received from Linton which gives an account of Bernadotte's proposals.[1] It looks bad and it is made still worse by the information that this is a result of Anglo-American agreements. I am quite certain that the President does not know anything about it, and he ought to be informed of it at once. Will you see to it that our distinguished representatives get a move on and do something. I am sending a copy of the same letter to Judge Rosenman with a note.

That is about all I can do from this side. Let me know what has happened.

All the best,

Affectionately yours,
Ch. Weizmann

218. To Lawrence Berenson,[1] New York. *Glion, 13 July 1948*
English: Copy. T.W.: W.A.

My dear Dutch,

Very many thanks for your letter and for the enclosures.[2] I have read Sumner Welles' letter with great interest. He seems to be rather disappointed that the Zionists have not paid more attention to his book,[3] which is very wrong of them.

The man to whom you should address yourself on this subject is not Cohn but Eban, who would probably do his best to see that the Zionists spread this book. I believe Neumann may be useful in this respect, and a word to him would do good.

My plans are changed for the time being, and I am waiting to hear of developments in England. There is some sensation on news concerning the attitude of the Arabs.[4] But probably you have read

---

217. [1] See No. 215, n. 1.

218. [1] Attorney. Represented W. in late 1920s in patent negotiations. Member of Z.O.A. Administrative Committee, he was the Zionists' main contact with Welles.

[2] 7 July (W.A.). Enclosed were copies of an exchange with Welles, and a letter to Congressman Claude Pepper, all of which are untraced.

[3] *We Need Not Fail*—see No. 192, n. 2.

[4] Ref. unclear. But the British Government announced 12 July that until the situation in Palestine had been clarified, and in particular the attitude of the Arabs to an extension of the truce, payment of the current quarterly subsidy of £500,000 to Transjordan for the Arab Legion would be suspended.

it in the American Press, and I shall wait for further confirmation without saying any more about it.

With very cordial regards and thanks for your letter,

Yours most sincerely,

Ch. Weizmann

219. To Ernst David Bergmann, Rehovot. *Glion, 14 July 1948*
English: Or. Copy. T.W.: W.A.

My dear David,

I don't know how letters go to Palestine, but I assume they arrive somehow if one writes them. Only those letters do not arrive which are never written, but I presume that since we are a Government you acquire all the characteristics of such, chiefly the negative ones.

The purpose of my writing concerns my voyage. It is true that I do not intend to travel until the last week in September, but seeing the speed with which things move on, one cannot begin too soon to worry about it. I understand that there are no boats going to Palestine, and if there were, the protocol demands that I should not go by them except if it is our own boat placed at my disposal. We have only the *Kedmah,* which is a nice little boat if it is washed and cleaned, but I am sure that I could not go on it without an escort, particularly through Egypt waters. The simplest thing would be to fly, but my state of health does not permit me to fly unless it is a Constellation. So here is the problem. I have discussed it with Remez when he was here, and he quite readily promised that everything will be in order, but I am somehow sceptical. I would therefore like you to be so good and get definite information and an undertaking that my transport will be arranged. I would also like to know whether it is correct to assume that if I go by boat it would be from Marseilles and by plane it would be from Geneva. The latter would certainly be the simplest, if one can get a pressurized plane.

There is one more matter I would like to put to you, namely: Could you come over here in September, and we shall return together? I shall be glad to hear from you without delay.

Looking forward to see you soon,

I remain, with much love, also from Mrs. Weizmann,

Yours very sincerely,

P.S. We are sending a copy of this letter to Goldberg in Paris because it might be forwarded quicker to you from there.

220. To Aubrey Eban, New York. *Glion, 14 July 1948*
English: T.W.: I.S.A. 93.03 (64/3).

My dear Aubrey,

I am extremely sorry to add to your burdens, which—I am afraid—are many, but I feel that there is nobody whom I could ask to go over this epilogue[1] and to fill out some of the missing data except you and possibly Meyer. I am therefore sending this material on to Meyer again, who will no doubt communicate with you; and between you two, you will settle the final text. I think it should not prove too difficult and time consuming. Needless to say that I am grateful in advance for all you may do in this matter, and I remain with best regards as ever

Yours very sincerely,
Ch. Weizmann

P.S.   I hear on all sides of the very excellent way in which you represent our cause in Lake Success. I have never doubted the fact that you will do so. Still it is good to hear a confirmation. I offer you my best congratulations and good wishes for further successful endeavour.

221. To James G. McDonald, Washington. *Glion, 15 July 1948*
English: T.: W.A.

Shall be happy meet you in Switzerland on your way Israel, first week August.[1] Kindly send timely information care of Doctor Erlanger,[2] Lucerne, Switzerland. Best regards.

Chaim Weizmann

222. To Hugo C. Heiman,[1] Haifa. *Glion, 16 July 1948*
English: Or. Copy. T.W.: W.A.

My dear Doctor Heiman,

I was very much moved by your kind message[2] and good wishes, which I gladly reciprocate. It is always a source of great satisfaction

---

220. [1] Of *T. and E.*—see No. 203, n. 4.

221. [1] That day Weisgal had cabled (W.A.) that the envoy-designate wished to see W., but for purposes of protocol W. should send an official invitation to State Department.
    [2] Lily Erlanger, W.'s secretary during the Swiss visit.

222. [1] B. 1896. Professor of Industrial Chemistry, Haifa Technion 1936–64; then professor emeritus.
    [2] Heiman had wired 25 May (W.A.) on the great honour W. had brought to the chemical profession.

to me to be connected with the Technion, which I am sure may look forward now to a rapid development. I believe it is essential that the new State should possess schools which in their scope and effectiveness must not fall behind any Swiss schools. We could do it; we have the forces to bring it about. I am sceptical whether our Government fully appreciates the value of high education for the State. I believe that Switzerland owes its flourishing of industry and agriculture primarily to its School system, and of course to the nature of the people, which is hard-working and law-abiding.

We have to conquer many deserts still and therefore intensify our scientific effort. I know that you are doing all you can in this direction, and I look forward to the time when we shall meet and discuss the problems of higher education.

I believe that in view of the peculiar situation which Jerusalem is likely to occupy in our State for a long time to come, a new University will have to be erected within the limits of the State. There is only one objection to it: it might be interpreted as if we renounce Jerusalem. But it can be made abundantly clear that that is not the case.

All these questions and many more will form the subject matter of a discussion which I would like to initiate with the representatives of our institutions of higher learning and of the Government.

Thanking you once more, I beg to remain, with kind regards,

223. To Aubrey Eban, New York.   *Glion, 18 July 1948*
English: Or. Copy. T.W.: W.A.

My dear Aubrey,

I was happy to receive your letter,[1] for which I was really waiting impatiently. I have also read part of your speech before the Security Council,[2] which is very impressive and no doubt will not fail to produce certain results. Nevertheless, I am somehow feeling that our situation is not stable until the following two things have happened:

1) Entry into the UNO as a member State;
2) Recognition by the French.

About the latter, I have been trying to do something while in Paris but, of course, it is a subject on which the local people have to work

---

223. [1] 10 July (W.A.). It was a survey of the situation at U.N., reviewing Eban's discussions with delegates and assessing Truman's current attitude.

[2] Eban informed the Security Council 16 July that Israel would comply with the cease-fire resolution, applying this also to Jerusalem, provided the Arab Governments did likewise.

steadily and systematically, and as you may know, these qualities are not to be found easily amongst our workers in Paris. They get enthusiastic and promise you the moon and the stars, but forget all about it as soon as you have turned your back. I am now sending them reminders. The only man who could really produce an effect is Mr. Blum. But, of reasons best known to himself, he is hesitant. It is quite true that he is not too well, but I am going to write to him again and ask him to make an effort. The longer one drags it out, the more difficult it becomes. Yesterday, I was informed that André Philip, a member of the French Political Commission, has gone specially to Israel to see how things stand, and that he had come back enthusiastic, willing to do his utmost to further the cause of recognition.[3] I shall try and find out a little more about it one of these days and let you know. That the French should be so much under the thumb of Mr. Bevin seems to me grotesque. All that he has done for the French was that he threw them out of Syria.[4] Still, from what I hear, it is not so much the Arabs of North-Africa, but Downing Street which is the cause of the inaction.

I could also write to Mr. Truman on this matter, but I did write to him a few days ago, asking him to warn the Arabs that they should stop their fighting, and I am reluctant to worry him with another matter. Nevertheless, I am prepared to do so if you send me a telegram to that effect.

There is nothing very much to report from here. All the interests are concentrating either in America or in Israel. Europe is a desert as far as we are concerned.

I propose to stay here—I mean in Switzerland, not necessarily in this hotel—for another few weeks, and I shall be glad and ready to move on to Palestine.

You write in your letter that you intend to be in England in August. I hope that you will come here for a few days. Then, we could talk over the whole situation better than we could do it in a letter.

I was informed that Robinson is drafting something of a constitution, and that he is sending me on the pages conc. the presidential duties and rights.[5] I shall be very curious to read it.

Will you kindly see that this is really done. I suppose the heat

---

[3] See Goldberg to W., 16 July (W.A.). Philip (b. 1902), a Socialist Deputy, had been Minister of Finance and of National Economy 1946–47.

[4] Due in large part to pressure from its British ally, France relinquished its claim to, and control of, Syria in 1946, ending a quarter century of direct French presence there.

[5] See No. 231 and n. 1 there.

is intense in the States, and you will be glad to finish with Lake Success and come into more clement surroundings.

Both Mrs. Weizmann and myself, we are sending to you both our affectionate regards, and I remain,

As ever yours,

224. To Léon Blum, Jovy-en-Josaz.   *Glion, 18 July 1948*
French: Or. Copy. T.W.: W.A.

My dear Friend,

Allow me to return once more to the question of France's recognition of the State of Israel. I am very worried by the delay because France's example of non-recognition is being followed by other Western countries, such as the Netherlands, Italy, etc.

This greatly harms our cause in the eyes of enemies such as Bevin and his Arabs. I would remind you that Jews the world over have always supported France, especially in time of crisis. Now, when we need a service which is so easy for France to give, we are refused a simple act of justice.

I am convinced that France's attitude will cause harm to both sides. I have been informed that our American friends are astonished to see the French Government take sides with our worst enemies— Bevin and his Arabs.

It is possible that France will one day need the support of Jewish public opinion, as has already been given twice in the past twenty years.

If recognition is not granted by September, it is possible that at the U.N. Assembly convened in Paris for September they will bring up modifications of the decision taken on 29.XI.1947, either by modifying our borders or by changing the content of the decision. I should point out to you that the young State of Israel will resist these efforts with all its force. They have already tried, firstly to assassinate us and then to amputate us. They didn't succeed, and they will not succeed in the future. But all of this produces tension and victims, and prevents the normal progress of a new State.

I can see no logic in France's attitude, unless it be Mr. Bidault's desire to please his friend Bevin at our expense. The only good thing that Mr. Bevin did for France was to get it out of Syria.

Therefore, my friend, I am begging you to do your best to encourage the French Government to give us the fundamental justice which it owes us.

I understand that Mr. André Philip went to Palestine for a few days and that he came back very enthusiastic and desirous of working on the Political Commission [of the French National Assembly] for recognition. I hope that this enthusiasm will not dwindle away too quickly, and that it will give some tangible results.

While I was in Paris, I charged Mr. Spanien (Loulou) with this whole affair, but I have heard nothing from him since. Perhaps you would be good enough to remind him. I am sure that he is capable of doing something, if he puts some energy into the affair. I forgot to tell him that we are prepared to give him all the money he needs if there are any expenses to be paid, provided that he arrives at a positive result as quickly as possible.

I hope that you and Mrs. Blum are well. We have been here for more than a week but, as yet, we haven't seen any sunshine. It's cold and damp, and my wife has unfortunately been ill for the past week.

Allow me to remind you once more that the problem I have described is urgent.

With all good wishes, I remain,

Yours sincerely,

225. To Abraham Goldberg, Paris.   *Glion, 18 July 1948*
English: T.W.: Photostat W.A.

My dear Goldberg,

I have received the enclosed letter from a certain Miss Henriques,[1] who apparently has done very good work in recovering some of the Jewish property and fortune of which our people have been deprived by the Germans during the last war. Judging from the letters, which she has sent in original written by the Joint and the *Fédération des sociétés juives de France,* she seems to be a competent person quite capable of continuing this good work if she is given some means, which apparently she has exhausted. I do not know to whom I could turn and therefore send you this note with a request to address yourself to the head of the above *Fédération.* Perhaps they could do something. I think the case is sufficiently important to warrant an effort. I beg of you not to let slide the affair. I do not know the lady at all, but judging from the testimonials it is a serious case deserving attention.

I now turn to another matter. From a letter which I have received

---

225. [1] Unidentified; her letter untraced. Goldberg promised support for her activities, within official limitations—his letter of 23 July (W.A.).

from America[2] it follows clearly that the recognition by France is a matter of importance. Of course you ought to understand that the Jewish State does not stand or fall with French recognition, and I believe that this action is as important for us as it will eventually be for the French. But apparently Mr. Bidault is so much under the influence of Bevin that he dare not take this step in spite of all the sympathy to which the French have given so much expression publicly. Sympathy is all very well, but the act of recognition is a deed of importance. It is essential that one should approach Blum at once, and that he should really take some trouble in this matter and not let it drag out endlessly. I know that many people are probably away this month, but the Government functions and Mr. Schuman[3] ought to be approached energetically, that he should give [an] order to Bidault to do what is necessary. Instead of Jarblum running away to Palestine at present, which he would do much better to postpone until after the heat season is over, he should concentrate on this subject. I understand that he is always meeting members of the French Cabinet. What is the good of all that if he can get no result. Again and again I repeat that French recognition is of importance *vis-à-vis* the Arabs, the Benelux Countries and even England.

Did you meet Spanien? What has he done? I shall be most grateful for a full report on this matter, and perhaps you will be good enough to send me Spanien's address. I shall write to him directly[4] and if Jarblum is still in Paris, will you tell him my opinion, which is not very flattering at the moment.

I remain, with best regards,

Yours very sincerely,
Ch. Weizmann

P.S. Enclosed copy of my letter which I just addressed to Mr. Blum.[5]

---

[2] In his letter of 10 July (W.A.), Eban reported being told by Parodi that British pressure alone was responsible for delay in French recognition.

[3] Robert Schuman (1886–1963). A founder of Roman Catholic *Mouvement républicain populaire* (M.R.P.); Prime Minister Nov. 1947–Sept. 1948; Foreign Minister 26 July 1948 (succeeding Bidault) until Dec. 1952.

[4] No such letter traced.

[5] See No. 224.

226. To Aubrey Eban, New York.   *Glion, 20 July 1948*
English: Or. Copy. T.W.: W.A.

My dear Aubrey,

I am grateful to you for yours of July 16th.[1] Meanwhile several important things have happened: the cease-fire has been accepted by both sides.[2] How long it will last is difficult to say. I was particularly glad to read your remarks about Bernadotte's remarks and his schemes.[3] Although I have never met the man, I am deeply prejudiced against him; and my only reason is his great friendship with Himmler. He is naturally in the tow of Mr. Bevin and his friends, and only yesterday there was a curious statement in the Swiss press that Bevin considers from now onwards the Germans as the most favoured nation. So Bevin and his friends, Bernadotte and his friends form a nice kettle of fish, which we should try and avoid like poison. I therefore was extremely happy to read of your stand against him. I have no doubt that attempts will be made at the next session of the UNO in September to reopen our question. And the more recognitions we can get from the Western Powers here, the more difficult we can make it for our enemies to try and revise.

I would like to utter a warning against the Galilee-Negeb exchange.[4] The two territories are not comparable. If Western Galilee is left alone to itself at present with so many Arabs having gone from it, it will in the course of time fall to us automatically, whereas the Negeb represents a vast territory—true, empty and desolate now—but with water can be made to hold a very considerable population. In fact it is the only empty place in Palestine to-day, and we must hold on to it for dear life.

I think President Truman understood it very well when I had the opportunity of talking to him about it, and we must see that he is kept well informed about it.

Incidentally, that touches also the problem of Akaba, on which, as you will remember, the President was very keen. I hope you will be in Europe soon and it would be wonderful if you could come over here. We might talk things over and prepare for the next meeting of the Assembly. Do not let Josef, who seems to be sticking on to the judge [Rosenman] as hard as he can, interfere too much at this stage.

---

226. [1] Acknowledging receipt of No. 214 (W.A.).

[2] It went into effect 18 July.

[3] Eban wrote that the fact that no Government would support Bernadotte's proposals, while both Israel and the Arabs rejected them, had had 'a chastening effect' on him. Eban and his colleagues hoped to enhance this effect by persistent pressure and criticism.

[4] Eban felt the only one of Bernadotte's proposals liable to U.S. endorsement was the Negev-Galilee exchange.

The judge is a nice man, but as you rightly say,[5] he knows too little to be very effective at present. I am warning Josef to keep his hands off.[6]

I have got a long report from him,[7] but it does not convey very much. When is the Security Council actually finishing?

I remain with affectionate regards,

Yours very sincerely,

Ch. Weizmann

227. To Josef Cohn, New York.   *Glion, 21 July 1948*

English: Or. Copy. T.W.: W.A.

Dear Josef,

Thank you for your note of July 16th and for the information contained therein.[1] Without wishing in any way to underrate your connection with the Judge, I am beginning to fear that there should be no interference with Aubrey's work. I am afraid that the Judge—with all my respect and affection for him—is not a match for Lovett, who knows too much and can always produce doubtful facts and specious arguments. I am acquainted with this sort of conversation from the days of Shuckburgh[2] in the Colonial Office. And this kind of officials are the same on both sides of the Atlantic. In fact, they are interchangeable.

I now understand that Henderson has gone as Ambassador to India. I hope he stays there a long time. Please let me know whether Dewey [Stone] has seen the President and what has happened.

I did not see Adele [Levy], and if she does not telephone here I have no intention of looking her up in Geneva.

With kind regards,

Yours sincerely,

---

[5] Of Rosenman's interventions with Truman, Eban stated that he appeared 'more willing than effective'.

[6] See No. 227.

[7] See No. 227, n. 1.

227. [1] W.A. This described Cohn's latest meeting with Rosenman, who was concerned with drafting the Palestine portion of the Democratic Party platform. Rosenman had discussed with Truman and Robert Lovett of State Department both *de jure* recognition of Israel and a lifting of the arms embargo, and subsequently reported that State Department in general would now be much more cooperative.

[2] Sir John Shuckburgh (Biog. Index, Vol. X). At C.O. from 1921, with responsibility for supervision of the Palestine Mandate.

P.S.   We are writing to Reva Ziff that she should send to me short statement conc. the £3000. For some reason, you only mention £2000 in your letter of the 6th inst.³ Could you please explain this to me?

228. To Ernst David Bergmann, Rehovot.   *Glion, 22 July 1948*
English: Or. Copy. T.W.: W.A.

My dear David,

I was delighted to receive your long letter of the 6 inst.¹ It has only arrived this morning. The airmail is obviously very slow.

I do not know what the reason is. I understand there is a direct mail once a week from Paris to Israel and return. But if you miss this some of the letters go via Egypt, and I shall not be surprised if they are tampered with.

At any rate yours has arrived, and I was glad to hear of the important program of work which we are pursuing. I do not know how long this truce will last, but it may give you a chance to catch your breath. I am somewhat worried about your handling so many explosives and cannot caution you enough not to take unnecessary risks.

A young man, Mr. Atlas,² rang me up yesterday. If I remember rightly he is one of Brailowsky's boys. He tells me he is here to buy things for us and I have asked him to come and see me next Sunday, because I am most anxious to hear all about our workshop. And if possible I propose to contact Brailowsky and extract from him some stuff for our workshop.³

I just sent you a telegram about Benji's joining the Citrus Board.⁴ I have also sent the same to Kaplan. Knowing Kaplan as I do, he will probably not be in a hurry either to do something or to answer. He is a very good fellow, but he always pleads being too busy, and that covers a multitude of sins. My experience is just the opposite: the busier a man is, the more careful he is in attending to his cor-

---

³ Relates to W.'s enquiry as to his personal funds. Cohn had stated that £5,150 was available for withdrawal in England, Israel or Switzerland. As to the discrepancy of £1,000 referred to here, see W. to Reva Ziff, 21 July. See also Cohn-W. exchange, 2, 6 July (all in W.A.).

228. ¹ W.A. This described morale in Israel during the truce and projects completed or undertaken by the Institute in connection with the war. These included production of light equipment and explosives, Chloramin T for use against mustard gas, and the manufacture of propellants in large quantities for mortars and rockets.

² Moses Atlas.

³ M. Brailowsky—see No. 46.

⁴ See No. 194 (see also cables to Bergmann and Kaplan, 23 July, W.A.).

respondence. Will you be so kind and go and see him and give him my very best regards and read him out the passage of this letter. I would like if possible to have Benji attached to the Citrus problem. And as he has a great experience in handling of fruit and excellent connections in Covent Garden, in France and Italy it might be to the mutual advantage, and should not be thought of lightly. I am reluctant in pleading for my own son and would never have done it unless I was thoroughly convinced of his efficiency and usefulness. Please do not let it slide, see Kaplan and read him out this letter and ask him to do something. It is not often that I ask others to do something for me. The whole of my life it was just the reverse.

And independently of Kaplan, could you consult some more people like Tolkowsky,[5] e.g. Anyhow, I would like them to do something. There is nothing much to report from here. Mrs. Weizmann has not been well for now over ten days. She is improving, but the illness has left her limp and weak. We are moving on to another hotel, as from the 28th inst. The address is: Grand Hotel, Vevey, Switzerland. It is just on the lake and probably will suit little David[6] better than here on the heights.

Kind[7] has promised to come, but the last minute has postponed his visit, and I expect he may turn up next week. I am rather anxious to see him and to hear when their factory goes into production.[8] I think they ought to pay some royalty even if they do not produce according to the contract, but I have not got the faintest idea what the terms of our contract are. Probably Max[9] would know it. Anyhow, do not trouble about it. I shall find it out in good time.

As soon as I know about my transport, I shall be able to determine when I come to Israel. And the transport depends upon the availability of steamers. I understand that the protocol demands my going on a Jewish boat. And in one of my letters, I have asked you to discuss this with Remez.[10] You cannot do it too soon. And I do not wish to get stuck here after mid-September. Well, give my love to everybody in the Institute, particularly to my sister [Anna] and Miss Goldschmidt. You might next time when you write say

[5] Samuel Tolkowsky (Biog. Index, Vol. VII). Chairman Citrus Exporters Association 1934–40; Consul-General of Israel in Switzerland 1949–51; Minister 1951–56.

[6] W.'s grandson.

[7] Franz Kind (1902–55). Czech chemist; founder and Managing Director of Manchester Oil Refinery, Ltd.

[8] The Manchester Oil Refinery was establishing a pilot plant developing a process invented by W. for the simultaneous production of aromatic hydrocarbons and olefinic gases.

[9] Max Sulzbacher b. 1901. Chemist; refugee from Germany; worked with W. in England 1934–48.

[10] See No. 219.

something about what Rosenfeld[11] is doing. I hope he is helping and not staying out. I would not like it. I think Felix [Bergmann] and Hirschberg[12] ought to return as soon as possible. And I have written to Meyer [Weisgal] accordingly. There are many problems I would like to discuss with you, but I prefer to do it orally. I hope to see you here in September, and we go back together.

   With best love,

Yours

Ch. Weizmann

229. To Oscar Fehr,[1] London.   *Glion, 22 July 1948*
English: Or. Copy. T.W.: W.A.

My dear Professor Fehr,

Miss Erlanger has just read to me your very kind letter,[2] and I am most grateful to you for your good wishes and solicitude. I am not sure that my sight has gone much worse, but I might have it tested somewhere in Zurich or in Geneva, because I am afraid I shall not be in London for some time. I intend to go from here directly to Palestine in September.

I think there is a very good oculist both in Zurich and in Geneva. I wonder whether you know their names and whether you would recommend an operation now. I do not feel as if I would like it, particularly in view of the fact that my left eye is not at all good, and if anything goes wrong during the operation with my right eye, I can become practically blind. Perhaps you would be kind enough to let me have your opinion.[3]

I did hear that you were in U.S.A. As I did not know exactly where you were and how long you were staying I have not tried to bother you, much as I would have loved to see you. I wish you would have come to see me in New York, even if I was in bed. It is quite true that this trip to America was very much interfered with by almost continuous sickness. I am much better now, but unfortunately my wife is not too well. However I hope she will improve soon. Are you by any chance coming to Switzerland for a short holiday? It would be wonderful to meet you here.

[11] Bruno Rosenfeld, b. 1903. Biochemist; at Sieff and later Weizmann Institute 1933–52.

[12] Yehuda Hirschberg (1903–1960). Physical chemist; from 1933 with Sieff and later Weizmann Institute.

229. [1] London eye specialist.

[2] Untraced.

[3] Fehr recommended (26 July W.A.) that W. have his eyes examined by a prominent Swiss eye-surgeon.

I hope all is well with you, and I remain with very kind regards and many thanks for your good wishes,

Yours very sincerely,

230. To Moshe Shertok, Tel Aviv.   *Glion, 23 July 1948*
English: T.: W.A.

Yours mh 782:[1] Am rather doubtful whether I could competently advise on a matter which although merely symbolic is of importance for generations to come. My advice would be to consult a heraldic expert, who probably might be found at the University or in the school for archaeology. My personal opinion, which should count for little, is to keep the old symbol with the Lion of Judah holding in one paw the Tablets of the Law. This like the Bible is not clericalism, but I believe the foundation of human civilisation. Kindly discuss with Premier question of my transport mid-September. I understand protocol demands travelling on our own boat under escort by some corvettes. Have written in detail to Bergmann with request[2] consult Remez.

Affectionately,
Weizmann

231. To Jacob Robinson, New York.   *Glion, 25 July 1948*
English: Or. Copy. T.W.: W.A.

My dear Robinson,

I am most grateful to you for having sent to me the notes concerning the head of the State.[1] I have not had time yet to read it, but I shall do so to-day, probably, and I'll then try and get in touch with Leo Kohn and see what he has produced.

I hope you are all well and probably very busy making constitutions. My opinion would be not to have a constitution in all its

230. [1] See Shertok telegram 22 July (W.A.). He was consulting W. on a State flag. The Government had intended creating a completely original design, distinct from the traditional form, so as to preclude the interpretation that the traditional one signified allegiance to Israel by Diaspora Jews. But certain American Jewish visitors had reacted strongly against this idea, arguing in favour of the Lion of Judah embracing the *Torah*, revered by Jews the world over.
[2] See No. 219.

231. [1] Robinson wrote 21 July (W.A.) that he had completed his observations on the first 46 Articles of Kohn's draft constitution, but had not yet reached the chapter on the President. Nevertheless, he was sending a paper prepared on the subject by Prof. Ezekiel Gordon. He thought this offered a realistic approach to the problem, worthy of consideration.

details, but a few great general principles laid down, and wait for two or three years, and see how the thing works in the light of real experience. A constitution is like a straitjacket, and it may fit a mentally sick man but not a young organism in the state of development. Still, this is only an opinion of a layman. I am sure that you lawyers are having a field day now. And if Leo Kohn gets on to it, God help us all. He is a good fellow, very slow, but apt to write volumes, of which I am terrified beforehand.

    With very kind regards,

Yours very sincerely,

232. To D. Werner Senator,[1] Jerusalem.   *Glion, 25 July 1948*
English: Or. Copy. T.W.: W.A.

Dear Doctor Senator,

    I beg to thank you for your note of the 13th inst.[2] It is almost the same to me when you wish to call the Board of Governors; as long as it is in Jerusalem, after September I can attend it. I intend to be there probably the 3rd week in September. In view of the latest development and my own position I of course cannot serve any more as chairman of the Board of Governors, and you will have to look out for somebody else. I do not know whether Brodetsky[3] would take it or would be elected. He seems to have other ambitions. At any rate, you will have to think hard in order to find a suitable person. For the time being, I do not see anybody I would like to recommend, but we may possibly discover somebody in France or in U.S.A. At the first sight, I would like to think of a man like Mandelbroit.[4] He is a brilliant mathematician, occupies a very distinguished position in the *Collège de France,* is interested in the University and is from all I hear a very good Jew. He is young, knows a good deal about universities, and may be suitable. But that is merely a rough idea. I have not spoken to him and would not do anything until I have heard something from Jerusalem.

    There is one other matter which exercises my mind of late. You may or you may not agree with the political settlement, but it is there; and it is going to stay, and one has to reckon with such a hard fact. According to this settlement, Jerusalem is outside the Jewish

---

232. [1] Biog. Index, Vol. XIV. Administrator of H.U.

   [2] W.A. Relating to forthcoming meeting of H.U. Board of Governors and W.'s contemplated resignation as its chairman.

   [3] Selig Brodetsky was also W.'s candidate as the next H.U. President.

   [4] Szolem Mandelbroit, b. 1899. Professor at *College de France* from 1938; Vice-President Friends of H.U., France.

State. What will happen 25 years hence, nobody can foretell, but I fear that the fact that Jerusalem will be international and the Jewish position there different from that in the State itself will no doubt affect the life of the University.

It is a tragic fate of ours that our capital and our unique University should fall outside the boundaries of the State. I am convinced that we must begin to think of a second University. It does not mean that we renounce Jerusalem, but I think that in one year or two Palestine could do with a second University. I have calculated out that in Switzerland there is about one University or high Technical School per population of 450,000. There is no doubt that in about 2 years we shall have 1 million Jews in Palestine. And therefore we could have another University in Tel Aviv. Think that over. You may talk it over confidentially with some friends. It is a matter of supreme importance that the new State of Israel should be symbolized by a great University. We could now get first class people easier than we did 25 years ago. And I believe the money would be forthcoming. I am only throwing out this idea for you and your colleagues to think about it. Whatever is in my power to do to help it on, I shall certainly be happy to do so. Please let me have your news care of: Grand Hotel, Vevey, Switzerland, without much delay.

With kind regards,
Yours very sincerely,

233. To David Ben-Gurion, Tel Aviv.   *Vevey, 26 July 1948*
English: Or. Copy. T.W.: W.A.

My dear Mr. Prime Minister,

I am addressing myself to you on the subject of my journey to Israel, which I propose to start about the second or third week of September. As you may be aware, there are not too many boats plying between European ports and Haifa.

Besides, I am informed on every side that it would not be proper for me to go on any boat except our own. Therefore, there remains the only way to travel by the *Kedmah,* if she could be sent to Marseilles about the 15th September or thereabouts.

It is also essential to have this boat escorted while passing in the vicinity of Egyptian waters. I understand that we have armed corvettes and they could either meet me in Marseilles or somewhere in Greece, say near Crete. But I believe that something of that kind should be organized.

One could also fly to Israel, but I could only go in a pressurized plane. An ordinary plane is rather dangerous for my health. Of course, that would be the simplest and the quickest. I have discussed these possibilities with Mr. Remez, when he was here. Perhaps he has gone into it with the authorities concerned, but so far I have not heard anything, and it is essential that I should know about it a reasonably long time before the actual departure takes place.

There is nothing I could say from here, as we are living a very retired life and can only watch events from afar.

The only piece of news which I would like to communicate is that with the new Government in France, which includes Mr. Blum and Mr. Reynaud and some other friends,[1] the chances of our recognition seem to have somewhat improved. You know that I have made a considerable effort while in Paris, but have not been very successful. My friends tell me now that it may be easier to get recognition at present. Frankly, I am sceptical. I have not had the impression that Mr. Blum is going out of his way to press forward our claim. It is also a great pity that Jarblum has suddenly left Paris for a jaunt to Palestine. He should have stayed in Paris and kept trying. But they are all so volatile.

You will understand that I am eager to get back to Israel before *Rosch Haschanah* and we would then have an opportunity of going over the whole situation.

I hope that the strain of your Office is not trying you too much, and looking forward to your speedy reply,[2]

I remain with all regards and respects,

Yours very sincerely,

233. [1] The new French Cabinet as announced that day included Blum as Vice-Premier, and Paul Reynaud as Finance and Economic Minister. Others known to W. were Schuman (Foreign Minister), Moch (Interior), René Mayer (National Defence), Yvon Delbos (Education) and Daniel Mayer (Labour and Social Security).

[2] Ben-Gurion replied in English (15 Aug.) asking W.'s forgiveness for not replying sooner. He wrote that he spoke in the name of the entire people in looking forward to seeing W. in Sept. and promised to 'do our best to make suitable arrangements for your reception', which would be 'as festive as possible'. He understood that the Foreign Ministry was making the necessary arrangements for W.'s arrival aboard the *Kedmah* (I.F.M. 2449/150414). Writing again, in Hebrew, 17 Aug. (W.A.), he reported their inability to despatch a corvette to Marseilles. 'We also feel the need for calling elections soon in order to give the State and the Government permanency and stability. You will doubtless find the atmosphere of elections somewhat disagreeable—but it cannot be escaped.'

234. To Sir Wyndham Deedes, London.   *Vevey, 26 July 1948*

English: Or. Copy. T.W.: W.A.

Dear Wyndham,

It is a long time that I wish to send you a word but somehow I did not get down to it. In fact there is so much to say that one fights shy of beginning to discuss matters. It is thirty years since we met first in Egypt and then in Palestine, and it seems that it was only a short time ago, because so much was crowded into these years that the march of time was unnoticeable.

Now, we have reached the end of a road and the beginning of a new one. I am only dreadfully sorry that your health does not permit you to take an active part in this new phase of our affairs as you did before. But the purpose of my letter is really a somewhat different one.[1] I would like to ask you to come to Israel in the autumn and stay with us for how long as you may like. You may come whenever it suits you. We shall be there about the third week in September, staying continuously without moving too much. We have had so much travelling in these years that we would like to come to rest now. I need hardly tell you that you will be a most welcome visitor not only in our house, not only in the little city of Rechovot, but everywhere you would care to show yourself. We will try to keep you as quiet as possible and warn off all intruders, and we shall not force you to eat. So you see, I offer you all the advantages. You only have to say when you can come, the rest can be arranged. I think it will do your heart good to see the results of the work of which you were one of the first architects. It will do all of us good to have you amongst us. If you care to be in Palestine during Xmas, so that you could combine a visit to us with a pilgrimage to the Holy Places, that might be an additional attraction. Our own program is as at present advised as follows: We shall stay in this country until about middle of September, and then we shall begin to think of taking up our quarters in Palestine. And we intend to stay there practically permanently. Now you know what we are doing, and if you really wish to come, which I hope you do, you can easily fit in your movements with ours.

234. [1] A comment by Miss May in a letter to W. 14 July (W.A.) may explain the background to this letter. She stated that in the wake of statehood an administrative reorganization was being carried out. The J.A. London office was in process of liquidation. Some employees, including herself, were joining Goldmann in establishing the Israel 'Representation' which was to be located in Palestine House, 'after ejecting the Deedes outfit'. She therefore thought it would be 'a kindly deed to send a personal word to Wyndham, just to say how much you have appreciated all he has done'.

I hope that your health is not giving you too much trouble and that you are not overworking.

We are having a quiet time here, and I shall be looking forward to your reply with great eagerness.

I remain as ever,

Your old friend,

235. To Aubrey Eban, New York.   *Vevey, 27 July 1948*
English: T.W.: I.S.A. 93.03 (64/3).

My dear Aubrey,

I was glad to read your telegraphic report about your conversation with Parodi.[1] But I am anxious to warn you that you should not accept all these encouraging statements at their face value. Parodi speaks very nicely, and perhaps he means it while he speaks. But when it comes to performance this falls far short of the promises. This experience is general with Frenchmen, who are quick to promise and slow to carry it out.

The Minister for Foreign Affairs at present is Mr. Schuman. He is not unfriendly but very obstinate and always producing the 20 million Arabs in North Africa. So we will have to go very slowly there. It is true that we have Mr. Blum and Mr. Reynaud, but I would not rely too much on them. I think Parodi is right not to press the question of admission unless you are sure to get a satisfactory reply. A rebuff would be highly unpleasant. Apart from prestige, I do not see of what importance the whole matter is, and I would waste neither time nor breath on it. I believe we attach too much value to finding ourselves in the good company of other nations. I confess, I have not got the slightest desire to do it and would concentrate all my energy on making the Jewish State strong, intellectually powerful, in fact—if possible—a model of social and political organization. All the rest will then come by itself, and if it does not come we need not cry over it. As it is, I fear we are losing too much energy on externals quite insignificant in themselves.

One thing e.g. which is in my thoughts very much at present, and which if realised would mean much more than recognition by the Assembly or other bodies, is the creation of a University in the Jewish State.

---

235. [1] This was a copy of Eban's telegram to Shertok, 23 July (W.A.), reporting a discussion with Parodi. The latter had declared that French recognition of Israel was inevitable, though he could not commit himself as to timing. Further, he cautioned Eban against a premature formal application for Israel's admission to U.N. without assuring success in advance.

Jerusalem is outside the State, and for a long time our institutions there will be in a precarious position, even if we occupy it now by force. Besides we shall soon perhaps reach a million population, and two Universities are not too much for such a population. A performance of that kind would mean more to the world and to us than all the bickering about recognition, or admission, or any other formality like that. I may be mistaken. I have never been strong on formalities. In fact, I hated it. I like business, big facts, which signify something to the Jews and to the world at large.

I am giving you my opinion for what it may be worth. I shall be looking forward to seeing you in Europe, and I hope you will come to look me up in Switzerland. My address here is Grand Hotel, Vevey.

Give my best regards to Robinson, who was good enough to send me the document about the rights and prerogatives of the Head of the State. It is a very learned document, and I am almost frightened to be saddled with all these so-called rights and privileges. Again, I dislike that as much as all the other formal things, and I am not so sure whether on arrival to Palestine I will not hand over the whole bag of tricks to somebody who would like to take it; and I am sure there must be plenty of candidates. I dislike it more and more. Well, that is all for to-day.

My best wishes to you and your wife,

As ever yours,
Ch. Weizmann

236. To Abraham Goldberg, Paris. *Vevey, 27 July 1948*
English: T.W.: Photostat W.A.

My dear Goldberg,

I am most grateful to you for your kind letter[1] and also for sending me the book of Lamartine.[2] As for Mr. Wolzok's book,[3] I am not so mightily impressed by it and so far, it remains unread. Mrs. Weizmann is better, and to-morrow we move on to the Grand Hotel, Vevey. We also expect our children on Thursday.

With regard to the recognition, I am somehow less optimistic than you are and fear that neither Mr. Blum nor Mr. Reynaud will put themselves out, particularly if Mr. Bevin asks them not to do so. If

236. [1] Of 23 July (W.A.).
[2] *Travels in the Holy Land, 1832–33,* publ. 1835.
[3] Dr. Wolzok of Monte Carlo, whose book (untraced) had a dedication to W.

there is a choice between us and Mr. Bevin, they are sure to choose the latter.

However, I may write to Blum, but I think I shall give him a day or two, until he is settled down in his new Office. I realize that one has to write quickly, because he may be thrown out to-morrow.

The fact that Mr. Schuman is in the *Quai d'Orsay* is not too encouraging. He is a nice man and not unfriendly, but in my last conversation with him I had the impression that he would like to wait. How long he wishes to wait, God alone knows. But I am sure he has all the time at his disposal. Still, if Blum and Reynaud would wish it, they could probably put it through. Will you please find out for me if Blum has been approached by Fischer or anybody else; or should we wait for Jarblum to return from his excursion?

There is nothing new here, and the news from Palestine seem to be somewhat confusing. I do not quite see what the Government has done with Jerusalem. If it means destroying Bernadotte's plans, I am delighted. I never thought much of this Gentleman, and the more I read about his doings, the less confidence he inspires. But one has to await further development before passing any judgment.

Well, I hope you will keep me informed and remain with kind regards,

Yours,
Ch. Weizmann

237. To Léon Blum, Jovy-en-Josaz.   *Vevey, 29 July 1948*
French: Or. Copy. T.W.: W.A.

My dear Mr. President and Friend,

I am sorry that I am forced to come back to the thorny problem of our recognition. I do not know if you are aware that France's attitude towards recognition gravely damages our cause as far as the Arabs and our other adversaries are concerned. I also do not know if the change which has cropped up allows us to hope that recognition will be shortly granted to us.

Mr. Schuman, to whom I talked during my stay in Paris, expressed his agreement to the idea of recognition, but thought that it was necessary to wait a little while until the situation becomes more stable.

Moreover, Mr. Parodi recently stated publicly that the military successes of Israel's army completely refuted any doubts of the stability of the State of Israel.

Even the English press has stated that the State of Israel should be seen as a stable entity which is here to stay.

Therefore, I think all Mr. Schuman's conditions have been ful-filled, and I see no reason why we should not be granted recognition.

I beg your pardon for bothering you with all these problems, which perhaps seem small in comparison with those you are dealing with at the moment,[1] and, wishing you the best of success with your new and difficult task,

I remain,

Most sincerely,
Your friend,

238. To Meyer W. Weisgal, New York.   *Vevey, 30 July 1948*[1]
English: Draft. T.W.: W.A.

My dear Meyer,

Although I have not heard yet from you, I suppose one of these days there will be a letter. The purpose of my writing is a rather earnest one:

Since the establishment of the Jewish State, I have been trying to obtain some clear information both about politics and projects. I have been telegraphing and writing, and so far I obtained no satisfaction. In fact, no reply has been forthcoming. Whether this is due to bad communications, as I am being told, or to some other causes, I cannot say. But I feel that it has reached the stage that I must take a definite decision.

I am informed that communication via U.S.A. is much easier and quicker, and this is why I am addressing this letter to you in the hope that you may forward either a copy of this letter or a telegraphic gist of it to Shertok and Kaplan.

From time to time, I get glimpses of a byzantine display of power and quasi military strength but nothing else. As you know, these are things which produce no echo in my soul. I realize that they are at war, but it seems to me that the moloch of militarism is having everything and everybody in his grip. As far as I am concerned, this cannot go on much longer, and as I do not see any hope of a change, I have decided to sever my connection with the Office which has been foisted on me. I am not in a position to cover with my name all that is going on at present in Palestine and to accept everything which the Government does without being able in any way either to influence it or to prevent it. It may be that if I were on the spot

---

237. [1] I.e., the political instability of the Fourth Republic.

238. [1] Dated as given, but apparently despatched 3 Aug. See No. 242.

I might think differently or see things in another light. But I am not there and not likely to get there until the second half of September. Meanwhile facts are being created which one would have to face, and I am not prepared to do so.

I really do not wish to create any trouble or difficulties for the new State, which is already beset by a great many difficult problems, but I cannot reconcile myself to being a sort of passive partner in an enterprise which is run on lines of which I cannot approve fully, anyhow cannot acquiesce in them without knowing all the facts. And the facts are definitely withheld, whether intentionally or not, I cannot say. I appreciate that the main actors in the new drama are very busy but that is neither a reason nor an argument for keeping me entirely in the dark.

You will—I beg of you—send a copy of this letter to Shertok. That should serve as an announcement of my resignation. As soon as I know that this letter has reached them, I would announce it publicly.

Now about another matter, equally serious and equally unpleasant, and that is the Institute.

Again, I have no information of what is really going on there except some scanty communication to the effect that the whole Institute is switching over to what is called war work. This means that the entire scientific basis of the Institute has been changed. This has been done without any previous consultation or advice. Again, I understand the pressure under which our people are working, but as in the previous case, there was no reason why the information should not be forthcoming in time. Equally there is no reason why the whole of the scientific work, into which so much energy, devotion and love has been poured, should be replaced by something which is not science but making of explosives. I consider myself as the head of a scientific centre, but if this centre changes its character without even as much as "by your leave," I find that this relieves me of my duties, and I rather have nothing to do with the whole thing. And I shall be grateful to you if you would take cognisance of it and inform your board accordingly.

I am quite certain that Dr. Bergmann could carry on without me, and if one day he reverts back to science he would probably do quite well whether I am connected or not.

My hatred for all these military performances is so profound and ingrained in me since my childhood that it literally hurts me to feel that the Institute to which I have devoted so much energy and so many hours of endeavour should be desecrated in a manner which I can neither explain nor acquiesce in.

As you see, I am shaking off two oppressive burdens and I shall be looking forward with great joy to come to Palestine untrammeled by any ties of Office.

I find that it is about time at seventy-four to think of retreat, and this is a wonderful occasion which I would not like to miss.

I hope your trip to Mexico was successful and that you are really thinking of taking some sort of a holiday with your wife and family.

We are here in a very nice place, but we have not been too fortunate in as much as Mrs. Weizmann was seriously ill. She has now got over it, but it has left her rather weak, and she must go very slowly.

I have indicated in my letter of yesterday[2] that our further plans depend upon information which is expected from Israel; but as you already know, they are extremely slow. Much love to you and to your family, and let us hear something from you soon.

As ever yours,

239. To Oscar Fehr, London.   *Vevey, 1 August 1948*
English: Or. Copy. T.W.: W.A.

My dear Professor Fehr,

I am most grateful to you for your kind letter[1] and for the offer to write to a surgeon in Switzerland. I am most likely to be in Geneva very soon, and perhaps you would be good enough to write to Prof. Franceschetti. I shall then get in touch with him, when in Geneva. I do not quite understand the phrase in your letter "the prognosis of the operation is good." Does it mean that you have no serious objection to an operation on the cataract on my right eye? I was under the impression that you would not make it because you think that it does involve a certain amount of risk, particularly as I have really only one eye.

But if there is no danger in such an operation I would rather like to have it done, because to recover full sight would mean a great deal to me. I shall be glad if you would let me know.[2]

I hope you had an interesting time in U.S.A. and with all my kind regards, I am,

Yours very sincerely,

[2] W.A.

239. [1] See No. 229, n. 3.

[2] Replying 7 Aug. (W.A.), Fehr stated that he had already conveyed to Franceschetti in Geneva a full case history. He now felt the risks attached to an eye operation to be insignificant, and he would favour an operation.

240. To D. Werner Senator, Jerusalem.   *Vevey, 1 August 1948*
English: Or. Copy. T.W.: W.A.

My dear Doctor Senator,

I am really grateful for your very interesting letter,[1] which has given me information about the University, which I wanted to have very much.

I am extremely sorry about the severe losses which our staff has sustained, and it won't be easy, I am afraid, to replace such men as Do[l]janski, Bonaventura or the others.[2]

But one will have to look round very soon in U.S.A. or in Europe to find appropriate candidates, and I wonder whether Palestine is capable of supplying any suitable personnel. I doubt it. But it ought not be entirely impossible. There must be a series of young men who left the University and went abroad, and maybe some of them might come back.

When I read about the attack on the omnibus I felt sick at heart, and I also felt that it was improvident and incautious to have the University Bus travelling over this dangerous road at this time of trouble. However, it is easy to criticize from an armchair. Still, the severe lesson will probably teach you all that the road to the University must be made safer. This brings me to another order of ideas.

It is quite right of you to say that the institutions on Scopus are destined to strengthen morally and intellectually Jewish Jerusalem. But important as this function is, one must always bear in mind that Jerusalem will never be Jewish in the same sense as Tel Aviv or Haifa or Tiberias. It is an international religious centre, and Christianity has a great claim on Jerusalem. So have the Moslems. You know how much I am attached to this University, to which I have given a great part of my life. And we shall try and foster its development as much as possible. But the existence of the University in Jerusalem will always be precarious, and the time has come to think of another University in the midst of the Jewish State and not outside it. It is quite true that the Jewish State has got a great deal of other things to do at present and is probably short of money, but it could do nothing better which would signify the coming into existence of Israel than the foundation of a University in the Jewish State.

It may begin with a faculty of law, perhaps, which was always planned to be placed in Tel Aviv; also a faculty of commerce and

---

240. [1] This, 22 July (W.A.), spoke of the damage caused by Arab shelling of the University buildings and of the death of people indispensable for H.U.'s work.

[2] Enzo Joseph Bonaventura (b. 1891), Professor of Psychology, was, with Doljanski, among those killed in the attack on the H.U. convoy, March 1948.

with some modest nucleus of a science faculty. But it should do so without very much delay. And if I come over in September, I am prepared to devote a good deal of time to this matter, which I consider most important.

You will remember perhaps that it was Fichte who struggled for the foundation of a University in Berlin at the time when they passed through a dark period in their history.[3]

With regard to the decreased income from U.S.A.,[4] I believe that it is not merely due to the illness of Mr. Leo Schwarz, but as far as I realized when in U.S.A., the gross sum in pledges was the usual amount if not more than usual, but the actual income in cash was small. Therefore, there is hope that some of the pledges may still be recovered, and if you press the Friends for more cash you are likely to get it.

Dr. Wechsler is a great optimist and has ambitious plans, but it is my conviction that his performance does not stand in adequate proportion to his plans. However I may be mistaken. Neither do I know that he has been able to penetrate into the Zionist masses, which would have been a good thing. I have not got the slightest idea how he stands with Silver, who is the dictator of American Zionism, neither do I know what sympathies Silver has for the University. I have never spoken to him nor met him in U.S.A. But only to-day I hear that Neumann is on his way to Europe, and he has promised to visit me here. That may be a good opportunity for bringing up the whole matter of the University because I think Neumann is the brains of the concern, and Silver is the loudspeaker. At any rate, I am glad that the Government is beginning to take an intelligent interest in the University, and I shall be more convinced of it when I see what place the higher institutions of learning occupy in the budget.

When we meet in September, we shall talk it all over carefully. I do not think that the real budget of the State will be made up before the elections. So we shall have to struggle for it, and with a good chance of winning our case. We hope to leave from here in September. I cannot give an exact date, because I do not know what arrangements are being made by my colleagues for my transport. But it is all likely to happen before *Rosch Haschanah*.[5]

Once more I beg to express my profound sympathy to the University and to the families of those who have lost their lives in the sav-

[3] Johann Fichte's 'Addresses to the German Nation', 1807–08, were an important factor in founding the University of Berlin 1809.

[4] Senator wrote that he was informed by Leo W. Schwarz, director of the American Friends of H.U., that they should anticipate $235,000, not $350,000 as previously promised.

[5] The Jewish New Year fell 4–5 Oct. 1948.

age attack. It is more than I can put in words when I think of those innocent victims who have been carrying out so much distinguished work and with a great scientific career before them.

I remain, dear Doctor Senator,

Yours very sincerely,

P.S. I am told that there is an excellent jurist, former *Appellationsgerichtspraesident* of Berlin, living now in Tel Aviv: Dr. Paul Galewski, Gnessin Street 3, Tel Aviv. I suggest you contact him and find out whether he is ready to take Dr. Freimann's place.[6]

If you wish to write to me, your letter will reach me on the above address, and shall be forwarded should I eventually leave this place. As far as I can see from the date of your letter it took about 8–9 days to come here which, considering all the difficulties, is not too bad. I also understand that there is a regular air-mail service once a week to Paris, I think on Wednesday. This could also be made use of by you. I understand if you post a letter in Tel Aviv on Tuesday it could reach Paris on Thursday or Friday and—of course—from Paris it could reach me here by air-mail the same day or a little later, but, at any rate, it would take less than 8–9 days.

241. To Moshe Shertok, Tel Aviv.   *Vevey, 2 August 1948*
English: T.W.: W.A.

My dear Moshe,

In spite of your promise to write to me, I have seen no trace of your communication so far.

Although you have not deserved it at all, I am sending you a copy of a letter which has reached me to-day from Elliot,[1] and which no doubt will interest you. I also send you copy of a few sentences which I have written to Senator,[2] which gives in my opinion some data about communication between the President of the State and his colleagues. But so far the communications were entirely unilateral. You will hear no more from me, because it is only a source of irritation to repeat always the same reproaches to people who are

---

[6] Abraham (Alfred) Freiman (b. 1889). Lecturer in Jewish Law, he was killed in the H.U. convoy.

241. [1] Elliot had written 29 July (W.A.) relating that in a recent talk with Churchill the latter had sent W. warmest personal regards, but added: 'The Palestine position now, as concerns Great Britain, is simply such a hell-disaster that I cannot take it up again or renew my efforts of twenty years. It is a situation which I myself cannot help in, and must, as far as I can, put out of my mind'.

[2] Reference unclear.

apparently not sensitive to them. I shall therefore have to rely on the Palcor[3] for news. As for State Secrets, which may or may not exist, I will have to restrain my curiosity.

I am not offended but greatly irritated because this treatment which is meted out to me only indicates the lack of respect to your own institutions; and that is a Balkan trait, of which I did not think that you would all acquire it so quickly.[4]

Best regards,

Yours,
Ch. Weizmann

P.S. Enclosed please find copy of a telegram which I just received.[5] In spite of the approval of the *Agudah,* I still believe that the symbol proposed by me is very appropriate.

242. To Meyer W. Weisgal, New York.   *Vevey, 3 August 1948*
English: T.W.: W.A.

My dear Meyer,

It is a long time since I have written to you and equally long since I have heard something from the other side. In your case, I understand the silence because you were away to Mexico.[1] I was glad to see that the results of this trip seem to be satisfactory. It is after all a small community, and they produced quite a respectable sum. I hear comparatively little from Palestine, and only by constant prodding and telegraphing one succeeds occasionally to extract a short message from our Government.

How they are doing is difficult to say, but it seems on a whole quite well, considering the cares which they have found on taking over office.

Bergmann is suffering now from the same vice. He, who used to be such a regular and accurate correspondent, has lost this valuable quality. Maybe the war has upset their nerves. I do not know in which state the building of the institute finds itself. Everything is of course

[3] Palestine Correspondence—news agency of J.A.

[4] The day the letter was written, this cable arrived from Shertok: 'Deeply distressed you have been left without personal reports for such long time. Pleading guilty as this due solely my desire report you personally. Long letter already dictated. Waiting free hour for concluding chapter. Hope despatch it next couple days. Meanwhile sending you all papers of interest. Please forgive' (W.A.).

[5] Dated 30 July (W.A.) by an official of the religious party, *Agudat Israel.* This thanked W. for endorsing the Tablets of the Covenant as the fitting symbol for the Israeli flag (see No. 230) rejected by other Government leaders.

242. [1] On a fund-raising mission.

dreadfully delayed because of lack of labour. On the other hand, I hear that the Institute has been the great centre of the war effort and the manufacture of war material, of which our people were so lamentably short.[2]

Anyhow, there is a letter of David [Bergmann] theoretically on its way with a promised full report, and God help him if it is unsatisfactory.

I have read also in the press somewhere that the great Rabbi Silver is preparing to descend upon Palestine with a view of becoming a citizen and probably taking part in the elections. I do not know whether it is true, but it sounds very much like a Silver enterprise.[3]

Neumann has been spreading a good deal of sunshine round him, and he is threatening to be here some time in August, and of course he is most anxious to see me. Is he already preparing to throw over his master? I do not know. But it somehow feels like it. I shall no doubt hear something when he appears on the shores of the lake. I cannot get any clear answer from our Authorities how they propose I should come to Palestine in time for the inauguration. But I believe that that is going to be found in David Bergmann's report.

When are you coming out to Palestine? In case I really go the second half of September on the *Kedmah,* it would be a very good opportunity for you to join us. We would probably have a quiet and fairly comfortable passage, without too many of our fellow citizens milling around. We could have the inauguration of the Institute coincide with all the other inaugurations, of which there are going to be plenty, and finish it all up before the New Year.

You can write to me here and please do it soon. My love to you and to your family from both of us,

Ever yours,
Ch. Weizmann

P.S. Enclosed a copy of a letter recently received from Mr. W. Elliot[4] which will no doubt interest you and which you will perhaps show to Aubrey.

I also enclose a draft of a letter which I have written on the 30.7.48.[5] I did not send it off in the hope that some message would come from Palestine which might bring me some relief. And true enough, yesterday came a telegram from Moshe, of which I enclose a copy. This renders the sending off of the letter less urgent. But I am doing it nevertheless *ad memoriam,* because I am quite convinced

² See No. 228, n. 1.
³ Silver did not visit Israel at this time, and never became an Israeli citizen.
⁴ See No. 241, n. 1.
⁵ See No. 238.

that a similar occasion will arise again. The letter is meant entirely for yourself, and you can destroy it after having read it. Still I am anxious to point out to you that I am unhappy to head a Government with whose personnel I have not much in common, with exception of one or two personalities.

David Bergmann's behaviour is equally distressing, and I really do not know what has come over the people. Is it the war, is it the statehood, or is it the effect of both? I shall be interested to hear your opinion, and do please write in your usual frank way.[6]

Yours as ever,
Ch. W.

P.P.S. Since this letter has been dictated, your telephone message[7] came through, and many of the questions which I have raised have been answered, for which I am most thankful.

243. To Aubrey Eban, New York.   *Vevey, 4 August 1948*
English: T.: W.A.

Grateful your letter of 29th concerning epilogue and agree your suggestion.[1] Regards you and Meyer.

Weizmann

244. To C. David Ginsburg, New York.   *Vevey, 4 August 1948*
English: Or. Copy. T.W.: W.A.

My dear David,

I am grateful to you for your letter of the 28th ult.,[1] and I do hope you will visit us on your return journey. There are certain things which one could only discuss personally. I am not so optimistic as to believe that one could come to terms with Egypt before the Assembly in September.

---

[6] Weisgal replied 13 Aug. (W.A.) inviting W.'s understanding of the strain under which the people in Tel Aviv and Rehovot were working in the midst of war; hence their failure to reply to all his communications.

[7] This was 4 Aug., and in a letter the same day (W.A.) Weisgal noted that W.'s recent irritability had now been replaced by cheerfulness.

243. [1] See No. 220. Eban now wrote (W.A.) suggesting that he and Weisgal extend the epilogue to *T. and E.*, as an impressive last chapter necessary for historic perspective.

244. [1] (W.A.). Ginsburg wrote of his anxiety lest Zionist support decrease in U.S. after the Nov. Presidential Election. He felt that direct, independent negotiations with the Arabs, leading to a settlement without Bernadotte's intervention, should be conducted before the Sept. session of U.N. General Assembly in Paris.

In spite of what Afifi Pasha[2] said,[3] Egypt is still fighting against us, being encouraged by Great Britain.

Usually, our representative, Mr. Sasson,[4] goes to Egypt, but the situation is to-day such that they cannot cross the border, and they had to go to Paris in order to communicate with the Egyptians. How deep this hostility is is difficult to say, and things may change, but I do not know whether it will go so quickly.

What you say about the prospects of the Paris Assembly is very disquieting. But it is difficult to believe that one Assembly will cancel the decision of another one, without making of itself a laughing stock for the whole world.

There is no doubt in my mind that attempts will be made to revise the decisions of November 29, at any rate insofar as the frontiers are concerned. But not—I believe—as far as the principle itself goes. It all goes to prove that we have still a long struggle in front of us.

I believe our people in Palestine are fully aware of it. Hoping to see you soon, I am with much love from both of us.

Yours very sincerely,
Ch. Weizmann

245. To Samuel I. Rosenman, New York.   *Vevey, 4 August 1948*
English: T.W.: W.A.

My dear Judge Rosenman,

I am sorry to trouble you again with our affairs, but our difficulties seem to be never ending.

I have now received the enclosed letter from Major Aubrey Eban.[1] It is self-explanatory. There seems to be still a doubt about the full validity of the recognition. As I am convinced that the British will make every effort at the September Meeting of the Assembly in Paris to do us as much harm as possible, it is essential that there

---

[2] Hafiz Afifi Pasha (b. 1886). Egyptian Foreign Minister 1928–29; Minister 1930–34; Ambassador in London 1936–38.

[3] Ginsburg cited a conversation between a close friend and the Egyptian politician, in which it was emphasized that Egypt had territorial ambitions in the Negev but was primarily concerned with cancelling British influence in the Middle East, exercised directly or through Abdullah in Transjordan. He presented this as evidence of the possibilities for direct Arab-Israel negotiations.

[4] Eliahu Sasson (Biog. Index, Vol. XVIII; d. 1978). Head of J.A. Arab Department 1930–48.

245. [1] This (29 July, W.A.) informed W. that a memorandum was being sent to Rosenman for his use in further meetings with Truman. It indicated that there was no legal basis for the assertion that the provisional nature of the Israel Government compelled only *de facto* recognition.

should be no flaw in the American attitude. It is only when U.S.A. stands absolutely firm that the British attempts to destroy us will fail. I do not know exactly what can be done in that matter, but on reading the enclosed you will no doubt with your legal mind see for yourself what can be done. As you know, I am only a chemist.

With affectionate regards to you and Mrs. Rosenman,

I remain

Yours,

Ch. Weizmann

P.S. Enclosed copy of a letter of David Ginsburg received this morning.[2] The other enclosure, sent to me by Eban as mentioned above, is an opinion[3] given by Robinson, our legal adviser in NY and Mr. Lauterpacht,[4] who was professor of international law at the University of Cambridge.

246. To Winston S. Churchill, London.   *Vevey, 6 August 1948*
English: Or. Copy. T.W.: W.A.

I was more than delighted to receive Mr. Walter Elliot's message from you.[1] This emboldens me to address these few lines to you. I meant to write before, but I somehow felt instinctively that you do not wish to enter into a discussion of Palestine affairs. I quite understand and respect this sentiment and have no desire of raising these problems in this letter. I would like however to say that I wholeheartedly agree with your definition of the situation as a "hell-disaster."

My mind goes back to the time when British statesmen like Mr. Lloyd George, Mr. Balfour and yourself had laid the foundation of the Jewish National Home, and in spite of many vicissitudes and very serious difficulties it has progressed and can enjoy the privilege of statehood. It is a small State surrounded by many enemies and will have to ward off deadly perils, but the major part of the Jewish population of Palestine are men of courage, vision and integrity, and

---

[2] See No. 244, ns. 1, 3.

[3] The two legal experts took the position that, although Truman had extended *de facto* recognition only to the Provisional Government, it implied full status to the State of Israel.

[4] (Sir) Hersch Lauterpacht (1897–1960). Professor of International Law at Cambridge 1938–55; member Hague International Court of Justice from 1955.

246. [1] See No. 241, n. 1.

they face an enemy who may be numerically far superior but possesses no stamina and no courage. The headlong flight of hundreds of thousands of Arabs from Palestine at the mere approach of the Jewish Army and the very poor military performance of Egypt in spite of its wealth and equipment testifies to the quality and the spirit of the Arab world; this is the spirit we have been hearing so much about for the last twenty-five years.

It is a matter of deep distress to me, who laboured for a quarter of a century for the cooperation between the Jewish and the British peoples, to see this work at any rate temporarily jeopardized. Instead of making the new State a friendly outpost of Great Britain in the East, the present Government prefers to build on the quicksands of Arab loyalty.

I shall not weary you with an examination of the causes which have produced such a tragic situation. I pray that it may prove merely a temporary aberration, and that the tradition of friendship which began with Cromwell and continued for so many years will revive under the pressure of realities.

Permit me to say that you, as practically the only survivor of this great group of architects in the British Isles, might find it possible some day to overcome your present understandable reluctance, and speak to us as only you can do about the ways we have to tread.

I have very little to say for myself. A heavy burden not of my seeking has fallen on my shoulders, and I intend to do my best in guiding the first steps of the young State on the path of peace, integrity and good intelligence with the world at large.

I have little hope at present that our Arab neighbours will change their attitude. Only when they see that their fellow Arabs in the Jewish State are treated on equality with the Jewish citizens may they possibly change their minds.

Already at Lake Success I was approached by the Indian and Burmese Delegations about cooperation between their countries and Palestine in the intellectual and scientific fields. This is the first case of a great Eastern Power seeking such cooperation with us.

I have always believed that Providence selects the small countries to dispense its most precious gifts to humanity. Athens was merely one small city, and Palestine was always a poor country subjected to pressure from North and South; yet what they gave to the world is still the bedrock of human civilisation. It is thrilling to think that after a desert in time of two thousand years, the ancient glories of Jewish culture may be revived again in a modern form.

But I am afraid I have let myself go too much, and I would like to conclude by once more expressing my profound gratitude and asking you to forgive the length of the letter and submitting the request that if you feel like it, perhaps you might send me a word at your convenience.[2]

I remain, dear Mr. Churchill, with all my affectionate good wishes for your health,

247. To Ernst David Bergmann, Rehovot.   *Vevey, 8 August 1948*
English: Or. Copy. T.W.: W.A.

My dear David,

I was very glad to receive your letter of the 6th ult.,[1] but I am still without a reply to the main questions, namely a) what arrangements are made for my transport? Time is getting short, as I would like to leave here on or about 15th IX. b) Are you coming or are you not coming? If you do not come, I shall have to get somebody to accompany us. c) Can I count on the *Kedmah* being in Marseilles on or about the 15th IX?

I have received the following telegram from Kaplan:[2] "Israelgovt 22. Citrusgrowers delegation leaving for London next few days; will contact Benjamin there to receive his proposition. Warmest regards. Affectionately yours, Eliezer Kaplan."

Unless Kaplan takes the trouble to really urge this delegation to do something, nothing will happen. And it is no use Kaplan putting me off with this sort of stuff. So kindly see that something substantial is done. And please do answer my main questions.

I do not want any long letters, but I want short and precise answers to precise questions. It would make life much easier. I shall not write about the Institute and its work, neither shall I trouble you about the workshop except for asking you: How did you imagine Atlas to pay for the goods he intends to acquire?[3] Atlas seems to be under the impression that I shall place at his disposal the necessary sums. I would gladly do so, but it is entirely outside my competence. It is a matter for the Treasury of the Institute in U.S.A. Would you please answer these questions by telegram, as time is getting dreadfully short. And the long intervals between one communication and another one makes correspondence a most painful performance. I realize that you are all at war. I also realize that the whole scientific basis of the Institute has been changed. Whether it

---

[2] Churchill did not reply.

247. [1] W.A. At Weisgal's request Bergmann had also cabled W. 3 Aug. (W.A.) reassuring him on the safety of personnel and the work at the Institute.
[2] See Nos. 194, 228.
[3] See No. 228.

is a good thing or not I propose to discuss personally. Meanwhile I expect a clear answer to my questions.[4]

Affectionately yours,

Ch. Weizmann

248. To Walter Elliot, London.   *Vevey, 9 August 1948*
English: T.W.: W.A.

My dear Walter,

I was extremely happy to receive your note,[1] and I am most grateful for it. You and Deedes seem to be the only two English people who have ever sent me a word. Now, I can include Mr. Churchill, which is something, and we have now a visit from Dr. Crossman.

I would very much like to know how you are and what are your plans.

Vera has not been well for some time, but I am happy to say she is pulling out of it now. We intend to go to Palestine on about September 15, if we have proper transport.

I wrote a short note to Mr. Churchill.[2] There is nothing very much to report. Things in Palestine seem to go normally in spite of initial difficulties. The West European Powers are very slow in recognizing us, and we shall have to make up our mind to do without it. And in the end, it will be more harmful to them than to us, and this stupid policy will bear Dead Sea fruit.

I am told by certain people[3] who have seen Mr. Bevin recently and have talked to him that he is just modelling himself on our old friend Mr. Hitler. Well, there is no accounting for taste, and the lesson of Hitler has apparently had no effect on Mr. Bevin.

If you have nothing better to do, please drop me a note. I would very much like to know how things are with you.

I remain, with affectionate regards,

Yours ever,

Chaim

[4] Bergmann cabled 18 Aug. 'Firstly, am dealing [with] your transportation arrangement. Secondly, everybody believes *Kedmah* unsuitable. Have written and cabled regarding Benji. Believe you need not worry. Regarding Atlas, have neither asked him [to] approach Chief [i.e., W.], nor buy any equipment apart smallest items, nor authorised him stay longer than required [for] family reason. Am prepared recall him immediately. Fifth, very distressed Chief dissatisfied present activities Institute.'

248. [1] See No. 241, n. 1.

[2] See No. 246.

[3] W.'s informant was McDonald, who had a meeting with Bevin in London on 3 Aug. and visited W. on 5th. Of his meeting with Bevin, he told W. that he recalled feeling 'as if I had heard the echo of Hitler's words about telling a big lie'. (James G. McDonald, *My Mission to Israel,* London 1951, pp. 25–26).

249. To Ernst David Bergmann, Rehovot. *Vevey, 11 August 1948*
English: T.: W.A.

Thanks telegram and all you have done for Benji.[1] Am entering hospital on Friday for cataract operation. Hope to be back Vevey about end month. Please wire definitely when you are coming. Affectionately,

Weizmann

250. To Eliezer Kaplan, Tel Aviv. *Vevey, 11 August 1948*
English: T.: W.A.

Most grateful what you have done for Benji. Appreciate it very deeply.[1] Affectionately,

Weizmann

251. To Harry S. Truman, Washington. *Geneva, 6 September 1948*
English: Or. Copy. T.W.: W.A.

Dear Mr. President,

I have received from our friend Mr. Eddie Jacobson an account of the conversation which he was privileged to have with you a few weeks ago on the subject of the proposed loan to Israel.[1] In his letter, Mr. Jacobson tells me that when he left you he felt confident of good news at an early date.

I should have written earlier, but I have had to undergo an eye operation, and I have only just come out of the clinic. May I now express my deep appreciation of the keen interest which you have taken in this project?[2] In sanctioning this loan you will be giving assistance to those schemes of refugee welfare and economic and social development which have always attracted your interest in connection with Palestine and the Near East.

---

249. [1] Representatives of Citrus Board had tentatively offered the post of fruit inspector in England to Benjamin W.

250. [1] See also W. telegram to Kaplan 19 Sept. (W.A.).

251. [1] Jacobson to W., 6 Aug. (W.A.), reporting on his meeting the previous day with Truman, at which the President spoke about a loan to Israel. Truman authorised Jacobson to tell W. that he would 'give us action' in the very near future. Further, Jacobson thought it wise for W. to send the President a note of appreciation in advance.

[2] The request had been for a $100 million loan to Israel. Despite this early private assurance to Jacobson and W., Truman announced authorization of the loan only 19 Jan. 1949.

In his letter Mr. Jacobson also informs me that he raised the question of *de jure* recognition of Israel and our entry into the United Nations. I feel that with these two steps you will be in a position to complete a political solution of this grave problem along lines which fully conform with the historic assistance which you gave on November 29th and May 14th.

I am certain that Jews and Zionists everywhere will always remember with gratitude your constant and effective support in critical times.

With warmest good wishes and personal regards,

Very sincerely yours,
Chaim Weizmann

252. To Leonard J. Stein, London.   *Geneva, 17 September 1948*
English: T.W.: W.A.

My dear Leonard,

I cannot tell you how glad I was to receive your note,[1] for which I am very grateful, and which reflects to a certain extent my own thoughts and opinions, especially with regard to the British. Here is something we built and nurtured for 30 years, and which has been destroyed in so short a time by the unthinkable behaviour of one or two men only. It has engendered a great deal of hatred and of ill will quite unnecessarily. The British could have gone out of Palestine in an atmosphere of friendship; I know that it was everybody's desire, and it probably still is, to continue in some way the tradition of friendly relations.

What hurt me most was the fact that the British have allowed Arabs from outside to invade Palestine, at a time when they were still in control of the northern frontier and the Mandate. They knew that the Arabs intended to massacre the Jews; like everybody else

---

252. [1] Stein wrote (13 Sept. W.A.) expressing happiness that W.'s eye operation was a success. He continued: 'I have been really troubled in my mind by my omission to write to you on your acceptance of the Presidency of Israel. I was torn by conflicting emotions—on the one hand, my natural impulse to say what I felt on so moving an occasion and, on the other hand, my deep distress at the emergence of Israel in circumstances reflecting so painfully the collapse of the British connection and all that it had signified . . . Knowing as I do how much you had staked on the British connection as the corner-stone of your policy, I realise how keenly you must have felt the unhappy series of events—not least the clumsy and short-sighted handling of the situation on the British side—which led to the ending of the Mandate in an atmosphere of mutual resentment'.

they did not realise the military strength and the devotion of the Jewish army, which has prevented a great disaster.

The attempts of Glubb Pasha[2] and his Arab Legionnaires to seize Jerusalem, and put Abdullah on the throne of David is something which will be remembered in history as a cynical desecration of the Holy City by a nation which calls itself Christian.

All that has upset me no end, and it will take a long time to get over it. Neither Churchill nor anyone else of the elder British statesmen has found the time or the opportunity to give expression to what they must have felt to be a most miserable performance of their own country.

However, that is all gone and passed, the Jewish State is established and seems to be working very satisfactorily so far. I think that everybody in Israel realises how much the attention of the world is centered on them, and they will, no doubt, try to live up to our expectations. We shall make mistakes, we shall blunder about for some time; but I believe that in the end we shall get on the road to some considerable achievement.

I expect to leave here at the end of the month, and settle down in Rechovot for practically the whole of the year, and shall, of course, try my best to advise and to guide the Government and the *Yishuv*, in accordance with the principles for which I have lived and toiled all my life.

I wonder whether you will have time in the course of the winter or the early spring to come out and spend a few weeks with us, for the mutual benefit of both sides.

We shall be trying our hand at a constitution, and my view is that we should not hurry to lay down a hard and fast constitution before two or three years of empirical government have passed. We must gain our own experience. Moreover, there is going to be a very considerable immigration in the next few years, and it would not be fair to face the newcomers with a completed constitution without giving them a chance for their contribution to or their criticism of it.

Still, I do not know what the Government has in mind to do, I haven't discussed it with them yet, and I will have to do it when I get out there.

The one thing I hope for is that the end of this war should be speeded up, as it is eating up all our national resources, which could have been useful for important constructive tasks.

---

[2] Lieut.-General (Sir) John Glubb (b. 1897). British soldier; commanded Arab Legion of Transjordan 1939–56; author, works on Arab politics and culture.

The Arabs are in a still worse financial plight, but that is little comfort to me. I am afraid that the war was a matter of necessity; we had to ward off the danger. But indefinite truce, which some of the British would like to continue, is equally dangerous. May be that when the rainy season comes passions will cool down, as they always do; and happily this is not far away.

Well, my letter has become somewhat rambling and unduly long. I do hope that you might find time to come out to Israel, you know you have a great share in it; and whatever your misgivings may be,[3] you will find a warm reception there, and you will, also, I am sure, rejoice in seeing the people going about their work in an atmosphere which has, from all I hear, a great deal of happiness about it—and in the world there are few communities nowadays about whom that can be said.

My best regards, and again thanks for your letter.

Affectionately yours,
Ch. Weizmann

253. To Gustavus V, King of Sweden,[1] Stockholm.

Geneva, 18 September 1948

French: T: W.A.

Deeply distressed by news of terrible assassination of Count Folke Bernadotte;[2] a cowardly and stupid criminal act deplored by the whole Jewish people, in Israel and elsewhere. I beg your Majesty to accept my deepest and most sincere condolences for all the bereaved family[3] as well as the Government and people of Sweden.

Chaim Weizmann
President of the State of Israel

[3] Stein had opposed Jewish statehood and was alienated from the Zionist leadership after W.'s removal. His letter expressed his reservations about visiting Israel.

253. [1] 1858–1950 (King from 1907).

[2] Having circulated his controversial peace proposals, rejected by both sides, the U.N. Mediator was assassinated 17 Sept. in Jerusalem by members of a Jewish dissident group not under the national discipline of the Jewish leadership. The assassins were never found.

[3] Bernadotte was a nephew of the King.

254. To Samuel I. Rosenman, New York.   *Geneva, 20 September 1948*
English: T.: W.A.

Understand proposals being mooted again[1] to cut off Negev from Israel. In my opinion there is no justification whatsoever for such truncation our territory, and arguments, which I had honour of submitting to President Truman in November 1947 for inclusion Negev are equally valid today. For us it is only large area within our boundaries which comparatively uninhabited. We have made not unsuccessful efforts at colonisation and have shown that with labour, capital and devotion Negev can be made fruitful. I believe that we shall be able to settle in time some hundreds of thousands refugees. Without us Negev will remain profitless desert. Akaba in Israel will grow into sizeable port and become centre of Israeli-Arab cooperation in economic development. Without us it has remained backward fishing village. Removal Negev from Israel will increase bitterness and stimulate irredentist feelings. It will become centre of unrest from which neighbouring areas of Israel will be harassed by Bedouins and Egyptian bands as is happening now. Beg you do whatever possible and convey gist this cable to President Truman.[2] Warmest regards.

Chaim Weizmann

255. To Meyer W. Weisgal, Tel Aviv.   *Geneva, 20 September 1948*
English: T.: W.A.

Thanks telegram,[1] but am most anxious have definite news when plane arriving take me back. Surprised Bergmann's silence. Waiting becoming increasingly difficult.

Chaim Weizmann

254. [1] W. had received copy of a telegram from Eban in Paris to Shertok (19 Sept., W.A.) with advance summary of the Mediator's revised main proposals, submitted before Bernadotte's assassination. Eban noted that Bernadotte had moved towards Israel's position since his original suggestions. Thus he now relinquished the idea of a political or economic union with Transjordan and saw the need for separate States. Lydda and Haifa were not to be internationalized, while Jerusalem would be accorded separate treatment rather than incorporation within the Arab State. Finally, proposals about the Arab refugees left the door open for compensation and resettlement as well as for repatriation. Israel was being offered the whole of Galilee; the Arabs the whole of the Negev. Eban cautioned in a further letter to W. the next day (W.A.) that it would be 'only realistic to understand at this moment that at least a partial relinquishment of the Negev will be inevitable'.

   [2] Rosenman replied 21 Sept. (W.A.) promising his good offices.

255. [1] 20 Sept. (W.A.), stating that a plane was being prepared for the Weizmanns' transportation.

256. To Oscar Fehr, London.   *Geneva, 21 September 1948*
English: Or. Copy. T.W.: W.A.

My dear Professor Fehr,

I should already have written to you before, to tell you that my operation has passed successfully. The scar is healing well, and my sight has, naturally, greatly improved. Still, I feel that it was a very deep intervention, which has required a long period of convalescence, which is almost over now. When the sun is very strong, as happens here in the warmer days of autumn, I have to put on my dark glasses, and I will probably have to do the same over in Israel. I am sure, though, that I will get used to this condition.

I am very grateful for your advice, and I must say that Franceschetti is a first class man.

I hope all is well with you, and that you have good news from your children, and that you do not work too hard.

I am leaving for Israel in about 10 days, so that a line from you could still reach me here; and I would be very happy to hear from you.

I remain most sincerely, and with kindest regards,

Yours

257. To Doris May, London.   *Geneva, 21 September 1948*
English: Or. Copy. T.W.: W.A.

My dear Miss May,

I am most grateful to you for your kind letter[1] and also for your cable.[2] We seem to be doing our best in critical moments to make our task impossible. The fatal series which began with Moyne[3] seems to continue, and it is no use to try to apportion blame, as we are paying for all the sins to some extent. I never thought the Jews will be as stupid as that; I am sorry to say they are.

We hope to get away in about a week or ten days, and I am most anxious to do so. My trouble is that I cannot get any sense out of our people in Israel. I cannot pin them down to a definite date when they will send a plane, and the suspense is great trouble to me. However, I am still hoping to hear something in a day or two, and then we shall be going between the 27th and the 30th.

257. [1] 16 Sept. (W.A.).

[2] This, 18 Sept. (W.A.) was in reaction to the murder of Bernadotte. She hoped W. would be given strength 'to endure through this valley of the shadows'.

[3] Lord Moyne (Biog. Index, Vol. XX). For his assassination while Minister of State in Cairo by members of Stern Group, 6 Nov. 1944, see Vol. XXI.

I do hope I might see you when we have settled down in Israel. I shall write to you about it when the time comes.

There is one small request. Linton mentioned to me that Locker, in reading some part of my memoirs concerning a conversation with Passfield and some Labour people, has found some errors. I am anxious to correct them, but Linton did not make it quite clear enough. Would you please be so kind and ask both Linton and Locker about it.

There is nothing to report from here, apart from the fact that we are having some wonderful autumn days, which I wish I could enjoy more than I am able to at the moment. You can still write to me to Geneva and tell me how you are. How is your work? And with whom are you working chiefly?

I am sending you my affectionate regards, and remain

Yours ever,

258. To Moshe Shertok, Tel Aviv. *Geneva, 24 September 1948*
Code: T.: W.A.

Believe considered reply must be given to antisemitic attacks charging whole Jewish people with crime of Bernadotte's murder. Never were the English charged with the responsibility for the murder of General Wilson[1] and similar cases. Regards.

Chaim Weizmann

259. To Edward Jacobson, Kansas City. *Geneva, 27 September 1948*
English: T.: W.A.

Regarding new proposal to cut off Negev from Israel: In my opinion there is no justification for such amputation our territory, and arguments which I had honor of submitting to your friend in November 1947 for inclusion Negev are equally valid today. For us it is only large area within our boundaries which is comparatively uninhabited and therefore suitable for settlement numerous immigrants without interfering with anybody. We have made not unsuccessful efforts at colonisation and have shown that with labour, capital and devotion Negev can be made fruitful. I believe we shall be able to settle in time some hundreds of thousands refugees. Without us Negev will remain profitless desert. Akaba in Israel will grow into

258. [1] Sir Henry Hughes Wilson (Biog. Index, Vol. IX). Assassinated by Irish nationalists in London 1922.

sizeable port and become center of Israeli/Arab cooperation in economic development. Without us it has remained backward fishing village. Removal Negev from Israel will increase bitterness. It will become center of unrest from which neighbouring areas of Israel will be harassed by Bedouins and Egyptian bands, as is happening now. Only intervention of your friend, who has done so much for us, can avert the worst dangers. Please go and see him without delay, reminding him of Democratic Party pledge that no change boundaries would take place without consent Government of Israel, but above all his own encouragement to me, on which we all very implicitly rely, and for which we shall be eternally grateful. Cordial greetings and best wishes.

Chaim Weizmann

260. To James C. Chuter-Ede,[1] London.   *Geneva, 28 September 1948*
English: Copy. T.W.: W.A.

Dear Sir,

As you probably know I was elected President of the State of Israel soon after the State was proclaimed on the 14th of May, 1948. For reasons of health it has not been possible for me so far to return to Israel to take up my duties there. I am now, however, on the verge of departing for Israel, and I am sure that it will be appreciated that it is appropriate that I should arrive in Israel as a citizen of the country. I am, therefore, taking steps to acquire Israeli citizenship immediately, and assume that as a consequence I will be automatically relieved of British citizenship, which it has been my privilege and honour to enjoy for the past forty years.

In these circumstances I return herewith the British passports of Mrs. Weizmann and myself, with expressions of the deepest appreciation for all that I was able to do and to become during the time I lived and worked in England. It is still my earnest hope that in my new capacity I shall be able to work for the reestablishment of the traditional friendly relations between Great Britain and Israel.[2]

I am, Sir,
Yours faithfully,

260. [1] Later, Lord Chuter-Ede (1882–1965). Home Secretary 1945–51.

[2] The Home Secretary replied only on 22 Mar. 1949, pleading legal technicalities: under English law British nationality could not be renounced unless the British subject in question was a national of a foreign country recognized by His Majesty's Government. With Britain's *de facto* recognition of Israel on 30 Jan., Chuter-Ede was prepared to accept from W. a declaration of renunciation of citizenship. He thanked W. for his warm words of appreciation for the past and of hope for the future: 'May I say how much we all look forward to happy relations between our two countries.'

[On 30 Sept. 1948 Chaim and Vera Weizmann, travelling by D.C. 4 of Israel's Air Transport Command that was specially painted and converted for the purpose, arrived in Israel for the first time since proclamation of statehood and resumed residence at their home in Rehovot. As to the flight, see Munya Mardor, *Strictly Illegal,* London 1964, pp. 228–29.]

261. To Edward Jacobson, Kansas City. *Tel Aviv, 4 October 1948*
English: T.: W.A.

It gives me great pleasure and happiness to convey to you from here my best wishes for New Year and my cordial thanks for all you have done to help bring about establishment of Jewish State.

Chaim Weizmann

262. To Pierre Bigar,[1] Geneva. *Rehovot, 10 October 1948*
English: T.W.: W.A.

My dear Pierre,

Let me first of all wish you, Madeleine and the rest of your family, including Dr. Blum and Thérèse, a Happy New Year and all the best. I am here now almost a fortnight and have been fairly busy, first with the Institute, then in my own house, and have had no time yet to go around and see the country. Although our people are extremely courageous and confident, there is a depression and fatigue noticeable which is quite understandable. It is an unequal fight which is painfully reminiscent of Spain. On the one side is courage and determination—on the other are numbers and a great deal of equipment. We have now more equipment than we had at the beginning, but I am informed on very good authority that there were times when our people had to fight tanks with bare arms. It is much better now, but it has cost us a great deal. We have lost in this war ten thousand young men—and they are of the best. Still, it is very remarkable that one hears few complaints, few criticisms and comparatively little grumbling.

The problem I want to write to you about is a comparatively simple one, and I believe that if anybody can find a solution to it it is yourself. The Egyptians are attacking us from the air very severely, and although they are not very skilful the attacks are painful, because our defences are not what they ought to be. We have no anti-aircraft guns worth speaking of, while the Egyptians have

---

262. [1] 1889–1966. Department-store owner. Friend of W. Madeleine was his wife, Thérèse his daughter and Blum his son-in-law.

plenty, and in addition to that, long-range artillery. The total quantity of anti-aircraft guns in this country in Jewish hands is fifteen—whereas we ought to have something like five hundred to a thousand in order to meet the enemy on equal terms. The only place where one can get these guns is Oerlikon,[2] but I understand that they do not want to sell them to us. There may be reasons of neutrality, but from what I hear the owner of this factory is rather anti-Jewish. I am sure that you are in a position to find out the exact state of affairs, and we would all be extremely grateful to you if you could let us know whether and how many guns we can get, what are the conditions of payment, and we would then send you the money over at once.[3] I do not think I need waste your time in long explanations on how important all that is to us. If we would have the necessary equipment, we could finish the job in about a month, and it is essential, both politically and economically, to do so as soon as possible.[4]

That is all for the time being. We shall be looking forward to your visit in the early spring, and please do not disappoint us. We are all well, and Rehovot has been spared so far, although a very short time ago it was the object of many attacks.

We send you all our best love and remain, with kindest regards,

Yours ever,
Ch. Weizmann

263. To Leopold S. Amery, London.   *Rehovot, 24 October 1948*
English: T.W.: W.A.

My dear Amery,

I wanted to write to you before, but I was anxious to really get the feel of the land prior to expressing an opinion on the situation

---

[2] Oerlikon Machine Tool Works, Bührle & Co. of Zurich, armaments manufacturers specialising in anti-aircraft artillery.

[3] Replying by secret, coded telegram 1 Nov. (W.A.), Bigar stated that he had located in Geneva 100 Hispano model cannons available immediately at a reduction, with prospects of another 50 each month after Nov. Purchase could be made through a neutral country approved by Switzerland. The Israeli Government could send a buyer to Geneva to negotiate. Writing again 18 Nov. (W.A.), Bigar informed W. that, having put Israeli agents in touch with well-placed Swiss arms dealers, he considered his task finished. Nevertheless, he remained entirely at W.'s disposal.

[4] Shaul Avigur (Meirov), of the Defence Ministry and one of the leading figures engaged in arms purchases, wrote W. 19 Nov. (W.A.) that the sources of supply indicated by Bigar were known to them, and a considerable quantity had been purchased from one of the firms.

here. I must admit that I have not yet got used to the fact that one can travel from Beer-Sheva to the North without meeting either an Englishman or an Arab. The total number of the Arabs in Israel is about 60,000, or slightly over, and there are practically no Englishmen except a few officers who stayed behind with the Jewish Army and some officials of the Haifa Refinery. All dire prophecies which were so freely spoken of before the British left have proved completely false. The Arabs were told and encouraged to believe that as soon as the British go they can sweep down on the Jews and throw them into the sea. They might graciously condescend to leave us Tel-Aviv and its immediate neighbourhood, and even that would have been emptied out to a very considerable degree. And true enough, all the preparations for such an event were made, and on the 15th of May the British allowed about 10,000 Arabs from the North to invade the country. They stood by watching; they knew very well what the intentions of the Arabs were, and they were ready to witness the destruction of the work which they themselves had helped to build up.

Of course, they were greatly surprised when they saw the resistance of the Jews, and I still read in the press that neither they nor a great many other people in the UNO have got over this surprise which has completely upset all calculations. I see in to-day's press that they talk quite glibly in the UNO that the Negev will be divided between the British and Trans-Jordan. I do not think that an inch of territory will be yielded by the Armies of Israel to anybody. The conquest of the Negev has cost us many hundreds of dead and many thousands of wounded, and the account is not yet closed, and the Jews are not prepared to shed their blood either for Mr. Bevin or Mr. Abdullah. If they want the Negev there are two ways: they would either have to negotiate with the Jews or they can take it. You know what my relationship to the British was and still is, but the fact that they permitted the invasion of Palestine while they were still in the country has given me a shock which I have not got over yet. The tragedy of it is that the British could have left Palestine as friends with the Jews, and could have secured for themselves in a peaceful way whatever interests they were in need of, either in the Negev or in other parts of the country. It will now require a long period before all that is forgotten, and the good which the British have done to Palestine is remembered.

The policy of the Foreign Office is fatal. I cannot describe to you in detail the chicanery to which we have been subjected here. They left Palestine in a completely chaotic condition, no railway, no port or telegraph, many water sources were polluted, but in a fortnight everything was put in order, and the State functions much more effi-

ciently than at the time of the Mandate. So, for instance, letters
from Jerusalem to Tel-Aviv, which used to take anything between
10 to 14 days, arrive now in a day or so. The roads are clear, and we
shall very soon have at least two roads to Jerusalem, which have
been cut off by the Arabs in Latrun. If it was not for the present
Truce, the Arabs would be thrown out of the country mercilessly.
The only thing which saves them is the Truce, which they break and
utilise to bring up reinforcements. As you may have read in to-day's
papers the UNO observers seem to have discovered that the Egyptians had doubled their forces during the Truce period. But even if
they tripled their forces, it would be of no avail; they do not stomach
the fight, and run for their lives as soon as they are faced with a
real attack. I do not think that there can be any question of the Jews
yielding any part of the Negev, and I do not believe that they can be
forced to do so after these battles.

I am writing about the same question to President Truman,[1] as
I would not like to leave him under any misapprehension concerning
our intentions.

I know that the British have considerable interests both in the
Negev and in Haifa—these will have to be dealt with in a peaceful
and friendly way, but not under pressure and threats. It is quite possible that the Foreign Secretary would not like it, but that is a matter
of secondary consideration to us at present. It is he who encouraged
the Arabs, it is he who will have to reap the results of this bitter
disappointment.

As a side light on the situation you may be interested in the following report from Egypt of two days ago. As soon as it became
known that the Egyptians signed the agreement for a truce, a vast
mob filled the streets of Cairo and demonstrated against their Government, saying that they had been betrayed. If they were so victorious as the Government had presented it to them all these weeks
and months, then there was no reason to agree to a Truce; this
agreement seems to indicate that they have been fed on false information. The situation threatened to become ugly, and the only
way to disperse this mob was to sound the sirens announcing an
air-raid by the Israeli Air Force. The mob dispersed, but it is inevitable that they will get to know the real state of affairs very soon,
and like some of our British Ministers, Farouk[2] and his people

---

263. [1] See Nos. 269, 271.

[2] Farouk I (1920–1965). King of Egypt until deposed and exiled in the revolution of
July 1952.

will have something to answer for. The Egyptians have been printing every week special stamps on which were depicted their victories; I am getting a collection of these stamps and intend to send it on to the F.O. as a memento.

The Haifa Refinery is for the time being idle, and the Iraqis do not let their oil through the pipe, but we shall have tankers coming from various parts of America and we can run the Haifa Refinery with our own forces. We have done so before for about six weeks in spite of the warnings and threats of the I[raq] P[etroleum] C[ompany]'s engineers.

I am afraid my letter has become somewhat long and discursive, but I was anxious to inform you that the State of Israel is running quite smoothly in spite of the war both in the North and the South of it. If the Egyptians felt that they could expect no encouragement from the British they might quickly come to terms with us. If the British do not tell the Egyptians the truth, well, the thing will have to be fought out, and it might have serious consequences for the regime in Egypt, and it will certainly discredit the British in the eyes of the Arabs who relied so much on British judgment and advice. For about thirty years the British dominated the Middle East; they had their High Commissioners, their Ambassadors, their technical advisers, their Military advisers from the Euphrates to the Nile, and all this time they overestimated the strength of the Arabs and underestimated the strength of the Jews. These are two serious mistakes which a great power in possession of all the facts should not have made.

I am sorry to have to say all this, but I have no doubt in my mind that the British intended to sweep us into the sea with the help of the Arabs. If it did not happen, it is only because the Arabs proved a broken reed.

They could have had the State of Israel as a bulwark of friendship for the British, based on a long tradition and on community of interests. Instead of doing that they have chosen to build on the quicksands of Arab loyalty, and here are some of the results. I do not know what the British press is writing about all this, but I was anxious to let you know some of the truth.

I should be grateful if you would care to show this letter to Walter Elliot. I may be writing in a few days to Colonel Stanley.

I hope all is well with you and Mrs. Amery, and send you my fondest love and all the best,

As ever,
Yours,
Ch. Weizmann

264. To Sir Simon Marks, London.   *Rehovot, 24 October 1948*
English: Or. Copy. T.W.: W.A.

My dear Simon,

Meyer Weisgal is going to London, and he is bringing you our personal good wishes and greetings for the New Year. I am sending you a copy of a letter which I have written to Mr. Amery[1] and which is self-explanatory. Marcus[2] no doubt will have brought you some firsthand news; his travelling forwards and backwards is of great importance to all of us. I hope he will soon come back again.

I do not know what the British press is writing, but the situation here will have grave repercussions in the whole Middle East, and will affect the position and the credit of Great Britain and its prestige in the eyes of the oriental population for many years to come, unless they choose to alter their course radically.

Mr. Morgenthau is here and is going about the country like in a dream. He never thought he will find things as he is seeing them. Yesterday he spent the whole morning at the Institute and the Experiment Station,[3] and I am quite sure that even the Massachusetts Institute of Technology, which is of course a colossal institution with a budget of many millions of dollars annually, is not as impressive as all one sees now in Rehovot. Well, Meyer will tell you all about it.

I have been watching the work of the young Government, and although many things seem somewhat amateurish and hesitant, they have done extremely well on the whole under very difficult circumstances. B.G. as Prime Minister and Minister of Defence has proved a great success. Whether he will be the same success in peace time I am not prepared to say; he reminds me somewhat of Winston who is good in war and less so in peace. However, it is too early to draw any conclusions. He is thoughtful, calm, resolute and a man of enormous courage. I think he enjoys the support of all parties and rightly so.

Morgenthau thinks he could find some extra money outside the budget of the U.J.A. for certain purposes, and I am sure that he will do his best to carry his intentions into effect. My impressions are

---

264. [1] See No. 263.

[2] (Sir) Marcus J. Sieff, b. 1913. Son of Israel Sieff. His British military service in W.W.II included Staff work in Middle East. At this time he was engaged in activities on behalf of Israel Defence Forces in Tel Aviv. Later, chairman of Marks and Spencer, London. From Nov. 1976 chairman of Board of Governors, Weizmann Institute. Late 1948 he sent a memorandum to the British Government urging recognition of Israel (W.A.).

[3] The Sieff (Weizmann) Institute and the Agricultural Experimental Station at Rehovot.

not all yet properly settled down and organised, and I am writing somewhat at random and not too systematically, but I do not want to postpone sending you a word of heartiest greetings, both to you and Miriam[4] and the family. Please give my love to Harry,[5] and I hope his health has been restored; naturally also my love to Israel [Sieff].

With all best wishes for a happy New Year and looking forward to seeing you soon, I am your old friend,

Ch. Weizmann

265. To David Ben-Gurion, Jerusalem. *Rehovot, 26 October 1948*
Hebrew: Or. Copy. T.W.: W.A.

Dear Mr. Prime Minister,

Knowing that in these days your time and thoughts are occupied with matters of the greatest importance, I am directing my request to you most reluctantly. I am certain, however, that only you are in a position to be of assistance in this matter.

In order to complete the new Institute at Rehovot, we need 75 permanent labourers. At the moment we have had placed at our disposal, after great difficulties, only 10% of the required number, and even they come and go, and are not on the job regularly. I am certain that there is no need to explain to you the vital function which the Institute serves in carrying out its tasks for the war effort, and how important it is to increase the number of completed, operational laboratories.

Please forgive my troubling you on this matter, which I hope you will agree is by no means a trivial one.

With cordial greetings,
Ch. Weizmann

266. To Beatrice Magnes, New York. *Rehovot, 28 October 1948*
English: T.: W.A.

Our affectionate sympathy is with you in your bereavement. Your husband[1] will be remembered as one of the great leaders in the

---

[4] Lady Marks.

[5] Harry Sacher (Biog. Index, Vol. V). Lawyer and journalist. Formerly on Zionist executive in Jerusalem; Marks' brother-in-law.

266. [1] Judah Leon Magnes (Biog. Index, Vol. IV). President of H.U., he had died in New York.

upbuilding of our country and as an example of untiring devotion to the work which will remain sacred to the Jewish people.

Vera, Chaim Weizmann

267. To Edward Jacobson, Kansas City.　　*Rehovot, 4 November 1948*
English: Or. Copy. T.W.: W.A.

Dear Mr. Jacobson,

I should like to send you heartfelt greetings on this day,[1] which means much to us all, and I know means particularly much to you. We here in Israel have watched the ups and downs of the Presidential contest in recent weeks with bated breath, and I know that I am speaking the mind of the bulk of our people here when I say that we feel deeply grateful at the outcome of this election. The next few years will be critical ones for the State of Israel. Our enemies are trying to achieve by intrigue and calumny what they failed to bring about by brute force. Much will depend on the attitude of the President of the United States, who has been elected under such auspicious circumstances and with such a large measure of national support. And a great responsibility devolves upon you, my dear friend. I need not say much on the subject, for I know that you are deeply alive to that responsibility.

Kindest regards and all good wishes,[2]

Yours

268. To Harry S. Truman, Washington.　　*Rehovot, 4 November 1948*
English: T.: W.A.

Most happy result of elections. Respectfully offer sincerest congratulations. All good wishes for most successful term of office for the good of your country and humanity.

Chaim Weizmann

---

267. [1] On 2 Nov. Truman had been re-elected President over his Republican rival, Thomas Dewey.

[2] On 29 Nov., first anniversary of the U.N. Resolution, Jacobson acknowledged receipt of this letter and No. 261 (W.A.). He reported that Truman had given assurances on at least two recent occasions of his continued friendship towards W. and Israel.

269. To Harry S. Truman, Washington. *Rehovot, 5 November 1948*
English: Or. Copy. T.W.: W.A.

Dear Mr. President,

Permit me to extend to you most hearty congratulations and good wishes on your re-election. We in this country have been watching the progress of the Presidential contest with bated breath, and I am sure that I am speaking the mind of the bulk of my people when I say that we feel deeply thankful that the people of the United States have given you the opportunity of shaping the policies of your country and the affairs of humanity at large during the next critical four years. We interpret their vote as an emphatic endorsement of the policy of peace, security and ordered progress in world affairs, for which you have stood since you assumed your high office, and for the continued prosecution of which men and women in every part of the globe pray with all their hearts. May you be granted health and strength to carry out your noble purpose.

We have special cause to be gratified at your re-election, because we are mindful of the enlightened help which you gave to our cause in these years of our struggle. We particularly remember your unflinching advocacy of the admission of Jewish refugees to Palestine, your determined stand against the attempts to deflect you from your course, your staunch support of our admission to statehood at Lake Success, and your recognition of the fact of its establishment within an hour of our proclamation of independence. We pray that your assistance and guidance may be extended to us also in the coming years. We have succeeded in the past twelve months in defending our independence against enemies from every quarter—north, south and east, as in Biblical times—and in setting up the framework of our State. Enemy armies are still on the borders of our country, maintained there, I regret to say, by the vacillating attitude of the United Nations, which have imposed a truce that is becoming ever more not a forerunner of peace, but an instrument of war. Our essential aim is peace and reconstruction. While the eyes of the world have been turned on to the battlefields in the south and the north, we have succeeded in liquidating one refugee camp after another in Europe and bringing the chance of a new life to thousands of ruined men and women whom the world has all but forgotten. We have brought over 62,000 since we attained independence. To develop this great effort at human rehabilitation we need, above all, three things: first, peace; second, recognition; and third, financial and economic support for the execution of those large projects of agricultural and industrial development which are essential for the absorption of newcomers and the economic progress of the country.

The most important requirement at this moment is that this unreal and untenable truce be brought to an end and be supplanted by a speedy and enduring peace. Over two months ago we asked the Mediator to call both sides to the conference table, but the other side rejected our offer. We have no aggressive designs against anyone, and we are at any moment ready to negotiate a peace settlement. Our enemies have failed in their efforts to beat us by brute force although they outnumbered us by 20 to 1. They are now endeavouring through the medium of the Security Council to undermine the decision taken by the General Assembly last November and to deprive us of the undeveloped areas of the Negev which offer space for new homes for many thousands of our uprooted people, and which will remain a desert land if they are annexed by the neighbouring Arab states, as is evidently intended. This is the real purpose behind the Security Council's Resolution introduced by Great Britain, which to my deep regret was supported by the American Delegation.[1] We have no choice but to oppose this design, which would destroy last November's decision of the General Assembly and would reduce us to a state of permanent insecurity and vulnerability.

I pray with all my heart that you, Mr. President, may use your high authority to put an end to these hostile manoeuvres. We have successfully withstood the onslaught of the Arab States, who were sent against us by the British, almost like a pack of hired assassins. I am saying this with deep pain because I have throughout my life been deeply attached to Great Britain and have suffered for that attachment. But the evidence unfortunately all points in this direction, and even as I write we are receiving constant reports of Great Britain re-arming the Arabs to enable them to re-start hostilities against us. Having failed in her efforts to wipe out our young commonwealth, she now appears bent on detaching the Negev from our State. I feel emboldened to ask for your intervention in this matter, remembering the deep sympathy and understanding which you displayed when I had the privilege of stating to you our case on the Negev and displaying to you maps showing its potentialities for settlement. It was with a deep feeling of elation that I

---

269. [1] Hostilities had resumed in Oct., during which the Israeli Army made important gains in the Negev against Egypt. The Security Council, meeting in emergency session 19 Oct., gave unanimous approval for an immediate cease-fire and for an Anglo-Chinese Resolution of 14th which stipulated, *inter alia,* that both sides withdraw from positions not hitherto occupied.

left you on that day, and it is this which now encourages me to plead for your intervention to prevent this part of the country, which was allotted to us last November, from being detached from our State. Sheer necessity compels us to cling to the Negev. Our pioneers have done yeoman work in opening up this semi-arid country; they have built pipe lines through the desert, set up agricultural settlements, planted gardens and orchards in what was for many centuries a barren land. They will not give up this land unless they are bodily removed from it.

I venture to hope that clear and firm instructions be issued on this vital matter to the American Delegation in Paris which has of late, apparently, not received directives corresponding to the views which, I know, you hold on the subject. I would further plead that you may find it possible to direct the competent authorities to enable us to secure that long-term financial assistance which is urgently needed for the execution of the great scheme of reconstruction which I had the privilege of submitting to you in the Summer.[2]

With every good wish,[3]

Sincerely yours,

270. To Felix Frankfurter, Washington.   *Rehovot, 7 November 1948*
English: Or. Copy. T.W.: W.A.

Dear Felix,

Many thanks for your charming letter.[1] I can hardly put into words how deeply I felt receiving your and Marion's greetings. I was particularly glad to read that you were thinking of coming out here. I hope you will come soon. You will be a most welcome guest in this country. Do come as soon as you can.

I don't know what kind of reports are reaching you about things here. Things are getting more stable from day to day. I do hope that this unreal truce will soon come to an end and the road be opened up to a stable and enduring peace. You will probably have heard Morgenthau's report. He had the opportunity of seeing things at

---

[2] See No. 173.

[3] Truman cabled acknowledgement of this letter 15 Nov. (W.A.). On 29 Nov. he replied fully, noting their recent parallel experiences: 'We had both been abandoned by the so-called realistic experts to our supposedly forlorn lost causes. Yet we both kept pressing for what we were sure was right—and we were both proven to be right.' He expressed his full agreement with W.'s estimate of the Negev's importance for Israel—and 'I deplore any attempt to take it away from Israel'. He further assured W. of American willingness to help develop the new State through financial and economic measures (W.A.).

270. [1] 2 Oct. (W.A.). A note of tribute on the occasion of W.'s arrival in Israel.

first-hand, and, though not given to easy enthusiasms, I believe he was very deeply impressed and formed a businesslike view of the situation and the prospects it holds out for the future.

Once more, come soon. We are beginning already to fatten the calf.

Yours ever,

271. To Harry S. Truman, Washington.   *Rehovot, 9 November 1948*
English: T.: W.A.

Feel moved address you urgent appeal that United States Government use its influence in counsels of United Nations view preventing detachment Negev,[1] whose potentialities for large-scale Jewish settlement I put before you last summer, from State of Israel contrary to last November's decision General Assembly United Nations. On May fifteenth fully equipped Arab armies were allowed invade Israel from north, east and south with evident purpose destroying our young commonwealth. Our people almost unarmed withstood the onslaught and successfully defended their independence. Since then under guise maintenance truce sinister efforts have been made by interested parties bring about reduction area State Israel, in particular annexation Negev in whole or part by neighbouring States. Strongly feel that present Assembly United Nations should concentrate upon speedy liquidation present unreal truce which fraught grave danger resumption hostilities when Arab States have received necessary rearmament. Venture to suggest that durable peace can only be achieved by direct negotiations based on speedy withdrawal invading armies, full recognition State of Israel and its admission to United Nations. Encouraged by your sympathetic attitude and deep understanding of this problem I beg approach you with this request on which hinges peace and stability of our young State to whose establishment you have contributed so much. Sincerely hope you may find it possible instruct United States Delegation work for such comprehensive settlement. Thankfully and respectfully,

Chaim Weizmann

---

271. [1] W. may have been moved in this message to reinforce the plea in No. 269 by a cable from Morris Margulies in New York, 7 Nov. (W.A.). This suggested that W. offer a presentation of the facts to Truman, because the American Press was 'badly muddled' and the current Zionist leadership 'either impotent or incompetent'.

272. To Isaiah Berlin, Oxford.   *Rehovot, 10 November 1948*
English: Or. Copy. T.W.: W.A.

My dear Isaiah,

I can scarcely tell you how happy and moved I was in reading your letter.[1] I apologise for not having answered it at once—simply because on arrival here there were so many impressions and so many things to see that it took some time to get one's bearings. It is all like a dream. The country is just flourishing; the Jewish community is working, there are very few Arabs about and so far no hostile forces to impede our progress. I have no notion how all that reflects itself in the British press, but I can see from the little I glimpse from the Hebrew papers that Mr. Beeley[2] is doing his best; what he means to achieve seems quite clear, but I think he will fail like many other of our detractors before him. It is all a great pity, and I am sure you feel it as much as I do. Why they should do it, I do not know; it serves no useful purpose to the interests of England, but apparently the evil is always stronger than the good instincts, for a time at any rate.

Remembering our conversation in Paris, I am afraid it is no use repeating my invitation to you to come over even for a short time, but it seems to me that perhaps a short interruption in the midst of your arduous labours may do you good. One can fly out here in about twelve hours, and if you say the word I could arrange for our own plane to pick you up in Paris and bring you here; all this can be done without much waste of time. Even if you stay here only ten to fifteen days it will be of an enormous pleasure to us, and I am sure it will give you a great deal of encouragement and hope. Just say the word and we shall do the rest; you can easily do it at Xmas, I suppose.

Much love to you and all good wishes,

As ever,
Yours,

272. [1] 16 Sept. (W.A.). Berlin had written from France the day following a visit to the Weizmanns in Geneva. He stated that he now intended to pursue his academic interests with greater intensity. The only way he knew of serving Israel was by 'serving you, for reasons which you will not want me to put into banal words ... My association with you has been in all my life the thing in which I felt more pride and moral satisfaction than anything else'.

[2] (Sir) Harold Beeley, b. 1909. Secretary of Anglo-American Committee of Inquiry 1946; F.O. expert on Middle East 1946–49, when he was regarded by the Zionists as one of their principal opponents through his influence with Bevin. Ambassador to Egypt 1961–64.

273. To Selig Brodetsky, New York.   *Rehovot, 10 November 1948*
English: Or. Copy. T.W.: W.A.

My dear Brodetsky,

I was much interested in reading your important letter[1] and am grateful to you for having written to me in such detail. I am afraid you are labouring under some optimistic illusion if you think that you can get a substantial sum now from the Government or from the Zionist Organization. Our Government at present has no money, and for the time being I do not see anybody here who really is interested enough in higher education so as to feel the necessity of making a substantial contribution. This is a matter of education which, as you know, is a slow process.

I have not had an opportunity of speaking to Ben-Gurion about it, but I shall find time very soon to do so. I know what the answer will be: (a) they have no money and (b) whatever little comes in will be required for projects which are more immediate and more urgent.

Of course you realise that the war is eating up practically the whole of the budget, but I am hoping that this plague will soon be over. It will then be time to raise your question, and if you are here in December,[2] I think we ought both to make a dead set on the Government that they should at least begin to do a bit more than they have done hitherto. At any rate, I am extremely happy that you will be here soon, but for the present I advise you to get as much out of America as you possibly can. You know that Morgenthau has been in this country and went back very elated. He might be of some use to you, although he is not too much interested in academic problems.

With kindest regards and looking forward to seeing you here soon, I am,

Yours ever,
Ch. Weizmann

274. To Richard Crossman, London.   *Rehovot, 10 November 1948*
English: Or. Copy. T.W.: W.A.

My dear Dick,

I am writing to you on behalf of Vera and myself to ask you and your wife to come over to Israel as our guests at your earliest con-

---

273. [1] 27 Oct. (W.A.). Brodetsky was about to visit U.S. to raise funds for H.U., and had raised the question of contributions from the Z.O. and Government of Israel.

[2] For the meeting of H.U. Board of Governors.

venience. I do not know when your parliamentary duties will permit you to absent yourself for some time, but it must not be just for a few days. You must stay here long enough to get the feel of the country, and to be able to go round; I also want to go round, but could postpone my trip until you are here. I need not tell you how welcome a guest you will be; the rooms are waiting for you. So please let me know when you can come, so that we should make the necessary preparations.

I have been here now about six weeks and am still walking about like in a dream. The country is quiet and stable. The people work hard and in spite of the dire prophecies by our British friends I think you will find that things here look in many respects much brighter than in a great many countries in Europe, including England and France. I am terribly sorry that the relations with England have become so strained, and I do hope that a visit of yourself and of one or two of our friends in England—I am afraid there are not many left; I am thinking of Walter Elliot and Sir Wyndham Deedes, whom I would like to invite as soon as I have heard from you— might do something towards re-establishing of proper relations and towards giving the English public a real impression of what is going on here. The British could have left this country in all glory, leaving thousands and thousands of friends behind them, and it is a terrible tragedy that the clumsiness of one or two people has brought about a set of circumstances which have made this contingency impossible—I hope temporarily.

My love to you and to your wife, and I hope to hear soon from you when you are coming out.[1]

Yours ever,
Ch. Weizmann

275. To the Committee of Sereni House, Givat Brenner.

Rehovot, 18 November 1948

Hebrew: Or. Copy. T.W.: W.A.

Dear Friends,

Most unfortunately my crowded schedule does not permit me to participate in your meeting, so that I am obliged to express my good wishes and admiration to the Sereni House project by letter. I was pleased to learn of the success of your first steps in founding a memorial worthy of the character of the man after whom your

274. [1] Crossman replied 30 Nov. (W.A.) that he hoped to come late Dec.

project is named.[1] Even in our independent state, the *Yishuv* will have one source of strength—its bond with world Jewry. Our task, however, is not only to gather and cherish the treasures of the past. Rather, it is our duty to serve as guides to Diaspora Jewry, as a living wellspring from which they may draw.

It is my hope that Sereni House will serve this dual purpose, and that this responsibility will find expression in your meeting. As in the past, I shall endeavour to assist you to the best of my ability.

With warm greetings,
Ch. Weizmann

276. To Meyer W. Weisgal, New York.   *Rehovot, 23 November 1948*
English: Or. Copy. T.W.: W.A.

My dear Meyer,

I was very glad to hear your voice on the telephone, and please talk to me again soon.

From copies of letters which I enclose you will see what the situation is, at least as it reflects itself in my mind. You have no doubt heard a full account from Henry Morgenthau, who has worked very hard here and has really seen a good deal. We are still in the throes of a war, and it would be rash to predict when it will end. It is quite possible that the rains may put an end to it automatically, and I am sure that the Arabs are more tired than we are. But there is no denying that we are tired, and our boys need a rest so that they could turn to constructive work and opportunities, which await them plentifully.

As you may read in my letter to James de Rothschild,[1] if we could only settle down to working on the land and to building we could easily create possibilities for a quarter of a million immigrants next year, and I consider such a figure essential if we wish to stabilise the position in a manner that our enemies would be powerless to harm us.

It is, therefore, more than deplorable that the Rabbi in Cleveland[2]

275. [1] The project was a cultural centre, a memorial to Enzo Sereni (Biog. Index, Vol. XVI), a founder of Kibbutz Givat Brenner, who had been executed by the Italians in W.W.II after having parachuted on a mission behind enemy lines. W. had been active in raising support for the project.

276. [1] See No. 280, a draft of which was typed 19 Nov.

[2] Silver, at the U.J.A. annual convention 6 Nov., charged that U.S. representatives at U.N. were not acting as Truman instructed in the Bernadotte Plan debate, and thus implied that the President could not control his Administration. (See Joseph B. Schechtman, *The United States and the Jewish State Movement*, New York, 1966, p. 377.)

does not begin to understand all the terrible harm he is doing to the young State in making its initial steps so dreadfully difficult and dangerous. It is inconceivable that a community like the American, which has done so much for the up-building of Palestine should tolerate such a position. On the other hand, the performance of the fleet which is conducted in part by Becky Schulman's boy,[3] or the behaviour of young Dunkelman,[4] make up largely for the failings of Silver and his cronies. Still, he will never be forgiven for the harm he is doing.

It is important to uphold the hands of your *Nasi*,[5] who is no doubt working under heavy pressure, that he should stand by the promise he has given me concerning the Negev. His very charming telegram[6] gives me hope; but the British are working overtime, and I am not sure that Mr. Marshall fully realises that because of British oil interests he is ready to support the selling-out of a part of Palestine which, if the British have their way, will remain a desert as it was for the last 2000 years. But I do not believe it can possibly happen without serious upheavals. They will have to carry away bodily every settler from our places in the Negev. This will lead to bloodshed, and if the British come into the Negev, the Russians will no doubt try to prevent it. This may lead to untold complications; I dread to think of it. Neither the presence of the British nor the advent of the Russians means any good to us, and I cannot understand why men like Felix [Frankfurter] and the others do not make it clear to the President, who at such distance may perhaps not fully appreciate the dangers and difficulties which are inherent in the situation and which are a direct road to a world war.

Here in the Institute everything is beautiful; the people are working and we hope to see the finish of the building at the end of the year, but let us say certainly by February. Your house is already under roof, so that the rain will not prevent it from being completed in time. It will be a fine mansion, and you had better invite some of your cronies to stay with you, because for two people it seems to me much too big. At any rate I am glad that you will have such a beautiful house; it will perhaps make you stay here. I am deriving an enormous amount of joy from watching the growth of the place,

[3] Nachman Paul Shulman, b. 1922. Son of Rebecca Shulman, Hadassah leader. Commander of Israeli Navy 1948, and later adviser to Minister of Defence.

[4] Benjamin Dunkelman, b. 1913. Son of David and Rose Dunkelman, Toronto Zionist leaders. Commander of Seventh Brigade of Israel Defence Forces, which distinguished itself in the fighting in the north, reaching the Litani river in Lebanon.

[5] Hebr.: 'President', i.e. Truman.

[6] Of 15 Nov. (W.A.).

and as soon as a laboratory gets ready we push in one of the workers, who all seem to me to be very happy and contented.

Will you come out with the people you are bringing for the opening,[7] or will you come before? Let me know your programme.

Your *Nasi* has to be given all the information, and he should not be misled by some of our friends in the State Department.

Well, there is nothing more I can add. I have taken note of the date of Mendy's[8] wedding. I suppose it is still the same girl; I would be greatly disappointed if he has changed his mind in the meantime.

With much love from both of us to you, Shirley and the family,

As ever,

Yours,

277. To Frieda Warburg,[1] New York.   *Rehovot, 29 November 1948*
English: Or. Copy. T.W.: W.A.

My dear Frieda,

It was very kind of you to remember to send us a telegram[2] for our birthday, and we both thank you most heartily for it. I wonder whether you will still be travelling to Europe or to here. If your state of health does not permit you to undertake a long journey, please send your children, Carola for instance. There must be a connection between Israel and the Warburg family, and it must not be allowed to disrupt.

We are here at present taking part in the life of the new State, which is struggling, but on the whole doing not too badly. With further sympathetic support from the U.S.A., we shall overcome the initial difficulties; and once this young organisation becomes stronger, it will be a real factor for peace and stability in the Middle East. I wonder whether it is clearly understood in the U.S.A. that the attitude of the British is likely to throw some elements in this country into the arms of Russia. I have been trying to make the White House understand the situation, and I hope that Jimmy McDonald, who is likely to be in the States soon, will make it clear beyond any doubt.

Give my love to the children and tons of it to yourself,

As ever yours,

Ch. Weizmann

---

[7] Of the Weizmann Institute.

[8] Weisgal's son, an actor known professionally as Michael Wager.

277. [1] Biog. Index, Vol. XIV. Widow of Felix Warburg. She was herself a philanthropist and communal leader.

[2] Untraced. Both the Weizmanns' birthdays fell at the end of Nov.

278. To Walter Elliot, London.
English: T.W.: W.A.

My dear Walter,

I should have written to you before, but on arrival here I was taken up with a good deal of business; I also did not want to write before I had formed some idea of how things run here.

I spent last week touring the country and have seen a good deal of what is going on.

I do not see the English press nowadays—only occasionally do I read extracts in the local papers—but I should like to inform you that things here seem to me to be very stable, and in spite of all dire prophecies the country is definitely moving towards peace and consolidation. Those Arabs who have chosen to stay in the country are contented, as I could convince myself during my trip. Those who left are now dispersed between Trans-Jordan and Syria, and from what I understand are not very welcome in either place. A small fraction of them will, no doubt, come back, but only on condition that they cooperate and abstain from sabotaging our work. I do not know who advised the Arabs to run away; it was not merely fear that drove them out; they were not subjected to either threats or pressure from our side. I understand that the Mufti was anxious to collect the Arabs in one place and form them into an army which would attack and destroy Israel. Whether he did it on his own or whether he was misled by some of his advisers—I am sorry to say amongst them also some Britishers—I am not prepared to affirm. One thing is clear: the British advisers of the Arabs made some serious miscalculations: they anticipated that the Jews would be wiped out by the Arabs as soon as the British Army had left the country and that thereupon the partition scheme would collapse in its entirety. In both respects the wish was father to the thought. It was to me a terrible shock when, on May 15th, in the full sight of British troops—of whom a good many remained in the country for weeks thereafter—the country was invaded by Syrians and Iraqis, who were allowed to come in full daylight on the main roads with tanks, jeeps and shining armour. The idea was that these hired assassins would wipe out the Jews in about a fortnight. This miserable adventure has ended disastrously for the Arabs, and although the Jews had practically no arms at that time and had to meet tanks with revolvers or rifles, they drove them off. This fact so impressed the Arab population that they began to run, and to-day you can travel the length and breadth of the country and meet few Arabs except in the triangle of Jenin-Nablus-Tulkarem. Even Jenin is practically empty. I do not know what is being written about all this in England, but I would like you to understand that we did nothing to cause this mass flight. Whoever organised it must be a very disappointed man by now. The British could have come out of Palestine leaving thousands and thousands of friends behind them. But all that has been thrown to the winds because of the whim and deepseated anti-semitism of the man who inspires the policy of the British Foreign Office. It is a very great pity.

To me it is a nightmare. I am waiting for the day when all this will blow over and decent relations be established between the British people and ourselves. I would be happy to have a word from you as all this oppresses me very much.

I have just had a telegram from President Truman in reply to the message of congratulations I sent him upon his re-election. His reply was most cordially worded and conveyed his good wishes for health and happiness and for the peace and prosperity of Israel. I see in it evidence of his genuine friendliness to us and of his determination not to be led astray by the intrigues that are being spun in other places.

There is one other thing I should like to propose. In spite of everything that has happened, I believe a world of good could be done if you could come out here some time at Xmas. You need not fear that you will meet with hostility. You will naturally stay with us, and you may be interested to see what is going on. A great lesson is to be learned from recent developments here, and I still believe that just as after the Boer War England and South Africa became friends, this may happen again in our case. Men like you and Colonel Stanley could play a very important part in this respect, serve your own country, help us and make a substantial contribution to peace.

Well, I am afraid this is becoming a lengthy epistle, and you may think me sentimental, but there is one recent impression about which I would like to add a word. I have seen proofs of creative activity here which have astounded even me, who have always believed in the latent forces of the Jewish people. A few days ago I was invited to inspect the "Fleet of Israel." There is no fleet in the ordinary sense of the word; they are a few very nice corvettes, beautifully kept and manned by an extremely courageous and efficient crew which has grown up in the last year or two. Nevertheless, I am convinced that these people will be able to hold their own and protect Jewish shipping in the Eastern Mediterranean. You may have heard that some weeks ago they were attacked by the Egyptian Navy, which suffered a crushing defeat; their flagship *King Farouk* was ripped open within two minutes and sunk with all men aboard. It was a deadly blow to the Egyptians. No doubt they are trying to recuperate, being helped by British instructors. British officers, I understand, are also building up the Egyptian and Transjordanian Air Forces. Unpleasant as it is to find the British on the side of our deadly enemies, nobody fears these preparations on the part of Egypt or Trans-Jordan. As in ancient times we have the Philistines in the west and the Egyptians in the south, and as in ancient times we shall, with God's help, hold our own against them.

Well, come here and you will see it all for yourself. I have little hope that even you may be able to convince Bevin that he is on the wrong road; still, his regime is not eternal, and it might be extremely useful that men like yourself or Colonel Stanley should get a real insight into the position. We must do what we can to prevent the situation deteriorating further. The only effect of Mr. Bevin's policy is to create extremists here in Palestine, and foster anti-British feeling in the United States. I assure you that we are not interested in that.

Will you present my very kind regards and respects to Col. Stanley, and if you find it convenient, perhaps show him this letter. I would have written to him myself, but I am somehow fearful lest I embarrass him. However, if you tell me, I shall certainly send him a line. At any rate give him my best regards and respects.

Vera and myself send you our best love. I shall be waiting anxiously to hear from you,[1] and remain,

As ever,
Yours,
Chaim

279. To Richard Crossman, London.   *Rehovot, 1 December 1948*
English: Or. Copy. T.W.: W.A.

My dear Dick,

I am sending you copy of a letter which I have just written to Walter Elliot,[1] and I am doing so in order to save a little time. I do not quite agree with the views expressed in the *Statesman,* and quoted in the press here, that the Jews are unbalanced because they are victorious, or words to that effect. In my opinion the contrary is correct. I have seen no glee in their deportment and conversation.

---

278. [1] Elliot replied 21 Dec. (W.A.) regretting his inability to accept the invitation at that time; he had become involved again in Conservative Party politics, because he felt strongly the damage being done to British interests, and indeed to world affairs, by the Government's actions. However, he arrived as W.'s guest in Jan. 1949.

279. [1] See No. 278.

On the contrary, I find them all quiet, extremely serious, bent on the dangerous task in hand and certainly not boastful.

Well, all I can say is: come and you will see for yourself. I hope that you will confirm my view.

Let me know when you are coming. Xmas is almost at the door, and if you could spare the time, it would be a great thing if you could come. You will, of course, both stay with us. We shall give you a short run through the country, and I promise you a warm reception in spite of the December weather. Please let me know as soon as you can.

Much love and greetings from both of us to both of you.

Yours ever,
Ch. Weizmann

280. To James de Rothschild, London.   *Rehovot, 1 December 1948*
English: Or. Copy. T.W.: W.A.

My dear Mr. James,

I should have written to you before, but I wanted to gauge something of the spirit of the people and the country before writing to you. I recently made a short trip through the North, and have seen the possibilities which are now open for our work. There are about five million dunams of land at least which could be taken under plough almost at once, but we have not yet got the people. In the district between Ramleh and Latrun there are about two million dunams of the best land in Palestine, for which, if we had to buy it, we would have to pay at least LP.50–60 per dunam, and, as you know, one could never buy land between Ramleh and Latrun. Now it is all free, overgrown with weeds and it is very doubtful whether the Arabs will ever come back to work it. Everybody seems to think that they have gone for good, and that with the exception of about 70,000 who are here and who never left, the Arab population has to all intents and purposes disappeared. In my opinion some of them will drift back when things have settled down, but the rich effendis, on the one hand, and the landless fellaheen, on the other, can easily settle down in Syria, Iraq, Egypt or Transjordan. So an opportunity is open to us which may not recur for centuries, if ever. Our present trouble is that most of our young men are in the Army, and the newcomers are apparently not too willing to settle on the land. They will have to be gently persuaded to do so, but I am sure that they will come to see that this is the best way for them to build up a reasonable existence for themselves. I have no heart to blame them, for they have suffered so much that their whole mentality is out of gear. All they want at present is to be left alone for a time, so that they can regain their balance.

We may have some little trouble with these newcomers—still, we have to face it. Now that we have land we have no people—when we had people we had no land. But we must get over it and we must try and bring over during the next year or two as many of them as we possibly can, because that is the only way of saving them.

Amongst the remarkable phenomena which I have noticed during my trip is the Jewish fleet, which consists of a few corvettes kept in excellent condition by a group of young men who are good sailors and hope one day to control the Eastern Mediterranean. I think they will—if they are not crushed by some unforeseen events. You have no doubt heard or read their exploit in getting rid of the Egyptian flagship which had come to attack our shores. It was a battle which lasted exactly two minutes. The ship was ripped open by a torpedo; all was done noiselessly, and without any people being seen or heard about. The Egyptians lost about 700 men, among them high-ranking officers and some members of the Royal family. Since then no Egyptian ships have been seen, and I believe are not likely to be seen, in the waters of Israel.

I hope you are both well, and wonder whether you and Mrs. de Rothschild would consider coming over here when the weather becomes warmer and the rains cease. As you know, March or the beginning of April is the best time, and I believe after all that your father and yourself have done for this country, it is right and proper that you should come and see the new period upon which we have entered and which in my opinion is a lineal descendant of the work of your family. I have no doubt that it would give you great satisfaction, and the people would be happy to see you and would, I am sure, receive you in the same spirit as they did your father in the times gone by. I would be greatly obliged if you would send me a word whether this is at all possible.

Judging from the press the position in the UNO and the attitude of Great Britain is extremely confused. This uncompromising hostility may give satisfaction to certain members of the F.O., but it will do them no good in the end, and I am genuinely sorry about it. Why the British people should have been involved in a destructive policy after having initiated a project which could have served the British Empire, the Jewish people and the peace of the world, I fail to understand. I am afraid it is a sign of decline, which always begins with anti-semitism. However, I had better spare you all my thoughts about the political situation in England, of which I know very little and understand still less.

I repeat my request. Please come, it will give you satisfaction and pleasure in a way that I could scarcely put into words.

Both Mrs. Weizmann and myself send you and Mrs. de Rothschild our best wishes and kindest regards.

As ever,
Yours,

P.S. I have seen Mr. Wolfsohn;[1] Mr. Gottlieb[2] happened to be away when I was in the North.

281. To Henry Morgenthau, Jr., New York.

Rehovot, 3 December 1948

English: T.: W.A.

Most thankful your great broadcast speech[1] text just received. As you see from the press the Negeb situation is still serious owing to British incessant pressure. Would respectfully suggest that you see the President, give him gist of your own speech, and also point out that I fear that this action of the British may bring in the Russians and is fraught with the greatest danger. I believe that Edward Jacobson of Kansas City, who is friend of the President, may be very useful. Affectionate regards.

Chaim Weizmann

282. To Isaiah Berlin, Oxford.

Rehovot, 9 December 1948

English: Or. Copy. T.W.: W.A.

My dear Isaiah,

I have read your letter[1] with great joy, and with the help of some friends here we managed to decipher almost all of it except for two words, which defied all the efforts of the people who think themselves graphologists. But somehow we can do without them.

---

280. [1] Harry L. Wolfson, General Manager P.I.C.A. in Palestine 1934–50.

[2] Robert Gottlieb, P.I.C.A. Director in Paris until 1957.

281. [1] Apparently relates to Morgenthau's speech of 18 Nov. on occasion of Dinner to ex-Governor Herbert H. Lehman, when he warned that a truce or armistice would necessitate a scale of military preparedness for Israel that would hamper its up-building and economic development. A prompt peace through direct negotiations between Israel and the Arab countries would enable the new state to develop as a bulwark of democracy in Middle East. Therefore American Government and U.N. should urge such negotiations on all concerned—Jewish Telegraphic Agency, 19 Nov. 1948.

282. [1] 1 Dec. (W.A.) concerning Berlin's impending departure for Harvard.

I was happy to hear that you are well and setting out for Harvard very soon. This brings you mine and Bergmann's best wishes for God's speed and for a successful stay in the States—and please make it short and come back here.

We are expecting Dave Ginsburg here, and I believe he is now helping us in Washington—which is very good. The situation here is, of course, very substantially affected by the war, which absorbs a great deal of our material resources and moral power. In spite of the victory, and perhaps because of it, the British are pushing the Arabs both in Egypt, Syria and Trans-Jordan into the furnace, and the more they lose the less the British are inclined to call a halt to all this absurd game which is not doing any good to anybody. The latest development is that of Akaba.[2] Abdullah does not want the war, but he is being drawn into it by the British F.O., who apparently does not see that if this phase develops a little further it may bring about a conflagration which our rulers do not seem to appreciate. The British Foreign Secretary is blinded by his hatred of the Jews, and by the failure of all his manoeuvres, and is trying to hit out right and left without taking into consideration the serious consequences which may follow. In spite of the fact that about 100,000 of our best young men are tied up on the various fronts, life and development of the country has perhaps slowed down somewhat, but is certainly going on, and if we get peace, as I hope we shall, there will be a very marked upward movement scientifically, intellectually and industrially.

I am impatiently looking forward to the time when you could come out here and see it all for yourself. I quite understand your situation, and I sympathise most deeply with it; and I think you are doing right by pursuing the course which you have mapped out for yourself. But I do want you to know that in my opinion you will find Israel infinitely more interesting than Oxford.

There is a great deal more I have to tell you, but I have a long list of letters to send off, and am reluctantly cutting myself short. I shall write again fairly soon.

Both Vera and myself are well and happy. We are fairly busy trying to do two or three things at a time and always remembering Professor Willstaetter's[3] saying "You can only do one thing well, and that is difficult." I am delighted to hear that your mother may be

---

[2] Concerned at the Israeli military thrust southward, the British were considering invocation of the Anglo-Transjordanian treaty of alliance of March 1948 and sending British troops to Akaba.

[3] Richard Willstaetter (Biog. Index, Vol. XVI). German organic chemist and Nobel laureate.

coming out, and please tell her that we are much looking forward to seeing her.

We all send you our best wishes. Look after yourself and come back soon.

Affectionately yours,

Ch. Weizmann

283. To Lord Melchett,[1] New York.   *Rehovot, 9 December 1948*
English: Or. Copy. T.W.: W.A.

My dear Henry,

I was very happy to receive your cable,[2] and I hope that you are well and your health improves. I take it that Gwen[3] is staying with you. Is it too much to ask you or Gwen to drop me a note giving me some details about your health and of the sort of life you are living now? I would be most grateful for it.

We here are carrying on as best we can, and are faced still with a great many problems which may in the future cause us some trouble. But the fact that Israel exists and that the Government functions with great regularity and considerable efficiency has happily put out of face all the dire prophecies of our enemies and our previous friends, who have been waiting impatiently for their Arab friends to come and sweep us into the sea. This did not happen, but the stuffing has been knocked out both of the Egyptians and the Syrians, and that makes our British friends rather angry. They had misled their Arab friends and have put a noose round their necks. At present they are looking for all sorts of ways how to help the Arabs—and really help themselves primarily. Now they have fastened on Akaba and are playing a very dangerous game. If they get hold of Akaba it is almost certain that the Russians will lodge a protest, and there are all the elements of a world war in it. Abdullah would like to have peace; if he loses one or two battalions of his force—he will eventually lose his head and his throne, and he knows it. He is most anxious to get into direct conversations with us, but is being prevented by the British, who are ready to fight to the last soldier of the Arab Legion. It is a most complicated situation, which can only be explained by the stupidity and obstinacy of a man who has lost his game and is trying to throw good money after bad.

283. [1] Henry Mond (Biog. Index, Vol. XIII). Industrialist. Former M.P.; Chairman of J.A. Council 1942; Hon. President Maccabi World Federation.
[2] Untraced.
[3] Lady Melchett.

Meanwhile, in spite of the war and in spite of some lack of experience—which is understandable—the country is carrying on, and every Jew here and, I understand, outside has straightened out and grown at least two inches. If they do not grow too quickly and keep the sense of proportion, the State of Israel will be a wonderful home for all those who want to come to it.

I wish you and Gwen could come and see it—you have such a stake in the country.

My fondest love to you both, and please let me hear from you,

As ever yours,
Ch. Weizmann

284. To Edward Jacobson, Kansas City.   *Rehovot, 14 December 1948*
English: Or. Copy. T.W.: W.A.

My dear Mr. Jacobson,

I want to write to you to-day about a problem which has become increasingly urgent during recent weeks, and of which I fear we shall yet hear a good deal in the days to come. You will probably have read in the papers that the British have been putting out allegations about the infiltration of Jewish forces into Trans-Jordan territory, particularly in the neighbourhood of Akaba. There is not a word of truth in this, but it is important that you should know the background and the reason why these stories are being put about by our enemies.

The Gulf of Akaba is an arm of the Red Sea, bounded by four different countries—Saudi Arabia, Trans-Jordan, Israel and Egypt. Israel possesses a coastline of some nine kilometres along the northern shore of this Gulf, and this piece of land, known as the Coast of Eylat, is, by the United Nations' decision of 29th November 1947, every bit as much part of Israel as Tel-Aviv or Haifa.

The Gulf of Akaba takes its name from a small town called Akaba which lies on that part of the shore which belongs to Trans-Jordan. It is not part of Israel territory, and Israel has no designs on it whatever.

The recent British propaganda campaign about Israel forces advancing towards Akaba is deliberately designed to mislead world opinion by suggesting that our forces are invading the territory of Trans-Jordan. As I have already told you, there is not a word of truth in this, and it is clear to all of us here that some people in England have an ulterior motive in spreading such tales. They have a Treaty with Trans-Jordan, under the terms of which they can be called upon for military help if Trans-Jordan territory is attacked.

Now that their attempt to strangle Israel by political and diplomatic pressure in the United Nations has so palpably failed, somebody in London is apparently seeking an excuse for military intervention in order to crush us by the force of arms. If Israel forces were invading Trans-Jordan, this would give the British the excuse they are looking for to send their Army against us.

Our friends in America should be on their guard against manoeuvres of this kind. Armed intervention by Britain in the Palestine conflict would not pass unnoticed in the capitals of other countries and might easily kindle a flame which it would afterwards be hard to put out.

To put it in different words: neither Trans-Jordan nor Britain nor anyone else has any right to interfere with our sovereignty over the Coast of Eylat, and we have no right and no design to interfere with Akaba itself or any of the adjacent territory of Egypt, Trans-Jordan and Saudi Arabia. I am sure that we can come to terms with our Arab neighbours on the basis of mutual respect for each other's territorial rights, and that there is every chance of a peaceful solution as long as Britain and other outside forces do not step in. We have quite enough to do to consolidate Israel politically, socially and economically, without embarking on pointless adventures against neighbouring countries. If ever you hear anybody say that Israel has aggressive intentions against Akaba, you can straight away deny it.

How are you keeping? I should be happy to have a word from you about how things are shaping at your end. I am very busy here putting the final touches to the Science Institute, which is to be opened early in the Spring.

    With kindest regards,

Yours ever,

285. To Ada Sereni,[1] Givat Brenner.   *Rehovot, 24 December 1948*
English: H.W.: W.A.

Dec. 24th/48.

My dear Ada,

    I have meant to write to you soon after your last visit to us, but there was the death of my friend,[2] which has affected us very

---

285. [1] B. 1905. Widow of Enzo Sereni. She received hon. Fellowship of Weizmann Institute 1976.

[2] Albert K. Epstein of Chicago, who had worked consistently for Weizmann Institute, died in Tel Aviv 22 Dec. 1948.

much. I shall be short and what I'm telling is said in the spirit of our old friendship and affection, which has not changed and is not likely to change ever.

We belong to different generations—and to different schools of thought. What you politely called the "prophetic" outlook is translated into modern terms something "soft", "forgiving", liberal—not "tough" and dictatorial. I'm ready to accept it and am not ashamed of it. What the other school will do still remains to be seen. We have saved a good many thousands of Jews from the furnaces of Hitler and from other destructive influences, and we have made Palestine a place where civilised human beings can live in dignity.

Come to see me soon and we will talk about it. Perhaps you will telephone to me if possible on the receipt of this note.

Affectionately,
Ch. Weizmann

286. To Felix Frankfurter, Washington.   *Tel Aviv, 31 December 1948*
English: Or. Copy. T.W.: W.A.

My dear Felix,

As you may have heard, there is a dinner put for February 19th, ostensibly in favour of the Institute, but it gives, of course, an opportunity for getting in touch with American Jewry again.

The President promised to come to this dinner, and Abe Feinberg[1] and also Meyer Weisgal are naturally anxious that I should come.[2] In my present position it is not a very easy matter unless some other purposes can be achieved by this trip. What I have in mind is (a) the loan, (b) the *de jure* recognition, (c) some pressure on the part of your Government on the French and the British, (d) convincing you people that the rumour which is being insidiously spread by our enemies that Israel is showing Communist tendencies is malicious and false. Of course, the Russians are standing with their arms outspread to receive some part of the *Yishuv* in their embrace, and possibly strangle them afterwards. Unfortu-

---

286. [1] Abraham Feinberg, b. 1908. Merchant, founding-President of Americans for *Haganah*. President, Development Corporation for Israel; President, American Committee for Weizmann Institute; later, chairman, Board of Governors of Weizmann Institute.

[2] They had telephoned W. 23 Dec., urging him to attend the Weizmann Institute Dinner which Truman had promised to attend. W. expressed doubts as to whether his physician would permit the trip (see Feinberg to W., 23 Dec. 1948, W.A.; V.W. to Weisgal, 30 Dec., W.A.).

nately the attitude of England, America and France has encouraged certain groups of the *Yishuv* to look to the Russians as our great saviour. The clearer the American attitude is, the less chance the Russians have. Without wishing to make predictions, the elections[3] will show how feeble the Communistic tendencies in this country are, but Bevin is helping the Russians very considerably, and the only people who could counteract the vicious atttitude of Bevin and his friends are your friends.

I wonder whether you would, under the circumstances, advise me to come. You know everything better than any man in the world, and you know what your advice means to me. Perhaps you will be good enough to call in Dave Ginsburg and Dave Niles, and send me a short telegram.[4] I don't want to burden you too much, but Meyer Weisgal's opinion is important as far as the effect on the Jewish masses goes.

Needless to say, I shall be more than glad to see you and Marion again, when we will have a good deal to talk over.

Much love to both of you,

Yours,
Ch. Weizmann

287. To Harry S. Truman, Washington.   *Rehovot, 2 January 1949*
English: Draft: T.W.: I.F.M. 2449/150414.

I have seen the communication from Mr. James G. McDonald to the Provisional Government of Israel expressing your anxiety and that of the Government of the United States with regard to the fighting on the Egyptian side of the border at El Arish.[1] Official assurances have already been given on behalf of the Government of Israel to the effect that the presence of Israeli forces on Egyptian territory signifies no political or territorial claims by Israel at Egypt's expense. Assurances have also been given that Israeli forces operating on Egyptian territory will be speedily withdrawn.

---

[3] Forthcoming elections to First *Knesset*.
[4] Frankfurter replied 12 Jan. 1949 (W.A.), encouraging W. to attend.

287. [1] The Israeli army's Oct. offensive against Egypt had carried it past Beersheba and within several miles of Gaza. Despite the U.N. demand for both sides to withdraw, Israel remained at its forward positions pending final armistice negotiations. A cease-fire came into operation in the Negev 7 Jan. 1949, and on 10 Jan. Israel announced that withdrawal of all its troops from Egyptian territory had been completed.

There are, however, certain basic facts connected with this incident on which I feel impelled to address you personally.

The presence of Egyptian forces in the Negev confronts the United Nations and the United States with the duty of understanding where the guilt of aggression lies. It cannot possibly be denied that Egyptian forces invaded Palestine with the object of destroying the State of Israel, while Israeli forces have not invaded Egypt with the intention of destroying the kingdom of Egypt. The presence of Israeli forces in the Negev is in conformity with the Resolution of the General Assembly. The presence of Egyptian forces in the Negev is a conscious and deliberate defiance of that Resolution by the use of force. By every principle of the Charter and of decent international conduct it is clear where the responsibility of aggression lies.

Apart from the question of responsibility, there is the question of initiative. On the 15th May the Egyptian army marched into Palestine, brutally bombarded the civilian population at Tel Aviv, killing men, women and children, and destroyed Jewish villages and water installations in the Negev. The Jews had not touched a hair of any Egyptian head; they had neither committed nor planned, nor have they committed or planned to this day, the slightest infringement of the territory, sovereignty or freedom of Egypt. Egyptian forces proceeded to advance to positions which they held until recently by defying and rejecting successive cease-fire orders of the Security Council at the end of May and in mid-July. Egyptian forces in the Negev have therefore arrived at places where they have no right to be by methods which are strictly forbidden by international law.

Against this background of Egyptian responsibility and Egyptian initiative, it is most disturbing to note the unequal reactions of the Powers to Egyptian aggression and Jewish defence respectively.

When the United States attempted to secure Security Council action for stopping the Egyptian and other Arab invasions, those resolutions were defeated owing to British initiative. Great Britain is therefore responsible for allowing the Egyptian invasion to reach the point which it reached. Now that Jewish counter-measures are throwing the invaders back, Great Britain springs to the aid of the aggressor. There is also the circumstance that practically all the armaments used by Egypt in this wanton aggression were officially supplied by Great Britain in recent years. British policy has therefore been clear. Its aim has been to enable the Egyptians to advance into Palestine and to prevent them by every means from being ejected. The deep and passionate resentment at British policy which animates me today is shared unanimously by all sections of Israel's population. The great constructive contributions which you, Mr.

President, have made to the solution of this problem have been significant precisely because they indicated a refusal to follow British calculations and policies, which have proved to be universally unsound.

The candour and frankness which you have always encouraged me to use in our conversations and correspondence force me to say a word on the attitude of the United States. When the forces of Israel pursued the aggressive invader back to his base, the United States threatens to review its relations with Israel. As far as we are aware, when Egyptian forces launched their brutal invasion of Israel, the United States did not threaten to review its relations with Egypt.

We are now told that United States support of Israel's application for membership in the United Nations[2] would have to be reviewed if Israeli forces remain on Egyptian territory. Yet at a time when Egypt was invading, attacking and bombarding Israel, the United States not only refrained from questioning Egypt's membership in the United Nations, it positively encouraged and sponsored Egypt's membership in the Security Council—the body charged with the maintenance of international peace and security. At this time the Egyptian invader sits as a colleague of the United States in the very Council which is supposed to suppress aggression. Egypt therefore appears both as the aggressor and as a member of the court which ought to condemn its aggression. In these circumstances I am forced to remark that it is wholly disproportionate and out of place for Israel's right of membership to be questioned merely because the momentum of its defence temporarily took its forces onto Egyptian territory.

I might add that El Arish, which was penetrated by Jewish forces, is one of the air bases from which Egyptian bombers periodically set out to attack the cities and villages of Israel. My own scientific institutes at Rehoboth are frequently under Egyptian attack. United States missions in Israel have themselves been affected. Although Israel as a matter of principle had decided not to interfere with Egyptian control of El Arish, it should not be ignored that by so doing it is voluntarily allowing its enemy the free use of a base for attack upon Israel.

My final point is that Egypt is not only defying the General Assembly Resolution of November 1947, the Egyptian government has also not complied with the Security Council's Resolution of Novem-

[2] On 29 Nov. the Provisional Government of Israel made formal application for membership of the U.N.

ber 16th or the General Assembly's Resolution of December 11th, both of which contain an unconditional order to the parties to enter into negotiations for a peaceful settlement.

I hope, Mr. President, that the above considerations may assist you in determining where the initiative, responsibility and guilt properly lie for all the unhappy events which have followed upon the Egyptian invasion of Palestine and Israeli defence against that invasion.[3]

288. To Henry Morgenthau, Jr., New York. *Tel Aviv, 5 January 1949*
English: T.: W.A.

Find it difficult convey to you our deep distress and anxious concern caused by your withdrawal from U.J.A., which you have raised to such unprecedented heights during your chairmanship. Your labours and statesmanship in organizing and inspiring American Jewry to unique achievement past two years form integral part very foundations of State Israel. We now facing stupendous task, while still fighting for our very existence, of filling framework attained by past two years labours and sacrifices with living content. Our first objective absorption during 1949 of three hundred thousand homeless Jews who cannot continue in their present untenable position. This tremendous task with all its ancillary problems can be solved only if American Jewry continues during coming year contribute on the scale which you have taught them. No one familiar with true facts situation can have any doubt that you and you alone can organize the decisive effort demanded by this historic hour. You who were with us only few weeks ago have seen our achievements and our struggles. None other than you can convey to American Jewry the sense of the stupendous mission which is theirs to perform in 1949. We cannot conceive you should permit unique effort you started during past two years remain torso. For sake Israel, for sake our young State and for sake long suffering homeless Jews we beg you rise above ephemeral difficulties and come back to resume reins of U.J.A. Cannot believe you will fail us this crucial hour.[1]

Weizmann, Ben-Gurion, Kaplan

---

[3] This was cabled in abbreviated form 3 Jan. (I.S.A. 68/11). See also No. 290.

288. [1] Morgenthau withdrew his letter of resignation and remained chairman until 1950.

289. To Ada Sereni, Givat Brenner.   *Rehovot, 8–9 January 1949*
English: H.W.: W.A.

Saturday 8/49.

Ada dearest,

I do hope that you have carried out your intention to go to the Negev. It is a godly day and it will do you good to get out of yourself, if only for a short time. You are in my mind all the time and I wish I could do something to give you a little joy. At any rate I hope to see you more often than it was the case hitherto. You are greatly mistaken if you think that your letter[1] is a "waste of time" for me; I have read and reread it many a time, and it means to me a good deal, more than I can say. I am distressed to detect sadness in it every time I read it. But you will—I am sure—still do great things, as it befits your character and your abilities. You must collect and organise your thoughts. If I can help in some small way I shall consider it a great privilege and a labour of love. You will—I trust— not hesitate to call on me at any time. I hope that you feel it as much as I do.

My book[2] will—I hope—have shown you how much I had to suffer from my Jewish "friends", and besides I had no non-Jewish society worth speaking of which could compensate me. But I took it all in my stride as a matter of course: מהרסיך ומחריביך ממך יצאו .[3] I once had a long talk on this subject with Bialik,[4] who was a sage and a man of a tender heart. One day I will tell you about it. I have suffered mostly from those people who climbed to notoriety on my back. It is so human. Where would they all be if not for the Balfour Declaration, and they will never know how much of myself has gone to obtain it. *You* understand, and that is for me a great reward.

Be of good courage and don't let yourself get under by buzzing flies.

All my love
Ch. W.

Jan 9th, 49.

As for young Daniel,[5] we were happy to read that he has got off with a slight wound, and please God he may be free from dan-

---

289. [1] No letter from Ada Sereni to W. traced.

[2] W.'s autobiography, *Trial and Error,* was on the point of publication.

[3] 'Thy destroyers and they that made thee waste shall go forth of thee' (Isaiah 49:17), meaning those who do most to tarnish Israel's fair name come from her own camp.

[4] Chaim Nachman Bialik (Biog. Index, Vol. X). National poet of the Hebrew revival.

[5] Daniel Sereni, her son, was wounded in the Israel War of Independence; in 1954 he and his wife were killed in an air crash at Kibbutz Ma'agan.

ger in the future. The war is practically at an end and I hope that your anguish ends with it. I can feel with you deeply. My son Michael used to convoy ships to and from Ireland, to and from Gibraltar and whenever we used to go to bed on a winter night I thought of him on his lonely flight on a winter night; and that went on for $2\frac{1}{2}$ years until he had reached his journey's end over St. Nazaire in France on Febr. the 11th. We still went on hoping that he is a prisoner with a changed name in German hands, and the agony lasted practically to the end of the war. May you be spared all these tortures. Give Daniel our love. He used to be a great favourite of Mrs. W.— and I believe he still is. Perhaps one day you will bring him along. He is of course a big man and a warrior now. Give him our very best love and good wishes. Looking forward to see you soon.

I am affectionately yours,
Ch. W.

290. To Harry S. Truman, Washington.   *Tel Aviv, 9 January 1949*
English: Or. Copy. T.W.: W.A.

Dear Mr. President,

I was profoundly moved by your letter of November 29th which has just reached me.[1] It was very kind of you to compare your outstanding achievement with my humble experience. We may indeed say in the words of the Psalmist: "The stone which the builders rejected is become the chief cornerstone."[2] But, as you truly observe, it is not taking long for our bitter and resourceful opponents to regroup their shattered forces for a new attack, and we have had evidence of it in these very days. That is why we are all the more grateful for your sustained and active sympathy.

I was also deeply touched by your gracious acceptance of the invitation to attend the dinner to be given on February 19th in support of the Science Institute at Rehovot with which I am associated. Friends in the States have urged me to come over for this function. My physicians, as is the way of physicians, feel some qualms about my undertaking this trip in winter time, but in view of your presence I have decided to come. I am looking forward very much to renewing our personal contact and discussing the great problems which we both have so much at heart.

I am very grateful for your renewed assurance concerning the Negev, all the more so as the British Foreign Secretary and his

---

290. [1] See No. 269, n. 3.
  [2] Psalms 118 : 22.

associates have apparently not abandoned their design to deprive us of this large and important area. It is thus that I interpret the events of the past few days and the panic which Mr. Bevin and his assistants have been trying to work up regarding the incident when some of our detachments crossed the Egyptian border while in hot pursuit of the invaders of our country.[3] In view of the threats addressed to us by the British[4] and of the reports received of an imminent British military intervention in Palestine and on the Egyptian border, I took the liberty of addressing to you a telegram[5] in which I endeavoured to set out the facts and equities of the situation. As explained therein, the presence of Israel forces on Egyptian territory was not part of any premeditated plan motivated by political or territorial claims at Egypt's expense. Our troops in the course of chasing back the Egyptian invaders found themselves on the other side of the frontier and were duly withdrawn by our High Command.

Our position in this matter is the very reverse of that of the Egyptians. The Egyptian Army in May of last year invaded Palestine in defiance of both the U.N. Charter and the Assembly Resolution of November 29th for the avowed purpose of destroying the State of Israel. Our forces did not cross the border with the intention of destroying the Kingdom of Egypt. We had every right to be in the Negev: the Egyptian Army had none. When they invaded Palestine, none of the Great Powers suggested the imposition of sanctions. The Resolutions introduced at the time by the United States in the Security Council for stopping the Egyptian and other Arab invasions were defeated through British influence. Yet, when our forces, in throwing out the invaders from the Negev, are led by the impetus of the attack across the frontier, the British Government, which all along encouraged and armed the invaders, rises up in righteous indignation and throws out ominous warnings of an impending British intervention should Egypt invoke the Anglo-Egyp-

---

[3] The crisis came 7 Jan., when Israeli fighters shot down five R.A.F. reconnaissance planes on the Egyptian side of the frontier.

[4] On 8 Jan. a British memorandum to Israel Government declared that Britain took a grave view of the incident, which resulted from 'unprovoked attacks by Jewish aircraft over Egyptian territory' and that it wished 'to make a strong protest to the Jewish authorities at Tel Aviv and to reserve all rights both with regard to claims for compensation and to all possible subsequent action'. The Israel Government refused to accept the memorandum as Britain did not recognize Israel and it was addressed to 'the Jewish authorities in Palestine'. Israel on 11 Jan. formally called upon the Security Council to investigate Britain's 'menacing attitude' and her creation of an 'artificial crisis'.

[5] See No. 287 and n. 3 there.

tian Treaty of 1936,[6] which Egypt has shown no inclination to do. The great constructive contributions which you, Mr. President, have made to the solution of this complex problem have been significant precisely because they indicated a refusal to follow the disastrous policies pursued by the British Foreign Secretary and his advisers. But the warning we received through your Special Envoy on December 31st that U.S. support of our application for U.N. membership might have to be reconsidered on account of our forces having crossed the Egyptian border[7] would seem to indicate that some section of American official opinion was unfortunately impressed by Mr. Bevin's mischievous propaganda.

I believe that the incident and the renewed British attempt to swing American opinion against us may now be regarded as a closed chapter. The Egyptians have at long last declared their readiness to meet us at armistice talks,[8] and I hope these will now begin. But I would be less than candid if I failed to warn you, Mr. President, that the British Foreign Secretary may still be in no mood to acquiesce in the establishment of our State and that similar shock tactics and intrigues may be expected in the near future. We have had new evidence during the last few days of the continuance of these tactics. They will not, I assure you, deflect us from our pursuit of peace and reconciliation. I only pray that they may not succeed in misleading and embarrassing our friends.

There have of late been some indications that important sections of British opinion, both Labour and Conservative, do not see eye to eye with Mr. Bevin in his squalid feud with Israel. The recent speeches of Mr. Churchill and Mr. Eden in the House of Commons are deeply significant,[9] and I understand that in the Labour Party, too, the Foreign Secretary's policy on Palestine is meeting with growing opposition. That policy has indeed brought nothing but discredit on himself and his country. The evident purpose was to undermine

---

[6] Article 7 of the Treaty of Preferential Alliance between Egypt and Great Britain, signed 26 Aug. 1936, provided that should either of the contracting parties become engaged in war the other party would immediately come to its aid in the capacity of an ally. However, Britain invoked its 1948 Treaty of Alliance with Transjordan to justify sending a British force to Akaba.

[7] McDonald conveyed Truman's message to Ben-Gurion and Shertok, transmitting also the British demand that Israeli troops withdraw from the Sinai Peninsula, together with a U.S. declaration that Israel must comply at once (see McDonald, *op. cit.*, pp. 107–12).

[8] Armistice negotiations between Egypt and Israel commenced in Rhodes 13 Jan. under the chairmanship of the Acting Mediator, Ralph Bunche.

[9] A two-day debate on foreign affairs was opened 9 Dec. 1948 by Bevin, who made no reference to Palestine. Anthony Eden, for the Opposition, demanded *de facto* recognition of Israel, and on the second day Churchill, reviewing a 'lamentable tale of prejudice and incapacity', stated that Israel 'cannot be ignored or treated as if it does not exist'.

our young State, and by exploiting the military weakness of the Arab States to bring them again under British heel. In both respects he has earned failure. Far from destroying us he has forced us to mobilise all our latent strength, while the Egyptians have not been slow to understand the ominous implications of his invocation of the 1936 Treaty and of the military aid he tried to force upon them.

The most pathetic exemplification of Mr. Bevin's policy is to be found in his obstinate retention in Cyprus of eleven thousand men, women and children who were forcibly transferred there before May 15th, after having reached the coast of Palestine. Seven months after the termination of the Mandate and three and a half years after the end of the War these pathetic survivors of Nazi persecution are kept indefinitely in detention in a Cyprus concentration camp for no other crime than that they endeavoured to reach their national home, and for no other purpose but to satisfy Mr. Bevin's malice.[10] While the gates of Palestine are open—and we have succeeded in the course of 1948 to bring in as many as 130,000 new immigrants, most of them from Europe—these unfortunate people are still kept behind barbed wire in flagrant defiance of all international law and decency. It passes comprehension how the British people and the civilised world permits this shameful scandal to continue.

I am deeply grateful for your kind interest in the matter of the proposed long-term loan to Israel. Our Government have submitted detailed propositions to the Export-Import Bank, and I hope that the loan will soon materialise. We are most anxious to commence our work of reconstruction and settlement.

In conclusion I cannot sufficiently stress, Mr. President, the urgency of every possible influence being brought to bear upon the Arab States with a view to promoting their acceptance of a true and lasting settlement. These States have domestic difficulties of their own making to overcome, and I am afraid that British influence in the Middle East, so far from being wielded in the interests of peace, is actually directed towards prolonging the present state of unrest and tension. It is of the utmost importance that the Government of the United States should use its undisputed authority for impressing both upon the British and upon the Arabs the vital necessity of a speedy and enduring peace settlement.

---

[10] When the Commons reassembled 18 Jan. after the Christmas recess, Bevin announced that the remaining Jewish immigrants (those of military age) detained in Cyprus would be released as soon as the Israeli authorities provided the necessary shipping.

Looking forward very much to seeing you, Mr. President, in February, and thanking you once more for your very kind letter,

I am,

Yours very sincerely,

Ch. Weizmann

291. To Winston S. Churchill, London.   *Tel Aviv, 18 January 1949*
English: T.: Draft: W.A.

Emboldened by your recent statement House[1] and encouraged by progress Rhodes negotiations[2] would urgently appeal you use your authoritative influence view lessening present utterly unwarranted Anglo-Israel tension and averting acts of intervention which may produce grave consequences. Desire reaffirm to you my recent statement *Times*[3] that Israel has no aggressive designs whatever on any of its neighbours and is most anxiously concerned for speedy and enduring all-round settlement. Please forgive my insistence, which is prompted by real concern general situation.[4] Kind regards.[5]

Chaim Weizmann

292. To Harry S. Truman, Washington.   *Tel Aviv, 20 January 1949*
English: T.: W.A.

On behalf people of Israel I desire to convey to you our grateful appreciation of decision U.S. Export-Import Bank grant Israel loan of thirty-five million dollars and earmarking sixty-five million dollars for subsequent use. We interpret this momentous decision as expression confidence and goodwill of United States towards Israel and as first instalment international assistance for Israel's

---

291. [1] See No. 290, n. 9.

[2] See No. 290, n. 8.

[3] W. was interviewed at Rehovot 12 Jan. by *The Times* and *Manchester Guardian*. He expressed deep concern at the deterioration in Anglo-Israeli relations, spoke of his lifelong friendship for Britain and appealed to the British people not to pursue a course which must lead to war; rather, they should 'utilize their unique influence in the Middle East to help towards peace and reconciliation'. (See *The Times,* 13 Jan. 1949.)

[4] Churchill replied 9 Feb. (W.A.): 'My dear Weizmann, thank you so much for your telegram. You will no doubt have read my public declaration. I look back with much pleasure on our long association.' He ended the typed note with a final salutation in his own hand: 'The light grows'.

[5] W. also cabled Amery and Elliot, urging that they too use their influence to lessen the tension (W.A.).

constructive development. We are deeply aware of how much we owe you personally for this most helpful decision. Respectfully and gratefully,

Chaim Weizmann

293. To Meyer W. Weisgal, New York. *Tel Aviv, 20 January 1949*
English: T.: W.A.

Thanks for your call. Was deeply sorry to disappoint you,[1] knowing how much is at stake but am still hopeful for the best. My illness began a week ago with severest possible attack of neuralgia, which has at present subsided, but cold and rain prevailing here makes recovery slow. Zondek[2] opposes every attempt of travelling. Mrs. Weizmann suffers presently from flu. We all hope for the best another three weeks. Appreciate fully importance trip, and disappointment if it does not materialise, but must give you plain facts. Shall keep you informed very often. You might communicate yourself with Zondek, who is extremely helpful. All phone conversations overheard.[3] In future send cables through Eliahu [Epstein]. Much love.

Chaim Weizmann

294. To Lady Melchett, London. *Tel Aviv, 23 January 1949*
English: T.: W.A.

Dear Gwen, we are both deeply grieved by your bereavement and want convey to you our deepest sympathy.[1] We have both lost a dear friend, and Jewry one of its most respected representatives. Our thoughts are with you.

Chaim, Vera Weizmann

---

293. [1] W. had told Weisgal on the telephone that his journey to U.S. was now unlikely. See Weisgal's telegram, 20 Jan. (W.A.).

[2] Samuel Georg Zondek (1894–1970). Physician; head Internal Medicine Department, Hadassah Hospital, Tel Aviv.

[3] I.e., by the Censorship Dept. of Israel Government. A letter from Gershon Dror, the Chief Censor, to Yigal Kimhi, Secretary of the President, 20 Mar. (W.A.) stated that the President and his wife were henceforth to use specially marked envelopes giving him absolute immunity.

294. [1] Melchett died 22 Jan.

295. To Joseph I. Linton, London.   *Rehovot, 1 February 1949*
English: Or. Copy. T.W.: W.A.

My dear Ivor,

I was very glad to receive your letter[1] and your cables[2] and to know that you have re-established normal relations with our friends. Now that recognition has come, it opens up, as I hope, a chapter of normal and friendly intercourse, which I consider very valuable for both sides.

As you know I am due to be in the States about the 20th of April and I shall start my trip from Paris. I would love to pay a visit to England now that the recognition has been awarded; I would love to see my children, my old friends and, perhaps, get in touch with some people of the Government. Would you kindly sound it out and send me a cable embodying your views? Talk it over with Mr. Amery and I shall talk it over with Walter Elliot, who is at present staying with us, and we could then take some decision. I would otherwise stay in Paris and from there take the plane which President Truman is sending for me. Prof. Zondek here is not in favour of my frequent changing of altitudes, but if I stay in Paris most of my friends would come over and by this avoid the complication. Anyhow, I shall be happy to hear from you soon, and may I again repeat my best wishes for your work and continuous progress. Please give my very kind regards to Miss May, whom I hope to see on my way to America.

Affectionately yours,
Ch. Weizmann

296. To René Mayer, Paris.   *Rehovot, 3 February 1949*
French: T.: I.F.M. 2449/150414.

Warm thanks your telegram 25 January.[1] Deeply appreciate help you kindly brought to our cause.[2] Shall be happy to receive you in

---

295. [1] 14 Jan. (W.A.). This reported favourable British reactions to W.'s Press interview—see No. 291, n. 3. Linton also described the confused situation over British troop deployment in Akaba, which he saw as one more attempt to wrest the Negev from Israel.

[2] Cable of 13 Jan. (I.S.A. 93.04.37/33II) commended W.'s Press statement as timely and helpful in dispelling misinterpretations. The second (W.A.) was received at Rehovot 31 Jan. Linton informed W. of his meeting 29 Jan. with Bevin, at which he was notified of Britain's *de facto* recognition of Israel. Bevin had expressed the desire for a restoration of amicable relations and told Linton that he had often meant well, but was limited in his freedom of action. Britain accorded *de jure* recognition 27 Apr. 1950.

296. [1] Untraced.
[2] Mayer was then Defence Minister.

our country. Sincerely trust that future friendly relations between France and Israel will contribute to maintenance world peace and strengthening spirit of solidarity among nations.

Weizmann

297. To Sir Simon Marks and Israel Sieff, London.

Rehovot, 4 February 1949

English: T.: W.A.

Deeply touched by your cable.[1] My first thought when I read the news was with you, remembering the days of trial and tribulation we shared and enthusiasm with which you both helped overcome all obstacles. Am convinced also in future Jews of British Commonwealth will have to play important part in fulfilment our task. I know I can always count on you. God bless you.

Chaim Weizmann

298. To Clark Clifford,[1] Washington.   *Rehovot, 20 February 1949*

English: Or. Copy. T.W.: W.A.

Dear Mr. Clifford,

I am taking the opportunity of my friend Meyer Weisgal's return to the States to send you these few words together with an autographed copy of *Trial and Error,* which I hope you may have a chance to glance through.

Our mutual friend Abraham Feinberg has kept me informed of doings in Washington, and especially of your magnificent cooperation in many critical situations. In these days of struggle and readjustment we are desperately in need of understanding friendships, and it is good to know that we have in you a genuine friend of our cause. I can assure you, and I wish you would in turn assure your great Chief, that we desire nothing but peace and amity with our neighbours, and that we have no aggressive designs on any of them. We shall always be mindful of the Biblical injunction: "Zion will be rebuilt in Justice."[2]

---

297. [1] 1 Feb. (W.A.). Their congratulations on British recognition.

298. [1] B. 1906. Lawyer. Special counsel to Truman 1946–50; U.S. Secretary of Defense 1968–69.
   [2] Isaiah 1:27.

I am looking forward with great anticipation to my revisit of the United States, and hope we shall have an opportunity to meet again soon.

With kindest personal regards and best wishes,

Yours very sincerely,

Ch. Weizmann

299. To David Niles, Washington.   *Rehovot, 20 February 1949*
English: Or. Copy. T.W.: W.A.

Dear David,

Meyer has been telling me of the fine cooperation we are receiving at your hands. Need I tell you of my profound appreciation? We are living in great days; it is perhaps too soon to evaluate their meaning for history. For many years now you have played no insignificant part in the making of this history, and I feel certain that when you look back upon these years you will have good reason to be proud and satisfied that it had been given to you to help bring about a proper understanding of the ideals of our cause in high places in Washington.

May I ask you to please convey to your great Chief my warmest greetings and to express to him my profound gratitude for all he has done and is doing for us.

I look forward to our meeting again,

Sincerely yours,

Ch. Weizmann

P.S. I am sending you with Meyer an autographed copy of *Trial and Error*; I hope you will have a chance to read it.

300. To Meyer W. Weisgal, New York.   *Rehovot, 20 February 1949*
English: T.W.: W.A.

My dear Meyer,

Now that *Trial and Error* is published and is in process of translation into the *shiv'im leshonot*,[1] I have been thinking about the many unpublished documents and letters of the past forty years and more that might be of some public interest. These letters and documents are scattered all over the world and in many hands. The main sources, however, are London, Jerusalem, Rehovot and New York. I should

---

300. [1] Hebr., lit. 'seventy tongues', i.e. the languages of the world.

very much like to see them collected in one place and prepared for proper editing and ultimate publication. Would you be willing to undertake this task? I know it is quite a job and will involve a great deal of collaboration and probably several years of work. I cannot think of anyone other than yourself to whom I would entrust this work with the feeling that it will be done with responsibility and fidelity. Will you undertake it? If so, let this be your authority to begin gathering the material and approach any and all persons or organizations in whose possession these letters or documents may be.

I shall appreciate greatly if you will let me know what your views are and how you propose to proceed in the matter.[2]

Yours ever,
Ch. Weizmann

301. To Abba Hillel Silver, Cleveland.   *Rehovot, 21 February 1949*
English: T.: I.F.M. 2449/150414.

Sincerest thanks your felicitations.[1] I pray that I may be granted strength and wisdom to discharge my duties in this fateful historic hour for our people. Never before have we been faced with so great a challenge and equally great an opportunity. It is therefore incumbent upon all of you, irrespective of temporary differences, to rally to support of Israel with same consecration as have done our sons and daughters in defence of our country. It is my fervent hope that you will use your great influence with American Zionists to ensure concentration all forces on enormous effort that must now be made through U.J.A. to help us in ingathering of exiles. Feel confident you will not fail us in this momentous hour.[2]

Chaim Weizmann, President

---

[2] This was Weisgal's formal appointment as General Editor, *The Letters and Papers of Chaim Weizmann*. See his General Foreword in Vol. I, pp. ix–xvii.

301. [1] Cable of 19 Feb. (W.A.) following W.'s formal election and inauguration as President of Israel in Jerusalem 17 Feb.

[2] On 23 Feb. W. received a second cable in which Silver sought his intervention in a dispute among American Jewish leaders which threatened to harm U.J.A. and other campaigns. W. was advised by Kaplan and others to leave Silver's cable unanswered, lest his name be misused in a conflict in which the other side (e.g., the non-Zionist element in U.J.A.) were employing 'unscrupulous tactics' (Locker to W., 27 Feb., W.A.).

302. To Mr. Lazrus,[1] New York.   *Rehovot, 27 February 1949*
English: Or. Copy. T.W.: W.A.

My dear Mr. Lazrus,

I understand from Meyer [Weisgal] that you and your friends intend to pay tribute, in a fitting manner, to Professor Albert Einstein on the occasion of his seventieth birthday; I am indeed very happy about this plan. The high esteem in which Professor Einstein's personality and scientific achievements are held has reflected credit upon the Jewish people everywhere. The suggestion that the tribute to him should be connected with Israel, is, therefore, very appropriate.

Perhaps never before has the need for science, for research in Israel, been as vital as at this juncture. Our successes in the war against the Arab States have been largely due to the availability in this country of scientific knowledge and technical skill. The constructive task with which we are now confronted demands the mobilisation of our scientific forces to an even greater degree. It is fortunate, therefore, that just at this time our new Institute of Physics and Physical Chemistry has been completed in Rehovot, to which our friends in America have devoted so much effort.

I believe it would meet with Professor Einstein's approval if you were to establish in Israel an Einstein Fund for Research Fellowships. This Fund should enable gifted young scientists to continue in this country their studies after they have graduated from the University—an opportunity which at present is given only to very few of them due to the limited means at the disposal of the scientific institutions in this country. We would thus be able to increase the scope of research which is being carried out now, and we would have a better possibility of judging the talents of the young scientists, which often reveal themselves only some time after they have left the University.

I do not want to trouble you in this letter with the formalities of such a Research Fellowships' Fund. I would only like to put before you this suggestion and would be grateful to know your reaction to it.

With kindest regards,

Yours sincerely,
Ch. Weizmann

302. [1] Probably Ralph Lazrus (1898–1959), of the family which owned the Benrus Watch Co. and was prominent in Jewish philanthropic activity.

303. To Clement Davies,[1] London.   *Rehovot, [?] February 1949*
English: Or. Copy. T.W.: W.A.

Dear Mr. Davies,

I would like to express in these lines my grateful thanks for your very kind message,[2] which you were kind enough to send me on the occasion of the recognition of the State of Israel. It is, of course, a great departure, and I still do not know why this heavy mantle has fallen on the shoulders of this generation. I fully realise the enormous responsibility which rests on the people of Israel, who must make the most of this opportunity.

We shall be tried and tested in the next few years very severely. Every act of ours will be scanned and scrutinised by the whole world, and we shall be working, so to say, with the full light turned on us.

It is a great opportunity and a great ordeal. Whether it has come to us too soon or not the next few years will prove. We shall need the help and guidance of men of good will, of which you are one, and this is why I am so grateful to you for your words of encouragement.

I may be passing through London in about two months and hope to have then the opportunity of seeing you. Meanwhile I send you my renewed thanks and good wishes.

With kindest regards,

Yours very sincerely,
Ch. Weizmann

304. To Moshe Shertok, Jerusalem.   *Rehovot, 2 March 1949*
Hebrew: T.W.: I.F.M. 2485/9429 I.

Dear Mr. Foreign Minister,

Please forgive my addressing you in such a formal manner, but I am obliged to turn to you in connexion with the following matter.

A few days ago I was visited at Rehovot by the Swedish ambassador in Cairo, and among other things he spoke about the assassination of Bernadotte. He did not file a formal complaint—but his words tended in that direction. It is true, he explained, that the Swedes are a Nordic people and do not become overly excited about events, but it would be a mistake to regard their attitude as apathy. The Swedish Government takes the whole matter of Bernadotte's

---

303. [1] 1884–1962. Leader of the Parliamentary Liberal Party 1945–56.
    [2] 15 Feb. (W.A.), rejoicing at Britain's recognition of Israel.

Chaim Weizmann is sworn in as President of Israel, February, 1949.

The President of Israel with Ambassador James G. McDonald of the U.S.A. (*left*) and Ambassador Paul Yershov of the U.S.S.R.

Jan Smuts arrives in London for a commemoration of Weizmann's 75th birthday. With the South African leader are, *from left,* Lord Nathan, Lord Samuel and Sigmund Gestetner.

assassination very seriously. The ambassador added that there is a growing impression that we are not doing enough—or that what we are doing is not being done energetically enough—to find the assassins. He complained that the Swedish Government has not received any interim report on the steps we have taken.[1]

I promised the ambassador that I would pass on his complaint to you—which I am now doing. I think that it is advisable to forward him an interim report on the efforts of the police in this matter, as well as on the steps which the Government intends to take. During our conversation the ambassador was courteous—but very agitated.

With cordial greetings,
Ch. Weizmann
President of the State of Israel

305. To Maurice B. Hexter,[1] New York. *Rehovot, 3 March 1949*
English: Or. Copy: T.W.: W.A.

My dear Maurice,

I am most grateful to you for your kind letter[2] and for bringing up the reminiscences of the days when we both fought and suffered, dreamt and planned. In spite of the Shiels[3] and the Passfields,[4] Bevins and many others, it has come off, and even the British have to admit, grudgingly of course, that the Jewish State is a reality. Considering the enormous difficulties with which we are faced, and the difficulties which the British have prepared for us, the curse much desired by them has not materialized, and the State affairs are running remarkably smoothly, and sometimes I think we are all day-dreaming.

There is an enormous immigration pouring in—so far without any check, but I believe that some sort of control will be necessary soon if we are not to be flooded. Knowing as you do the conditions in this country you can easily imagine that this immigration brings

304. [1] In Feb. 1949 leaders of the Stern Group were brought to trial, although not directly on the charge of planning and ordering the assassination of Bernadotte. The murderers were never apprehended. In 1950 the Israel Government paid symbolic compensation to the U.N., in whose service Bernadotte had died; and a forest was planted in Bernadotte's name near Jerusalem.

305. [1] Biog. Index, Vol. XVII. Non-Zionist member of J.A. Executive, Jerusalem 1929–38.

[2] Hexter wrote 15 Feb. (W.A.), congratulating W. on his speech in inaugurating the First *Knesset*, 14 Feb.

[3] Hexter had recalled an instance in 1930–31 when he had sought the assistance of the then British Under-Secretary of State for the Colonies, Drummond Shiels (see Biog. Index, Vol. XIV).

[4] Sidney James Webb, Lord Passfield (Biog. Index, Vol. XIV). He was responsible for the Palestine White Paper of 1930, known as the Passfield White Paper.

with it problems and difficulties of all kinds, but there is such an elation and high spirits that it is likely to be an important factor in carrying us over these difficulties. One feels for once that the Almighty is on the side of the Jews, and one realises how good a partner he can be if he chooses to.

I do hope to see you in the States where we intend to go for a short visit at the beginning of April.

Affectionately yours,

Ch. Weizmann

306. To Frieda Warburg, New York. *Rehovot, 3 March 1949*
English: Or. Copy. T.W.: W.A.

My dear Frieda,

Your letter of February the 16th,[1] written with so much sympathy and affection, has brought up many memories and many recollections of important steps which we discussed together in your beautiful house in 1015 Fifth Avenue. I hope we shall be able to go over it briefly when I have the privilege of seeing you in New York very soon. As at present advised we are leaving here between the 2nd and 4th of April. We shall stop in Paris for a few days to see the children, who will come out there from England to meet us, and then we proceed to the States, hoping to arrive there about the 11th. I think the dinner with the President is on the 23rd of April, and we shall probably be leaving very soon after that.

We had a very moving time all these weeks; but things are becoming a little more settled just now.

Now with regard to your criticism about my book, which criticism I value very highly, I would like to explain as follows:

I have been hard pressed for space; Harper advised to have only one volume, and even this should be a little more handy than the volume which actually appeared. I had to shorten as much as I could, the description of all the persons, however dear, with whom I have worked. You may perhaps not know that I have never had the privilege of meeting your father.[2] When I came to America

---

306. [1] W.A. This was one of many letters received by W. at this time on publication of *Trial and Error*. While evoking the plaudits and memories of the majority, it also prompted various criticisms, relating to factual data or W.'s interpretation of them, and to his failure to mention or commend certain individuals.

[2] She had written: 'I want to add how avidly I read each word of your Autobiography. My one regret is that as you devoted only one line apiece to my father [the banker and philanthropist Jacob Schiff—see Biog. Index, Vol. VI] and to Max [Warburg], you speak of them so slightingly and also that you do not do justice to Felix [Warburg] as a man and as a co-worker.'

first in 1921 and then the following two times, I have never met anybody of your family. I came in contact with Felix only on my third visit to the States, and have found him very friendly and charming as usual, but certainly not disposed to cooperate. It is only after I have convinced you that you should come to Palestine, and only after your return, that the ice was broken, and happily it never froze again. Had I written about your father from hearsay, I would certainly not have done him justice, and I have made up my mind only to write about those people whom I knew personally.

With regard to Max,[3] I do not wish to do injustice to his memory, but he has never been friendly, although he seems to have changed slightly during his visit to Palestine. It was not easy for me to write about the Warburgs without giving the slightest offence and attempting to do justice. I took note of your criticism. I shall have to revise the book very soon—in fact I hope to do so next summer—and I may correct some of the errors which are unavoidable in a first edition which has been written under very great pressure.

If you look at the Epilogue you will realise that I have devoted just a few lines to the fundamental historical fact of the emergence of the Jewish State. I simply could not do more at that time.

We are both well and much looking forward to seeing you soon. Meanwhile, I remain with affectionate regards,

Yours ever,
Ch. Weizmann

307. To Hersh Z. Cynowitz,[1] Bombay.   *Rehovot, 4 March 1949*
English: T.: W.A.

Am dispatching detailed letter for transmission Shiva Rau.[2] Our proposals as follows: Firstly willing dispatch two experts agricultural problems to India. Secondly believe that Indian Government after studying our proposal should send here group chemists, engineers. Discuss on spot production power, alcohol, vitamin prep-

---

[3] Max Warburg (Biog. Index, Vol. XIV). Banker, philanthropist and communal leader in Germany; brother of Felix.

307. [1] B. 1907, Poland. Arriving in India 1941, he became a merchant and communal leader there, representing J.A. 1942–50. Represented W. in negotiations with Indian Government 1948–49.

[2] See No. 36. Cynowitz cabled Rehovot (23 Feb., W.A.) requesting early despatch to the Indian leader of a formal proposal for scientific and technical cooperation; this could serve to initiate a mutual relationship and influence the Indian attitude during the forthcoming U.N. session.

arations from molasses. Thirdly Rehovot Institute, Haifa Technion and when Jerusalem situation clarified also Hebrew University happy accept number research fellows various branches natural and technical sciences. Would be grateful indication how many research fellows and which special fields are desired to be sent. Please convey Shiva Rau contents this cable and answer third point soonest possible.[3] Regards.[4]

Chaim Weizmann

308. To Lady Violet Bonham-Carter,[1] London.

Rehovot, 13 March 1949

English: Or. Copy. T.W.: W.A.

Dear Lady Violet,

I am in receipt of your letter of February the 23rd.[2] I am very sorry that you should have fallen a victim to the campaign of vilification that is now being waged against our young State. British people have a reputation of being able to see the other side even in times of conflict and tension. There is little evidence of this where we are concerned. You use strong language about our terrorists and their deeds. Has it occurred to you that there might be grievous reasons for the appearance of so unbelievable and unprecedented a phenomenon as "Jewish terrorism"?

The Jews are not a people given to violence. For many centuries force has not been our weapon. Our colonisation in Palestine was an outstanding achievement of non-violence. We maintained the peace even when our fields and settlements were set on fire, and peaceful men, women and children were murdered. For three long years before the Second World War we were the target of a ruthless guerilla war, which the Mandatory failed to stem. We did not retaliate.

---

[3] Cynowitz replied 26, 28 Mar. (W.A.) that India requested training facilities in Israel for two or three persons in agriculture and well rigging (W.A.).

[4] Before leaving for U.S. 7 Apr. W. entrusted the matter to the Agriculture Ministry in Tel Aviv (see W. to Cynowitz, 6 Apr.).

308. [1] Later, Baroness Asquith (1887–1969). Daughter of Herbert Asquith, Prime Minister 1908–16. She was President, Liberal Party Organization 1945–47.

[2] Declaring her sympathy for the tragic wrongs and sufferings of the Jewish people and referring to her efforts over the years on their behalf, Lady Violet continued that she felt no friendship for the new State of Israel. Her disillusionment stemmed from a universal dislike of murder, terrorism and inhumanity 'as much when it is practised by Jews as by anyone else.' Having read of conditions in the Arab refugee camps, she condemned the Jews for having 'chosen' innocent people as their victims. She had no doubt that in time Israel would be accorded full recognition by England, 'but it has lost the hearts of all its truest friends in this country' (W.A.).

And what was the outcome? The Arab gunmen won the political battle. The British Government in the 1939 White Paper fixed a final limit to Jewish immigration, closed the bulk of Palestine to Jewish settlement and announced that within five years Palestine would be placed under Arab rule. It was then, for the first time, that the ominous saying was heard among Jews here that violence paid with the British Government.

We—I mean the Jewish leadership—set our face against that dangerous current. We mobilised our manpower and industrial resources for the war against Hitler. Nearly 30,000 of our young men and women enlisted under the British colours. The Arab leaders went to Berlin—after having engineered an anti-British rising in Baghdad.[3] Then came the agonising reports from the gas chambers and the crematoria in which six million of our people, a third of the entire Jewish nation, were being done to death. Few hands were lifted to save them. Palestine Jewry was ready to receive them, but the doors were bolted by the White Paper, which was administered with a ruthlessness and thoroughness worthy of a better cause.

Day after day the reports of the death chambers in Auschwitz and Maidenek poured in; day after day frantic cables came through Geneva begging for certificates, begging merely for the promise of a certificate. Even the Nazis were ready not to deport if you could show proof that a certificate will be forthcoming. Day after day the lesson was hammered in that it was British policy which prevented any help from being extended to the fathers and mothers, brothers and sisters. Neutral governments intervened. The Swedish Government promised to take in 20,000 Jewish children if the British Government were to undertake their transfer to Palestine after the war. The offer was turned down, and these children, like hundreds of thousands of others, went to the gas chambers. The same happened with a group of Rumanian children on whose behalf I put in a personal plea with the then High Commissioner. It proved of no avail, because the Home Government was adamant.

A small number of the doomed managed to escape and tried to reach Palestine on precarious craft. Some foundered at sea. Exactly seven years ago the *S.S. Struma* went down with over 700 men, women and children off Istanbul, after the British Government, following weeks of urgent pleadings, had refused to admit them to Palestine. A few thousand refugees who reached Palestine were sent off by force to Mauritius and kept there till the end of the war. Even when the war was over, the White Paper continued to be in

---

[3] The abortive pro-Axis coup of Rashid Ali al-Kailani in 1941, supported by the Mufti of Jerusalem, which was suppressed by British troops.

force against the survivors. Few things have caused more bitterness among our people than the cruel expulsions to Cyprus and the detention of these worn-out men and women in the British camps on the island. The return of the *Exodus* with its passengers to a German port is a case of unparalleled cruelty.

You are surprised and disgusted that we have terrorists. I can only affirm that any nation which would have to go through the cruel ordeal through which the Jews have passed under Hitler would have produced such growth as terrorism and even worse. I cannot help feeling that a good deal of the self-righteous indignation with which the British press abounds in these days springs from an uneasy awareness—perhaps only subconscious—that the guilt rests with the accusers.

You are annoyed with Israel and its Government for having declared a general amnesty which benefited also the terrorists.[4] It so happens that I had nothing to do with this matter because it is outside my province, although I share the responsibility for it, but you are very much mistaken if you think that this decision implies any truckling to terrorism or any fear of its agents. The Provisional Government of Israel showed that it knew how to deal with insubordination when it did not hesitate to open fire at a Jewish boat, the *Altalena,* which was bringing in arms in defiance of the truce. Not many old-established governments would have acted with such firmness in a situation of this kind. If that Government and the Council of State have decided now to proclaim a general amnesty, it is because they felt—and presumably had good reason to feel—that that was the most effective way of liquidating, not the terrorists, but terrorism. It may be that they were mistaken; only the future can tell. But if the assumption is correct that this evil thing was the result of a holocaust such as the world has not seen and of the heartless policy of those who bolted the doors of Palestine against the victims, there may be ground for hoping that the normalisation of our national life may eradicate this cancer more effectively than savage punishment, however well deserved by ordinary standards. The hangman and the jailer, on whom the British Administration relied for fighting terrorism, have as you know certainly not produced results. This is not an age of humanists, but speaking for myself I still believe that there is boundless wisdom in Goethe's dictum that if you want to change the hearts of men, treat them as though they were already what you want them to become.

There is one more point in your letter which I cannot allow to

---

[4] On 10 Feb. the Israel Government granted amnesty to all prisoners except those serving life terms.

pass unanswered—your reference to the "dispossession of some 800,000 Arabs now ravaged by starvation, disease and death." The actual number is about half of that figure, but that is irrelevant. Undoubtedly there is starvation, disease and death among these unfortunate and ill-used people. But whose responsibility is it? Did we declare war on the Arabs and drive them out of the country? Was it not rather the Arab States that invaded our country on the 15th of May and even before—under the very eyes of the British Army and with the definite conviction that Britain was supporting them? The poor Arabs were misled by promises that the Jews will be exterminated in a very short while and then they would be brought back to what they had left, and more than they had left, by the victorious armies of Arabistan led by a good few British officers. It was not part of our plan of campaign to dispossess the Arabs. When the flight started—long before the British Administration left Palestine— we tried hard to persuade them to stay. Nor have we any intention to take by force the lands which they have deserted. They will be duly compensated. Would that those with whom rests the responsibility for their flight did anything material to help them. I feel sick at heart when I read in the British press heartrending accounts of the plight of these Arab refugees, all pointed against us, when only ten months ago, these same papers, in scarcely veiled form, encouraged the Arab invasion of Palestine which has brought forth all this misery and suffering. I could say a great deal more on the subject of your letter, but my reply became already unduly long.

Something very great and significant has happened here during these twelve months. The spirit of freedom is alive again in this ancient land, and it is producing miracles as in the days of old. There is a great hope in this, not only for us, but also for our neighbours, and certainly for those Arabs who are staying with us or those who intend to come back. It is sad that all this is hidden from your vision, which is usually so clear.

Yours sincerely,
Ch. Weizmann

P.S.   I am enclosing an article on the Arab refugee question which appeared yesterday in a local paper from the pen of a non-Jewish Englishman.[5]

[5] Apparently a reference to David Courtney's 'Column One' of 1 Mar. in *Palestine Post.* Courtney maintained that neither the Jews nor the Arab refugees were themselves to blame for the refugee problem; the responsibility was to be shared by 'those who were able, from the beginning, to exercise moderating influence upon the Arab States', but who instead supplied them with guns, ammunition, officers and incompetent advice—i.e., the British. The article concluded that only an internationally backed scheme could provide a future for the unfortunate Arab refugees.

309. To Albert Einstein, Princeton.   *Rehovot, 15 March 1949*
English: T.: I.F.M. 2449/150414.

On behalf of the Government and people of Israel and of its learned institutions I beg send you warmest congratulations and heartiest good wishes on your seventieth birthday. Although far away from us you are today very much in the hearts of the people of Israel. They pay homage to you as the greatest Jew of our generation, who has shed fresh lustre on the name of Israel and given a new interpretation to the ancient spiritual and moral ideals of our people. They gratefully remember how at the zenith of your scientific achievement you proudly identified yourself with our downtrodden people and lent your name and efforts to every cause designed to relieve Jewish suffering and raise Jewish dignity and self-respect. The active support you gave to the Zionist Movement during some of its most critical phases and your association with the building up of the Hebrew University of Jerusalem and the Technical Institute in Haifa will forever remain unforgotten. The people of Israel are anxious to pay personal homage to you as one of the builders of the New Zion and extend to you warm invitation visit their liberated country.

Chaim Weizmann

310. To Albert Einstein, Princeton.   *Rehovot, 15 March 1949*
English: T.: I.F.M. 2449/150414.

Would like to add to my official message on behalf of Israel my own and my wife's heartfelt personal greetings. Your association with Zionism will forever remain one of the happiest recollections of my personal life. We particularly recall your first trip with us to America in 1921, which was milestone in the awakening of Jewish America for Zion. We wish you health and strength and many happy years to come.

Chaim Weizmann

311. To John Gunther,[1] New York.   *Rehovot, 17 March 1949*
English: Or. Copy. T.W.: W.A.

My dear John,

     I am most grateful to you for having sent us your latest book,[2] which both Vera and myself have read with the greatest possible

---

311. [1] 1901–70. Roving journalist and author of the best-selling *'Inside'* series.

   [2] *Death Be Not Proud*, which told of the death of his son in 1947 at the age of 17, after a struggle against a brain tumour.

interest, and were deeply moved by the great tragedy which you describe in such simple and such moving words.

All I can wish you and Frances[3] is that you may find comfort in your literary pursuits which have been so many and so important. Few people can feel so deeply with you as we do, and therefore I do not think I need say many words.

My love to all of you and let us meet very soon.

Yours ever,

312. To Leopold S. Amery, London.   *Rehovot, 21 March 1949*
English: T.W./H.W.: W.A.

Dear Amery,

I was very glad indeed to receive your letter of February 19th.[1] I deeply appreciate your kind words. They reflect the sincere friendship and helpful attitude which you have maintained towards our effort in good and evil days. I am wholeheartedly with you in hoping that the estrangement of the last few years may soon be healed and that the vision of Balfour and his associates may again become a reality in the relations between the British people and Israel.

The problem of Jerusalem is admittedly a complex one. I need hardly tell you of all people what Jerusalem means to us. For eighteen centuries our spiritual attachment to Palestine has been compressed in that one word: Jerusalem. All that is noblest in our aspirations is summed up in the conception of Jerusalem Rebuilt. When the United Nations took its historic decision on November 29th 1947, the exclusion of Jerusalem from the Jewish State was a very bitter pill for our people to swallow. And then came the six months of the attack upon Jewish Jerusalem, with the bombardment of the Jewish quarters by the Arab Legion from the east and the Egyptian army from the south. There was no water or food in the city, and no one lifted a finger to save it from a fate that I don't care even to imagine. They held out, these men and women and children in Jerusalem, although their numbers were decimated, and every one of them suffered intensely. In the light of that experience and the inaction of those who had indulged in such noble phrases about the inviolability of Jerusalem, you will appreciate that none of us is now pre-

---

[3] Gunther's former wife, mother of the boy.

312. [1] W.A., congratulating W. upon his inauguration. Amery looked to an end to the estrangement between England and the Zionists. He saw room for compromise on the future status of Jerusalem and wondered whether it was impossible for the Jews, while not abandoning their claim to Jewish Jerusalem as part of Israel, to entrust it voluntarily to an international authority.

pared to entrust the safety of the city and the hundred thousand and more Jews living there to an international regime—dependent for its defence on the support of who knows how many governments and armies having no direct interest in the city. As you know, we are ready to accept any suggestion for ensuring the safety of the holy places and the freedom of access to men of all faiths. We should like to see the Old City turned into a dignified centre of religious and learned institutions of the three faiths to which pilgrims from near and far would come and derive real inspiration—a thing which was hardly possible under prevailing conditions. The placing of the Old City under Arab rule, which is apparently demanded by King Abdullah, would hardly be calculated to bring about such a development.

With kind regards and every good wish,

Affectionately,
Ch. Weizmann

I may be in London on my way back from the States and shall be hoping to see you.[2]

313. To Walter C. Lowdermilk,[1] Berkeley.   *Rehovot, 22 March 1949*
English: Or. Copy. T.W.: I.S.A. 68/11.

Dear Dr. Lowdermilk,

I was very much moved by your kind letter of February 17th.[2]

There is great truth in what you say about the spiritual significance of the events of the past year. We are yet too close to these great happenings to appreciate their full import.

There is also deep and sad truth in your observation that it was the prowess in arms of our people rather than their constructive work during the past half century which won the respect of the nations of the world. Yet I believe that it is our work of reclamation in this long neglected country which will be recorded by history as having pre-eminently established our claim to independence and political statehood. I need hardly tell you that for us such statehood is but an instrument for continuing that great work. The tasks which you set out in your letter are very much in our minds in these days. We have not, unfortunately, passed entirely out of the realms of the conflict

[2] Postscript handwritten.

313. [1] 1888–1974. U.S. land conservation and hydrology expert.

[2] Expressing 'Christian religious joy' at W.'s inauguration as Israel's President, Lowdermilk hoped for the full implementation of his scheme for a Jordan Valley Authority as developed in his book *Palestine—Land of Promise* (London 1944).

that was forced upon us by the invasion of last year. There are, however, good prospects that, unless external agents hamper us, we may succeed in the course of the next few months in achieving, if not full peace, at least the preliminaries of a peace settlement. The economic tasks that are pressing on us are hard and urgent. As you know, immigration has risen to unprecedented figures. We are liquidating one after another of the infamous camps in Europe, and are at the same time taking in Jews from the Middle Eastern countries whose position is becoming ever more precarious. We shall be able to settle them effectively only if we can carry out those large works of development and reconstruction to which you refer. It is by such settlement alone that we can give a sense of real home to these long-suffering people and redeem the soil that has for so long lain fallow.

I have made grateful note of your kind offer to assist in this wide field.

With kindest regards,

Yours sincerely,

314. To Dame Caroline Haslett,[1] London. *Rehovot, 31 March 1949*
English: Or. Copy. T.W.: W.A.

Dear Miss Haslett,

I was extremely happy to receive your note,[2] and Flora,[3] who has been staying with us until to-day, has been telling me about you a good deal.

One should not be overjoyed even if one reaches an important milestone like this on the road. The first days of exhilaration are over, and the great task which the present turn in our events is imposing on us begins to tower on the road ahead. I know how difficult it will be for those who follow us to do justice to the expectations which are connected with the Jewish State. It is a very small State, scarcely more than a county in England or Scotland, but if measured by the yardstick of human history it is very large; and I always bear in mind that Athens was only one city, and still it has shaped the civilisation of the Western world. I would feel happy if I could carry the conviction that Jerusalem and the cities which form our

---

314. [1] 1895–1957. Feminist, first British woman to obtain recognition as qualified engineer. Founding-editor, *The Woman Engineer*; President, International Federation of Business and Professional Women 1950–56; appointed Dame of British Empire 1947.

[2] 1 Mar. (W.A.). She had earlier visited the Weizmanns in Rehovot and wrote of her appreciation of W.'s sense of achievement.

[3] Flora Solomon, daughter of Gregory Benenson (see Biog. Index, Vol. VII). Wife of Col. Harold Solomon and a close friend of the Weizmanns.

State may contribute their part to the rehabilitation of the East, which stands in need almost of everything at present. We are facing to-day a large immigration, urgent problems of reconstruction and a war—a very serious war—but it will all pass if we do not lose faith. I think we won't!

With very many thanks and kindest regards,

Yours ever,
Ch. Weizmann

315. To Lord William Percy,[1] London.   *Rehovot, 31 March 1949*
English: Or. Copy. T.W.: W.A.

My dear Lord Percy,

Please forgive me for answering your charming note[2] by a type-written letter. As you may have heard my eyes are in such a state that I must avoid writing by hand.

I have no words to express my thanks for your lines, and on re-reading them memories of all these past years are coming up; our talks in Bir Salem, in Jerusalem and in London. It is all a long cavalcade of pictures and men; it was my good fortune to meet real men—you are one of the rare representatives of a friend who may be critical at times, but stout and reliable. I wonder whether you remember our talks in the Mess Room of the camp of the late Gilbert Clayton.[3]

I do not know when I shall be in London again, but it is quite possible that I may be on my way back from the States, where I am betaking myself to on Sunday next.

Mrs. Weizmann and myself send heartfelt greetings to you and Lady Percy, and if you do happen to meet Eustace[4] give him my very best love.

Affectionately yours,
Ch. Weizmann

---

315. [1] 1882–1963. He had served with the British Forces in Palestine in W.W.I and became an Aide to the Military Governor of Jerusalem, retiring 1919.

[2] 3 Mar. (W.A.). Percy recalled their first meeting 30 years earlier and sent 'the tribute of my great respect and admiration for your journey'.

[3] When the Zionist Commission, led by W., arrived in Palestine 1918, Army H.Q. was at Bir Salem (today Kibbutz Netzer Sereni). Clayton (Biog. Index, Vol. VIII) was Chief Political Officer in the force.

[4] Lord Eustace Percy (later Lord Percy of Newcastle; 1887–1958), brother of Lord William; Unionist M.P. 1921–37; Minister without Portfolio 1935–36.

316. To Harry Pirie-Gordon,[1] London.   *Rehovot, 31 March 1949*
English: Or. Copy. T.W.: W.A.

My dear Pirie-Gordon,

Your note[2] revived all the memories to which you refer, and which I remember so well. Bir Salem, Jerusalem, Haifa, the North, the Paris Conference, the Foreign Office in Downing Street, and all the gallery of persons who directly and indirectly helped to shape the Jewish State—sometimes without knowing it, sometimes without wishing it. But it was written in the stars that the redemption of Israel should come about, and in spite of many adversaries it has come to pass, and I am confident it will stay if we keep to the path of justice and righteousness.

I do remember not only conversations we had here (you know that I see from my house in Rehovot the little hill and grove of Bir Salem) and in the office of the *Times,* and on many other occasions. It was extremely good of you to have written to me and I appreciate it deeply.

I send you my kindest regards and good wishes, and I still hope to see you at not too distant a time in London.

As ever yours,
Ch. Weizmann

317. To Lady (Caroline) Schuster,[1] Maidenhead.

Rehovot, 31 March 1949

English: T.W.: W.A.

My dear Cary,

What a long journey it was from Kent House to here, and how much we all went through in this span of life, which may be long for human beings, but short compared with the history of an ancient people.

---

316. [1] Editor of Military Government weekly *Palestine News* in W.W.I and Allenby's Press Officer.

[2] 2 Mar. (W.A.). Letter of congratulation prompted by memories of W.W.I associations. Pirie-Gordon expressed the wish that Israel would find it possible to come to a satisfactory agreement with 'another old friend of mine on the other side of Jordan', King Abdullah.

317. [1] Biog. Index, Vol. V. She and her husband, the physicist Sir Arthur Schuster, had befriended W. during his early days in Manchester.

I am extremely sorry about the mistake[2] which I made in the Book, which, I am afraid, I cannot correct now, because it is already published both in England and the States. It was already too late when your dear letter arrived, but I bear it in mind and shall certainly correct it in the next edition, which I hope to republish in the course of the summer. There are many things which have to be supplemented. As you will have noticed, the last part, which is perhaps the most important, namely, the creation of the State, etc. is skimpy, and I have not done any justice to it at all. All that requires thought and work, and I rely on the possibility of doing it during the summer holidays. If you have any more criticism and any more memories of Manchester, I would be more than grateful to you if you could let me know.

Meanwhile we both send you and the family our fondest love. I wonder where Norah[3] is at present; I have not heard anything from her since we met at the wedding.

We are going to the States for a very short visit and hope to be back here in harness at the end of April.

All the best and all our love,

Yours ever,
Chaim

318. To Juan Domingo Peron,[1] Buenos Aires. *Tel Aviv, 1 April 1949*
French: Or. Copy. T.W.: I.S.A. 130. 02/2391/70.

Your Excellency,

I was very moved to read your handwritten letter,[2] which was given to me by Mr. Sujer Matrajt,[3] and I very much regret that the state of my eyesight does not permit me to reply to you in a like manner.

---

[2] Her letter offering congratulations (23 Feb., W.A.) referred also to an apparent misstatement in *T. and E.* relating to her late husband, whom she felt was wrongly described as the student, rather than the mentor, of the mathematician J. J. Thomson. She noted that she was quoting from a pre-publication article in J.C. The mistake appears in a special limited edition, and was subsequently corrected.

[3] Norah Nicholls (formerly Schuster; Biog. Index, Vol. V). Pathologist; daughter of Lady Schuster.

318. [1] 1895–1974. President of Argentina from 1946 until exiled 1955; returned to power 1973.

[2] 18 Mar. 1949 (I.S.A. file as above). A message of goodwill to Israel and to W. personally, and expressing the desire for strengthened ties between the two countries. Argentina had accorded Israel recognition the previous month.

[3] Prominent Jewish communal figure in Argentina.

For a long time now I have been very much aware of the sympathy and interest shown by yourself and the noble Argentinian people for our young state, and I was so very pleased to find the confirmation of this in your kind letter.

In fact, we are only at the beginning, and we very much need the goodwill and friendship of the major nations of the world. We have obtained our independence. Our task at the moment is to make it into a living reality. Our future essentially depends on the agricultural and industrial development of our country and the sensible exploitation of its natural resources. In order to achieve these ends, the example of your large country can serve as a precious model. The enormous amount of agricultural and industrial development in Argentina can serve as an inspiration for those among us who, on a far more modest scale, are endeavouring to launch the country economically.

Permit me to send you the sincerest wishes of the people of Israel for the progress and prosperity of your beautiful country, and also allow me to add my own wishes for your personal happiness.

With all friendly assurances, I remain, Your Excellency,

Your sincere friend,
Ch. Weizmann
President of the State of Israel

---

319. To Selig Brodetsky, London. *Rehovot, 2 April 1949*
English: Or. Copy. T.W.: W.A.

My dear Brod.,

Your letter of February 20th[1] reached me too late to reply to you at your Australian address: I hope my reply will find you in London.

The question of the administration of the University has occupied me for the last few months, and I believe I have now a good picture of what the University needs. It is essential that the Head of the University should devote all his time and all his energy exclusively to the reorganization of the whole structure of that institution. The University has lost a good many of its members and promising

---

319. [1] (W.A.). Brodetsky was due in Israel to examine the administration of H.U. But he was first to visit Australia, returning briefly to London before travelling to Israel. He wrote of reports that W. had endorsed another's candidacy for the post of H.U. President although he had earlier encouraged Brodetsky to accept the office. He felt that if W. still held to his earlier view this should be made clear to any members of the Board of Governors W. might meet while in U.S.

students during this war, and the interruption of the studies, too, has contributed to a certain disintegration of the whole structure.

If your other obligations will make it possible for you to concentrate on the University, I believe that no other candidate would come into consideration besides you.[2]

With kindest regards,

Yours very sincerely,
Ch. Weizmann

[The Weizmanns left for the U.S. 7 Apr., arriving on 13th. On 23 Apr. W. addressed a gathering arranged by the Weizmann Institute Committee at the Waldorf-Astoria Hotel. President Truman was unable to attend, but he gave a luncheon for the Weizmanns at the White House 26 Apr., thus affording the two Presidents an opportunity to discuss Israel-American relations, the forthcoming Arab-Israel negotiations at Lausanne, the question of Jerusalem, and the problem of Arab refugees—see W. to Truman, 26 Apr., I.S.A. 93.08 375/19. On 4 May W. addressed a U.J.A. celebration of Israel's first anniversary. The next day he and his wife embarked on the *Queen Mary,* stopping in Paris for a meeting with President Vincent Auriol of France on 12 May, and returning to Israel 16 May.]

320. To the Stephen Wise Family, New York.

New York, 19 April 1949

English: T.: W.A.

On behalf of my wife my son and myself deeply distressed by the tragic news death of your father our dear friend Stephen.[1] He was a great leader of our people and he adorned everything he touched. He leaves behind him a gap which will never be filled, and he will be mourned by his fellow Zionists in and outside Israel, and also by innumerable members of the non-Jewish community. We send you our heartfelt sympathy in the hour of your tragic loss. May you find comfort in the thought that he leaves behind him a glorious memory and that he lived a full life for the benefit of his own people and mankind.

Chaim Weizmann

[2] Brodetsky's appointment as H.U. President in succession to Magnes was announced 27 May.

320. [1] Wise died that day.

321. To Albert Einstein, Princeton.   *New York, 20 April 1949*
German: Copy. T.W.: W.A.

Dear Professor,

I was very pleased with your kind letter.[1] As you know, I am always greatly overworked for the first few days after my arrival, and am replying with a slight delay, which I hope you will excuse.

I really hope to see you while I am here. I intend to stay until May 5th and then to return directly to Israel. Should you come to New York, I would greatly appreciate it if you would let me know one day in advance. I would very much like to discuss with you the University and other institutions in Israel. If we want to absorb a large immigration, a scientific and technological base must be created, and it is becoming very urgent to put everything in order now.

I hope you are in good health, and I should anyhow be glad to receive a few lines from you. In the meantime please accept my own and my wife's best regards.

321A. To Harry S. Truman, Washington.   *Rehovot, 4 May 1949*
English: T.: I.S.A. 93.03 67/2.

Your message of greetings and congratulations on the occasion of the first anniversary of the independence of Israel is most warmly and gratefully appreciated. The people of Israel will never forget the part played by your great country as well as your own personal sympathy and helpful attitude at all times in the achievement of their national independence.[1]

                                                    Chaim Weizmann

322. To B. B. Appleby, Chicago.   *Rehovot, 5 July 1949*
English: T.W.: W.A.

Dear Mr. Appleby,

Thank you very much for your letter of May 3rd,[1] which has just reached me. Despite the brevity and the circumstances under which we met I have a distinct recollection of our meeting in New York following the affair at the Waldorf-Astoria. It was indeed a

---

321. [1] 4 Apr., anticipating a meeting during W.'s visit to 'Dollaria' (i.e., U.S.).

321A. [1] For a detailed discussion of American-Israeli differences at this time, see W.–Truman exchange in Appendix I.

322. [1] (W.A.), requesting suggestions for a 'Motol Project' in Israel.

pleasure for me to be able to shake hands with the son of Moshe Yudel, the Doctor.

I knew your father when I was still a young boy, and in later years I often heard my parents speak of him in very warm terms. All of us, I am sure, have travelled a very long way since those early beginnings, and I am happy to know that the seeds that were planted in Motele many years ago have not gone lost, as is evidenced by your own warm interest in the rebuilding of Israel.

I am particularly happy to know that the Moteler Progressive Club has undertaken to establish a permanent memorial in Israel in my honour and also to bear the name of Motele, which has always been very dear to me. As you know, my whole life's work has been devoted to science and to the rebuilding of *Eretz Israel*. I have tried to integrate these two in a manner which would be most beneficial. If, therefore, as you say, your organization is interested in making a contribution of $100,000 towards some specific project in this country that would bear my name and that of Motele, I can think of nothing more appropriate than the establishment of a well-equipped scientific laboratory in Rehovot.

The needs for scientific development are great—it is the life blood of this country. Specifically I should like to recommend a laboratory for Experimental Biology (Cancer Research) to be conducted by Dr. I. Berenblum of Oxford University, one of the most eminent authorities on the subject. He was recently invited by the United States Government to undertake a similar project and has been in the States for two years. A most unusual honour has been bestowed upon him, both as a Jew and as a Scientist, when he was invited by the Vatican recently to attend a Scientific Congress under its auspices and to lecture on the subject of his experiments.

Dr. Berenblum is now in Israel, and we invited him to join our staff of distinguished scientists to head the department of Experimental Biology. I am happy to say that he has accepted and will begin his work here in the fall of 1950. Your contribution of $100,000 would make it possible for us to begin work at once on the setting up of his laboratory, the entire cost of which, incidentally, for the initial stages only, would be approximately $300,000. But we would be happy to give the Department the name you suggest. Dr. Berenblum's work here would be of enormous importance, not only to Israel but to the world at large. I hope you will find my suggestion feasible and accept it.

I am quite sure that when you and your friends will come to Rehovot and see what we have already accomplished by way of scientific development in this country, you will have every reason to be proud and happy to be associated with such an enterprise.

In conclusion may I suggest that for further details you contact Mr. Weisgal, who is now in Rehovot, and to whom I gave your letter and copy of my reply.

With warm regards and best wishes,

Very sincerely yours,
Ch. Weizmann

323. To Winston S. Churchill, London.   *Tel Aviv, 18 July 1949*
English: T.W.: Mordechai Eliash Papers.

Dear Mr. Churchill,

I have much pleasure in introducing to you by these lines Dr. Mordecai Eliash,[1] the first Minister of the State of Israel at the Court of St. James.

Dr. Eliash, before assuming his present mission, was a distinguished member of the Palestine Bar. He is also an eminent Jewish and Oriental scholar. He has undertaken the worthy, if difficult, task of rebuilding the old bridges and renewing under the new conditions the friendly associations between Zionism and Great Britain, which were so tragically disrupted in recent years. He will need all the help he can get from those who stood for that earlier tradition, among whom I count you as one of the foremost. That is why I commend him to your wise counsel and informed guidance.

With kind regards,

Yours very sincerely,
Ch. Weizmann

324. To Meyer W. Weisgal, Rehovot.   *Burgenstock,[1] 12 August 1949*
English: T.W.: W.A.

My dear Meyer,

I don't know whether you have seen the pamphlet published by the Jewish Theological Seminary in New York. It came into my hands when looking through the scrapbook which you have given me; I have found it in the worst possible taste, which can only do harm both to the book and the author.[2]

I have written to Mr. Gotshal asking him to make representations to the Jewish Theological Seminary for causing me unpleasantness

---

323. [1] Biog. Index, Vol. X. He had previously been legal adviser to *Va'ad Leumi*.

324. [1] The Weizmanns left Israel 19 July to vacation in Switzerland, returning 10 Oct.
   [2] The pamphlet is untraced, and the cause of W.'s grievance is unknown.

by such a publication. I enclose herewith a copy of Mr. Gotshal's reply.[3] There is nothing I could add to it, except to request you that in future I might be informed of any steps which you wish to take with any important organization, such as the Jewish Theological Seminary, whenever my name is involved, so as to avoid unpleasantness.

I would like to thank you for your cable. It is more explicit than your previous one[4] about "everything under control," which, in my opinion, covers a multitude of sins without giving a real picture. I shall be looking forward both to your letter and Bergmann's report announced in the telegram, but I would like to add that I am uneasy because of the lack of a real sincere statement concerning the Rehovot situation. If it is done with the purpose of saving me worry, I am anxious to point out once and forever that this method—well intentioned as it may be—has just the opposite effect.

With all good wishes,

Affectionately yours,
Ch. Weizmann

325. To Meyer W. Weisgal, Rehovot.   *Burgenstock, 18 August 1949*
English: T.W.: W.A.

My dear Meyer,

I am in possession of your letter of 12th inst.,[1] and also of your letter to Dewey [Stone], Harry [Levine] and Gestetner, of 8th inst.[2] I know that you will believe me if I say that I have read and reread your letter several times and I think I have grasped the full meaning of all that you give expression to, and even of the implications— I'm sorry that you seem to meet with considerable difficulties, and I'm particularly sorry about Shirley. I know from my own experience that the question of adaptation is much harder for a woman than for a man, and it is my fervent wish that you should both get over the initial difficulties and that life would become gradually normal and smooth.

[3] Sylvan Gotshal, a New York lawyer, wrote 3 Aug. (W.A.) that he was pursuing the matter. W.'s letter to him is untraced.

[4] Weisgal was preparing for the Weizmann Institute's inauguration on 2 Nov. Only one telegram has been traced, of general reassurance (10 Aug., W.A.).

325. [1] Dated 11 Aug. (W.A.). This hinted at difficulties at the Institute without specifying their nature, Weisgal stating that he preferred to discuss them personally with W. He also spoke of problems of adaptation in Rehovot for himself and his wife.

[2] This (W.A.) discussed the Institute's financial problems and scientific achievements.

I have taken note of your admonitions on the front page of your letter of the 11th inst. to reserve judgment and treat things with kindness and fatherly love. I was doing so for almost 15 years, and the relations between me and Bergmann were impeccable—I have however found a profound change in him on my arrival to Israel in September 1948. Of course, I was not aware of the "profound psychological factors," to which you are referring, until somewhat later and only after having taken cognizance of it I realized the full importance of the change wrought in Bergmann. There was nothing more to do. And that is the situation to-date. It is, in my opinion, very unsatisfactory, both as far as the Institute is concerned—which is the main thing—and as far as my relations to the man are concerned, to whom the Institute owes a great deal and whom I have certainly considered as a loyal and devoted friend, and have never ceased to consider as such.

Nothing which has happened in the last few years of my life has hurt me so much as the above-described situation, and, as you may already have noticed, I am not given to overstatements. For the time being, I am afraid I do not see any solution to the problem except, perhaps, to withdraw quietly from the Institute, which step commends itself to me very much.

I wish you could come here for a short time when we could talk all that over, but my views are not quite crystallized and a good deal will depend on what Mr. Van Leer[3] will do in Israel. As I have already cabled to Bergmann,[4] Van Leer has gone to Israel with the intention to build an Institute for technical physics. Whether this project will be carried out or not depends largely upon the impression which Van Leer will carry away from Rehovot. Should he decide in a positive sense, there will be a fair amount to do outside the routine of the Institute, and in my present state of mind it might suit me very well. Of that we ought to know very soon, as Van Leer is due back in less than a fortnight. Should this hope not materialize, I shall have to look for another avenue, because I certainly don't want to identify myself with the establishment in its present condition.

I must add in parentheses that Joseph [Cohn] has done a good piece of work both with Mr. Van Leer and Mr. Zalmanowitz,[5] whom he has interested in our place.

---

[3] Bernard van Leer, of Amsterdam. A manufacturer of oil drums, he endowed a workshop for precision instruments attached to the Institute. His son Oscar created the Van Leer Foundation, with a Research Academy in Jerusalem.

[4] On 14 Aug. (W.A.).

[5] Jacques Zalmanowitz. Of Lithuanian origin, he resided in Geneva and was head of the commercial organization *Société Générale de Surveillance*. Contributed substantially to the Institute.

I was extremely glad to read that Dr. Dostrovsky[6] has at present been appointed as temporary scientific director. I think it is an excellent appointment and might be made permanent in some different form; he is a good and solid man and very serious in spite of his young years.

I was glad to read the opinions which you quote in page 3 of your letter to Dewey and Harry, but I confess that I was somewhat astonished to read the sentence on the same page which begins "considering the conditions they were compelled to work in the last few years, etc." Frankly, I don't understand what it is addressed to, the work in the Sieff Institute was, in my view, much more comfortable and convenient than in many great academic institutions which I had the opportunity to see, and I have seen the University of Manchester, the laboratories in South Kensington, in Oxford, in the Sorbonne, and in the Pasteur Institute; I don't think for one moment that the conditions in the Sieff Institute—even in its modest beginnings— were in any way falling behind the conditions of the places mentioned. The contrary is true. I therefore fail to understand your reference to the so-called difficulties.

I was pleased to see you writing that our people are gaining recognition in international scientific circles, and find favour with visiting scientists, but without wishing to put too many flies in the ointment, I would like you to know that I have heard also other opinions from friendly sides, and they all allude to a certain state of affairs which has worried me so much.

I begin to doubt whether the date chosen for the opening, namely 2nd November, is exactly suitable. It is just the beginning of the academic year, when every scientist is busy with his duties, and would find it difficult to get away. It seems to me after mature reflection that the first week of January is much more suitable: it is Christmas Vacation, and people go willingly to warm countries. I leave it to you to think it over and to decide.

I have said almost all I intended to, we are thinking of returning about the end of September, and I must confess that although I am always happy to return home after an absence, this time the feeling is marred by a certain pain which I can't get rid of.

I think I finished my story and can conclude my letter by saying that I am extremely happy to know that you are in Rehovot during this crucial period. I am sure that although things appear troublesome and confused at present, it will sort itself out in the end.

[6] Israel Dostrovsky, b. 1918. Professor of Physical Chemistry, Weizmann Institute. Lecturer at University College of North Wales 1943–48; Vice-President of Weizmann Institute 1971–73, then President until Oct. 1975.

I shall be awaiting further and more explicit news from you, and remain with much love to both of you from both of us.

Yours ever,
Ch. Weizmann

P.S. The despatch of this letter has been delayed by the arrival of Dr. Bergmann's cable,[7] and I should now like to add that it is extremely difficult when one sends a cable to a country 3000 miles away to realize what effect is produced by completely innocent statements, or steps that impose themselves.

I am surprised and pained to see you taking offence after so many years of harmonious cooperation, which have never been marred by any misunderstandings. I can only explain it by the tension which exists in Rehovot.

Affectionately,
Ch. Weizmann

326. To Meyer W. Weisgal, Rehovot.   *Ascona, 29 August 1949*
English: T.W.: W.A.

My dear Meyer,

I was somewhat surprised to receive two communications from you, both rather unpleasant: one, dealing with the Wavell passage[1] and the other dealing with Mr. J. Malcolm.[2] You did not deem it

[7] This related to a grievance of Weisgal's caused by van Leer's stipulation that, on arrival at Rehovot he was to discuss his project exclusively with a scientist, and he was not to be approached with financial requests. W. had asked that Bergmann alone have dealings with van Leer. See W.'s telegram to Zondek, 14 Aug.; Bergmann to W., 16 Aug. (W.A.).

326. [1] Lord Wavell (Biog. Index, Vol. XX) had taken exception to a passage in *T. and E.* This appears on pp. 529–30 of the London 1949 edition, and purports to describe a statement by Wavell to Jewish leaders in Palestine to the effect that, as a result of Rommel's 1942 offensive, the British Army was to be withdrawn towards India and the 'Jews would be delivered up to the fury of the Germans, the Arabs and the Italians'. In fact, Wavell had left the Middle East one year earlier and he denied having made the statement. W.'s London publisher, Hamish Hamilton, in contact with the Field-Marshal's solicitors, believed the offending passage should be taken out, lest legal action ensued. Further, the publisher informed Weisgal that Wavell was hurt by W.'s failure to write to him personally on the matter. In the event, Wavell received public and private apologies. See Hamish Hamilton letter and cable to Weisgal, 12 July, 8 Aug.; W. to Miss May, 18 Aug. 1949 (all in W.A.).

[2] W. had failed in *T. and E.* to acknowledge the role of James Malcolm (Biog. Index, Vol. VII) in the pre-Balfour Declaration period in 1917. George Malcolm Thomson, biographer

necessary to add a word of comment or advice, as if you were simply a transmitting agent and a complete stranger.

I am thinking the matter over, I have come to the conclusion that you must be offended by something, and it can obviously be only the Van Leer incident, which I have already explained to you by cable and by letter.[3]

I never imagined that vindictiveness could be peculiar to your character.

So far I have only had the unpleasant side of the book, but I understand that various payments are due. However, as all the arrangements were made by you, I am completely in the dark and would be most grateful if you would enlighten me on the subject.

I did not want to apply to Harper's or to Hamish Hamilton directly, and I am, therefore, writing to you and hope to have a full report from you soon.

Best regards to Shirley and yourself from Mrs. Weizmann and myself.

> Yours ever,
> Ch. Weizmann

327. To Oscar Vasella,[1] Fribourg.   *Geneva, 16 September 1949*
French: T.W.: Photostat W.A.

Your Eminence,

Before leaving Switzerland I would like to extend my most cordial greetings to yourself, to all the professors of the University of Fribourg,

---

of Lloyd George, raised this matter in *The Times Literary Supplement,* 22 July 1949, citing W.'s own admission, and that of other historians of Zionism, that it was Malcolm, President of the Armenian National Committee in London, who had put Sir Mark Sykes, one of the architects of the Balfour Declaration, in touch with the Zionist leaders. Thomson concluded that the omission in W.'s autobiography was no doubt due to a lapse of memory. But he insisted that 'in view of the historical importance of the matter and in justice to Mr. Malcolm, I feel that the true facts should be clearly stated'. For W.'s interpretation of Malcolm's contribution, see Vol. XVIII, No. 427. Further, on 4 Dec. 1947 W. cabled Malcolm: 'You stood with us from the Balfour Declaration till present day, and you have given us unstinted support and sympathy in these stirring days' (W.A.). Thomson again emphasised Malcolm's role in a letter to *The Times* on 2 Nov. 1949, anniversary of Balfour Declaration.

[3] See No. 325 and n. 7 there. To assuage Weisgal, W. had telegraphed Bergmann and Weisgal jointly 20 Aug. (W.A.) explaining that van Leer had wished to deal with one individual only, preferably a scientist. 'Most certainly my attitude [towards] Meyer unchanged, but guided by necessity only.'

327. [1] Professor and Rector at University of Fribourg, where W. had studied (see Vol. I).

and especially to the Professors de Diesbach, Blum, Weber and Müller, and to thank you once more for the honour and attention which were so generously shown to me by my old and well-loved *alma mater* of Fribourg.[2]

Please accept this expression of gratitude together with cordial regards on the part of my wife and myself.

Chaim Weizmann

328. To Ernst David Bergmann, Rehovot.

La Croix,[1] *28 September 1949*

English: Or. Copy. T.W.: W.A.

My dear David,

I was delighted to receive your telegram as well as Meyer's.[2]

With you, I wish ardently that things should settle down and that the Institute should work as harmoniously as before.

I scarcely remember anything in my life, which certainly was not poor in troubles, which has given me so much pain as what happened in the last few months; and I would not like to go through it again. And I am sure we shall all try to avoid it.

I have written to various chemical works like Schuchardt Goerlitz; I. Merck Darmstadt; Bender & Hobein Zurich asking them for their respective catalogues and whether they could send 250 gr. of pure hemipinic acid (ANH). I am doubtful, of course, whether they would send any, and we shall probably have to produce it ourselves. Could you put somebody on to try some preliminary experiments on a small scale? If successful, he could try somewhat larger quantities.

I suppose Schmidt[3] is already working on the new Microscope. As for the required photographic attachments, it will take a month or two before they arrive to the Institute.

When I return, I would like to try and photograph, together with Fry,[4] my bacterium on the Electronic; I seem to remember you mentioning to me that he did begin to work it and to have done nicely.

Our final programme is to leave La Croix on the 1st Oct. for Paris

---

[2] W. received an honorary degree at a special ceremony at the University 12 Sept. 1949.

328. [1] In France, Department of Var, country home of Joseph Blumenfeld.

[2] Bergmann's telegram untraced. Weisgal wired 27 Sept. (W.A.) upon his return to Rehovot that 'everything so far calm, serene and fine. Hope will remain so'.

[3] Gerhard M. J. Schmidt (1919–71). Chemist, b. Berlin, received doctorate at Oxford. Joined Sieff Institute 1948 and became Head, Department of Chemistry at Weizmann Institute. Vice-President of Institute 1969–70.

[4] Ephraim Heinrich Frei, b. 1912, Vienna. Head of Department of Electronics, Weizmann Institute. Weizmann Prize 1957.

and we shall take the plane for Israel on the 9th. Any cable could reach me at the Meurice Hotel.

With all best wishes and much love; my love to Meyer and thanks for his cable.

Yours ever,[5]

[The Weizmanns returned to Israel 10 Oct. 1949. On 2 Nov. they participated in the dedication ceremonies of the Weizmann Institute in Rehovot. Postponed several times, either because of the political situation or because of W.'s absence abroad, the dedication was conducted in the presence of leading public figures and distinguished scientists. Many congratulatory messages were received, including one from Truman (see W.'s acknowledgement, 13 Nov., W.A.). On 27 Nov. W. celebrated his 75th birthday, an event marked in London by a public banquet, with Smuts arriving specially from South Africa to be chief speaker, and when the fundraising campaign to plant the Weizmann Forest in the Jerusalem Hills was launched—see W. to Smuts, 29 Jan. 1950, I.S.A. 68/11.]

329. To Vincent Auriol,[1] Paris.   *Rehovot, 8 December 1949*
French: T.: I.F.M. 2449/150414.

Very worried by yesterday's vote at General Ad Hoc Committee of United Nations Assembly.[2] Separation of State of Israel from

---

[5] W.'s alienation from Bergmann had been growing for months. On 17 June Bergmann sent a note to V.W. that he had just had 'a very upsetting conversation' with W. He felt the situation was due to no objective cause but to 'the vile gossip to which Dr. Weizmann had listened and against which I am powerless'. Thereafter there was little if any contact between the two men. Thus Bergmann submitted a detailed report on Institute research activities to V.W. 5 Aug., and he wrote to her 22 Aug. of his unhappy situation and sense of isolation, which, he added, he did not attribute to Weisgal. Though he found V.W.'s support a source of strength, he referred to 'unjustified, unfounded and libellous' personal attacks compelling the conclusion that 'I have no place in the Institute any longer'. He had not written to 'the Chief' about resignation, 'as he has not chosen to talk to me, but only *about* me in this whole affair' (W.A.). Late that August Bergmann went on an extended lecture tour on behalf of the Institute in South America, and wrote to Weisgal 26 Aug. of his determination to resign. Returning via Paris, he apparently had a discussion with Blumenfeld, and as a result withdrew his resignation. See Meyer W. Weisgal, ... *So Far*, London 1971, pp. 274–75; Barnet Litvinoff, *Weizmann; Last of the Patriarchs*, London 1976, pp. 248–49.

329. [1] 1884–1965. President of France 1947–54.

[2] The Ad Hoc Political Committee on 24 Nov. commenced consideration of the proposals of the U.N. Conciliation Commission for an international regime for Jerusalem, but were informed by the delegates of both Israel and Jordan that those countries would refuse to accept internationalization of the city—though fully prepared to give free access under U.N. supervision to the Holy Places—and would adhere to the existing arrangement whereby Jerusalem was partitioned between them. Nevertheless a proposal that Jerusalem and its adjacent area, including Bethlehem, form a separate entity under the administration of the U.N. Trusteeship Council was adopted by the committee 7 Dec. by 35 votes to 13, with 11 abstentions. The vote in the plenary session on 10 Dec. for adoption of this Resolution was 38–14, with 7 abstentions. Some countries changed their votes of 7 Dec., but France consistently supported the trusteeship plan.

Jewish Jerusalem with its hundred thousand Jewish inhabitants and eternal tradition is completely unacceptable to all sections of Jewish people. Could only be imposed against determined opposition of entire population. Proposed internationalisation would provoke permanent conflict and industrial depression rather than assure security of Holy Places. Find incredible that after desperate efforts and happy realisation seen last year to re-establish peace in the Holy City, peace once again endangered by actions of U.N. itself. Find even more incredible fact that last disastrous action undertaken with support of France, which had shown such deep understanding of idea Israel's rebirth. People of Israel agree that security and accessibility Holy Places be safeguarded and that United Nations should have certain amount of control, but under no circumstances would they accept separation from ancient cradle of our resuscitated State. With sincere regards to your Excellency,

Chaim Weizmann
President of the State of Israel

330. To L. Denivelle,[1] Paris.   *Tel Aviv, 1 January 1950*
French: Or. Copy. T.W.: I.F.M. 2449/150414.

Dear Mr. Denivelle,

I was very pleased to receive your letter of December 15th[2] which, unfortunately, only got to me on the 30th.

Since my telegram to President Auriol,[3] the General Assembly has adopted the unfavourable decision of December 9th, with its prospective separation of the State of Israel from Jerusalem, with its hundred thousand Jews and all its large Jewish institutions, and its subjection to outside international rule. This decision was due to a surprising alliance between the Catholic countries under strong pressure from Rome, the Soviet bloc, who want, above all, to drive Abdullah, whom they consider to be a British protégé, from the Old City, and the Arab bloc, for whom the internationalisation of Jerusalem, as such, has very little importance, but who see in the problem an unexpected opportunity to mobilise the entire Christian world against Israel, of undermining its reputation at the United Nations and also to prepare the ground for the renewal of hostilities against us. It is extremely painful for me to acknowledge the fact that France took an active part in the adoption of this disastrous resolution.

---

330. [1] Lecturer at *Conservatoire National des Arts et Métiers*, Paris.
 [2] I.F.M. file as above.
 [3] See No. 229.

The United Nations' decision is both absurd and cynical. Because of an area constituting only two percent of all Jerusalem—*the major part of which area is not in our hands, but in those of Abdullah*—housing the Holy Places of the three monotheistic religions, the entire city will be placed under international rule. The hundred thousand Jews of Jerusalem and the State of Israel are to be punished because Abdullah has in his possession the Church of the Holy Sepulchre and the Church of the Nativity in Bethlehem. Any person having the smallest amount of knowledge of international affairs knows very well that such an international rule in an isolated city is absolutely inapplicable, and can lead to nothing but insecurity, conflict and economic decline. In Jerusalem's case, being a city cut off from everywhere, without any contact with the outside world, squeezed in between Israel and Trans-Jordan, without the slightest economic life of its own—international rule would only serve to multiply these disastrous effects. If anyone wanted to put the Holy City and its sacred relics into a state of permanent insecurity, he could find nothing better than to put it under international rule.

This decision also reaches the heights of cynicism. After all the suffering undergone by the Jews of Jerusalem last year in defending their city against the aggression of the Arab states, when the United Nations showed complete indifference, they are now to be deprived of their political right to look after their own interests, a fundamental right guaranteed to all the nations of the world by the United Nations Charter. The Jews of Jerusalem have declared in unequivocal terms that they will not accept this cynical decree, and that they will continue to occupy a part of Israel as they have always done. Abdullah has also made it quite clear that in no circumstances will he give up his possession of the Old City. So what will the United Nations do?

That is a grave and extremely urgent problem. A solution must be found to this dilemma in which the United Nations has got itself stuck. Territorial internationalisation is obviously out of the question because of the given facts. The only thing that should concern the world in general in Jerusalem is the safe-guarding of the Holy Places and the free and safe access to them of all those wanting to visit them. This legitimate interest can be efficiently provided for by adequate security measures and guarantees, which we are only too ready to give as far as our own territory is concerned, and which I am sure would be reciprocated by Abdullah for the Old City. With a minimum of common sense and good will the whole problem can be solved by a general agreement. It would certainly be agreed generally that such an agreement would be more efficient and more durable than any solution which would have to be imposed, even if one considers that it could be imposed.

A very grave responsibility now rests on France as far as this matter is concerned. The President of the Trusteeship Council, on whom the next development of this embarrassing situation now depends, is the French representative.[4] He will most certainly have realised at that moment what an impossible task had been imposed on the Trusteeship Council. It would be very good if his own Government could help and advise him, and facilitate his finding a solution which would be both practical and fair. You may assure all your friends that we will cooperate faithfully with any project which safeguards Christian interests and assures the security and accessibility of the Holy Places without separating the State of Israel from its ancient birth place.[5]

> Yours sincerely,
> Chaim Weizmann
> President of the State of Israel

331. To Otto M. Lilien,[1] London.   *Tel Aviv, 1 January 1950*
English: T.W.: C.Z.A. K11/10/14.

My dear Mr. Lilien,

I was greatly touched by your friendly letter of 16th December,[2] and I can only express my regret that I shall not be in London to participate in your father's[3] Jubilee Exhibition, which I would have liked very much.

Your kind letter brought up many pleasant memories of my association with your dear father and of days which we have spent together in Germany and in Switzerland.

---

[4] Roger Garreau of France was President of the Trusteeship Council during these deliberations on Palestine.

[5] On 20 Dec. 1949 the Council adopted a French motion expressing concern at the removal of some Israeli Ministries to Jerusalem, and calling upon the Government to revoke these measures and to abstain from any action liable to hinder the implementation of General Assembly resolutions. Garreau, in consultation with other Governments and interested religious bodies, drew up proposals for the Statute of Jerusalem, which he presented to the Council when it resumed its discussions in Geneva 30 Jan. 1950.

331. [1] B. 1907, Berlin. Engineer, specialist in printing technologies. War service R.A.F.; consultant to publishing companies, including Axel Springer Co., Hamburg, and *Daily Telegraph*, London, and to U.N. Technical Assistance Administration. Settled in Rehovot 1973.

[2] Untraced.

[3] Ephraim Moses Lilien (Biog. Index, Vol. I). Artist and lithographer. He collaborated with Herzl and was associated with W. in the Democratic Fraction at early Zionist Congresses. The exhibition of his work took place at the Anglo-Israel Club, London. W. had opened a similar exhibition 25 years earlier, in Berlin.

We were, as you may know, a group of five very intimate friends: your late father, Berthold Feivel,[4] Trietsch,[5] Buber[6] and myself. There are only Buber and myself left; and of Buber I see very little, unfortunately. There is no particular reason for it but we have somehow drifted apart.

I would be very interested to know, if I may, whether you are wandering in father's footsteps or have you chosen another profession. A note from you giving me some particulars about your life would be very appreciated. Are you married? Have you a family?[7]

Looking forward to your letter and with all best wishes for the success of the exhibition and with kind regards.

Yours ever
Ch. Weizmann

[For a letter to Truman, regarding status of Jerusalem, 3 Jan. 1950, see Appendix II.]

332. To Dewey Stone, New York.   *Tel Aviv, 12 January 1950*
English: Or. Copy. T.W.: W.A.

My dear Dewey,
I have sent to-day to Meyer the following cable:[1]

Happy to learn your efforts organising joint fund-raising campaign with Hebrew University. You have my best wishes for this undertaking, which hope will include soon Hebrew Technion. It has always been my conviction that the future of Israel depends on the scientific standing and technical effort of the *Yishuv* and on the generous help of Jews and Jewish institutions all over the world. The joint campaign will symbolise the unity of the scientists and scientific institutions in Israel in common effort to tackle the great problems confronting us. Shall write you about some more detailed plans we have been discussing recently. Regards.

Chaim Weizmann

I have done so not without doubts and hesitations, and I would like to apprise you of my thoughts, as I think they may be useful to you and to our other friends in your present efforts in the States.

I have always felt uneasy about the relations between the University

---

[4] Berthold Feiwel (Biog. Index, Vol. I). Editor, Zionist publicist, and K.H. leader.

[5] Davis (David) Trietsch (Biog. Index, Vol. I). Writer, and specialist in Jewish colonisation problems.

[6] Martin Buber (Biog. Index, Vol. I). Philosopher and theologian. Zionist thinker; at this time professor at H.U.   [7] He was married, with two daughters.

332. [1] W.A.

and the Institute. It is unfortunately a fact that the University has not done too well both in the organisation of its Science Departments and in its administration, and I would not like the Institute to be drawn into this circle. The independence of the Institute, both scientifically and administratively should be guarded very jealously.

Secondly, I am not convinced that it is better for two institutions to raise funds together than it is to do so separately. However, I am not in a position to judge the present situation in America from here, and I am relying on your and Meyer's judgment in this matter. I realise, of course, that it would not be dignified nor useful to either of the institutions concerned if they would start competing for the contributions of individuals or groups, and I am also aware of the necessity of taking care of the needs of the University. I understand that you have come to some agreement as to the distribution of the funds raised jointly, and I hope that the Institute will benefit from this arrangement.

Having said all this, there only remains to wish you and Meyer and all our friends full success in your effort; I hope you will keep me informed of any development.

With kindest regards,

Yours ever,
Ch. Weizmann

333. To the Chairman, Nahariyah Local Council.

Rehovot, 2 February 1950

Hebrew: Or. Copy. T.W.: W.A.

Some time ago the Nahariyah Local Council presented me with a gift of a tract of land along the coast.[1] Being rather doubtful whether I shall be able to make use of it, and not wanting the property to go unused, I'd like to suggest the following offer.

I am prepared to put this tract of land at the service of some public institution. It seems to me that one of our most sacred obligations is toward our war invalids. Consequently I am curious to know whether your Council, perhaps in conjunction with the neighbouring settlements, is willing to build on this land a modest building to be used as a rest home for invalid soldiers and their families. This, I believe, would be an appropriate way of utilizing the property and would link me even more with the residents of Nahariyah.[2]

Sincerely,
Ch. Weizmann

333. [1] In March 1938—see Vol. XVIII, No. 311.

[2] The property was sold, and the proceeds went towards the establishment of a convalescent and rest home for invalid soldiers.

334. To Yigael Yadin,[1] Tel Aviv.   *Rehovot, 8 May 1950*
Hebrew: Or. Copy. T.W.: W.A.

My dear Chief of Staff,

I am turning to you in the matter of Major David Arnon,[2] my aide-de-camp. I understand that his contract with the Defence Forces terminates on 1 June, and I request you to do everything possible to ensure his continuing service. He is competent in his present assignment, and I wouldn't want to replace him and have to adjust myself to someone else around me.

Major Arnon carries out his tasks to my complete satisfaction. His devotion is worthy of commendation, and I should like to give some tangible expression to my esteem for him. Therefore I would be most grateful if you could promote Major Arnon to the rank of Lieutenant-Colonel. I can't think of any other or more appropriate way of showing him my thanks, and I know you won't refuse my request.[3]

I would have preferred speaking to you personally about this request. But to my regret I haven't been well, and I don't want to delay arranging this matter.

With thanks in advance and regards,

Chaim Weizmann

335. To Israel Sieff, London.   *Rehovot, 23 May 1950*
English: Copy. T.W.: Sieff Archives.

My dear Israel,

I should like to thank you with all my heart for the kind, thoughtful and, indeed, moving letter you wrote to me on May 15th.[1]

What you said about our long association, the kind and sensitive and modest way in which you reflected about our work together, and your own development, evoked many memories in me. I, too, look back with a feeling of somewhat melancholy pleasure upon those "old days" to which you refer.

---

334. [1] B. 1917. Archaeologist. Chief of Staff of Israel Defence Forces 1949–52; entered politics as leader of Democratic Movement for Change 1976; Deputy Prime Minister from 1977.
[2] 1910–70. W.'s A.D.C. throughout his Presidency.
[3] Yadin was reluctant to make an exception in Arnon's case (see his letter to A. George Weidenfeld, Adviser to W., 17 May, W.A.). However, the request was fulfilled.

335. [1] (W.A.). Sieff wrote that he had received a personal report from Marks, just returned from Israel. The letter continued in nostalgic vein.

Simon's stay with us enabled me to recapture the many moments of happiness and intensely felt excitement which marked the early days of Manchester and London—the years of uphill struggle and spade work.

It would be really wonderful to see you again very soon. You know, no doubt, of Vera's and my movements. We intend to leave Israel in the first week of July for Buergenstock, where we were last year. There we hope to stay for the first part of our holiday and thence move to another cool and restful place in Switzerland. I should, of course, like to see you in Israel before our departure, but if this entails too many difficulties on your part, we hope to be able to welcome you in Switzerland instead.

Try to escape from your omnivorous business duties and spend a quiet week or two with us. Then we shall talk things over intensely, and yet, strangely peacefully, as in the old days.

With affectionate regards from both of us and many *Shaloms,*

Yours ever,
Chaim

336. To Leopold S. Amery, London. *Tel Aviv, 29 June 1950*
English: T.W.: W.A.

My dear old Friend,

Thank you very very much for your charming letter,[1] your book,[2] and the apposite touching poem![3] I could not be more pleased than to hear that you and Julian[4] enjoyed your visit, that you left with the sincere feeling that this country is making forward strides.

Both my wife and I were delighted with your visit. I shall treasure the many hours of stimulating conversation, roving far and wide over our joint past association and far ahead into the future beyond our lifetime.

I am about to leave for Switzerland and by the time this letter

---

336. [1] 16 June (W.A.), thanking the Weizmanns for hospitality to himself and his son Julian during their visit to Israel. Amery also indicated that he had not yet been in touch with Churchill but would certainly 'urge Winston' to consider seriously the possibility of visiting Israel at the first opportunity.

[2] *In the Rain and the Sun* (London 1946), which included a section on the non-political side of Amery's visit to Palestine in 1925.

[3] Amery was surprised that W. did not know of Robert Browning's poem 'Holy-Cross Day', with reference to Israel's Return.

[4] B. 1919. Politician and historian; son of Leopold Amery. Cons. M.P. 1950–66, and from 1969; Under-Secretary of State for War 1957–58; for Colonies 1958–60; Minister of Housing 1970–72; Minister of State, Foreign and Commonwealth Office 1972–74.

reaches you, I shall be, by the grace of God, at Burgenstock on Lake Lucerne. Should your own plans and perhaps Mr. Churchill's,[5] take you to that part of the world during the summer months, how very agreeable it would be to meet again!

Meanwhile, please accept the affectionate message of really genuine friendship from my wife and myself.

Yours ever,
Ch. Weizmann

337. **To Henry Hurwitz,[1] New York.**   *Rehovot, 30 June 1950*
English: T.W.: W.A.

Dear Mr. Hurwitz,

Meyer Weisgal called my attention to the $2,500 balance of an old pledge of $5,000 which I had made to the *Menorah Journal*.[2] I am sure you will realize that in my travels to and fro and other slight pre-occupations, this matter has entirely escaped my attention. You should have advised me of this oversight long before. I would have been happy to fulfil my pledge. Having been victimized most of my life by broken or unpaid pledges, I can fully sympathize with you. I have authorized, therefore, Mr. Weisgal to pay this sum to you on my behalf, when he returns to the States this Fall.

May I take this opportunity to thank you for sending me the original Struck etching with Herzl's autograph.[3] I shall be very happy to possess it and will see to it that it occupies a special place amongst my collection.

With best wishes,

Cordially yours,
Ch. Weizmann

---

[5] On 2 June 1950 Churchill acknowledged a note from W. brought by Marks. Commenting on reports he had received of Israel's progress, he concluded: 'I feel that it is under your leadership and guidance that Israel will enjoy prosperity and happiness' (W.A.).

337. [1] 1886–1961. Editor and educator; founded in 1915 *Menorah Journal* and was its editor until his death. Opposed political Zionism.

[2] See Hurwitz to Weisgal, 18 May (W.A.) recalling the pledge. Financial stringency compelled him now to ask whether W. could be reminded of the balance outstanding.

[3] Hurwitz had acquired the etching of Theodor Herzl in 1913—see his letter to Weisgal, 12 June (W.A.).

338. To David Ben-Gurion, Jerusalem.

Ouchy, Switzerland, 3 September 1950

English: T.: W.A.

Prime Minister David Ben-Gurion, please convey my heartfelt greetings to Jerusalem Conference of American Jewish communities.[1]

Deeply regret being unable participate in consultations to which attach paramount importance and only convalescence from serious long illness prevents me from attending.

Young State of Israel in addition overwhelming tasks its own consolidation and defence has undertaken truly gigantic effort of providing homes during next few years for hundreds thousands Jews who cannot stay where they are. Hitherto bulk responsibility caring for uprooted and impoverished Jewish communities has developed [devolved?] upon American Jewry, which spent untold sums on relief measures. Establishment State of Israel now offers unprecedented chance providing permanent homes to unsettled Jewries, Europe and Middle East, under conditions full equality among their own kith and kin. Situation presents unique challenge to American Jewish statesmanship and foresight. Problem can be solved only if American Jewry, faithful to its noble traditions of Jewish brotherhood, assumes predominant share not merely in financing but also in planning this vast effort of migration, resettlement and consolidation.

Please extend my personal greetings Jewish Agency and to representatives Joint Distribution Committee, Jewish Welfare Fund, United Jewish Appeal, United Palestine Appeal and Zionist Organization of America as well as to individual tried friends who attending conference. May your joint efforts result in working out agreed plan for greatest effort of constructive self-help in Jewish History.

Chaim Weizmann

339. To Viscount Samuel, London.

Rehovot, 3 November 1950

English: T.W.: Photostat W.A.

My dear Lord Samuel,

It gives me deep pleasure to write to you on the occasion of your 80th Birthday, and to wish you every happiness. So many tributes

---

338. [1] A gathering invited by the Prime Minister to review Israel's economic needs in the light of its expenditures for defence and immigrant absorption. It was decided to launch a popular loan (Bond Drive) in U.S. for $1,000 millions.

have been and will be most justly paid to you as a distinguished statesman, man of the World, that anything I can add might be only redundant and repetitive. I wish, however, to take this opportunity of saying something about our long association which stretches over thirty-six years.

I so vividly remember that December day in 1914 when our staunch friend C. P. Scott[1] took me to meet Lloyd George and yourself. The animated atmosphere and positive and responsive attitude towards our then so seemingly fantastic aspirations encouraged me more than I can express, and I remember how intense was my joy and, if I may say so, my surprise to hear from your own mouth such words of reassurance. You had stood till then in my view for established and assimilated Anglo-Jewry and yet it was you who, in your memorandum to Mr. Asquith,[2] put forward the bold thesis for a Jewish Commonwealth in Palestine to harbour three to four million people gathered in from the Diaspora. I remember your advice, always direct, tactful and wise, which shepherded me and my friends through the labyrinth of government ante-room, parliamentary lobbies and diplomatic meetings. You contributed so much to the culmination of our then diplomatic strivings, the Balfour Declaration, the basis upon which we have progressively built the Jewish State. The decade following the war saw us collaborate intensively and in various spheres.[3] It was a period of great and exacting tests and trials, of concord and quite often of disagreement, but never of lack of confidence and respect. Our paths may have been divergent at times, but we had so much more in common than we had at variance. We have and always have had a common bond in the conviction that integrity of knowledge and purpose and scientific method pursued for peaceful and constructive ends are the only solid foundation for any Commonwealth, and most certainly for the new Commonwealth we are building up in our Homeland in Israel.

May I then once again wish you all that you desire on this 80th Birthday, and express my wife's and my own hope that you and Lady Samuel may have a good many more happy years of work and life together.

Yours very sincerely,

Ch. Weizmann

339. [1] Charles Prestwich Scott (Biog. Index, Vol. VII). Editor and proprietor of *Manchester Guardian*; friend of W. and Zionist supporter from 1914.

[2] Samuel was then President of the Local Government Board. For his memoranda addressed to his Cabinet colleagues Jan., March 1915, see Vol. VII, pp. 147–49, 179.

[3] Primarily when Samuel was the first British High Commissioner for Palestine, 1920–25. Later, they worked together for the economic development of the country, for H.U., and for European refugees.

340. To Harry S. Truman, Washington. *Tel Aviv, 8 January 1951*
English: Or. Copy. T.W.: I.S.A. 105/1747.

My dear Mr. President,
 I take the opportunity of my good friend Mr. P. Lubianiker,[1] the Minister of Agriculture, going to the States of sending you my heart-felt greetings and good wishes for a prosperous and happy New Year.
 There is nothing very particular to report from here. Things are going on normally, and we all pray that the world's situation may not deteriorate. Like every young organism we stand in need of peace so as to develop some strength.
 I follow with anxiety your daily tribulations on whose overcoming so much depends for the peace of the world. The last few days have somehow strengthened the belief that we have passed the height of the crisis.[2] I hope this impression is right.
 Please accept my heartiest good wishes and I beg to remain, as always,

Yours very sincerely and devotedly,
Ch. Weizmann

341. To Walter F. White,[1] New York. *Tel Aviv, 8 January 1951*
English: Copy. T.W.: W.A.

Dear Sir,
 It gives me great pleasure to pay my tribute to Dr. Ralph J. Bunche[2] on the occasion of the dinner given by the Association for the Advancement of Coloured Peoples in his honour.
 Dr. Ralph Bunche will always be honoured in the memory of the people of Israel for his objectivity, tenacity and his devotion to the aims of the United Nations. He helped to end a savage conflict in the

---

340. [1] Pinhas Lubianiker (later, Lavon; 1904–1976). General Secretary of *Histadrut* 1949–50, 1956–61; Minister of Agriculture 1950–52; Minister of Defence 1953–55; member of *Knesset* 1949–61.
 [2] Reversals suffered by U.N. troops in Korea led to proclamation of a state of national emergency by Truman 16 Dec. 1950. On 4 Jan. 1951 the President sought to ease tension and fears of a global war by announcing that the U.S. probably would not bomb China without a formal Congressional declaration of war.

341. [1] 1893–1955. American Negro leader; Asst. Secretary 1918–29, Secretary from 1931 of National Association for the Advancement of Colored People.
 [2] 1904–1971. Nobel Peace Prize 1950 for his role as Acting Mediator in negotiations leading to 1949 armistice agreements between Israel and Arab States. He helped to organize the U.N., and was its director, Trusteeship Department 1948–54; Under Secretary-General 1967–71.

Near East and thus demonstrated to a sceptical world that the United
Nations can be an effective instrument in the attainment and preservation of peace. I rejoice that these achievements were deemed
worthy of the Nobel Prize for Peace.

I am proud to join in this tribute to him not alone because of his
service to world peace, but also because he is a distinguished cham-
pion of the cause of equality and fought against all manifestations
of discrimination and bigotry. In this struggle my people and the
people of Ralph Bunche have long been allies. I pray that such men
as he may continue to labour in that cause until the declaration of
human rights becomes the living faith of mankind.

Yours very sincerely,
Chaim Weizmann

342. To Shmuel Dayan,[1] Nahalal.   *Rehovot, 9 January 1951*
Hebrew: T.W.: Photostat W.A.

My dear Dayan,

I am writing these lines simply to thank you for your last visit here,
in the course of which you reminded me of an episode from the
distant past which, unfortunately, is completely omitted from my
book. The interesting and important episode to which I am referring
is the purchase of land in the Hauran, and in Trans-Jordan generally—a matter in which I too had a hand, after several members of
Hapoel Hatzair[2] harnessed my interest to it.

I clearly remember that visit to Nahalal in August 1924 together
with Lord Balfour.[3] During that visit you and your comrades drew
my attention to the problem of some tens of thousands of dunams of
Baron Rothschild's on the other side of the Jordan, in the Hauran,
which was under the jurisdiction of the British Mandate. In those
days deliberations were in progress between P.I.C.A.[4] and the Emir
Said, who owned the lands on which stood four villages near Mount
Tabor, concerning the exchange of properties. The proposition was
that the Baron should transfer his properties in Trans-Jordan to the
Arab Emir in exchange for the lands in the region of Tabor. This took

342. [1] 1891–1968. Pioneer of co-operative settlement in Palestine. Father of Moshe Dayan.

[2] 'The Young Worker'. Labour Party, founded 1905 by agricultural pioneers and later
part of *Mapai*. For the matters referred to here, see Vol. XIII.

[3] Balfour visited Palestine 1925—see Vol. XII.

[4] P.I.C.A. was founded by Baron Edmond de Rothschild for the purpose of buying land
to facilitate Jewish settlement. It was independent of W.Z.O.

place at about the time that Mr. Churchill, then Colonial Secretary, divided Eretz Israel into two parts—the eastern and the western.[5]

I recall that you rightly saw in such a transaction a national calamity in the fullest sense of the word. Being in full agreement with you, I took up your suggestion to meet with Baron Rothschild in order to cancel the barter transaction which had been proposed to him by a P.I.C.A. official, so that we should not lose our hold on Trans-Jordan, nor uproot the stake which we had driven there. Equipped with the report which was given to me by the members of the group which had travelled in Trans-Jordan, I held (if I am not mistaken) three discussions with the Baron at his house in Paris, in addition to several conversations with one of his senior secretaries, Mr. Wormser,[6] and I succeeded in averting the evil decree.[7] Thanks to this joint action— that of several of your comrades and of myself—we are to this day the owners of land in Trans-Jordan.

Another matter which you raised during our conversation was the attempt to find a way to purchase land in the areas under the former French Mandate for the purpose of Jewish settlement. Several people of your group then travelled to Damascus and discussed the matter with the French officials. At a later stage I made a special journey to Beirut in order to speak with the French High Commissioner of Syria, M. de Jouvenel.[8] I recall that he made a good impression on me, and showed an understanding of the problem and of our aims. As a consequence of my discussions with him, I met with several officials of the French Foreign Office during my visit in Paris. If my memory does not mislead me, these conversations were suspended because of hints I was given that the English regarded the matter unfavourably.

I further recall my conversations with you on different occasions, both in this country and during the Congresses abroad, on the great possibilities of buying land in various parts of Trans-Jordan, and near the Baron's estates, at a cost of half a lira per dunam, to be paid in convenient instalments—but all the funds (the Palestine Land Development Company, the Jewish National Fund and the Zionist Organization) were empty.

[5] For the Agreement in 1921 between Churchill and Emir Abdullah resulting in a local Arab administration in Transjordan and the exclusion of Jewish settlement there, although it continued to be part of the Palestine Mandate, see Vol. X.

[6] Gaston Wormser (Biog. Index, Vol. VI). Adviser and private secretary to Edmond de Rothschild.

[7] For accounts in Hebrew of these efforts, see S. Dayan, *In Days of Vision and Siege,* Tel Aviv 1953, pp. 16–41, 54–56; and Eliahu Elath, *Zionism and the Arabs,* Tel Aviv 1974, pp. 100–01.

[8] Henri de Jouvenel, French High Commissioner for Syria 1925–26.

You and several of your comrades of the *Hapoel Hatzair* party were active in all of the above transactions—as I was, too—and I am grateful to you for reminding me of this important episode in the annals of this Zionist enterprise of ours.

Yours,
Chaim Weizmann

343. To David Ben-Gurion, Jerusalem. *Rehovot, [January] 1951*
English: Draft[1]: T.W.: W.A.

Personal and Confidential

My dear B.-G.,

I am writing this note after a very considerable amount of thought and with a genuine desire to clear matters up and not to allow them to grow into misunderstandings. I can only do so by being perfectly frank and by giving expression to a certain amount of criticism which has been troubling me for some time.

I should remind you at the outset that I did not seek the office which I hold now. The proposal was brought to me by yourself and your colleagues in the Government first in New York and then on my arrival here. I did not accept it with any particular enthusiasm. Not that I don't appreciate the high honour which such an office implies, but I wasn't clear what rights and duties were conferred on the President, and nothing is more troublesome, to me at any rate, than the lack of clarity in a matter of such importance.

I have therefore tried very gently and carefully to make some inquiries what are the duties and privileges of a President, and I was met with replies which have contributed to my greater confusion. So for instance, I was told that the President is a symbol. I am still at a loss to know what this vague statement means, and who has decided on the symbolic significance of the President.

There is nothing in the constitution (which by the way is still hanging in the air) about the role of the President. The whole thing is arbitrary, open to interpretation or misinterpretation on every side and is bound to lead in the end to serious conflicts which must be avoided at all costs.

The purpose of this letter is to clarify the points which are left in dangerous ambiguity. Nothing stands in the way of my leaving the

---

343. [1] The copy of this letter in W.A. contains a note in Hebrew by Yigal Kimhi: 'This letter was dictated to me on a beautiful sunny day on the balcony of [W.'s] house facing east sometime in January. The President changed his mind about sending the letter.'

presidency at any moment. In fact, I would consider it as a great relief. I could serve my country by continuing my scientific work as I did all these years, and not without a certain measure of success. I am by nature and training a scientist. I hate petty politics, although my life has been forced into it against my will. There is only one thing which stands in my way of resigning now, and that is the international repercussion. Without being boastful or without desiring in the slightest degree to overrate my personality, it is only fair to say that my resignation at present would cause a certain amount of bewilderment in international circles who know me, and it would be a shock to public opinion in the world interested in Israeli affairs. I am therefore standing before an unpleasant choice of either continuing to work in a manner which to my way of thinking is neither dignified nor useful, or to cut myself adrift and create an unpleasant situation in the first formative years of the State.

This dilemma has been haunting me all these months, and I don't see what useful purpose it will serve my continuing this state of affairs.

The purpose of this letter is therefore to ask you to arrange a short meeting between me and some of the more responsible colleagues of the Cabinet before whom I would like to place, in a very short and friendly way, the few essential conditions which would render it possible for me to continue to hold the office which I am holding at present.

The main and pre[. . . . . .][2] condition is a proper definition of the duties and rights of the President. It may well be that after such a definition has been made, I will find that under such conditions I would not serve, and I am [. . . . . .][2] this post cleared up at the earliest possible opportunity.

I have a laboratory in which, contrary to a political life, everything is precise and definite. And if I concentrate on the problems there, I can render better service to the cause of the Jewish State than by [. . . . . .][2] with phantom, which I don't intend to do.

I know that you are not well, and I am sorry to add to your burdens, but you may have heard that I wasn't in the best of health lately, and I am writing this letter practically from bed. I therefore ask you to consider the suggestions that on your return from your holiday, which I hope will do you good, you should call a meeting of some of the important ministers, before whom I'll have the opportunity of laying my case.

Should it for any reason be inconvenient for you to accept my suggestion, I would like to tell you now and here that I don't propose

---

[2] Space in extant copy.

to continue my service, and that you better make arrangements to find a substitute for myself.

I think I have said as much as it is possible or desirable at this stage, leaving the rest to a discussion at the meeting as suggested above.

I would like in conclusion to say that I deeply appreciate your friendly references to me, and I shall be anxious to help in the difficult task guiding the State to the best of my ability in a private capacity as a citizen of Israel. I am afraid that these lines may cause a certain amount of confusion or pain, which I can assure you is not intended, but it was essential to disperse my illusions and to normalize the relations between us and between our colleagues.

It remains for me only to wish you every success in your difficult task which lies ahead before you.

With very best regards,

Yours very sincerely,
Ch. Weizmann

344. To Meyer W. Weisgal, New York.   *Rehovot, 24 February 1951*
English: Draft. T.W.: W.A.

My dear Meyer,

I am writing to you in great distress. The position at the Institute has gone much worse of late, and unless it is remedied fundamentally and very quickly, I, for one, shall go out and will be compelled to explain the reasons publicly.

The position is briefly as follows: Since the war our friend Bergmann is devoting himself entirely to this aspect of our life, and whereas there was such justification during the hostilities, I see no reason now why his energies should go into an effort which is neither urgent nor desirable.

Bergmann behaves like a Prussian junker. War seems to be his primary consideration, everything else, including the affairs of the Institute must, of necessity, be secondary. He disappears for a day or two without even saying where he is going, leave alone for what purpose.

The state of my health in recent months was somewhat unsatisfactory. I had no help from him, and for all I know the Institute was orphan. You know that whatever Bergmann does he does it fanatically. At present this fanaticism is applied to military affairs, although the war is over, and there is little prospect of its being reopened soon.

Matters have gone much worse since the death of his mother, who was a very fine woman and who had a decisive influence over him. I don't expect therefore any change or improvement in his relations to his work very soon, if at all. On the contrary, there will be a constant deterioration and as far as I am concerned I don't expect any change in his attitude. You know Bergmann has a mulish obstinacy, and nobody can teach him anything.

It is a matter of deep regret to me that you are not here, although you promised to come over for a short time. It seems that this war effort, whatever it may mean, may be the ruin of the Institute; as I have neither the intention nor the strength to face all these destructive tendencies. I therefore make you the straight offer to come over here without delay, even for a short time—Bonds or no Bonds![1]

I am afraid that I can't face it alone, and I don't think it's fair to me to throw this burden on my shoulders at this age and in my state of health.

I have told you the straight truth. If you wish the Institute to continue, then please come along and take your share in producing the changes which are required.

Fortunately I have one man here who is likely and willing to help, that is Dr. [Joseph] Blumenfeld. But his volume would greatly be enhanced if you would come over.

That is all I have to say now and please convey this letter to Harry [Levine] and Dewey [Stone] with love and best regards. Don't delay in sending me a telegram, which I would appreciate very much.

As ever yours,

345. To Aubrey Eban, Washington. *Rehovot, 19 April 1951*
English: Or. Copy. T.W.: I.S.A. 68/11.

Dear Aubrey,

About the same time that your last letter arrived,[1] I received one from Eddie Jacobson,[2] of which I am sending you herewith a copy,

---

344. [1] Weisgal was organizing the Israel Bonds campaign in U.S.—see No. 338, n. 1.

345. [1] 20 Mar. 1951 (I.S.A. 68/11). This, a political *tour d'horizon*, discussed the improvement in U.N. military position in Korea, intercession by supporters in Washington to assure military and non-military supplies to Israel, progress of the Israel Aid Bill in Congress, and Jewish fund-raising campaigns. Eban spoke of the U.S. and U.S.S.R. delegations at U.N. using the Israel delegation as a sounding-board on matters relating to a peaceful settlement of the Korean question, and of Russian fears of a re-armed, independent Germany.

[2] Jacobson had described a discussion with Truman in Florida, which had revealed good prospects for a $150 m. grant-in-aid to Israel—see Jacobson–W. exchange, 23 Mar., 19 Apr. 1951.

together with my reply. I am glad he continues to be so active and helpful.

I understand that Abe Feinberg is bringing a letter from President Truman,[3] which will give me an opportunity of writing to him in support of your efforts. I have been wanting to do so for some time, but it is much more helpful if the initiative comes from him.

Let me say how glad I was to receive your last full letter. It gave me a real insight into what is happening at your end, both in the international sphere and in our own affairs.

Please give my kind regards to Sam Rosenman, to David Niles and to Dave Ginsburg.

Yours ever,

346. To Harry S. Truman, Washington.   *Rehovot, 30 April 1951*
English: Or. Copy. T.W.: I.S.A. 68/11.

Dear Mr. President,

I was very happy to receive your friendly greetings on the occasion of the Passover season.[1]

It was heartening to hear from Mr. Abe Feinberg about your warm support of the idea of United States assistance to Israel. We are engaged in a vast enterprise of receiving and rehabilitating hundreds of thousands of people and of developing the country with the utmost speed. Within the first three years of Israel's existence its population has doubled. In this month of April the total of new arrivals is 30,000. We obviously cannot carry this staggering load alone and unaided. Every effort is being made to increase and speed up production and remarkable results have already been achieved, but immigrants must be provided for from the day of their arrival whereas they can become self-supporting only after a certain lag of time. Also, a great deal of capital must be sunk into works of development to render the country's latent resources fully productive. The gap is inevitable and it can only be bridged by outside assistance. If this is forthcoming over a limited period of time, the attainment of full economic stability will be well within our reach. I am confident that the United States will extend to us its helping hand.

These greetings are being brought to you by Mr. David Ben Gurion, the first Prime Minister of Israel, who has played an historic part in the establishment and defence of our State. He is going on a good will mission to the Government and the people of

---

[3] See No. 346.

346. [1] Conveyed by Feinberg (Truman to Feinberg, 18 Apr., I.S.A. 68/11).

the United States.² He will be able to present to you a true picture of our situation and of the tasks and difficulties that confront us. I pray that you may give him a sympathetic hearing.

The question which is uppermost in our minds at this hour is the preservation of peace, near and far. To us particularly this is a question of life and death, for without peace we can have little prospect of gathering in our people and of building up our country. We are following with anxious concern your noble and determined efforts to defend democracy and safeguard the peace of the world. May God's blessing rest on your endeavours.³

Very sincerely yours,

347. To Harry S. Truman, Washington.   *Tel Aviv, 18 May 1951*
English: T.: I.S.A. 68/11.

Have learned with deep apprehension proposal by American representative in Security Council to stop drainage of Huleh swamp¹ in order to appease Arab League that waged aggressive war against Israel. Drainage of Huleh is essential not only for reclamation of largest malarial swamp area in Israel but for agricultural development of arid zones throughout country particularly Negev. To hold up Huleh project means perpetuation of desert conditions in vast areas capable of providing homes for tens of thousands of immigrant settlers. Cannot conceive America lending hand to adoption of such calamitous decision² which affects very essence of our life. Pray you prevent grievous action.³ Warmest personal regards.

Chaim Weizmann

² Ben-Gurion arrived 8 May, to mark third anniversary of Israel's establishment by launching the Israel Independence Bond Drive.

³ Truman replied 5 June (I.S.A. 68/11), assuring W. of his country's continued goodwill.

347. ¹ 15,000 acres on both sides of Jordan river, but mainly in Israel territory adjacent to Syria. Part was a demilitarized zone according to Israel-Syria Armistice Agreement of 1949, and Syria maintained that its character could not be changed except by mutual agreement. Work had recently begun under police guard. Seven of the police were killed by Syrian fire, and the Israelis retaliated with air attacks on Syrian positions. Drainage was completed 1957, but incidents continued, culminating in the War of 1967.

² Security Council Resolution proposed by U.S. and supported by Britain, France, Turkey. Approved ten–nil, Russia abstaining. It required Israel to cease work in the demilitarized area; called on both sides to abide by cease-fire order and general Armistice Agreement; asked Israel to allow Arab civilians removed from the area to return to their homes; condemned Israel air attacks on Syrian positions. No condemnation was made of Syria for conducting military operations against Israel. Israel suspended work on seven acres of land owned by Syrian Arabs.

³ Replying 1 June, Truman emphasised that the sponsors of the resolution were motivated by the need to preserve and strengthen the Israel-Syrian Mixed Armistice Commission. They did not intend permanent cessation of drainage operations. Both sides had recourse to U.N. machinery if there were grievances.

348. To Aubrey Eban, New York.   *Tel Aviv, 20 May 1951*
English: T.: I.S.A. 68/11.

Wish express to you my deepfelt admiration for your courageous and brilliant stand in defence of Israel's rights.[1] When history comes to pass judgment on present dispute little credit will go to those who in deference to Arab aggression attempted hold up great effort sanitation and reclamation our country's largest malarial swamp. Feel confident that despite temporary setback your devoted efforts will result reversal this illguided decision. Warmest regards.

Chaim Weizmann

349. To Ernst David Bergmann, Rehovot.   *Rehovot, 2 July 1951*
English: Or. Copy. T.W.: W.A.

Dear Doctor Bergmann,

After due consideration I have come to the decision to relieve you of your duties and responsibilities as Scientific Director of the Weizmann Institute.

You will continue your functions as Head of the Department of Organic Chemistry.

It is, however, understood that you will take your Sabbatical leave as from the 15th July, 1951.[1]

Yours sincerely,
Ch. W.

---

348. [1] In debate on Security Council Resolution—see No. 347. Eban had described the move as 'unjust and one-sided . . . an insult to our gallant dead killed by Arab bullets. Israel attaches no moral value to this unjust presentation of the case'.

349. [1] See No. 328, n. 5. Differences between W. and his protégé were not resolved. Weisgal observed that W. 'has suffered more deeply about this thing than about anything else in the last few years, leaving its deep impress on his state of health', rendering the atmosphere inside Weizmann House 'beyond endurance' (Weisgal to Stone and Levine, 8 July 1951, W.A.). Bergmann for his part laid the blame for the deterioration of relations on Blumenfeld, now resident at Rehovot. In the ensuing deliberations, Bergmann was supported by the entire staff of the Institute. Finally, following extended, heated negotiation, a solution was arrived at as embodied in W.'s letter, to which Bergmann consented. See V.W. to Weisgal, 4 June, W.A.; Bergmann to W., 15 June, W.A.

350. To Edward Jacobson, Kansas City. *Tel Aviv, 27 August 1951*
English: T.: W.A.

Was happy receive copy your letter August 10th to Josef Cohn,[1] learn great role played by you grant-in-aid.[2] Please accept my heartfelt congratulations. I pray to God you be able continue your wonderful work for Israel many years to come. Pray give my kind regards to President and all my good wishes you and Mrs. Jacobson.

Chaim Weizmann

351. To David Ben-Gurion, Jerusalem. *Rehovot, 3 September 1951*
English: Draft. T.W.: I.S.A. 68/11.

Dear Mr. Ben-Gurion,

I was very happy to learn that the Government of Israel has decided to inaugurate a comprehensive effort for securing photostatic reproductions of Hebrew manuscripts from the great libraries of the world. All of us who in their young days have studied at foreign Universities and Libraries are aware that invaluable treasures of Hebrew literature produced in all ages and in every possible environment lie hidden in manuscript form in the great repositories of learning throughout the world. Much of this treasure is entirely unknown to scholars owing to the absence of facilities for its publication. I am convinced that the collection of photostatic copies of this material and its eventual publication will add a vast store of authoritative information on Jewish history and Jewish literature throughout the ages. I consider it a duty of honour of the State of Israel to take the initiative in organising and financing this great effort of collection and publication, and I should like to convey to all those engaged in this noble work my heartfelt good wishes for the success of their inspired effort.

Very sincerely yours,
Chaim Weizmann

350. [1] Untraced.

[2] On 22 Mar. 1951 Israel submitted a request to U.S. Government for a grant of $150 millions for the fiscal year 1 July 1951–30 June 1952 to help Israel absorb immigration and build up the national economy. The U.S. Administration at first proposed to Congress a grant of only $25 millions, but unremitting advocacy throughout the several stages of debate in Congress brought the amount to $65 millions: $50 millions for absorption of immigrants and the remainder for economic and technical aid. This grant-in-aid, the first by the U.S. to Israel, came into effect 31 Oct. 1951 when Truman signed the Mutual Security Act, and release of the funds began in Dec. (*Israel Government Year-Book,* 1952/53, p. 131).

352. To Meyer W. Weisgal, Rehovot.   *Rehovot, 7 September 1951*
English: T.W./H.W.: W.A.

Dear Meyer,

It has come to my attention that Dr. Bergmann has been corresponding with scientists here and abroad in a manner calculated to undermine the position of the Institute in the eyes of the scientific world. I regard this as a very grave offence and contrary to the spirit of our understanding.

I also understand that contrary to our regulations and instructions, Dr. Bergmann has refused to vacate the rooms in the Clubhouse. I consider his refusal to comply with these regulations as a deliberate defiance of our authority.

As you are aware, I was determined to sever all Dr. Bergmann's connections with the Institute. It was only because of special circumstances and sentiment that I allowed myself to be diverted from that course and agreed to the present arrangement. If Dr. Bergmann continues to defy our instructions and act in the manner described above, I shall be obliged to ask the Administrative Committee or the Executive Council to reconsider the whole question of Dr. Bergmann's future association with the Institute.

I shall be grateful if you will bring this matter to the attention of the Administrative Committee at once, especially in view of the fact that you are planning to leave on September 13th.

As always, affectionately,

Please don't procrastinate![1]

Chaim Weizmann

353. To Winston S. Churchill, London.   *Rehovot, 5 November 1951*
English: Or. Copy. T.W.: I.S.A. 68/11.

Dear Mr. Churchill,

May I extend to you my personal greetings and heartfelt good wishes on your reassumption of office.[1] I pray that you may be given health and strength to carry the heavy burden and that you may be able to write another great page in your unparalleled record of public service.

We all hope that your tenure of office may result in further strengthening the good relations that have developed during the last few

---

352. [1] This addition handwritten.

353. [1] The Conservatives had replaced Labour in the General Election of 25 Oct. 1951.

years between Great Britain and our young State. We are going through a period of great strain. The task which we have taken upon ourselves of providing homes for all Jews who cannot or do not want to remain where they are is taxing all our resources. We need help and sympathy from old friends and I know that we may count you among these, as one who has shown fearless support in the most difficult times for the Jewish National Home.

I am looking forward shortly to receiving your newly-appointed Minister to Israel who I hope will continue the fine work done by Sir Knox Helm.[2] I should like to add a word of warm commendation for Mr. Elath who represents us in Great Britain and of whose presence here I am availing myself to send you this letter.[3]

With kindest regards to Mrs. Churchill and yourself, in which my wife joins me,

Yours very sincerely,

354. To Alex Bein,[1] Jerusalem. *Rehovot, 18 November 1951*
Hebrew: T.W.: W.A.

Dear Dr. Bein,

Following our conversation at my home in Rehovot more than two weeks ago, at which I expressed my desire to edit a revised edition of *Trial and Error* which would correct errors and omissions of the first edition, I would request that you assist me in carrying out this task.

For purposes of this project you may utilize any and all documents not only under your control in the Central Zionist Archives, but in my private possession as well.

I would be grateful if you would confirm your willingness to accept this offer.[2]

Sincerely,
Chaim Weizmann

[2] Minister to Israel 1949–51. He became Ambassador to Turkey and was succeeded by Sir Francis Evans.

[3] Replying 19 Nov. (W.A.) Churchill stated: 'The wonderful exertions which Israel is making in these times of difficulty are cheering to an old Zionist like me. I trust you may work in with Jordan and the rest of the Moslem world. With true comradeship there will be enough for all.'

354. [1] B. 1903. Archivist, historian of Zionism and biographer of Theodor Herzl; for many years Director of Israel State Archives and Central Zionist Archives.

[2] Bein accepted the task, but the revision was never undertaken as W. fell ill shortly afterwards (personal communication from A. Bein, 14 May 1976).

355. To Dewey Stone, New York.   *Rehovot, 29 November 1951*
English: Or. Copy. T.W.: W.A.

Dear Dewey,

    The only redeeming feature of a birthday[1] for a man of my age is perhaps this: The years which have taken their toll of me have added the loot [*sic*] to the value of whatever achievement in which I may have a share. In this respect, national institutions are much better off than human beings: their endurance is greater. Thus, I willingly shift the weight of this birthday from my frail shoulders onto the solid framework of the Weizmann Institute of Science, and join you in dedication of an enterprise in which you of the American Committee have had so large a part.

    Of course, I should have liked to be with you, but I can't. It would have been a bracing interlude to spend a carefree evening with many of my friends in the States.[2] I must also forgo the genuine pleasure it would have given me to extend, personally, affectionate felicitations to my old friend, Louis Lipsky,[3] and to welcome my friends and associates of younger days, Sir and Lady Robert Robinson. However, I am grateful in the knowledge that the American Committee is steadfast in its devotion to our common interest—the Institute at Rehovoth, thus helping in the development of scientific research so essential both for the economy of our sorely beset country and for the free spirit of the mind.

    With all good wishes and affectionate greetings,

                        Chaim Weizmann

356. To Abram Berkowitz[1] and Mrs. Sol W. Weltman,[2] Boston.
                                Rehovot, 20 April 1952
English: T.W.: W.A.

Dear Mr. Berkowitz and Mrs. Weltman,

    I was very happy to hear from our mutual friend, Dewey Stone,

---

355. [1] W. had just celebrated his 77th birthday.

    [2] The message was sent to be read at the Dinner at the Waldorf-Astoria Hotel organised by the American Committee of the Weizmann Institute.

    [3] Biog. Index, Vol. VI. Representative of J.A. in U.S. 1933–46. The Dinner honoured his 75th birthday by establishing a Lipsky Fellowship at Institute.

356. [1] 1891–1971. Lawyer, co-trustee with Mrs. Weltman of Jacob Ziskind Trust. Active in cultural and social work.

    [2] Formerly Esther Ziskind, sister of Jacob. Board-member of educational and medical institutions in Massachusetts; Fellow of Brandeis University.

that you, as Executors of the Estate of the Late Jacob Ziskind,[3] have taken the first step toward the fulfilment of Mr. Ziskind's wish to have his name associated with our Institute at Rehovot. I remember meeting Mr. Ziskind at one of our Annual Dinners (I believe it was in 1949), when he expressed to me personally his keen interest in the work of the Institute. It is a great pity that he is no longer among us to be able to see for himself what we have thus far wrought in the Institute for the benefit of Israel and Science in general.

As you probably know, I have been ill for quite some time and confined to bed. I very rarely write letters these days, but news of support of the Institute sustains me more, I am afraid, than all my physicians put together.

I hope that your generous act will mark the beginning of a long association, and that both of you, as the Trustees of the Ziskind Estate, will have an opportunity at an early date to come to Israel and see with your own eyes the fruits of your interest.

I am giving this letter to Mr. Weisgal, Chairman of the Executive Council of the Weizmann Institute of Science, who is returning to the States shortly and will deliver it to you when he arrives there some time in May.

With best wishes,

Very cordially yours,

Ch. Weizmann

357. To Anglo-Israel Association, London.   *Tel Aviv, 3 June 1952*
English: Copy. T.W.: I.S.A. 68/11.

I am glad to learn of the formation of the Anglo-Israel Association and of the activities in which it is engaged.

The association of the Jewish people with Great Britain in the establishment of the Jewish National Home has come to an end with the proclamation of the State of Israel. A new era has begun, but the record of British support for our national aspirations will for all time remain a significant chapter in the annals of the British and the Jewish peoples. As one who has been closely associated with that phase from its very inception, I heartily welcome your efforts to give new meaning and content to this historical relationship by promoting understanding, goodwill and constructive cooperation between Great Britain and the State of Israel. In devoting itself to this task the

---

[3] 1899–1950. Industrialist, philanthropist. Benefactor of many institutions in New England and Israel. The trustees of his estate endowed the Ziskind Building for Experimental Biology and a Student Loan Fund at the Weizmann Institute in his memory.

Anglo-Israel Association is rendering high service to both countries and to the cause of international peace and good fellowship. May your efforts be crowned with success.

Chaim Weizmann[1]

<hr>

357. [1] This was W.'s last letter. He died 9 Nov. 1952 at 6 a.m. His body lay in state in the grounds of Weizmann House for two days while some quarter of a million people passed by in homage, and there he lies buried. His wife Vera died 24 Sept. 1966, and shares his grave.

APPENDIX I

The Road to Reconciliation with Arab World

To Harry S. Truman, Washington.   *Rehovot, 24 June 1949*
English: Or. Copy. T.W.: I.S.A. 68/11.

Dear Mr. President,

The Government of Israel have communicated to me the text of the Note transmitted to them on your behalf on the 29th May, as well as their reply of June 8th.[1] The matters raised in the Note are of such gravity that I feel impelled to address you personally on the subject. You have throughout taken such a warm and helpful interest in the affairs of our young State that I am most anxiously concerned that you, our great and good friend, should be under no misapprehension regarding our position and intentions concerning the issues now at stake. I wish, indeed, it were possible for me to talk matters over personally with you. That is always the best way of removing misunderstanding.

We have all been distressed at the slow progress made at Lausanne. It may be that the device of a Conciliation Commission, consisting not of officers of the U.N., but of delegates of three different countries, with different backgrounds and policies, was not the best way

---

[1] By a General Assembly Resolution of 11 Dec. 1948, the functions of the Acting Mediator, Bunche, were terminated and replaced by a U.N. Palestine Conciliation Commission (P.C.C.) comprising representatives of U.S., France and Turkey. It was to bring about a permanent settlement and to facilitate repatriation, settlement, rehabilitation, and compensation of Arab refugees not wishing to return to their homes. Meetings began in Lausanne 30 Apr. 1949 with separate negotiations between Israeli representatives and P.C.C., and representatives of Egypt, Transjordan, Lebanon and Syria with P.C.C. (the Arabs refusing to negotiate directly with Israel). Progress was hampered by insistence of the Arabs that the Arab refugee problem be resolved before a territorial settlement was discussed, while the Israelis demanded that negotiations proceed in the reverse order. Impatient at the rate of progress, for which U.S. blamed Israel, Washington replaced its principal representative, an independent personal nominee of Truman, by a State Department official. Further, U.S. accepted the Arab position that Israel both repatriate the refugees and make territorial concessions. Truman's Note had stressed the importance of Israel's making at least one immediate 'genuine and generous concession' regarding the refugees. Israel's reply had noted that the Arab States' refusal to enter into a peaceful relationship with Israel made the return of 'masses of refugees to Israel a quixotic undertaking which could not possibly be reconciled with any normal concept of national security'. The situation seemed at an impasse, hence this exchange of letters between the two Presidents.

of promoting a speedy settlement. It certainly appears to have been less effective than the mediation of one man pursued in the name of the United Nations as a whole. But be that as it may, we are trying our best to work with this Commission and have submitted to them a number of proposals, to none of which we have so far received any reply from the other side. Indeed up till now the Arab States have altogether refused to sit with our delegates under the auspices of the Commission.

When our Delegation first arrived in Lausanne on April 30th, they immediately announced that they had come with full authorization to negotiate a comprehensive peace settlement with the delegates of the Arab States covering all the matters referred to in the U.N. Resolution of 11th December, 1948. They specifically stated that Israel was ready to contribute towards solving the Arab refugee problem in cooperation with the United Nations and the Arab States. A few days later they submitted to the Commission a draft preamble and two articles of a proposed peace treaty to serve as a basis for discussion. In this draft they proposed, among other things, the final liquidation of the war, the establishment of normal political and economic relations between Israel and the Arab States, mutual guarantees of the frontiers, abstention from the use of force for the settlement of disputes, and international arbitration in case such disputes could not be settled by agreement.

To this day we have not received any reply to these basic proposals.

Coming to the question of the Arab refugees, our delegation gave repeated assurances to the Commission that Israel was ready to co-operate with the U.N. and the Arab States for a solution of the refugee problem. We pledged ourselves to guarantee the civil rights of all minorities within our territory; we accepted the principle of compensation for land abandoned by Arabs; we declared our readiness to unfreeze Arab accounts in our banks immediately on the conclusion of peace; we set up a Custodian of Absentee Property. Our delegation informed the Commission that the Government of Israel was ready to readmit members of Arab families separated by the war.

In conformity with the General Assembly's Resolution of December 11th, relating to access to ports and means of communication our delegation has offered to create a free zone in the Haifa port for the benefit of Transjordan. Various proposals were made by our delegation for the delimitation of the frontiers of Israel with the Arab States. Our delegation also elaborated our attitude on the Jerusalem question.

All these constructive proposals have not elicited a single reply from the Arab delegations. It would, indeed, appear that these delegations did not come to Lausanne with authority to negotiate a peace settlement, but solely for the purpose of arranging for the repatriation of the Arab refugees to Israel.

Our delegation subsequently proposed the establishment of a number of sub-committees to deal with the general principles and conditions of peace, the territorial settlement, the refugee problem, the Jerusalem question, and the economic development of the Middle East, pursuant to Clause 10 of the U.N. Resolution of December 11th.[2] We have not yet learnt the reaction of the Arab Delegations to these proposals. Finally, when members of the Commission suggested in a spirit of despondency that the Conference be suspended for a time, our delegation strongly opposed this course.

I feel you will agree, Mr. President, that in the light of these indisputable facts, we can hardly be charged with having failed to cooperate with the Commission. If so far nothing substantial has resulted from these talks, this is due essentially to the negative attitude of the Arab delegations and their persistent refusal to meet us under the auspices of the Commission. It is a great pity that the Commission failed to dislodge them from that negative attitude.

Permit me to add a few words on the two issues which are in the centre of the discussion: the territorial question and the refugee problem.

We have no aggressive designs against anyone and we are not looking for additional territory. But I think that no fair-minded man will deny us the right to retain that part of our ancient land which has become ours at a terrible cost of blood and treasure in the course of a war forced upon us by others. Most of the country which we hold beyond the boundaries set out on November 29th, 1947 was occupied by our forces during the second military campaign which was the result of the Arabs' defiant refusal to accept the Mediator's urgent plea for a continuation of the first truce. Bitter experience has shown that without that territory we are defenceless. Were we to give up the corridor to Jerusalem, that great city, whose people suffered so much and so heroically last year, would again be exposed to the danger of having its water supply cut off and of being starved into submission. In exactly the same way, Western Galilee holds the key to the defence of Haifa and the Valley of Jezreel, while the Ramleh area assures the safety of Tel Aviv from such menacing attacks as were launched upon it last year. None of these areas was ever allotted to any of the Arab States with which we are now negotiating. All of them are occupied by Israel legally under armistice agreements.

---

[2] This instructed P.C.C. to seek arrangements to facilitate economic development of the area, including access to ports and airfields and use of transportation and communication facilities.

The Palestine Arab State contemplated in the U.N. Resolution of 29th November 1947 has not come into being—not through any fault of ours—and there is no reason whatever why the neighbouring Arab States who invaded Palestine in flagrant defiance of their obligations under the Charter, should be appeased by territorial "compensation" at our expense. Incidentally, all these demands for compensation in the end boil down to the same old question on which you took so firm a stand last year—the Negev. It is the Negev, particularly the southern Negev, which appears again to be demanded from us. The reasons against it are just as potent as they were last year when you so strongly opposed our being deprived of that area which contains the country's sole mineral resources and which, in addition, is our only gateway to the East. What importance attaches to our having direct access to the Red Sea has been brought home to us strikingly by Egypt's closing of the Suez Canal to all ships—even British ships—carrying, or suspected of carrying, goods to Israel. Because of such closure we are compelled to bring vital supplies (wheat, etc.) from Australia and the Far East all the way via the Cape and Gibraltar. With the coast of Eylat in our possession and the Negev opened up by transport roads, we shall have free access to the sea routes which are vital to our existence.

Now as to the refugee problem. It is a grave issue, but it was not created by us. It was not the birth of Israel which created the Arab refugee problem, as our enemies now proclaim, but the Arab attempt to prevent that birth by armed force. These peoples are not refugees in the sense in which that term has been sanctified by the martyrdom of millions in Europe—they are part of an aggressor group which failed and which makes no secret of its intention to resume aggression. They left the country last year at the bidding of their leaders and military commanders and as part of the Arab strategic plan. But in spite of all this we are, for humanitarian reasons, ready to contribute as far as we can towards a solution of this problem. We have, in fact, done a good deal more under this head than could, for obvious reasons, be published. Your Ambassador has been given details under this head. We have been steadily re-admitting Arab refugees during the last few months. The number of those who have returned exceeds 25,000. We are ready to re-unite Arab families separated by the war, and we are now approaching the various Arab States through the Mixed Armistice Commissions for setting up special machinery to facilitate their return in organised form. We are prepared to re-admit more as part of a peace settlement. There are, however, two overriding considerations which limit what we can do in this sphere: we dare not again endanger our hard-won independence and security and, with all the good will in the world, we cannot undertake tasks which are economically beyond our strength.

So many malicious charges have been levelled against us in connection with this Arab refugee question, that I cannot help drawing attention to the basic realities of the situation. We are a small State, nine hundred thousand Jews wedged in between forty million Arabs. We held our own last year by a terrific effort and at very heavy sacrifices, losing some of our finest youth and suffering heavy damage. The Arab States are making no secret of their intention of resuming war whenever they are ready for it. Only two days ago Faris el Khoury, the former Syrian member of the Security Council and Chairman of the Syrian Chamber declared that the war against us "remains the corner-stone of Arab policy". Not a week passes without our being warned by authoritative Arab spokesmen of the coming "second round". The Arab States are rearming on a big scale, building up modern armament industries of their own and purchasing the most deadly modern weapons. A few weeks ago squadrons of British Vampire jet fighters were flown to the Suez Canal Zone—half an hour's air flight from our frontier—ready for instant delivery when wanted, while Egyptian pilots are being trained in their use close by. Egypt has also ordered British destroyers with 4″ and 6″ guns and submarines, while there is hardly any secret about the French rearming the Syrians. This rearmament, Mr. President, constitutes a direct threat to the peace of the Middle East and thereby also to the peace of the world. With this open threat of war hanging over us, can we ignore the security aspect of the admission of a large Arab population who, whatever their individual feelings might be, are likely to turn against us if war restarts?

Apart from the security question, which to my mind is paramount, there is the economic difficulty. When the United Nations in November 1947 voted in favour of a Jewish State, it was motivated pre-eminently by the purpose of solving once and for all the Jewish question in Europe, to get rid of the concentration camps and of the aftermath of Hitler's holocaust. I know, Mr. President, that this purpose was uppermost in your mind when you gave us your staunch and steady support in those critical days. We are now doing exactly what we were expected to do. We are liquidating one camp after another and have already brought over many thousands of their former inmates. Can we be expected at the same time to build up, alongside this big effort of reconstruction, a new Arab economy to absorb hundreds of thousands of Arabs? For let there be no mistake about it: the Arab economic and social structure as it was prior to last year's exodus has ceased to exist. The Arab refugee question can be solved in a big way only by a comprehensive effort of reconstruction. The crucial question is: is that effort to be undertaken in Israel,

with all the political, security and economic stresses and strains arising therefrom, or in the neighbouring Arab countries where vast
fertile areas are available for such resettlement and where these
people can find a home in the congenial surroundings of an Arab
society?

Our policy, as I stated before, is not one of absolute refusal to
readmit Arabs and we may, if real peace is established, be able to do
more in this respect than if the present atmosphere of latent war and
hostility continues. But an all-round solution can only be found as
part of a general development scheme for the benefit of the Middle
East as a whole. Towards such a development scheme Israel is ready
to make its contribution: I hope it will be a significant contribution.
But to achieve all this there must be negotiation, agreement and
peace. The most vital need at the present hour is for Arabs and Jews
to enter into direct negotiations and hammer out an agreed settlement. I plead with you, Mr. President, that you may use your unique
influence to induce the Arab States to face the realities of the situation and to take that decisive step.

With affectionate greetings,

Yours very sincerely,
Chaim Weizmann

To Chaim Weizmann, Rehovot.　　*The White House, 13 August 1949*
I.S.A. 105/1747.

Personal

Dear President Weizmann,

Thank you for writing me personally with regard to our note of
May 29, 1949, and your Government's reply of June 8. I appreciate
your desire to remove any misapprehensions regarding the position
and intentions of your Government. I am certain a personal talk
would be helpful. As this is not possible at the present time I shall
endeavor to answer certain of your points.

It is true that many long months have passed since the Palestine
question was first referred to the United Nations. On the other hand,
it is our belief that the United Nations has made remarkable progress
in view of the complexity of the problem. It may also be true that, in
theory, a single individual such as Count Folke Bernadotte or Dr.
Ralph Bunche would have been able to proceed more rapidly than a
commission consisting of three or more members. In practice, however, experience has demonstrated that a single individual can only
succeed with active assistance on the part of interested governments.
We believe that the present Palestine Conciliation Commission has
been able to function effectively, when one considers that it is

responsible for negotiating a longer range political settlement whereas the Acting Mediator's functions were confined to the achievement of shorter range military agreements.

The proposals which the Israeli delegation at Lausanne has advanced have undoubtedly been helpful to the Palestine Conciliation Commission. Although some of these proposals have not been adopted, it may be recalled that the representatives of Israel, Lebanon, Syria, Transjordan and Egypt on May 12, 1949, were signatories to a protocol[3] of the Commission which should have the effect of facilitating further discussion of all questions, including the refugee problem, and thereby of achieving a final peace settlement. It seems reasonable to consider the Arab agreement to the protocol of May 12 as a general reply to the Israeli proposals.

With regard to the general question of the Arab refugees, you may recall that the General Assembly Resolution of December 11 provided that the refugees wishing to return to their homes and live at peace with their neighbors should be permitted to do so at the earliest practicable date, and that compensation should be paid for the property of those choosing not to return. I am, therefore, glad to be reassured by your letter that Israel is ready to cooperate with the United Nations and the Arab states for a solution of the refugee problem; that Israel pledges itself to guarantee the civil rights of all minorities; that Israel accepts the principle of compensation for land abandoned by Arabs; that Israel declares its readiness to unfreeze Arab accounts under certain conditions; that Israel has set up a custodian of absentee property; and that Israel is ready to readmit members of Arab families.

It may be noted, however, that in making these proposals the Israeli delegation made them conditional, in general, on the conclusion of peace and other limiting factors, and that the representatives of the Arab states, on the other hand, considered the General Assembly Resolution as imperative and mandatory.

With regard to (1) access to ports and means of communications, and (2) the delimitation of frontiers, it again seems reasonable to believe that the protocol of May 12 might be considered as a con-

---

[3] This stated: 'The parties concerned agree to discuss all questions concerning refugees, respect of their rights and preservation of their property, as well as territorial and other questions . . . Territorial questions would be discussed only insofar as they affected the problem of refugees.' Walter Eytan, for Israel, made a verbal reservation in signing the protocol that Israel considered it only as a starting-point for discussion, and did not consider the partition map attached to the protocol as having relevance to future frontiers except as a point of departure for negotiations. This verbal reservation was not included in a progress report issued by P.C.C. 23 June.

structive basis on which these matters could be discussed. With regard to the Jerusalem question, it is my understanding that the Palestine Conciliation Commission has made excellent progress during which it consulted all interested parties and that it is presently in the process of preparing its report on this subject for the General Assembly in accordance with paragraph (8) of the General Assembly Resolution of December 11.[4]

In view of these developments at Lausanne, I believe one may conclude that the Arab representatives are prepared to enter into negotiations with the objective of achieving a peace settlement. This conclusion would appear to be reinforced by the Commission's communique of July 28, which reports that "the Arab delegations and the delegation of Israel have given express assurances regarding their intentions to collaborate with the Commission with a view to the definitive settlement of the Palestine problem and to the establishment of a just and permanent peace in Palestine".

The Commission has already activated a number of subsidiary groups, such as the General Committee, the Jerusalem Committee, and the Technical Committee on refugees. It is my understanding that the Commission now has your project regarding additional sub-committees under consideration and that the Commission might take advantage of your project to facilitate further discussions.

With regard to direct negotiations, it may be recalled that the General Assembly Resolution of December 11 provides for negotiations conducted either with the Palestine Conciliation Commission or directly. Thus far the representatives of the Arab states have been unwilling to enter into direct talks. It may be hoped, however, that further progress at Lausanne might make it possible to conduct negotiations both with the Palestine Conciliation Commission and directly.

With regard to the refugee problem, we are of the opinion that primary responsibility for a solution to this problem rests with Israel and the Arab states and that, assuming all concerned are willing to approach it realistically and constructively, the United Nations, including its individual members, might be willing to assist the states concerned in reaching such solution. It is reassuring that Israel, for humanitarian reasons, is ready to contribute as far as it can toward a solution of this problem and has been readmitting Arab refugees and is ready to reunite Arab families.

---

[4] This called for special and separate treatment of the Jerusalem area from the rest of Palestine, and instructed P.C.C. to present detailed proposals for a permanent international regime that provided maximum local autonomy for distinctive groups.

During your recent visit to the United States I talked to you about my feelings regarding the refugees and the question of a final territorial settlement. These views were repeated in the recent exchange of notes between your Government and mine. I would be less than frank if I did not tell you that I was disappointed when I read the reply of your Government to our note of May 29. Even after talking with Ambassador Elath, following his recent return from Tel Aviv, I am not certain that the present proposals of your Government will affect the current conversations at Lausanne in such a way as to achieve a lasting peace between Israel and the Arab states.

Whether or not one can say that Israel has cooperated with the Commission, it seems to us that the views of the Israeli Government are in many respects at variance with the General Assembly Resolution of December 11. The views of the Israeli Government may also be considered as failing to take into account the principles regarding territorial compensation advanced by the United States as indicated in our Aide-Memoire of June 24.

With regard to territory, your reassurances that Israel has no aggressive designs against anyone and that it is not looking for additional territory are appreciated. We can understand that you might be somewhat apprehensive on security grounds; nevertheless, it seems reasonable to believe that the conclusion of armistice agreements with the neighboring Arab states should prove reassuring and that both Israel and the Arab states on the basis of the General Assembly Resolutions of November 29, 1947, and December 11, 1948, should be able to discuss the territorial question.

I sincerely hope that both Israel and the Arab states will continue the discussions at Lausanne in a conciliatory spirit and with a greater understanding of the problems which exist between them. If both sides undertake an approach of this kind a settlement in Palestine would be greatly facilitated. Such a settlement would be an extremely important contribution to the stability of the Near East and the well-being of its peoples. It would, in addition, provide a basis on which it would be possible more constructively to plan for the future.

Very sincerely yours,
Harry S. Truman

Kindest personal regards.

H.S.T.[5]

---

[5] Postscript handwritten.

APPENDIX II

On the Status of Jerusalem

To Harry S. Truman, Washington.   *Rehovot, 3 January 1950*
English: Or. Copy. T.W.: I.S.A. 68/11.

Dear Mr. President,

I am very happy that Mr. Ewing's visit to Israel[1] gives me an opportunity to send you a personal letter. We spent a very pleasant hour together and although his visit to this country is of short duration, I am sure he will be able to convey to you a picture of the situation as it is and of the problems which are uppermost in our minds.

I cannot begin this letter without expressing to you our deep gratitude for the lead taken by the United States delegation at the recent session of the U.N. Assembly in opposing the disastrous resolution adopted by the Assembly on the internationalization of Jerusalem.[2] The view expressed by the spokesman of the United States that the resolution is both "irresponsible and impractical" will, I feel sure, be shared by all when calmer counsels come to prevail. This will provide an opportunity for reconsidering the whole question on more constructive lines and may possibly open the way for a solution acceptable to all parties. We are anxious to work with the Government of the United States towards that inevitable turning point.

Anyone familiar with international affairs knows that international regimes of this kind have invariably proved unworkable and produced nothing but insecurity, friction and economic decay. In the case of Jerusalem, a landlocked city wedged in between Israel and Transjordan, with no economic life of its own and no direct contact with the outside world, all these disastrous effects would be multiplied ten-fold.

---

[1] Oscar R. Ewing (b. 1889). Federal Security Administrator, had just completed a survey of social problems in Israel and Western Europe.

[2] I.e., General Assembly Resolution of 10 Dec. 1949 to internationalize Jerusalem. The vote was 38 in favour, 14 against, seven abstentions. Carried largely by a coalition of Arab-Catholic-Communist delegates, the following voted against: Canada, Costa Rica, Denmark, Great Britain, Guatemala, Iceland, Israel, Norway, Sweden, Turkey, South Africa, U.S.A., Uruguay, Yugoslavia.

The only significant concern which the world at large has in Jerusalem is the protection of its holy shrines and the provision of free and secure access to all who wish to visit them. In actual fact, the area containing these holy shrines represents not more than two percent of the whole of Jerusalem, and the bulk of this sacred area is not in our possession, but in that of King Abdullah. Is it then not the height of absurdity and injustice to force an artificial and unwanted international regime upon the whole of modern Jerusalem—with its hundred thousand Jews, its Hebrew University, and all its other great Jewish institutions—merely because these holy shrines and places are situated in a small area of the city which is not in Jewish possession? We are all in favour of providing special safeguards for the protection of these holy shrines and we are willing to give adequate guarantees for their free accessibility. But we cannot agree, and we cannot be expected to agree, that our ancient Mother-city be severed from the new commonwealth of Israel. Jerusalem has been our capital since the days of David and Solomon. It was the centre of our ancient glory, as the Psalmist described it, "beautiful in elevation, the joy of the whole earth, the city of the Great King". Jerusalem was the tribune from which the Prophets of Israel sent forth their eternal messages to mankind: "Out of Zion shall go forth the Law, and the Word of the Lord from Jerusalem." When Jerusalem was destroyed, our exiled fathers by the waters of Babylon took the awesome oath: "If I forget thee, O Jerusalem, may my right hand forget its cunning." Throughout the long ages of our exile, Jerusalem was the lodestar of our hope. To countless generations of Jews, ascent to Jerusalem and residence within its precincts was the highest that life could offer. During eighteen centuries this attachment and aspiration formed the central theme in our life and literature. And now that our national hopes have been realized and we have again become a free nation in our ancient land, is it conceivable that Jerusalem, the home and heart of our people, be detached from the State of Israel? It was an Archbishop of Canterbury who, a few years ago, commented on the absurdity of "realizing Zionism without restoring Zion" to the Jewish people.[3]

To all this has now been added the tragic experience of last year. How can any right-thinking man demand that the Jews of Jerusalem, who last year went through hunger, thirst, and deadly peril in defence of their city, should now be placed under alien rule? It was not the thirty nine nations who recently voted to turn Jerusalem into an

---

[3] Cosmo Gordon Lang (1864–1945). In House of Lords, July 1937, during debate on Peel Report.

international regime, but the soldiers and engineers of Israel, who last year saved Jerusalem from utter destruction. No wonder that the Jews of Jerusalem are determined to remain part of Israel, as they always have been.

We are most anxious to uphold the authority of the United Nations and we shall be glad to cooperate in any solution which safeguards Christian and Moslem religious interests without depriving us of our Mother-city. Such a solution can be worked out on the common sense principle that the holy places be placed under supervision of the United Nations, while the city is governed in accordance with the wishes of the people who live in it. That was the spirit and the intent of the proposals we submitted to the General Assembly of the United Nations, by which we still stand. I hope that the United States will wield its unrivalled influence in the United Nations for helping towards such a solution.

In my conversation with Mr. Ewing, I referred to another matter which is causing us great anxiety: the large-scale rearmament that is going on in the neighbouring Arab States with the help of Great Britain.[4] Mr. Ewing will be able to convey to you some of the facts and the dangers which are inherent in these warlike preparations. It is essential that effective steps be taken to put an end to this one-sided rearmament. We are desperately anxious for the peace of the Middle East and the peace of the world. We want to rebuild our ancient country and provide homes and security to the many thousands whom we are bringing over from Europe. We are trying to live up to the hopes which you placed in us when you gave us your generous support during those trying years, but to fulfil that task we need peace. I pray that you may do what you can to help preserve it.

With kindest regards,[5]

Yours very sincerely,
Chaim Weizmann

---

[4] In a letter following the discussion (W. to Ewing, 2 Jan. 1950, I.S.A. 68/11) he had detailed the large-scale rearmament of Egypt and had reinforced his figures from Press reports: some 400 light and heavy tanks, many artillery pieces, jet planes, Spitfires and frigates. W. requested Ewing to convey the information to Truman.

[5] Truman read this and the letter to Ewing in the latter's presence, and said 'that Israel could not be left empty-handed in the matter of arms to face Arab rearmament . . . he would take the matter up with Acheson'—see Kohn to W., 5 Feb. 1950, I.S.A. 105/1747.

OMITTED LETTERS

Items of minor significance or of a repetitive nature, which include a large number of replies to congratulatory messages received by Dr. Weizmann on his election as President of Israel, are detailed below and are available for reference at the Weizmann Archives in Rehovot.

1947   *Aug.* Ivor Joseph Linton; Herman Mark; Doris May (two items); Chaim Pozner; Meyer W. Weisgal.

Sept. Gershon Agronsky; Walter Baechler; Leo Baeck; Walter Baer (two items); Werner and Nelly Baer; Ernst D. Bergmann (three items); Benjamin Bloch; Willy Bloch; Lady Violet Bonham-Carter; M. Brailowsky; David L. Cohen; Josef Cohn; Reginald Coupland; S. W. Crickett; Samuel Daiches; Willy David; Angelo Donati; Blanche Dugdale; Eduard I. Echtman; Albert K. Epstein; Enrique R. Fabregat; Sigmund Gestetner; A. Gluecksmann; Nahum Goldmann; Akiva Goldstein; Mr. and Mrs. Sam Goldstein; Joshua Harlap; Freda Kirchwey; Nicolai Kirschner; Lola Kramarsky; Siegfried Kramarsky; Harry Levine; Louis E. Levinthal; Asher Levitsky; Chaya Lichtenstein; Fredman Ashe Lincoln; Louis Lipsky; Malka Locker; Lady Ebba Low; Judah L. Magnes; Lord and Lady Melchett; André Meyer; Henry Morgenthau Jr. (two items); Isaac A. Naiditch; Walter J. Neumond; Herbert Oppenheimer; W. Pease; O. Pernikoff (two items); Pinkas; N. Pollak; Walter Pollak; S. Pomerance; Moshe David Remez; Karl Rosenberger; James de Rothschild; Miriam Sacher; Mordechai Shenhabi; Leon Simon; Rose Singer; Celina Sokolow; Joseph Sprinzak; Dewey Stone (two items); Max Sulzbacher; Georg Tugendhat; Yizhak Volcani; Frieda Warburg; Meyer W. Weisgal (six items); Anna Weizmann; Sarah Wilkinson; Stephen S. Wise; Abraham Wix; Youth Aliya; Sam Zacks; Zionist Federation of South Africa; Leon Zuckerman (two items).

Oct. Ellen Ballon, Tammie Ryan and Ralph Gustavson; Jacob Blaustein; Benjamin Bloch; Joseph Blumenfeld; Judith Bookman; Maurice Boukstein; S. W. Crickett; Morris Eisenman; R. Foulkes; Stella Frankfurter; Harry Friedenwald; Elisha M. Friedman (two items); Lionel Gelber; Herman Gilman; Charles David Ginsburg (two items); Solomon Goldman; Joseph Gravitsky; *Habimah;* Maurice B. Hexter (two items); W. Peter Hohenstein; Baron Inverchapel; Chana Itin; Rose Jacobs; Marc Jarblum; Alvin Johnson; Ruth Kisch; Leibowitz; Samuel Lepkovsky; Mr. and Mrs. Abraham Lifshitz; Doris May; William S. Paley; Helen R. Reid; Eleanor Roosevelt; Morris Rothenberg; James de Rothschild; Ruth Schiff; Salman Schocken; D. Werner Senator; A. Spitz; Numa Torczyner; Abraham Tulin; Frieda Warburg; Sumner Welles; Maidie Weizmann; Sam S. Wishniak; Oscar Wolfsberg.

Nov. Frank Altschul; Max Ascoli; Mrs. Max Ascoli; Baum; James H. Becker; Adolfo Benarus; Niels Bohr; Frank W. Buxton; Louis F. Fieser; E. Louis Finkelstein; George S. Franklin; Eli Ginzberg; Mrs. David B. Greenberg; Mrs. Adolph L. Hamburger; Mrs. Samuel H. Hartley and Mrs. Morris Sprayregen; Baron Inverchapel; Leo Jung; Franz Kind (two items); Lola Kramarsky; Leo Lauterpacht; Herbert H. Lehman (two items); Ivor Joseph Linton (two items); Alfonso Lopez; John F. McCabe; Frederick Mann; Mrs. Henry Morgenthau; Herman Neaderland (two items); Walter J. Neumond (three items); J. Robert Oppenheimer; Mrs. Ogden Reid; Robert Robinson; G. Ronus (two items); Morris Rothenberg; Ada Sereni; Jan Christiaan Smuts; Dewey Stone; Henry A. Wallace; Frieda Warburg; Oscar Wolfsberg.

Dec. Walter Annenberg; Appel; Itzhak Araten and Maurice Gerzon; Walter Baer (two items); Lavy Bakstansky; Beau Rivage Hotel (two items); Benjamin Bloch; Hayyim Bograchov; G. K. Crichton; Wyndham Deedes; Dickler; Rose Dunkelman; Mordecai Ehrenpreis; Morris Eisenman; Walter Elliot; Albert K. Epstein (two items); Gershon Epstein; Arthur Felix; Gordon Ferguson; Harry M. Fisher; Felix Frankfurter (three items); Harry Friedenwald; Israel Friedlander; Gad Frumkin; Richard Gale; General Zionists; Sigmund Gestetner (two items); Leah Ginsburg; Eli Ginzberg (two items); Harold Goldenberg; Frieda Goldschmidt; Israel Goldstein; Sylvan Gotshal; Abraham Granovsky; Frances Gunther; *Habimah;* Hadassah, New York; Lola Hahn-Warburg; Isaac Hamlin (two items); Arthur Hantke, Leib Jaffe and Leo Herrmann; Isaac H. Herzog; *Hever ha-Kvutzot;* Siegfried Hoofien; Siegfried Hoofien and Aron Barth; Richard Jaffe; Barnett Janner; J. Leon Jona; Eliezer Kaplan (three items); Edmund I. Kaufmann (two items); Serge Koussevitsky; Herbert H. Lehman (two items); Samuel Lepkovsky; Adele Levy; I. M. Lewin; Ivor Joseph Linton; James Malcolm; Frederick Mann; Samuel Markewich; Lord and Lady Melchett; Fred Monosson; Rodney Moore; Henry Morgenthau Jr.; Nahalal; Jawaharlal Nehru; Simon S. Neuman; Emanuel Neumann; Louis Nizer; Ofboi Group (Labour Zionist Organization of America, Reseda, California); Herbert Oppenheimer; J. Robert Oppenheimer (two items); Palestine Transport Workers' Union; W. Pease; *Po'alei Eretz Israel;* Joseph Potofsky; Juda H. Quastel; Jill Rayner; Moshe David Remez; G. Ronus; Milton L. Scheingarten; Joseph M. Schenk; Jesse Schwartz; Ezra Shapiro; Carl Sherman; Mrs. H. Singer and Rabbi Jesse Schwartz; George Skouras (two items); Dorothy Spector; Oliver Stanley; Mrs. Stern; Samuel J. Stoll; Harry K. Stone; Georg Strauss; Hjordis Swenson; Paul Uhlmann; Yizhak Volcani (two items); Frieda Warburg; Meyer W. Weisgal; Stephen S. Wise; W.I.Z.O. Palestine Executive; Sam Zacks (two items); Zionist Federation of Canada.

1948   *Jan.* E. Alexander-Katz; Walter Baer; Isaiah Berlin (two items); Benjamin Bloch (two items); M. Brailowsky (two items); David Bronstein; H. Brough (two items); Josef Cohn (two items); S. W. Crickett (two items); Alan Cunningham; Morris Eisenman (two items); Felix Frankfurter; Sigmund Gestetner (two items); L. L. Gildesgame; Harold Goldenberg; Sylvan Gotshal; Marc Jarblum; Jewish Agency, New York; Eliezer Kaplan; Shlomo Kaplansky; Miriam Lane (two items); I. M. Lewin; Nancy MacKinnon; National Provincial Bank, Manager; Joseph Nedava; Fred Nettler; Walter J. Neumond (two items); William Rappard; Paul Rothschild; Harry Sacher; H. Shine; Ivan Shortt; Mr. and Mrs. Sinclair-Thomson; Jan Christiaan Smuts; Oliver Stanley; Esther Stott; Dorothy Thompson; H. W. Turner; Arthur G. Weidenfeld; Meyer W. Weisgal (four items); Abraham Wix; Isaac Wolfson; Benjamin J. Yahuda; Zionist Organization of Peru.

Feb. Shimon Bernstein; Benjamin Bloch; Madame Jacques Errera;

Louis F. Fieser; Maung Kyi; Jacob Landau; Herbert H. Lehman; Robert A. Lovett; Herman Mark; Jawaharlal Nehru; D. Werner Senator; Sumner Welles; Maidie Weizmann.

Mar. Lawrence Berenson; Ernst D. Bergmann (six items); Felix Bergmann; Benjamin Bloch; Samuel M. Blumenfeld; Elisabeth, Queen of Belgium; Herbert Evatt; Louis F. Fieser; Lionel Gelber; Sigmund Gestetner; Nelson Glueck; Seymour Herscher; John Hilldring; Jacob Landau; Herbert H. Lehman; I. M. Lewin; Arthur and Jeanette Lourie; Daniel Marsh (two items); S. Umberto Nahon; Martin Rosenblueth (two items); Jan Christiaan Smuts; Benjamin Weizmann; S. Zevuloni.

Apr. Anglo-Palestine Bank, Rehovot; Mrs. Barsby; Ernst D. Bergmann (six items); Benjamin Bloch (two items); Joseph Brainin; Jacob Chazan; Elisheva Furmansky; John Gunther; Freda Kirchwey; James G. McDonald; James Malcolm; George C. Marshall; Doris May; Henry Montor; *Motele Verein,* Chicago; Moshe David Remez; Herman Rosenberg; Morris Rothenberg (two items); Kurt G. Stern; Dewey Stone; Yaakov Uri; Meyer W. Weisgal (five items); Benjamin Weizmann; Maidie Weizmann; Yehiel Weizmann.

May   Agudat Harabbanim, New York; Harry T. Andrews; Shalom Asch; George Backer; Walter Baer (two items); Paul Baerwald; Lavy Bakstansky; Joseph Baskin; Crystal Bennett; Ernst D. Bergmann; Benjamin Bloch; Elaine Blond; Hayyim Bograchov; Selig Brodetsky (two items); Emanuel Celler; Cyril Clemens; Harriet Cohen; Bartley C. Crum; Max Davidsohn; David Dubinsky; Aba Elhanani; Albert K. Epstein (two items); Bernard Ettlinger; Abraham Feinberg; Felix Frankfurter; Freiman Family, Ottawa; Harry Friedenwald; C. L. Friedman; C. L. Gabriel; Marvin Gelber; Manfred George; Sigmund Gestetner; Frank Goldman; Frieda Goldschmidt; Mrs. Bert Goldstein; Israel Goldstein (two items); Paul and Romana Goodman; Sylvan Gotshal; Robert Gottlieb; Jennie Grossinger; Frances Gunther; John Gunther; Gutierrez; Charles Gutwirth; *Habimah;* Mrs. Samuel W. Halprin; Isaac Hamlin; Gottlieb Hammer (two items); *Hapoel Hamizrachi,* America; Benjamin R. Harris; Adolph Held; William Heller; Jacob Hodess; Siegfried Hoofien; Vincent R. Impellitteri; Henry Ittleson; Max Jacoby; Barnett Janner; Marc Jarblum; Alexander Kahn; David Kaminsky; Eliezer Kaplan; Edmund I. Kaufmann; Mr. and Mrs. Herman Klotz; Serge Koussevitsky; Lamon Family; Jacob Landau; Herbert H. Lehman; Louis E. Levinthal; Ludwig Lewisohn; Chaya Lichtenstein; Louis Lipsky; Manchester Zionist Association; Simon Marks; Doris May (two items); Lord and Lady Melchett; Asher Mibashan; Henry Morgenthau, Jr.; Louis Nizer; Edward A. Norman; Itzchak Norman; Philadelphia Jewish Community; David Pinski; David de Sola Pool; Joseph Proskauer; Mrs. Simcha Rabinowitz; Jill Rayner; Lady Reading; Abraham A. Redelheim; Rehovot Town Council; Joseph Reider; Moshe David Remez; Retinger; Simon H. Rifkind; Koppel Rosen; Martin Rosenblueth; William Rosenwald; Morris Rothenberg; Guy de Rothschild; Alexander Sachs; David Schapira; Isaac Schwartzbart; Vincent Sheean; Joseph Sherbow; Moshe Shertok (two items); Zippora Shertok; Rebecca Shulman (two items); Marcus Sieff; Silverstone; Julius Simon; Rose Singer; Jan Christiaan Smuts; Flora Solomon; Joseph Sprinzak; Max Swerin; Herbert Bayard Swope; Robert Szold (two items); Samuel A. Telsey; Dorothy Thompson; Harry S. Truman; Paul Uhlmann; Ben-Zion Meir Hai Uziel; Pierre van Paassen; Frieda Warburg; Judah Wattenberg; Israel S. Wechsler; Meyer W. Weisgal; Sumner Welles; Mrs. Joseph M. Welt; Ephraim and Ray Winer; Stephen S. Wise (two items); W.I.Z.O. Palestine Executive; Sam Zacks; Max Zaritsky; Zionist Executive, London; Zionist Federation of South Africa; Zionist Federation of Canada; *Zionita;* Samuel Zondek (two items).

June Walter Baer (four items); James H. Becker; Ernst D. Bergmann (seven items); Israel Brodie; Georges Brunschvig; Edward L. Cady; Israel S. Chipkin; Josef Cohn; S. W. Crickett; James and Frances Fergusson; Felix Frankfurter; Mrs. Isaac Friedenheit; Sigmund Gestetner; Charles David Ginsburg (three items); Nahum Goldmann; Mrs. Maude Grant; Gottlieb Hammer; Vladimir Ipatieff; Edward Jacobson; A. Jaffe; Eliezer Kaplan; Katherine von Kardorff; Franz Kind; Arthur G. Klein; Adele Levy; Ivor Joseph Linton; Miss E. Mandelstam; Daniel Marsh; Doris May (two items); Mme. René Mayer; William S. Paley; Chaim Pozner (two items); Mrs. William Prince; Juda H. Quastel; Lady Reading (two items); Hilde Rosenfeld; James de Rothschild; Otto M. Schiff; D. Werner Senator; Moshe Shertok (seven items); R. O. Smith; Jan Christiaan Smuts; Samuel Spanien; Joseph Sprinzak; Oliver Stanley; Dewey Stone; Max Sulzbacher; Herbert Bayard Swope; Meyer W. Weisgal (four items); Benjamin Weizmann; Mrs. Anita Wolf (two items); Charles E. Wyzanski; Reva Ziff (three items); Zionist Executive, London.

July Adolfo Benarus; Ernst D. Bergmann (four items); Joseph Blumenfeld; Serge Blumenfeld; Albert Cohen (two items); Josef Cohn; Richard Crossman; Charles David Ginsburg; Abraham Goldberg (three items); Ethel Hayman; Eliezer Kaplan; Franz Kind (two items); Ivor Joseph Linton; Doris May (four items); Lord and Lady Melchett; Robert Nathan; Emanuel Neumann; Chaim Pozner; Sir Benegal R. Rau; Joseph Sprinzak; A. P. Watt & Son; Meyer W. Weisgal (five items); Anna Weizmann; Benjamin Weizmann (two items); Maidie Weizmann; Stephen S. Wise; Reva Ziff; *Zionistes Generaux.*

Aug. Ernst D. Bergmann (two items); Albert Cohen; Josef Cohn; Eliezer Kaplan; Franz Kind; Ivor Joseph Linton; Doris May (two items); Emanuel Neumann; Theodor Thon; Meyer W. Weisgal (two items); Stephen S. Wise; Reva Ziff.

Sept. Walter Baer; Baumgardt; Ernst D. Bergmann (three items); Jacob Chazan; S. W. Crickett; Wyndham Deedes; Nahum Goldmann; Eliezer Kaplan (two items); Katherine von Kardorff; Lewenstein; James G. McDonald; Doris May; H. C. Medlam; Rodney Moore; Moshe D. Remez (four items); Jacques Salmanowitz; D. Werner Senator; Moshe Shertok (four items); Joseph Sprinzak; Frieda Warburg; Meyer W. Weisgal.

Oct. Walter Baer; A. Beret; Kurt Blumenfeld; Alexander Gezeldstein; Yehuda Kopelievitz; Ivor Joseph Linton (two items); H. Moss-Morris; Chanan Oppenheimer; Oscar Wolfsberg.

Nov. Walter Baer; Norman Bentwich; Maurice Bisgyer; Joseph Blumenfeld; Samuel M. Blumenfeld; Selig Brodetsky (two items); Thérèse Clay; Richard Crossman; Yaacov Dori (two items); Walter Elliot; Sigmund Gestetner; Sidney Goldstein; *Goveh Ha-Meches;* Hadassah, New York; Heinemann; Jewish National Fund, London; Franz Kind; Yehuda

Kopelievitz; Alex Lerner; *Magen David Adom,* Tel Aviv; Morris Margulies; Simon Marks; H. C. Medlam (two items); Martha Osborn; James de Rothschild; Harry Sacher; Ada Sereni; Moshe Shertok; Leon Simon; South African Zionist Federation; Stroun; Bernard Van Leer; Meyer W. Weisgal.

Dec. Irvin Bettman; Kurt Blumenfeld; M. Brailowsky (two items); H. Brough; Bartley C. Crum; L. Denivelle; Yaacov Dori; Abraham Feinberg; Charles David Ginsburg; Benjamin R. Harris; *Histadrut Nashim Zioniot,* Tel Aviv; Edward Jacobson; Ivor Joseph Linton; Misha Lubin; Simon Marks; Mishmar ha-Emek; Robert Robinson; Harry Sacher; Jesse Schwartz; Ada Sereni (three items); Arieh Shenkar; Israel Sieff; Marcus Sieff; Leon Simon; Meyer W. Weisgal (five items); Maidie Weizmann (two items); *Zionist Review.*

1949   *Jan.* Leopold S. Amery; Archimandrite Leonid; Aubrey Eban; Walter Elliot; *Jewish Chronicle;* Jewish National Fund, London; Simon Marks; Robert Nathan; James Parkes; Madame Rapkine; William Rosenwald; Ada Sereni; Leon Simon; Harry S. Truman (two items).

Feb. Aminacet, Ltd., London; Freddie Baer; M. Brailowsky; H. Brough (two items); Wyndham Deedes; L. Denivelle; Fitzpatrick, Graham & Co., London; C. L. Gabriel; Franz Kind (two items); Ralph Lazrus; Ivor Joseph Linton; James Malcolm; Frederick Mann; National Provincial Bank, London; Shiva Rau; Lewis Rosenstiel; William Rosenwald; Cecil Roth; Max Sulzbacher; Georg Tugendhat; United Jewish Appeal; Benjamin Weizmann; Eliahu Elath.

Mar. American-Israeli Shipping Co., New York; Anglo-Palestine Bank, Rehovot; Freddie Baer; Walter Baer (two items); Mrs. Barsby; Aron Barth; Selig Brodetsky; Hersh Cynowicz; James and Frances Fergusson; Louis F. Fieser; Agatha Forbes-Adam; Felix Frankfurter; Harry Friedenwald; C. L. Gabriel; Gidoni; Alexander Goldstein; Israel Goldstein; Sidney Goldstein; *Hashomer Hatzair,* Palestine; A. Jaffe; Kfar Szold; Ivor Joseph Linton (two items); Misha Lubin; Sammy Massel; Doris May; Rodney Moore; Robert Nathan; *Nisiut ha-Milve ha-Milchamti,* Tel Aviv; Lady Reading; David Rittenberg; Bruno Rosenfeld; Morris Rothenberg; Knowles A. Ryerson; Viscount Samuel; Zalman Shazar; Leon Simon (two items); Jan Christiaan Smuts (two items); Martin Solomon; Leonard J. Stein; S. Tocker; Harry S. Truman; Israel S. Wechsler; Meyer W. Weisgal (four items); Stephen S. Wise; Gisela Wyzanski; Reva Ziff; American-Christian Palestine Committee; Pierre and Madeleine Bigar; Sir Lionel Cohen; V. J. Murphy; James de Rothschild; Martin Solomon.

Apr. Benjamin Bloch; Selig Brodetsky (three items); Albert Einstein; Albert K. Epstein; Frances Gunther; *Hashomer Hatzair,* Palestine; Louis E. Levinthal; Ivor Joseph Linton; Joseph Sprinzak; Juan Trippe; Harry S. Truman; U.S. Secretary of State; Meyer W. Weisgal; Sumner Welles.

May George Backer; Walter Baer; Selig Brodetsky (two items); William Epstein; Avraham H. Frankel; George VI, King of England; Hadassah, New York; Gottlieb Hammer; Hebrew University of Jerusalem; Aubrey

Eban; *Jewish Exponent,* Philadelphia; *Knesset,* Israel; Menachem Kahany; Siegfried Kramarsky; Cord Meyer, Jr.; Herbert Oppenheimer; Carl Sherman; David Shimoni; Moshe Smoira; *Technion,* Haifa; Israel S. Wechsler; Meyer W. Weisgal.

June Walter Baer; Harry S. Truman.

July Edward Jacobson; Heinrich Levy; Robert Nathan; Yizhak Volcani.

Aug. Ernst D. Bergmann; Yigal Kimhi; Doris May; Robert Nathan; Meyer W. Weisgal; Samuel Zondek.

Sept. Marc Jarblum; Doris May; Robert Nathan (three items); William Rappard; Shmuel Tolkowsky; Meyer W. Weisgal (two items); Benjamin Weizmann; Eliahu Elath.

Oct. Leonie Landsberg-Frank; William Rappard; Moshe David Remez.

Nov. George Backer; Walter Baer; Shlomo Ben-Zvi; Maurice Bisgyer; Montague Burton; Joseph Cherner; David Dunkelman; Aubrey Eban; Albert Einstein; Eliahu Elath; Abraham Feinberg; Sigmund Gestetner; Frank Goldman; Jennie Grossinger; Benjamin R. Harris; Leonie Landsberg-Frank; Heinrich Levy; Mr. and Mrs. Harry Maizlish; Simon Marks; *Motele Verein,* Chicago; Edward A. Norman; Bernardo Rabinovitch; William Rappard; Charles Rosenbloom; Harry Sacher; Alexander Sachs; Jacques Salmanowitz; Ezra Shapiro; Israel Sieff; Flora Solomon; Harry S. Truman; Ben-Zion Meir Hai Uziel; Edward Warburg; Meyer W. Weisgal; Mordechai Eliash; Arthur Lourie.

Dec. Montague Burton; Moshe Cohen; Albert K. Epstein; Robert Gottlieb; Herman Mark; Juda H. Quastel; David Rittenberg; Victor Rothschild (two items); Mordechai Shenhabi; Eliyahu Shine; University of Vienna; Norbert Uri; Henry Wolfson; William O'Dwyer; Elpidio Quirino.

1950 *Jan.* Leopold S. Amery; Oscar R. Ewing; Franz Kind; Jan C. Smuts; Meyer W. Weisgal (three items).

Feb. Meyer W. Weisgal.

Mar. Robert M. Bernstein; Zvi Fein; King Frederick of Denmark; Juda H. Quastel; Meyer W. Weisgal.

Apr. Mr. and Mrs. Joseph G. Riesman; Martin Rosenblueth; Ralph A. Villani.

May A. Lasker; Robert Nathan (two items); William O'Dwyer; Allan Shivers.

June Brendan Bracken; Paul Guinness; Edward Jacobson; Robert Nathan; William Rappard; Israel Rokach; Isaac Wolfson.

July Benjamin Bloch; Frieda Goldschmidt; Robert Nathan; Dewey Stone; Harry S. Truman.

Aug. Yigal Kimhi.

Sept. Aubrey Eban; Israel Goldstein.

Oct. Mordechai Shenhabi.

Nov.   Harry S. Truman.

Dec.   Walter W. Johnson.

1951   *Jan.*   Leopold S. Amery; David Ben-Gurion; Maurice Bloch; Henry Ford; Franz Kind; William Rappard; Samuel Zemurray.

Feb.   Walter Winchell.

Mar.   Eliyahu Berligne; Abraham H. Frankel.

Apr.   Victor Berman; Joseph Blumenfeld; Sir Montague Burton; Edward Jacobson.

May   Trygve Lie; Isidor Schalit; Harry S. Truman.

June   Walter Baer; William Rappard; Tadeus Reichstein; Leopold Ruzicka; Jacques Salmanowitz; Charles Venn Pilcher.

July   Theodore R. McKeldin; Harry S. Truman.

Aug.   David Ben-Gurion; Rabbi Meltzer; Juda H. Quastel; Dewey Stone.

Sept.   Moshe Smoira.

Oct.   Martin Buber; Elpidio Quirino.

Nov.   Monnett B. Davis; Harry Scherman.

1952   *Jan.*   Joseph Levy; William Paley.

Apr.   Isidor Schalit.

BIOGRAPHICAL INDEX

For abbreviations see p. xxvii

BERNADOTTE, Folke, Count Bernadotte of Wisborg (1895–1948). Soldier and diplomat; nephew of King Gustavus V of Sweden. During W.W.II headed Swedish Red Cross, securing the exchange of many prisoners of war and inmates of German concentration camps. The Nazi leader Heinrich Himmler used his good offices in 1945 to forward peace proposals to the Allies. Appointed 20 May 1948 by U.N. Security Council to mediate in Arab–Israel conflict, and negotiated the first truce (11 June). He developed a peace plan which was rejected by both the Arab States and Israel and failed to achieve endorsement by U.N. General Assembly in Nov. 1948. Assassinated in Jerusalem 1 Sept. 1948 by Jewish extremists.

GINSBURG, Charles David (b. 1912). Attorney in Washington. Graduating from Harvard Law School 1935, he was attorney to Securities and Exchange Commission 1935–39; legal adviser to Government commissions 1939–46; in U.S. Army 1943–46; Deputy Director, Economic Division, Military Government Germany 1945–46; Deputy Commander, U.S. delegation, Austrian Treaty Commission 1947; adviser, U.S. delegation, Council of Foreign Ministers, London 1947; Adjunct Professor of International Law, Georgetown University from 1959. Author: *The Future of German Reparations* 1950.

JACOBSON, Edward (1891–1955). Merchant. Comrade-in-arms during W.W. I of Harry S. Truman, they engaged in business together for a period in Oklahoma and Kansas City, Missouri, and remained lifelong friends. After Truman became President, Jacobson discussed with him the Jewish refugee problem and Palestine partition issues. In March 1948, at a critical moment in the period preceding the establishment of the State of Israel, he persuaded Truman to receive Weizmann.

MARSHALL, George Catlett (1880–1959). Soldier and statesman. Served in France in W.W. I as Chief of Operations. Chief of Staff of U.S. Army 1939–45; Ambassador to China 1945–47. As Secretary of State, 1947–49, he introduced the European Recovery Programme, which became known as the Marshall Plan. Secretary of Defense 1950–51. Nobel Peace Prize 1953.

ROSENMAN, Samuel Irving (1896–1973). Jurist. Member New York State Legislature 1922–26; New York State Bill Drafting Commissioner 1926–28; Counsel to Governor F. D. Roosevelt 1929–32; Judge, New York Supreme Court 1932–43. Special counsel to President Roosevelt 1943–45, and to President Truman 1945–46, then continuing in latter's service as presidential adviser. Editor, 13-volume *Public Papers and Addresses of Franklin D. Roosevelt 1928–45;* author, *Working with Roosevelt,* 1952.

SAMUEL, Maurice (1895–1972). Author, lecturer and translator from Hebrew and Yiddish. B. Rumania, he was brought to Manchester in 1900, and following graduation, 1914, settled in U.S. Worked as publicist for Z.O.A. in 1920s, and member of its Administrative Committee 1927–29. He enjoyed a long association with Meyer Weisgal, through whom he came to collaboration with Weizmann on the latter's memoirs, *Trial and Error.* His prolific writings include fiction, works on Zionism, and Yiddish belles-lettres, besides an account of the Beilis Case, *Blood Accusation,* 1966.

INDEX

Cross-references to other volumes are given where appropriate.

INDEX

Ad Hoc Committee on Palestine, 11, 23, 38–39, 49; Weizmann's address, xii, 9, 17–19, 24, 30.

General Assembly, xii, 11, 16, 20, 24, 37–39, 42, 49, 51, 67, 97–98, 100–01, 107, 115, 130, 143, 178, 188, 199, 287, 322; Nov. 1947 Resolution, xiii–xiv, 32, 46–47, 58–61, 77, 80, 84–85, 93, 97, 99, 114, 116, 120, 146, 152, 156, 169, 175, 200, 220, 222, 239, 243–44, 248, 267, 313–15; Dec. 1948 Resolution, 245, 311–13, 317–19; Dec. 1949 Resolution, 284–86, 320.

Security Council, 37–38, 90–91, 97–98, 105, 109–10, 122, 133, 160, 166, 173, 179, 222, 243–44, 248, 303–04, 315.

United Nations (ship), 76.

United Palestine Appeal, 293.

United States Government, and Palestine/Israel policy, xii–xiv, 17, 23, 36–37, 47, 61, 67, 85, 91, 93, 143, 158, 221–24, 228, 236; arms embargo, 61, 91, 101, 109, 122, 130, 168, 179; British influence, 5, 129, 137, 143, 145–46, 168, 170, 239, 249; and U.N. resolutions, 222, 243, 303, 320. *See also* Truman, Harry S.

Israel: assistance, 129–30, 223, 302; differences, 242, 244, 249, 311, 319; grant-in-aid, 301, 305; loan, 130, 205, 241, 250–51; recognition, xiv, 109, 116, 118–20, 129, 158, 168, 179, 200–01, 206, 241.

Uruguay, 49, 320.

Va'ad Leumi, 91, 277.

Van Leer, Bernard, 279, 282.

Van Leer, Oscar, 279.

Van Niel, Cornelius B., 3.

Vasella, Oscar, 282.

Vishinsky, Andrei, 51.

Vishniak, Mark, his *Doctor Weizmann*, 57.

Waldman, Morris D., 19.

Warburg, Carola, 230.

Warburg, Edward, 19.

Warburg, Felix M., 19, 230, 260–61. *See also* Vol. X, Biog. Index.

Warburg, Frieda, 230, 260. *See also* Vol. XIV, Biog. Index.

Warburg, Max, 261. *See also* Vol. XIV, Biog. Index.

Watt, A. P., 7, 73, 155.

Wavell, Lord, 281. *See also* Vol. XX, Biog. Index.

Weber, Prof., 283.

Wechsler, Israel S., 55, 195.

Wedgwood, Josiah, 64. *See also* Vol. XI, Biog. Index.

Weicman (*formerly* Weizmann), Fruma, 14. *See also* Vol. III, Biog. Index.

Weidenfeld, A. George, 290.

Weill, Kurt, 46.

Weisgal, Mendy, 230.

Weisgal, Meyer W., xv, xviii, 7, 9, 11, 63–64, 73, 80, 96, 105, 107, 110–13, 137, 142, 145, 147, 151, 155–57, 163, 168–70, 172, 182, 191, 197, 199, 209, 218, 228, 241–42, 252, 254–55, 257, 277, 282, 288–89, 292, 309; jt. ed., *Chaim Weizmann, a Biography by Several Hands,* 85; appointed General Editor, *The Letters and Papers of Chaim Weizmann,* 256; and Bergmann's estrangement from W., 278, 283, 300–01, 304, 306; and *Trial and Error,* 7, 73, 78, 98, 155, 163, 199, 281; his . . . *So Far,* 284. *See also* Vol. X, Biog. Index.

Weisgal, Shirley, 113, 143, 164, 230, 278, 282.

Weizmann, Anna, 14, 97, 112, 181. *See also* Vol. I, Biog. Index.

Weizmann, Benjamin, 2, 22, 72, 102, 148–49, 180–81, 203–05. *See also* Vol. V, Biog. Index.

Weizmann, Chaim (*see also* subject headings throughout Index, and Vol. I, xxxvi–xxxvii, for Chronology); his address before U.N., xii, 17–19, 24, 30; birthday celebrations, xviii, 41–42, 46, 66, 284, 308; death, xi, xviii, 310; on higher education, 28, 173, 185; his historical perspective, 84, 201–02, 232, 262–65, 269, 314, 321; on Jewish refugees, 4–6, 76, 100, 129–30, 221, 250, 263–64, 315; on Jewish terrorism, xv, 3–4, 106, 208, 210, 262–64; his literary legacy, 255–56; memoirs, *see Trial and Error*; reminiscences, 66, 93, 124, 246–47, 254, 260–61, 266, 270–71, 276, 287–88, 290–91, 294, 296–97; his scientific processes, 1, 181, 283.

Arabs: aggression, 93, 100–01, 104–05, 122, 158–59, 166, 168, 206–07, 243–44, 285–86, 314–15; appeasement of, 17, 93, 101, 135, 146, 263, 303–04, 314; Arab-Jewish understanding, xii, 13, 32–33, 42–44, 58, 60, 104, 116–17, 119–20, 202, 212, 224, 240, 312, 316; British support and rearmament, xvii, 34, 93, 109–10, 113, 129–31, 146, 164, 175, 200, 202, 206, 215–17, 222, 231, 233, 237–38, 243, 248, 250, 265, 315, 322.

Health, xi, 10, 79, 85, 87–90, 102, 108, 111, 114–15, 119, 122, 165, 252, 309; eyesight, xi, 2, 134, 141, 182, 193, 205, 210, 270, 272.

Hebrew University, 55, 80–82, 90, 184, 194–96, 273; and cooperation with Rehovot Institute, 69–70, 81–82, 289; need for additional university, 173, 185, 188–89, 194.

Israel: on its establishment, xv–xvi, 116–17, 119–21, 131–32, 134, 140–41, 201–02, 207, 245, 256, 259–60, 265, 268–71, 293; boundaries, 36, 136, 144–48, 152–

INDEX